T0056558

WOOD

WOOD

A HISTORY

JOACHIM RADKAU

Translated by Patrick Camiller

polity

First published in German as *Holz* © oekom verlag, 2007

This English edition © Polity Press, 2012

The translation of this work was supported by a grant from the Goethe-Institut, which is funded by the German Ministry of Foreign Affairs.

Polity Press
65 Bridge Street
Cambridge CB2 1UR, UK

Polity Press
350 Main Street
Malden, MA 02148, USA

ISBN-13: 978-0-7456-4688-6

A catalogue record for this book is available from the British Library.

Typeset in 10.5 on 12 pt Sabon
by Servis Filmsetting Ltd, Stockport, Cheshire
Printed and bound in Great Britain by the MPG Books Group

For further information on Polity, visit our website: www.politybooks.com

CONTENTS

ACKNOWLEDGEMENTS

The publishers would like to thank the following for permission to reproduce copyright material:

Page13, photocase.com; 15, Schoningen spear 11 in its original position 1995 © Christa S. Fuchs NLD; 38, © State Archives Hamburg; 49, © C. Franke, Munster; 52, Deutsches Museum; 53, © iStockphoto.com; 56, © Ines Swoboda, oekem verlag; 62, © Heidelberg University Library, Sachsenspeigel Cod. Pal. Germ. 164, 10r; 67, © Deutsches Museum; 71, © Royal House Archives, The Hague. Nassau, Finaciewezen en Erbverein, C29-53a; 76, © National Library of Sweden; 77 Lithographie aus K.F. Jagerschmid: Handbuch fur Holztransport und Flosswesen zum Gebrauche fur Forstmanner und Holzhandler und fur solche, die es werden wollen. Tafelband. Karlsruhe 1827/28. Taf. 6, Fig 10-12, 20-22; 79 © Deutsches Museum; 82, © Deutsches Museum; 83, © Deutsches Museum; 85, © Deutsches Museum; 86, © Deutsches Museum; 89, © Kupferstich aus Roubo le fils: L'art du menuisier. In: Descriptions des arts et metiers, Bd. 4. Paris 1774. Taf 278, Fig. 10; 91, © Deutsches Museum; 93, Kupferstich von J. v. Montalegre nach Zeichnung von G. D. Zweiffel, 1715, eingebunden in: Stadtarchiv Schwaebisch Hall HV HS 89 (Schuler'sche Chronik der Reichsstadt Hall, 1775); © Deutsches Museum; 107, © German National Museum; 109, Bauzeichnungen – 1717, © Staatsarchiv Nurnberg, Waldamnt Sebaldi, Nr. 260; 111, © Royal House Archives, the Hague; 115, © Central State Archive Stuttgart, J 312 59; 116, © Central State Archive Stuttgart, J 312 59; 117, Kupferstich aus F.F. Jagerschmid (vgl. Abb. 11.). Taf. 24 (Ausschnitt); 120, Handkolorierter Kupferstichaus J.P Voit: Fabliche Beschreibung der gemeinnutzlichsten Kunste und Handwerke fur

ACKNOWLEDGEMENTS

junge Leute, Bd. 2. Nurnberg 1804, Taf. 20; 122, © Deutsches
Museum; 123, Itinerary of Jan Mandevill – 1420. British Library,
London, Add. MS 24189, fol. 16 (Ausschnitt); 124, Kupferstich
aus J. Kuncke: Ars vitraria experimentalis, oder Vollkommmene
GlasmacherKunst...Frankfurtund Leipzig 1679. Taf. E (beiS. 62);
127, © Stadtbibliothek Nornberg, Amb. 317.2°, f. 27v; 128, © Styrian
Provincial Archives; 129, Deutsches Museum; 135, © Ines Swoboda,
oekem verlag; 142, Ansicht von Unkel. Kupferstich von J. Ziegler
nach einer Zeichnung von L. Janscha. 1798. Rheinisches. Bildarchiv
Koln; 154, © Deutsches Museum; 173, © Deutsches Museum; 175,
© Deutsches Museum; 179, © Deutsches Museum; 180, © Deutsches
Museum; 183, © Adeva; 186, © Graphic Art Collection, Museums
of City of Nuremburg; 195, © Hertwig: Bauwesen. In: Technische
Kulturdenkmale (Hg. C. Matschoss/U.w. Lindner). Munchen 1932.
Abb 229, S. 116; 196, © A. Pech, Zweisel. Hier aus: Das Bayerland.
Illustrierte Halbmonatsschrift fur Bayerns Land und Volk (Hg. L.
Deubner), Jg. 46. Munchen 1935. Nr. 21, S. 658 (Ausschnitt); 199, ©
Styrian Provincial Archives; 203, © Deutsches Museum; 213, © J. P.
Baumer: Beschreibung eines zu Erspahrung des Holtzes eingericheten
StubenOfens...Berlin 1765. Taf. A; 216, P.G. Berthaultaus C.-N.
LedouxL L'architecture consideree sous le rapport de l'art des moeurs
et de la legislation. Paris 1804. Taf 15. (Ausschnitt); 219, © National
Library of Australia; 222, © A. Moles: Histoiredes charpentiers. Leurs
travaux. Paris 1949. Abb. 108, S. 107; 225, © Zeichnung – um 1830.
Sammlung E. Matthes, Hartenstein 69; 229, © Deutsches Museum;
231, © Deutsches Museum; 233, © Mercer Museum, Bucks county
historical Society, Doylestown. Ch. A. Foote; 235 © Th. A. SandeL
Industrial archeology. New York, Penguin Books Inc. 1978. S.99;
237, © Manchester Local Studies; 239, © photocase.com; 253, ©
Deutsches Museum; 257, © Deutsches Museum; 266, © www.manu-
factum.com; 270, © P. Morter aus: Dasgrobe Buchvom Holz (deutsche Bearbeitung J. Schwab). Munchen, Schuler Verlagsgesellschaft
1977. S. 48; 274, © Alamy/Look; 281, © 2011 Der Spiegel; 297,
© Ines Swoboda, oekem verlag; 312, © H. Hesmer aus ders.: Der
kombinierte land -und forstwirtschaftliche Anbau, Bd. 2 9 Tropisches
und subtropisches Asien). In: Wissenschaftliche Schriftenreihe des
Bundesministeriums fur wirtschaftliche Zusammenarbeit, Bd. 17.
Stuttgart, Ernst Klett Verlag 1970. Abb. 31, S. 192; 313, © Panos
Pictures; 320, © istockphoto.com.

INTRODUCTION: PRAISING WOOD, CARING FOR WOOD, SPLITTING WOOD – AND A HISTORICAL SYNTHESIS

> I marvel how our God has given so many uses to wood for all men in the whole wide world: building timber, firewood, joiner's, cartwright's and shipbuilder's wood, wood for rooms, wood for wheelbarrows, paddles, gutters, barrels, etc. Who can tell of every use that wood has? In short, wood is one of the greatest and most necessary things in the world, which people need and cannot do without.

This praise of wood as an indispensable, multi-purpose material, here taken from Martin Luther's *Table Talk* of 30 August 1532, became a leitmotif of early modern literature as people gave serious attention to supply problems instead of relying on the Good Lord to provide for them, even when they sinned against the forest. Later, Luther was said to have predicted that the world would one day 'lack three things: good coins, wood and good friends'. The sense of crisis sharpened this view of wood as the foundation of human existence, which had previously been given little thought. In fact, wood is a natural material that has marked human culture – not only in the 'Wood Age' of the past but right down to the present day. Recently we have been experiencing a renaissance of wood, as both fuel and construction material, that scarcely anyone would have considered possible a generation ago.

The more one goes into the significance of forest and wood in history, the more one can succumb to wood mania and start to feel that, in a way previously unsuspected by historians, it is a secret key to essential features of various cultures, and even to the rise and fall of great powers. Over the years and decades, my frequent travels inspired me to collect whole bookcases of literature on wood and the forest, until inevitably my colleagues gave me the nickname 'Woodworm'. But I was aware that in the wood scene this counts as

1

an honorific title. I was often overcome by the wealth of my discoveries, yet I found few books that even half satisfied my curiosity about the whole matter. Realizing that I would have to write my longed-for book myself, I was also seized with an ambition to show my disbelieving fellow historians that wood is one of the most important issues in the history of the world.

Or is wood so banal that it is not worth thinking about? In 1948 Sigfried Giedion published his magnificent work *Mechanization Takes Command* under the watchword 'For the historian there are no banal things' (Giedion 1948: 3). No one else has given such a fascinating description of the ways in which mentalities are embedded in furniture: the history of chairs, for example, which begins in the late Middle Ages, mirrors the history of bodily posture, and 'posture reflects the inner nature of a period' or 'the essence of the age' (ibid.: 262, 310f., 396ff.). Giedion's central question 'What happens when mechanization encounters organic substance?' (ibid.: 6) is a fateful one for human civilization, and also a central question in the present book. For Giedion it ultimately remains open: the history of man's dealings with wood brings forth a whole series of answers. Another vital question that history has lined up for us concerns the way in which societies manage on limited resources. It was already noted in the Middle Ages that the forests are finite, and more recently we have begun to grasp that the oceans and the atmosphere are finite too.

The history of wood and forest is all too often presented as a jumble of disconnected facts. Yet it provides much food for thought as soon as we broaden our horizons and look more deeply into the matter. Solid history here coincides with world history theory. In the 'modern world system' described by Immanuel Wallerstein, does the timber trade further widen the gulf between core and periphery, or do the forests actually give the periphery a special opportunity? Is Garrett Hardin's 'tragedy of the commons' decisively confirmed in the history of the forest, or are forest communities the best example of the model of local commons organization for which Elinor Ostrom received the Nobel Prize in 2009? Does rational choice theory provide the key to the technical history of wood, or does the power of tradition and emotion make itself felt everywhere in that history?

These are big issues of world history – and yet the literature is as split on them as a shattered wooden log. This is already visible in the concepts: the leader writer of the journal *Holzforschung und Holzverwertung* once complained of the 'massive, Babel-like, linguistic and conceptual confusion of the lumber industry' (Alfred Teischinger, in Heinzinger 1988: 236). And then there is the wider forest economy! Forest and timber are inseparable from each other, but the literature treats the history of the forest and the history of wood processing as if they belonged to two different worlds. Forest historians are reluctant to look beyond their chosen subject, yet the history of the forest cannot be understood if one looks only at the forest. 'Sustainable forestry', harmony between economy and forest, is a question not only of technology but even more of cooperation within a typically global field of tension between forest dwellers and tillers of open land, mountain and plain dwellers, herdsmen and farmers – a source of conflict present throughout human history.

The literature on wood processing is thoroughly opaque. Most of it refers only to discrete activities, from charcoal-burning to the art of wood-carving, and usually has a limited regional focus. Indeed, it is strange that regions closely related in terms of wood and forest know so little about one another. The bulk of published works offer a hotchpotch of facts that allows us to distinguish neither historical processes nor a coherent train of thought. The common idea seems to be that wood is mute, that it is not at all easy to make it speak.

Although in my heart of hearts I am a forest romantic, I have learned most of what I know about wood and the forest from thoroughly unromantic books. It was with surprise and enthusiasm that I discovered an American work virtually unknown in Europe: Stanley F. Horn's *This Fascinating Lumber Business*, published in 1943, whose author – a 'hardwood man', as he describes himself – founded in 1908 the *Southern Lumberman*, the 'oldest lumber trade paper' in the world. He vividly depicts how the striving for sustainable forestry can originate in practical problems and not necessarily, as many German historians believe, in academic research or the world of state administration. 'Hardwood people', we learn, are of a special mould. In an interview given in 1978, the 89-year-old Horn provided special insider's insights into how the timber sector in the American South organizes itself within the Order of the Hoo-Hoo, where conflicts similar to those of the old German student fraternities are worked off in a theatrical show of force. The European reader is astonished to discover that an old tradition of lamenting wood shortages survives in the forest-rich United States: 'Every time an old house is torn down there is somebody to shake his head in woe and say: "You can't get lumber like that any more." But the truth is that just as good lumber is being manufactured today as ever.' I had already delved quite deeply into the historical German fear that the supply of wood would run out. But Horn left me in no doubt that people elsewhere have had to take active measures to ensure that their supply holds up in the future.

3

Unsurpassed to this day is Bryan Latham's *Timber: Its Development and Distribution: A Historical Survey*, first published in 1957. Its author, founder president of the Institute of Wood Science, comes from a woodland dynasty stretching from James Latham I and James Latham II to James Latham V, whose trade in exotic hardwood began in Liverpool in 1757, exactly two centuries before the publication of the book. It is a unique work, in which one can sense this unbroken continuity of first-hand knowledge; the author tells us that 'timber is in my blood, as it has been in the blood of my ancestors for two hundred years'. The book's title is *Timber*, but its entire contents show that timber and wood cannot be separated from each other, in either nature or history. This is especially confusing for German readers, who have got used to the distinction between the two terms (for which there is no precise equivalent in German) only to learn that lumberjacks in the West shouted out 'Timber!', or rather 'Timber-r-r-r', when a tree fell.

Again and again we are confronted with the fact that wood is a special material which cannot be replaced with any other, and which, on closer inspection, decays in a range of quite different ways. Horn and Latham tell us that, both in the forest and in commerce, hardwood and softwood belong to different worlds, each with its own customs and histories. We would look in vain in their work for any trace of the common complaint about deforestation and wood shortages, since, in fact, a failing supply means a boom time for the business. Latham's book is full of stories, yet we see how wood – even when, as he does, we leave the vast realm of firewood – breaks up the historical narrative, and how difficult it is to divide up the history of wood satisfactorily.

Master narratives exist only for the forest as such. But, as the British historian Oliver Rackham mocked decades ago, they often amount to 'pseudo-history', copied down from others and resting on an uncritical attitude to the sources. Suspiciously, we find the same story in books about completely different forest regions, from Western Europe to Japan: first, a long bad period of unregulated plunder, then the great age of salvation, of sustainable forestry, under the supervision of a forestry administration. The darkness of the terrain encourages the development of myths and legends. And throughout history we find a constant vacillation between the idea that forests are endless and the fear of deforestation and shortage. My own debut in the matter was in 1981, at an international conference in Essen on 'Energy in History', where I questioned the thesis of a catastrophic shortage of wood in the eighteenth century. This triggered a controversy that rumbles on even today, thirty years later. For it has been the central myth of the proud German forestry that, ever since Germany began to revive in the 1800s, it has saved more and more other countries from the threat of a supply disaster. I was therefore called 'the German Rackham' and considered for a time as the foresters' enemy.

Fortunately, and for good reason, my relations with the forestry people have since become more amicable. For the critique of the traditional view of forest history opens up new perspectives for wood. If the lesson of history is that the 'Wood Age' did not end through ecological suicide, then the road to another wood age is not necessarily suicidal either. The Wood Age did not break down because of a shortage of wood, any more than the Stone Age broke down because of a shortage of stone. A broad overview demonstrates this better than a plethora of special studies can ever do. Environmental history as a critical discipline must also take pseudo-ecological statements apart.

Anglo-American naval history has long had a wood shortage controversy that is unknown in continental Europe. In the critical wake of Admiral Alfred T. Mahan and his famous work *The Influence of Sea Power upon History, 1660–1783*, Robert G. Albion published in 1926 the classic *Forests and Sea Power: The Timber Problem of the Royal Navy, 1652–1862*. Since it was ultimately timber resources, not the energy and courage of sailors, that ensured a country's supremacy at sea, the rise of the Royal Navy had gone hand in hand with constant supply fears – fears which, according to Albion, were well founded because of England's destruction of its forests. The inner contradiction of Albion's book, however, was that in the end he still attributed the naval victory over Napoleon at Trafalgar to Britain's superior timber resources. Later research showed that he had greatly exaggerated the country's deforestation during the period in question. The core of the problem – already in Albion's book – was not any real shortage but the power of the 'Timber Trust': while the British fleet was routing Napoleon, the Admiralty was allowing itself to be blackmailed by a gang of big timber dealers (Albion 1926: 58f.). As a naval official later mordantly noted: 'The real timber problem of the Royal Navy was the trouble with the wooden heads that guided its policies, and England did not have to import that kind of timber' (Horn 1943: 19f.).

But is the history of wood simply a matter of demonstrating particular causal relationships? Does wood not supply the material for 'big history'? Does the attempt to achieve a synoptic overview amount to

no more than ghost-hunting? Is there a reason after all for the unsatis-
fying character of the existing literature? Is 'wood' as such too general a
theme for a written history? Should we not stick to the usual narrower
subjects: the timber business, reforestation, woodcutting, charcoal-
burning, wood distribution systems, woodcrafts, wood-carving, housebuilding, the energy business, pitch, tar and potash production, and in
modern times the wood pulp and cellulose industry?

In my view, a general history of wood does make sense, because a
connection exists among all these themes – not only logically and in
nature, but also in history itself. Until the industrial age many users of
wood had a direct relationship with the forest, and all had to deal in
one way or another with the natural properties of wood. Craftsmen
in Lippe (in what is now North Rhine-Westphalia) defied the warden
in 1757 by searching in the forest for the tree of their choice instead
of having one allocated to them; otherwise 'they preferred not to have
any wood'. Typically, the scion of an old family of woodcrafters once
told me how his ancestors used to go into the forest to find the right
tree for a newly commissioned item. When I asked him when this
practice had ceased, he thought for a moment and said it had been
when the first woodworking machinery arrived. The whole pace of
work then speeded up, and people no longer had time to search the
forest for trees.

The American wood lover and technologist Bruce Hoadley is of
much the same view: 'Trees are a source of wood only for those
willing to expend much time and physical effort, because extracting
workable wood from the tree is no casual pastime' (Hoadley 1980:
203). Modern working speeds, together with modern transport and
distribution systems, have broken the direct link between the forest
and processing activity, and the grading of high-quality woods for
the market has become a centralized procedure. For many industrial
timber products, the natural qualities of a particular wood are no
longer of interest.

The whole forest and timber industry often strikes the outsider as
a world unto itself – an opaque, hermetically sealed black box. But
conflicts of interest that divide commercial forestry, sawmills, the
furniture business, the chipboard industry and the wholesale trade
find expression not only in lobbying activity but also in the specialist
literature. One might even say that different mentalities take shape
in all these sectors. In relation to the present and future, not only the
historical past, it is important to make ourselves aware of the over-
arching connection among these particular sectors. The first link is
the resource itself, wood; its finite character is today clearly apparent

on a world scale, as age-old fears of supply exhaustion, forgotten for some time, resurface alongside ambitious and varied plans for the exploitation of timber. At the same time, technological advances have given rise to what we might call programmatic connections. Modern technologies for the processing of timber waste yield new kinds of combined use: wood as raw material, wood as fuel, wood as input for cellulose production. Attempts were already made in the early modern period to exploit waste within such an interlocking system. Today, once again, these have a promising future ahead of them.

The various ways of using forest and wood have continually cut across one another. Today too, and into the future, there is a real danger that the different purposes will conflict: maximum use of wood as a resource capable of regenerating itself; optimum use of the natural properties of wood; and a return to an ecologically stable forestry. This too underlines the need to consider the 'forest and wood' sector more holistically than most analysts have done until now. Only then will it be possible to identify and overcome a conflict in aims before it is too late. As one 'woodworm' from Austria put it: 'If all parties interested in wood – from forest people through the timber industry to academic researchers – could be brought around a table, wood would be an unbeatable material' (Franz Solar, in Teischinger and Lex 2005: 117). But he knew that, for the time being, a Broad Green Alliance remains a pipe dream.

'America's Wooden Age was a wonderful era, specifically because of the nature of the prevailing technology which depended so heavily upon wood': so begins the collection *America's Wooden Age*, originally published by the National Museum of History and Technology (Hindle 1975: 12). Well, we might ask, if the Wood Age was really so wonderful, why didn't America stick with wood? A collection of American graphics and drawings from the nineteenth century, published around the same time by the Bettmann Archive in New York, bears the title *The Good Old Days – They Were Terrible!*, and the log cabin of legend appears in it as a stench-filled breeding ground for vermin (Bettmann 1974: 47). If one writes a history of wood filled with enthusiasm for the material, one finds oneself asking why it does not rule the world, instead of often being driven out by other materials. A critical approach is needed to avoid falling into illusions; if wood is to win back some ground, an explanation is needed as to how it lost that ground in the first place. Not infrequently, the advantages of wood have become evident only in retrospect. And the narrow horizons of the timber industry have prevented many an opportunity from being seized.

7

Here lies the attraction, but also the difficulty, of writing a history of wood: we are faced with a major context that has previously remained beneath the surface, little considered by historians. Our knowledge of how the forest has marked human existence down the ages, and of how it responded to human demands on it, is still full of gaps. There has been no lack of research, to be sure, but for olden times it is based mostly on the mass of forest ordinance. This by itself does not tell us what actually went on in the forest. As Oliver Rackham has repeatedly stressed, the real history of the forest should not be confused with the history of legal regulations.

Forest history also tends to judge earlier conditions from the point of view of the modern timber industry, for which the forest is productive of wood and little else. In the case of Italy, Gabriella Bonacchi has characterized the rise of the modern timber industry as the *vittoria del legno sulle foglie*, the 'victory of wood over foliage'. For farmers all over the world, the forest has been seen mainly as a grazing ground and a source of fodder for their animals, with fruit trees as the most valuable element in it; the Tree of Life in the final chapter of the Book of Revelation is a fruit tree. Thus, what for modern foresters is at best a 'marginal use', and at worst 'poaching', was for most of human history the main utility of the forest. What features stereotypically in many books as the bad age of the forest's ruin was the very time when the farmer's interests prevailed there, rather than an interest in maximizing timber production for the market. In certain periods, the production of pitch, resin, rubber and tannins also played an enormous role.

Since forest historians have focused only on their pet subject, they have shed little light on its connection with general history and economic-technological development. We know of the massive use of wood in many earlier trades but all too little about the wood policies of various cities or the strategies they adopted to ensure adequate provision in the future. General statements are made more difficult by the fact that local and regional differences are especially great in the timber industry.

Even the modern economic history of wood and the forest is less well known than one would like to think. Although wood continues to be the most versatile material, and a very important factor in the world economy, it has received relatively little attention from economists and technologists. Wood technology is not a 'cutting-edge technology', nor is the timber industry a headline-grabbing sector of large-scale industry – at least not in Central Europe. Wood is not (or is not yet) a material that holds out the prospect of a Nobel Prize. As in the past, wood is used in little-known ways in a whole number of sectors of the economy. Only a synoptic overview can reveal its full significance.

Although I am always susceptible to the romance of the forest, my main interest as a historian of wood and the forest has long been in the anti-romantic aspect of *rationalization*. For the fact is that, in modern times, human dealings with wood and the forest may be described as a series of rationalization drives. In this respect, I have unwittingly stood in the tradition of Max Weber – or, to be more precise, of the rationalization obsessive who has traditionally been the authority for rational choice theorists. In my own biography of Weber (Radkau 2009) I uncovered quite a different thinker: one who was aware of the ambivalence of rationalization and the force of passion in history – and who has left his mark on the present edition of this work. In reality, man's dealings with the forest cannot be rationalized through and through. As a Swiss expert noted, even 'cost unit accounting is virtually unknown' in the timber business (Höchli 1957: 35), and no one who plants trees can tell in advance what they will be worth by the time they are ready to be felled. To quote Hindle again, in order to write about the Wood Age, 'the first need is to develop a sensitivity to the ways of wood. This sensitivity cannot be fully conveyed in a written paper because the three-dimensional world of wood has important nonverbal aspects which can be apprehended only by seeing, or even by touching, the objects involved' (Hindle 1975: 4).

Such is the dilemma of all books about wood. The records are bare; you usually have to hunt for the emotions between the lines. The best way to get a feel for them is by talking with 'woodworms' – with people in the wood and forestry sector. But we should not forget that emotions also stir on the opposite side. Architects for whom 'modern' is a magic word drool over concrete as the pinnacle of design freedom and regard timber as a 'reactionary' material, even if they concede that it provides a pleasant indoor climate and that the freedom offered by concrete usually results in monotony.

Not surprisingly, emotions also permeate the literature on wood and the forest. Too often, though, they do not reveal themselves as such but are smuggled into the text, or else the author remains unaware of his subjective judgement. A forester and historian who loves mixed deciduous woodland once assured me that he would like to grab a colleague who is promoting conifer monoculture and string him up from the nearest tree! The forest is not the place of peaceful harmony that romantics like to imagine. Lovers of old-growth forest have no language in common with people for whom the giant trees are 'lazy journeymen' because of their slow rate of growth. The literary type who is fixated on ancestral woodland looks with indifference, or even disdain, on the reforestation projects that are the forester's pride. American forest rangers who take pride in the heroic struggle against fires hate pyromaniac lovers of the wilderness, for whom fire is part of the forest ecosystem. Wilderness fans see the timber industry as only one disturbing factor in the history of the forest, and consider those who see the forest mainly as a timber resource to be simply narrow-minded. And wood lovers who are fond of log cabins and lavish wooden furniture are the laughing stock of technologically minded moderns, who demonstrate the robustness of wood by making the most economical use of it. What a challenge to wood and forest historians! Max Weber's insistence on value-free science raises no more than a yawn among many of today's social scientists – but it is little short of revolutionary for the history of wood.

To knit together rational and emotional approaches would seem to be the most difficult challenge for historians of wood and the forest. It has not yet been convincingly explained how German forest romanticism links up with the simultaneous reforestation movement; there is evidently not a direct causal relationship. Today a coffee-table book entitled *Wood* promotes itself with the blurb: 'Access to the essence of wood opens up only when we give up counting, measuring and thinking' (Spring and Glas 2005). Even thinking we have to give up! When a wood-carver explained much the same thing to me, I countered by asking whether he didn't have to have a lot of intelligence in his hands when he was carving. Our intelligence is not present only in our brains. Only in combination with the intellect do our emotions become a productive force.

Theodor Heuss, who in the 1920s ran the Deutscher Werkbund (in many ways an offspring of the British Arts and Crafts movement) and in 1949 became the first president of the Federal Republic of Germany, looked back in 1951 at the 'cohabitation of romanticism and rationalism' in the Werkbund – 'a relationship that spawned very many children' (Heuss 1951: 13f.). Even the old half-timbered houses, which used prefabricated wooden components, required far more precise planning than brick buildings. Wood is conducive to identification and intuitive approaches, but these are capable of leading one astray. People think they know wood from long experience, but this very certainty can make them blind to new knowledge. In his book *Understanding Wood*, Bruce Hoadley attacked 'the mountains of misinformation available and commonly accepted by woodworkers' – for example, the idea that 'wood has to breathe'.

No, wood does not breathe in the sense in which animals do. 'Wood doesn't eat either, and it doesn't require feeding with furniture polish' (Hoadley 1980: 10).

In the existing ecological literature, two genres stand more or less side by side, unconnected with each other. One of these bewails the loss of forest all over the world; the other raves about wood as a natural material. But trees have to be felled for wood to be used. So how can the two attitudes be married? There is a lot of confusion on this score among nature lovers: many are shy of facing up to the contradiction. Georg Sperber, a leading forestry official in Germany, declared with a mixture of triumph and alarm: 'A new wood age has begun that threatens to sell off our natural heritage' (Knapp and Spangenberg 2007: 177). One resolution, at least symbolic, is the tree house – that is, a wooden construction built into a treetop. But the tree house is not exactly an optimal solution for mass housing. Are other syntheses possible? Or is it true that timber use inevitably leads to destruction of the forests? This book will also try to give answers to these questions; there is no single general answer.

For some time, the demand for a 'big history' has been in the air – one that links together human history and natural history. In view of the alarm bells about the environment and the global climate, the task is to understand both the historical past and the future in terms of a co-evolution of man and nature – a co-evolution which, in the absence of level-headed foresight, will eventually be marked by catastrophes. But historians have long had problems with writing such a new history in an empirically solid manner. Attempts at 'big history' are often banal or superficial, in line with the schema of 'modernization + globalization', and lack both the attraction of a hunt for sources and the surprise of unexpected discoveries.

If it is not to be completely colourless, a global history of the co-evolution of man and nature needs tangible material to work on. Wood might be one such material – a leitmotif for a history of the world with endless picturesque variants. For some centuries, a sizeable part of history may be seen as a constant to and fro movement between forest autonomy and timber industry dynamics – with agriculture as a powerful additional player. A new and dramatic culmination now seems to be shaping up. 'Sustainable development', set as the goal for the whole world economy at the 1992 environmental conference in Rio, was first applied – though this is now largely forgotten – to the forest, and especially the montane and saline forest of Central Europe. Forest policy, then, is the historical origin of modern environmental policy; and the historical, as well as contemporary, association between forest policy and power politics also reveals something about certain pitfalls of environmental policy. The structure of wood points to new paths for technology. 'So, the way in which a branch is joined to a tree trunk is such that no engineer can improve on it, in terms of tension and solidity' (Fellner and Teischinger 2001: 131).

Thirty years ago, when I began my researches, the history of wood was a *Holzweg*, in the sense meant by Heidegger, the philosopher from Todtnauberg in the Black Forest: that is, a path ending in thick undergrowth, where the walker turns back in disappointment and only the forestry worker can do any more. Because of the new timber boom, however, the story is now approaching a dramatic finale: the circle seems to be closing as many phenomena of the old Wood Age reappear, together with the fear of wood shortages and wood theft (a widespread crime typical of the eighteenth and nineteenth centuries). But we need to be careful. We are not at the end of history, even if storytellers are all too fond of creating that impression. A new wood age had only just been proclaimed when the crash of autumn 2008 arrived, and forest-owners were again complaining of falling timber prices. This is another oscillation that has been taking place for two centuries or more. The business press turns somersaults as it adjusts its words of wisdom from boom to depression, but one of the useful things about history is that it surveys longer time periods. This fits in well with the *longue durée* of the growth of trees. 'Learn from history' all too often means no more than finding contemporary analogies for certain fixed points in the past: 'death of the forest then, death of the forest now'. A more important lesson, however, is that history goes on.

— 1 —

PATHS INTO THE THICKET OF HISTORY

1 The 'Wood Age'

Do materials make history?

Wood is a special kind of material. From time immemorial, the skill of the human hand has developed by working wood, so much so that we might say the relationship with it is part of human nature. The handling of wood is a basic element in the history of the human body, and in the history of craftsmanship.

In a brown coal mine at Schöningen in Lower Saxony, eight wooden spears have been discovered since 1994 that date back 400,000 years – by far the oldest known wooden implements anywhere in the world (figure 1.1). This highly improbable find is in its way more spectacular than all those at Troy put together. It testifies to an amazing skill in woodworking, greater than anyone previously attributed to people in the Palaeolithic Age, and it shows just how early man developed a high level of competence in dealing with wood. An earlier prehistoric object – a yew spear unearthed at Clacton-on-Sea in 1911 – had already caused a sensation, but after the Schöningen find that was seen to be not just an isolated case but a representative example of Palaeolithic woodcraft.

The know-how associated with wood belongs, as it were, to 'human nature' – to a primal anthropological state. Hartmut Thieme writes of the Schöningen spears: 'The technical perfection of these ballistically balanced weapons points to a long tradition of using such implements.' The exciting conclusion is that humans were capable of big-game hunting hundreds of thousands of years earlier than we previously thought (Thieme 2007: 85). Since 1973 there has been considerable discussion of Paul S. Martin's thesis of 'Pleistocene overkill', according to which North American big game, with the exception of certain kinds of bison, were wiped out by human invaders within the space of a few centuries, some 10,000 years ago. Archaeological finds have indeed revealed a striking overlap between the appearance of humans and the disappearance of big game. The problem with the theory seemed to be that it was hard to imagine how these early humans could have technically mastered big-game hunting on such a scale. But, if we think of the art of perfect woodcraft stretching back into the mists of time, and applied precisely to hunting weapons, then the problem vanishes; the missing link is found.

The glacier mummy of 'Ötzi' from 5,300 years ago, which caused such a sensation when it was discovered in 1991 in the Ötztal in the Austrian Alps, had no fewer than seventeen different kinds of wood

Figure 1.1: Eight wooden throwing-spears were found in and after 1995 in an opencast brown coal mine at Schöningen, in the foothills of the Harz mountains. Dating back 400,000 years, they are the oldest hunting weapons to have survived intact. They were lying in a hunters' camp amid the bones of at least fifteen horses, which had presumably been hunted with these weapons on the shores of a lake. They prove conclusively that primitive man (and, later, Neolithic man) was not only a scavenger but a skilled hunter. But they also prove that people had developed technical skills in woodworking.

on it, each used for a particular purpose (Spindler 1994: 232–8). Archaeologists have also refuted Tacitus' claim that the ancient Germans built their houses from unhewn tree trunks; it appears again and again that the 'savages' were not as savage as we used to think. Ötzi has distracted public attention from oak-lined wells dug up in opencast mining areas in Saxony and near Erkelenz in the Rhineland, which dendrochronological datings have shown to be more than 7,000 years old. These completely unexpected finds have revolutionized our picture of prehistoric settlements in Central Europe, but most spectacular of all have been the wooden nails that make expert eyes as big as saucers. The archaeologist Susanne Friedrich commented: 'After these, anything is possible!' One is curious whether the 'Stone Age' will one day prove to have been a highly developed 'Wood Age'!

Since wooden implements have survived much more rarely than stone or metal objects, we long underestimated the extent to which human history rests upon wooden foundations. A whole culture of work depends on wood – from the Palaeolithic right down to the modern age. There has always been interaction between people and wood: the material made its mark on the hand, the muscular system and man's creative powers, and wooden implements bore traces of the hand that fashioned them.

The wooden machines of the early industrial age, however standardized in their production, sooner or later acquired an individual character from the people who worked on them – which is why these were less interchangeable than workers on iron machinery. Adjustments often needed to be made to wooden machines, and the workers themselves had to take charge of repairs. Wood was easy to work with, but wooden machinery wore out quickly and encouraged a lot of small improvements to be made all the time: 'Wood has been par excellence the material of innovation.' Two historians of the Japanese textile industry noted: 'Technological progress, therefore, penetrated more rapidly into factories equipped with wooden iron-reeling machines than it did with those of iron-machines only' (Clancey 2007: 130, 131).

Where the machines were made of iron, workers were sometimes expressly forbidden to make repairs themselves. Previously, wood had preserved a degree of autonomy for labour and also set limits to the increase in the pace of work. The natural fibrous structure of the various kinds of wood influenced the history of technology. Indeed, the effects of wood extended into social history and the consciousness that workers had of themselves.

Woodworkers played a pioneering role in the formation of the

16

German labour movement, providing a number of key leaders such as August Bebel, Carl Legien and Theodor Leipart. All three were turners – an occupation which, though low in the craft hierarchy, called for special skills of its own (Flade 1979: 231). Both Walter Ulbricht and Wilhelm Pieck, respectively the first party boss and first president of the German Democratic Republic, had originally been joiners. And, in the case of England, Edward Thompson has shown in his great biography that William Morris (1834–96) – who sparked new enthusiasm internationally for the crafts, especially carpentry – was not only a Romantic admirer of the Gothic style but also a passionate socialist.

The political consciousness of workers derived not only – as Marxist theory would have it – from the experience of capitalist exploitation but also from pride in craft skills. Carpenters may have stood out numerically, but when the various trades fused into an industrial union it called itself (after initial hesitations) the Deutscher Holzarbeiterverband, the German Woodworkers' Union (Gottfried Christmann, in Grebing 1993: 17ff.). And in 1966, when the German Wood Union (Gewerkschaft Holz) followed the technological realities and the practice of employers' associations by renaming itself the Wood and Plastics Union, this move triggered considerable disgruntlement: 'It's a new emblem that leaves our members cold'; 'even if we rechristen ourselves, we shall always remain the Gewerkschaft Holz' (Hans-Otto Hemmer, ibid.: 255). Wood shapes identity!

In commerce, too, wood created a world of its own. Buying wood is a matter of trust, since many defects are not visible from the external aspect of a tree. 'Lumber-grading requires considerable exercise of personal judgment', remarked Stanley Horn (1943: 219), at a time when wood was the object of intensive scientific research. And he knew what he was talking about. For this reason, long-lasting personal relations tend to develop between sellers and purchasers.

The Company of Woodmongyres, founded in London in 1376, lost its charter in 1667 when a number of cases of deception came to light; Samuel Pepys's diary contains details of this (Latham 1957: 31). Since the felling and transportation of timber was often subject to government regulation, large dealers often needed to have contacts in officialdom – and so it was that a network took shape, based on either trust or corruption, according to the situation and the way it was seen. 'Conservatism and corruption marked the system by which the navy received and used its timber', Albion tersely opens his chapter on naval timber procurement. 'Patron–client links . . . are central to the allocation and management of timber concessions', is how

Dauvergne describes the timber business in South-East Asia today (Dauvergne 1997: 8). And much the same can be observed in Europe too, throughout the history of the commercialization of timber.

We continually come across a special kind of human milieu in the world of wood – one sealed off on the outside but full of tensions inside. Today, when an ecologically aware public has become alert to illegal tree-felling and forest plunder, many timber firms claim not to know where their product comes from (see, for example, 'Gegen illegales Holz', *WWF-Magazin*, July 2009). Perhaps many really do not know: it would be further evidence of what Jürgen Habermas called 'the new obscurity'.

Wood, wood, everywhere!

Werner Sombart (1863–1941), one of the founders of modern sociology, never forgot – unlike many of his successors – that nature is the foundation of life on earth and that human culture is deeply marked by its handling of natural resources. In his view, the entire culture of pre-industrial times had an inner unity that was only apparent in retrospect but had never been taken into consideration by historians. This unity had a 'decidedly wooden character' (Sombart 1928: 1138).

Following Sombart, the concept of a Wood Age culture stretching over thousands of years from the Stone Age to the eighteenth century became central to the colourful panorama of the pre-modern world. Wood, wood, everywhere! The Stone Age was itself mainly an age of wood: this is too easily forgotten, because wooden remnants have survived from olden times only in exceptional cases. The Greeks also carved images of their gods out of wood: it is only an optical illusion that all their statues are marble.

For millennia, wood was the most important, often the only, substance used for fuel, building and craftsmanship; it was also central to the forerunners of the chemicals industry. A whole world may be seen under a wooden aegis – from woodcutters, rafters, charcoal-burners, potash-makers and glass-blowers, through salters, forgers and blacksmiths, carpenters, cartwrights, coopers and veneer sawyers, to the high art of woodcarvers and shipbuilders. In the early modern period, a eulogy of wood's many and varied uses became a rhetorical figure all the more forceful because of supply worries.

Wolf Helmhard von Hohberg, author of one of the leading works on agriculture in his time, wrote in 1682: 'If we had no wood, we would also have no fire – and then we would have to eat all our food raw and freeze in winter. We would have no houses, and also no brick, glass or metal. We would have neither tables nor doors, neither chairs nor other household equipment' (Hauser 1966: 38). Wood as fuel ranked quantitatively far higher than wood as craft material: it is estimated that, up to the nineteenth century, nine-tenths of wood was used for burning; the word 'coal', in Germany at least, nearly always referred to charcoal. In 1768 the Venetian naturalist Francesco Griselini called wood 'the most precious and most necessary good for the needs of humanity' (Vecchio 1974: 58). As to the forest, it was necessary to human life not only because of its wood but – even more important in some cases – as a grazing ground. It was the only pasture before a special technique was developed for the creation of irrigated meadows.

Someone who looks for wood and forest in history easily becomes obsessed with the subject, finding countless riches in Europe and other parts of the world. Wood as the foundation of human life, economy and culture is present everywhere: all one has to do is dig a little and learn how to read between the lines of the sources.

There is a transhistorical core to the relationship between human beings and wood. However, wood use and woodworking have been subject to (sometimes huge) historical change. The natural properties of the various kinds of wood have always been noted, but they represented *potentials* that were variously used and appreciated in different cultures and epochs. Wood inspires culture; it does not determine it. If there had been only a single 'Wood Age' culture from the Palaeolithic to the 1800s, world history would be truly monotonous. Historians would have to group Neanderthals and people from the age of Goethe in the same category, with the result that the Wood Age would become a night in which all cats were grey. But that is not how things are. Looked at more closely, history presents a *multiplicity* of 'wood ages' and 'wooden cultures', beginning already in prehistoric and ancient historical times. The following section will demonstrate this with the help of some striking examples.

Prehistory: in the beginning was fire

'Anyone who believes that in prehistoric times humans lived in harmony with nature has not the faintest idea of what really happened', Eberhard Zangger, an unconventional archaeologist, tells us. 'Whichever region one examines, the first phase of human-induced environmental instability was the most destructive, because it was at the very beginning that the most soil was lost' (Zangger 2001: 141). Zangger bases himself on the results of digs in Greece, but it is not only there that the evidence points to environmental crises of which no written testimony has come down to us. In the sandy soil of Lusatia, in eastern Germany, extensive forest clearances as early as the fourth century AD led to wind erosion on a scale that proved disastrous for agriculture. Around AD 400, the inhabitants of a village on the Teufelsberg near Briesnig 'gave up the struggle and abandoned a settlement on which sand deposits up to four metres thick had been laid down over the course of a century' (Spuren 2002: 278).

It was not natural instinct but hardship and a sedentary existence that led people to adopt a rather more sustainable way of handling natural resources. The early economy was based on plunder, and until modern times the threat of falling back into this repeatedly posed itself. In agriculture and livestock-raising – the two main kinds of farming – the effects of poor husbandry soon make themselves felt. But it takes longer in the forest, and it is there that the temptation of pillage is especially great. It can then take generations for the forest to recover.

But should the forest regenerate itself at all? As agriculture spread, the impetus to clear land was at first much stronger than concern for preservation of the forest. A turn to protection required a change in the form of economy. It may therefore be assumed that man's relation to the forest had some features of a drama – but when, where and how?

It was long thought that people in early times lived in quite straightforward harmony with the forest, since they would not have been able to clear large areas with their primitive axes. But, as experiments with stone tools have shown, this was to underestimate the capacities of prehistoric man. A Finnish pioneer of experimental archaeology demonstrated in 1953 that a Neolithic stone axe could fell a medium-sized oak tree in a mere half-hour (Radkau 2008c: 42).

The fact that humans soon learned how to make use of fire was also left out of account for a long time. Only since the 1960s has a combination of palaeobotanical and ethnological research made it clear to what extent human civilization had its origins in fire-assisted hunting and slash-and-burn cultivation, which left areas of cleared forest highly fertile for a few years before they became exhausted and had to be given up.

In the conditions of Central Europe, the forest managed to regenerate itself once humans moved on from these fire clearances. But things were not so easy in areas affected by drought. Much of Australia's savannah land came about as a result of burning by Aborigines, and tree cover returned only gradually when these practices were abandoned (Goldammer et al., in Schulte and Schöne 1996: 172). The dramatic character of man's early relationship with nature was mainly on account of fire. When it did not destroy the humus layer in the soil, lush and species-rich vegetation could quickly spring up over large areas. But the key question was how to keep fire under control if the wind suddenly gusted or changed direction.

Stephen J. Pyne, who, with the ardour of a pyromaniac, has uncovered the igneous beginnings of civilization all over the world, formed a general impression that fire very rarely destroyed a landscape all on its own. 'But fire and hoof, fire and axe, fire and plough, fire and sword – all magnify the effects by altering the timing of fire, its intensity, the fuel on which it feeds, the biological potential for exploiting the aftermath of a burn' (Pyne 1997: 39). The mountainous Mediterranean region, with its light soil and dry summers – an 'empire of fire', where sheep and goats followed in the wake of burning – was one of the fragile landscapes highly vulnerable to fire. And this brings us geographically to the world of classical antiquity.

Antiquity: the supposed crisis of the forest

In 1864 George P. Marsh, then US ambassador to Italy, published the most famous American manifesto against the destruction of the forests – *Man and Nature* – in which he argued that ancient Rome's 'brutal and exhausting despotism' over both man and nature was the *causa causarum* of the devastation of the Mediterranean (Marsh 1974: 5). In the same vein, travel guides written today maintain that the poverty of the Mediterranean forest is due to shipbuilding in antiquity. Later historical experience, however, gives reason to think that the exact opposite was the case: that forest conservation first became official policy as a result of intensive shipbuilding.

What do the ancient sources tell us? For those familiar with forest history in modern times, the great surprise is that the kind of complaints about deforestation that abound in sources in and after the sixteenth century are almost completely absent from the literary heritage of antiquity. The British ancient historian Russell Meiggs (1902–1989), who had practical experience in the field because of his responsibilities for the timber supply in the Second World War, already pointed to this previously unnoticed feature of the ancient world (Meiggs 1982: 377, 1ff.). Archaeological finds have provided evidence that early erosion as a result of mountainside deforestation occurred in the period *before* the first literary sources, whereas the Mediterranean ecology stabilized to some extent in the period of classical antiquity, not least because of the terrace cultivation of fruit trees, in a 'marriage of vine and olive' that has given the Mediterranean slopes their charm ever since.

Of course, people in antiquity were not more stupid than 'Ötzi': they knew a thing or two about the many and varied qualities of wood. They also knew that trees do not grow overnight and that saplings need to be protected against grazing animals. Aristotle, the most celebrated polymath of antiquity, lived in a world where there were already forest supervisors, but he did not consider it necessary to dwell on that institution (Radkau 2008c: 136). In 59 BC the Roman Senate appointed Julius Caesar on his return from Spain as supervisor of the forests and public lands, but this was only a vain attempt to curb the ambitious upstart's political ambitions (Meiggs 1982: 328). The geographer Strabo reported that the mineral ores of Elba (then Aethalia) would have to be shipped to the mainland for smelting, apparently because the woodland there was becoming exhausted, but he mentioned this only as a peculiarity of the island (Strabo V: 2, §6).

One of the very few references to extensive deforestation for gain (copper smelting and shipbuilding) comes from Eratosthenes, the other great geographer of antiquity, and refers to Cyprus, the ancient centre of copper production from which the metal actually got its name. But it turns out that, however much firewood man consumes, the tireless growth of the forest will prevail in the end. In order to promote agriculture, settlers eventually had to be given free rein to clear the land and allocated it as tax-free property (Strabo XIV: 6). Hans-Günter Buchholz, who is unique in having spent more than fifty years studying wooden remnants from ancient Cyprus, has estimated from the use of wood for copper smelting that the island must have been 'completely deforested much more than twenty times over' in antiquity – a quite astonishing figure! But presumably he thinks that the forest kept growing straight back again – otherwise how could copper smelting have been kept up? Cyprus, he notes, is still today 'the richest in forest among the Mediterranean islands' (Buchholz 2004: 33f.) – even though, as a British forester on a mission there snorted as long ago as 1881, 'the most instinctive hatred of trees is, perhaps, the only point of affinity between Greeks and Turks' (Thirgood 1987: 349). This was the view of a forest reformer from the North, who paid no heed to local fruit tree cultivation. But, as Turkish historian Faruk Tabak has shown, there is much evidence that this underwent a huge boom on the hills and mountains of the Mediterranean in the seventeenth and eighteenth centuries (Tabak 2008: 242–97).

If Herodotus is to be believed, the Persian king Xerxes must have used a third of his army to clear the forest as he made his way across the mountains of Macedonia in 480 BC (Herodotus VII: 131). According to John McNeill (1992), who has conducted field research on forest history in five adjoining mountainous regions of the Mediterranean, large-scale deforestation can be demonstrated in all cases since the nineteenth century. Modern Greeks have tried to blame the Turks for the bleakness of large parts of their mountainous regions, but even Kolokotronis, the hero of Greece's freedom struggle, complained that mountains in the Peloponnese, which were still covered in forest under Turkish rule, became bare slopes within a short time after liberation (Radkau 2008a: 134).

Archaeological finds suggest that these isolated shafts of light do not reveal the whole story. Thus, when modern archaeological methods were used in the 1950s to study buildings of late antiquity in the city of Trier, an examination of the kinds of wood in use came up with surprising conclusions. Contrary to all expectations, oak scarcely featured at all in either the Bishop's Palace or the Imperial Palastaula (known today as the Basilica); what there was instead was fir wood and even 'kinds of wood that were used hardly anywhere else in building construction: alder, hazelnut, poplar, birch and common dogwood' (Hollstein 1980: 155).

Many concluded from this that centuries of overuse must have led to a general shortage of oak in the region – a part of Germany famed for its abundance. In the modern climate of ecological doom, some even detected a general environmental crisis in the Roman Germania of late antiquity. It may be the case, however, that the ancient builders of Trier had practical reasons for preferring woods that later came to be thought of as inferior. A local shortage of certain kinds of trees does not mean a crisis. Many archaeologists were surprised to find that the Romans already recycled old beams in new buildings. Was this a sign of wood shortage? Not necessarily – for then, as later, timber from old buildings had the advantage of being seasoned and 'of proven quality' (Zwerger 1997: 11).

The situation was different in North Africa, the Near East and South and East Asia. An Egyptian papyrus text from 217 BC contains a complaint that is scarcely ever found in Mediterranean Europe during antiquity: 'We have looked for wood everywhere but hardly found one acacia' (Nenninger 2001: 63). In parts of the world without cold winters, however, it was not a basic necessity of life to lay up large stocks of firewood. And in regions with large irrigation systems the peasantry was not dependent upon forest grazing. Wood did not have the same strategic significance in such cultures that it had in Northern Europe; people could live with much smaller areas of forest. Indeed, until well into the modern age, political power usually displayed itself there in the clearance of forests, not in the kind of conservation policies that began to emerge in many parts of Europe in the sixteenth century.

When Buddha died in 483 BC, it was difficult to buy wood in sufficient quantity for the burning of his body (Schumann 1989: 253.). It was reported from medieval Arab cities that caretakers had to ensure that tenants did not take the doors with them when they left because of the high cost of wood (Cahen 1970: 117). A German apothecary who travelled in Turkey from 1587 to 1589 reported in amazement 'that in thousands of houses in Constantinople no fire is lighted all year round, and nothing is cooked, but everything is brought from cookshops because of the great increase in the price of wood. And the same cookshops have their pots and pans walled in, for they are exceedingly economical with their wood' (Koder 1984: 53f.). This shortage of wood was due not least to the fact that the population of the city had increased nearly tenfold over the previous century (Tabak 2008: 114). The wood supply must have grown subsequently, because full-timber (not half-timber) construction prevailed in Constantinople until well into the nineteenth century, despite the frequent outbreaks of fire. In any event, at the time of the apothecary's visit, the first literature on wood-saving measures was beginning to appear in Germany, although it seems to have had little success in changing people's habits until the eighteenth century.

In global terms it is clear that Europe – where by far the most complaints of wood shortages were made from the sixteenth century on – had plentiful resources in comparison with most other parts of the world. This abundance of wood in Western and Central Europe, which had originally been an element in its cultural backwardness, became an increasingly important factor in its prosperity and power. Nor was this the only example in which wood raised a peripheral region into a centre of power: Macedonia was another one in antiquity, as was New England in the modern age.

The Macedonian kings who preceded Alexander the Great were well aware of the significance of the forests for power politics, and they made wood a royal monopoly (Meiggs 1982: 126). Shipbuilding and metal processing, the two keys to power, depended on copious supplies of wood. In fact, generally speaking, we can see how shifts in the centre of power in and near the Mediterranean – from ancient Babylonia and Egypt through Macedonia and Rome to Spain, France and finally the British Empire – followed the availability of forest resources. Maurice Lombard has shown in a pioneering work how Islamic civilization, at its height from the eighth to the eleventh century, suffered from a shortage of wood that was fraught with consequences for the future (Lombard 1959; 1975: 177–81). Already in late antiquity the rise of Western and Central Europe was heralded by its role in economic activities related to wood: iron smelting, the making and repairing of carts, the production of barrels instead of fragile amphorae, even shipbuilding (Schneider 2007: 74f., 81).

In modern Europe, the nexus between forest and power was deliberately strengthened and institutionalized as it had never been before in history, so that it became a significant, though for a long time little noticed, aspect in the global position of the continent. One reason for the revolt of the New England states was outrage over the British Crown's claim to the tallest white pines, which provided the material for the best ship's masts. And one reason for the Americans' victory in the War of Independence was the superior resources of timber at their disposal (Albion 1926: 281–315).

Dependence on wood: time bomb or emergency brake?

The quotation from Werner Sombart to which we referred above suggested a reinterpretation of world history in which wood would occupy a place of honour. He characterized the transition from the Wood Age to the age of coal, metal and synthetic materials as a major turn from the 'organic' to the 'inorganic' – a turn that he deeply regretted later in life, when he became sceptical about the idea of progress. In his view, the whole of civilization before the nineteenth century had borne the 'imprint of wood', in a more than superficial sense; it had been 'organic also in its material-sensuous nature'. Human civilization had been closer to nature than it was in the modern industrial age.

Now, if anything followed from the 'organic' character of 'wooden civilization', it was surely the importance of gearing that civilization to self-regeneration, to 'sustainability'. Curiously, though, Sombart did not draw such a conclusion; he gave the impression, rather, that part of the vitality of 'wooden civilization' had to do with its prodigal use of wood, so long as it was still young, energetic and creative. A creeping ecological suicide was thus built into it from the start; the finite supply of wood became a ticking time bomb. Economic life, which experienced tempestuous growth in the late medieval and early modern cities of Europe, therefore faced decline in the eighteenth century as a result of shrinking timber resources – until coal appeared as the saviour and the dynamic of capitalism intensified still further.

In presenting this historical argument, Sombart could cite any number of complaints that people made at the time about the decay of the forest and the shortage of wood. These sound plausible to a modern ear, and have often been quoted in recent times in the context of a growing ecological consciousness. In 2006, a major work by the British geographer Michael Williams depicted the whole global history of the forests as one of advancing deforestation – a scenario that seemed to offer no hope. The mass consumption of wood means that concern about the forests continues to surface spontaneously. Ramblers are filled with unease when they see how a tree that took a hundred years to grow can be brought to the ground in the twinkling of an eye. A tree falls with a crash, but its growth is silent and imperceptible. We see how quickly wood burns in a fireplace, but we do not see the reserves of wood in the depths of the forest and the wide expanse of the planet. If we imagine the massive use that was made of all that wood in the pre-modern age, we are overcome with the feeling that 'it couldn't end well'. This was already a widespread feeling in the eighteenth century, the more that people wagered on economic growth and planned for the future.

But precisely *because* it had seemed evident for centuries that wood was a limited and endangered resource – in sharp contrast to the perception of fossil fuels in modern times – the reverse logic is also conceivable: that is, since fear of wood shortages regularly accompanied economic growth and dampened future ambitions by reminding everyone of the limits to growth, this 'wood brake' had a beneficial effect that stabilized the society of the time.

We do not have to follow Sombart in thinking of early modern capitalism as a racing car that continually started up with roaring engines and then came to a halt with a screeching of wooden brakes. Most goods were in short supply in pre-industrial times; and even if an abundance of wood encouraged rapid growth of the 'fire trades', food bottlenecks might well appear – not to speak of fodder for the horses that transported the wood. The old urban economy had no inner compulsion to unlimited growth – quite the contrary. The guilds watched over output restrictions, and the walled city saw itself as an association of burghers that admitted newcomers only under certain conditions. The 'wood brake' therefore helped to maintain the traditional order of the city.

If we bear in mind that people could use almost everything in the forest, almost every type of wood, as well as branches, foliage and dead wood, we might come to the conclusion that the Wood Age inevitably led to total plundering and the loss of all nutrients. This is a common belief among forest historians. But it is also quite possible to conclude that the very diversity of forest interests tended to preserve a rich species diversity there.

For the time being, this other logic of the Wood Age exists only as a model, only as an ideal type. The extent to which it corresponds to reality has to be determined on a case by case basis; human behaviour by no means always follows a hypothetical model. We cannot exclude the possibility that Sombart's great drama actually was played out in certain periods and in certain regions. There is more than one possible history of wood. But there are not an endless number: we keep coming across typical patterns.

Two contrasting histories of the relationship between man and the forest, and between man and wood, might be elaborated. The eco-pessimistic one would describe a centuries-long process of decline, in which wood has increasingly been replaced with other materials for building, crafts and fuel, so that today it is deformed beyond recognition, even when some use is still found for it. The alternative history, however, would point to technological advances that have uncovered useful new properties of wood; modern research, it would emphasize, has brought rational-scientific approaches to the fore, instead of the practical knowledge gained from experience that used to reign supreme.

In the Sixth Proposition of his 'Idea for a Universal History with a Cosmopolitan Purpose' (1784), Immanuel Kant wrote: 'Nothing straight can be built from such crooked timber as man is made of.' It is a proposition that cuts right across that philosopher's Enlightenment ideal. But does the wood metaphor hold up? Like most people, Kant thought primarily in terms of tall straight trees and associated wood with the idea of sturdy immutability. But even in those days craftsmen had plenty of experience of the pliability of wood. Though so firm in appearance, it could also be interpreted as a flexible bundle of fibres. Under a microscope, wood looked pretty much like a sponge.

Peer Haller, a technologist from Dresden who is more excited by wood's potential than by its nostalgic aura, has recently developed a process for giving squared timber a new solidity by first compressing it and then stretching it under heat. He argues that we must free our thinking from the influence of large trees and conceive of wood as a sponge in order to develop its technological potential; it is all too easy to forget that trees are made up largely of water – and of air. The textbooks tell us that wood consists of lignin and cellulose, but

27

a microscope also shows us the empty spaces in between, the pores. And Haller quotes from Lao Tzu's book of wisdom, the *Dao De Jing*: 'Nothingness is that which produces effect.'

In modern times, wood science textbooks repeatedly stressed that, for all our practical experience, we wrongly believed for thousands of years that we had a precise knowledge of wood. Generalization from experience also creates prejudices. This is particularly evident in the case of wood, which has so many individual characteristics that it continually flies in the face of general rules: not only rules derived from experience, but also the ones that modern scientific research comes up with. Although our familiarity with wood goes back to the most ancient times, its endless varieties have many properties, depending on type, location and use, that have only gradually become apparent. Only when some experience of building in concrete had been accumulated did people realize that wood affords a pleasant indoor climate and that, unlike concrete, it grows more beautiful with age. This is not the least of the reasons why the history of man's relationship with wood is a history without an end.

2 Man and Forest: Stories and History

History, voluble and silent

The global history of man's relationship with wood contains a multitude of different histories. The diversity of world history is reflected in the history of the forests. Yet forest historians who jump from one region to another, perhaps even from the central German uplands to the edge of the Himalayas, constantly have a sense of déjà vu. Many histories sound so familiar to them, however different the wooded landscape: conflicts between provision for the future and short-sighted egoism leading to massive deforestation and disruption of the hydrologic balance; conflicts between central authorities and local villages over forest use, or between foresters and farmers over pasture rights and slash-and-burn cultivation; recriminations flying in every direction over damage to the forest. Many stories of the forest have what Max Weber called 'ideal-typical' features – and this creates the opportunity to write *history* out of them. The best stories often contain a touch of invention. The extent to which these ideal types contain the whole history must always be established on an individual basis. Large stretches of man's relationship with wood, going back to primordial times, are still *terra incognita* and will probably remain so for ever. How people handled wood, and how it left its mark on them, is mostly a quite unspectacular, everyday history. Things that were once taken for granted are now discovered, if at all, between the lines of the written sources, so it is no wonder that there is much less historical research on everyday life than on the major wars.

The written sources frequently leave us in the lurch on the subject of wood. Historians therefore have to focus on *objects* – the material culture of an age – and to do so with the eyes of a connoisseur, drawing on the help of archaeologists, ethnologists, art historians and people who work with wood. Since the written sources usually register only woodcutting and methods of timber harvesting, not the actual growth of wood, a history that operated only with official records would almost inevitably be a history of deforestation. By walking in the forest, however, we can remind ourselves that it grows spontaneously (by no means always in planned ways) and that its history is not completely identical with the history of forest administration.

In the records we find much material about *conflicts*, so that it might appear that forest history is essentially a history of struggle. At least as important, however, though much less conspicuous, are the everyday arrangements that people with an interest in the forest came to (Ernst 2000: 345f.). The economic history of wood is definitely not only one of catastrophic plunder, but also one of co-evolution and recurring balance between man and nature. There have certainly been crises, but for long periods of time it has been a story of frugality and day-to-day coping with limited resources, in which people simply got on with it and made little fuss. Old wooden buildings tell us something about the state of the forest at the time of their construction.

The balance between man and nature had little to do with any 'natural' instinct on the part of human beings, but rested mainly on the omnipresence of scarcity and need. Where would a 'natural' instinct towards sustainability have come from, given that the forest had covered endless spaces since time immemorial? On the other hand, the need for sustainability within the household economy was so self-evident that people did not waste words over it. 'Sustainability' is emphatically proclaimed as an imperative when the circumstances are such that it is no longer a matter of course.

The link between wood and civilization is also partly reflected in the written sources. Arnold Toynbee, the most famous global historian of the twentieth century, felt sure that 'the extinction of the Attic forests compelled Athenian architects to translate their work from the medium of timber into that of stone and so led to the creation of the Parthenon', whose columns and capitals themselves recalled the form of trees (Toynbee 1946: 90). In his view, this perfectly illustrated his basic thesis that the great creative achievements of world history arose out of the challenge of an emergency situation. The Egyptologist Jan Assmann, for his part, explained the massive stone monuments of the pharaohs not by Egypt's lack of forest but by the pharaonic 'ideology of stone' (Assmann 2003: 76f.). Neither position can be proven with any exactitude. Plato even believed that the great buildings constructed under Pericles – a period he regarded as disastrous for Athens – had been partly responsible for the deforestation of Attica (Nenninger 2001: 197).

However it may be, a comparative survey of various parts of the world makes it clear that the dearth of forest in the Mediterranean in historical times went together with a prevalence of stone construction, whereas the abundance of forest in the North – and in Japan – went together with much longer traditions of wooden construction. The Old Testament King Solomon lavishly furnished the Temple with cedar, and the Bible repeatedly sings the praises of the wood (e.g., 1 Kings 6, 8–10), but the high price he had to pay King Hiram of Tyre for it was the beginning of the decline of the Israelite kingdom (Meiggs 1982: 69ff.). Where there are few massive trees to support massive buildings, rulers generally prefer to display their power in stone monuments. But sometimes the art of working with wood reaches its acme precisely where wood is most expensive. In Egypt, for example, the art of veneer (which applied wafer-thin layers of precious wood onto a much cheaper wooden base) was highly developed from a very early date. Thanks to the dry desert climate, no other Mediterranean civilization in antiquity has handed down so many wooden artefacts.

Some wood-based civilizations are typical of countries rich in forest, while others are typical of countries poor in forest. The Celts in their forests were ahead even of the Romans in cart construction and iron smelting. But it is necessary to be wary of forest determinism. The influence of abundant forest on architecture is double-edged: it can lead to wasteful practices such as the dysfunctional loading of buildings with heavy oak, but it can also – in so far as there is a free choice of types of wood – result in a highly developed 'material-specific technology' (Zwerger 1997: 227, 231). How wood is handled is a question not just of natural resources but also of cultural traditions. In the Alps, the border between German-speaking and Romanic villages is typically also the border between wooden and stone building traditions, even where there is no major difference in forest resources

(Bätzing 1984: 27). The Romanic villages express the cultural influence of the Mediterranean city not only in their wooden buildings but also in their general sociability (Cole and Wolf 1974).

Turning points in the economics of wood and forest

When, after millennia of prehistoric darkness, does the history of interaction between man and nature become a dramatic narrative? When does it become a field through which something actually moves? Three main factors can make this happen: 1) important types of wood that are much in demand become scarce and give rise to conflict, since their availability is a trump card in the competitive struggle; 2) technological development runs up against the limits of wood's natural properties; and 3) the culture in question holds wood in particularly high or low regard. Above all when these three conditions are present together, wood becomes, so to speak, the lead player in events.

From today's vantage point, the drama of man's relationship with wood really takes shape only with the coming of the modern age. This is in keeping with the emphasis of this book. The initial stage is the sixteenth century, in which some historians think they can detect a kind of first 'industrial revolution'. Then comes the period around the turn of the nineteenth century: one of industrial revolution in England, political revolution in France and 'proto-industrialization' in Germany. These historical moments mark turning points in the economic and technological history of wood – stages in the economic utilization of the forest, advances in the technologization and industrialization of wood processing. This may be illustrated at several levels.

1) At the level of scarcity and moves to a more 'economical' use of wood, it was in the sixteenth century that wood shortages first became a problem in need of special solutions. The period around the year 1800 saw the climax of supply anxiety and of technological efforts to reduce wood consumption. And today's world is faced with the threat of a new *global* shortage of wood, related to swiftly rising demand for it as a fuel, in a context of population growth and worldwide pillage of the forests. At the same time, however, new possibilities have emerged of making more efficient use of wood. The recycling of scrap wood is a red thread running through the technological history of the material, from the early modern period down to the present day.

31

2) At the level of the forest economy, the sixteenth century brought the first great advances in ordinance, the primary aim of governments being to gain maximum control of forest areas. Around the turn of the nineteenth century – especially in Germany – a breakthrough by the reforestation movement meant that the authorities now sought to regulate not only woodcutting but the growth of forest. Today this has reached a new stage, with the trend towards planned cultivation of wood and the development of new kinds of commercial woodland. The changing relationship between agriculture and forestry – a major theme in forest history since the Middle Ages – has played a role in all these processes.

3) It was in such historical periods that the various stages in the acquiring and processing of timber underwent rational organization. In the sixteenth century, timber rafting was already quite extensive, and some wood was being processed into boards in special sawmills. With the beginning of large-scale reforestation, attempts were made around the turn of the nineteenth century to make forest growth, too, the object of rational organization. But several stages of working with wood – from tree-felling to furniture production – became fully part of this process only during the final decades of industrialization, when they brought about a technological revolution. Major advances in the commercialization and marketing of wood first involved building construction, then extended to firewood and, finally, to wood waste.

The economic and technical history of wood is not, however, a story only of increasing rationalization, mechanization and marketization. Demands have repeatedly been made, and proclamations issued, for forestry to be put on a systematic economic basis, yet even today this has still not been achieved. A tree takes generations to grow, and there is no economic calculation that covers such time spans. A tension has always existed between the natural properties and growth conditions of wood, on the one hand, and economic and technical requirements, on the other. This too has been an element of dynamism in the history of wood.

What is a forest – and does the forest consist only of wood?

The accounts given in histories of the forest often deal only with large closed areas of full-grown trees, as if this were a matter of course. This reflects the point of view of the modern forester. A historian needs to operate with a broader concept, however. The woodland that was important to people's livelihood until the nineteenth century did not always consist of large forests. At least as important were small woods scattered about on farms, favourably situated riverside forest, and the scrub-like copses and pasture about which it has never been clear whether they should be seen as woodland or open field. And then there are the groves and orchards, containing the trees that everywhere in the world are the most valuable for farmers. In times of shortage, even foresters consider poplar-lined alleys, river banks and hedges on the edge of farmers' fields as valuable sources of wood. The histories of wood, forest and trees seem at first sight to form a single history. But they are to some extent different from one another, even if there are large areas of overlap.

For the forest authorities, the production of wood soon became the true purpose of silviculture; any other use was declared 'secondary', or even excluded as damaging to the forest, especially when 'scientific' forestry began to take hold around the turn of the nineteenth century. For farmers, though – who made up the bulk of the population until the nineteenth century – the main use of the forest, when it was not actually burned and cleared for agriculture, was often as a source of food for their livestock and fertilizer for their fields. In the nineteenth century, one 'secondary use' did acquire growing importance for industry and respectability in the eyes of foresters: that is, the extraction of oak bark as a tanning agent for the leather industry (Schenk 1996: 192ff.).

In many regions, agriculture and husbandry were completely dependent on the forest for such purposes until well into the nineteenth century. The philologist Jost Trier (1963: 52) claims to have demonstrated that one of the German words for forest, *Wald*, derived from the farmers' practice of plucking the foliage there. And the landscape planner Michael Machatschek (2002), who lives on a farm in the Alps, has produced a lot of material to show that, although foresters regard it as a bad habit harmful to the trees – especially since botanists started to teach that leaves are 'the lungs of trees' (Stuber 2008: 188) – 'pollarding' for fodder (*Schneiteln*) is a varied practice with its special know-how.

All these problems, which might be thought to belong to a remote past, have a core that remains as topical as ever. This may be defined, in Karl Marx's terminology, as the contradiction between use-value and exchange-value, which appears in exemplary fashion in the case of the forest. A really major split, or even sharp conflict, has often developed between the use-value of the forest for people living there and the exchange-value arising from forest produce that can be turned directly into money. In today's 'Third World', with its 'dual economy' in which the timber industry and local users of the forest are worlds apart from each other, this opposition manifests itself even more sharply than it used to do in Europe. It is a good example of how a look back at our history can shed light on many conflicts in the contemporary world.

The newly discovered ecological function of the forest has given a new form to the use-value/exchange-value contradiction. Since the significance of forests for climate, water balance, soil fertility and species diversity is a value that cannot be expressed in money or traded on the market, it has often been concluded that forests in general should be subject to far-reaching state control. Already before the early modern age it was argued – most vehemently by officials, of course – that the state is the best manager of the forest. This view was more typical in continental Europe than in Britain, where John Evelyn's famous manual on forestry (*Sylva*, 1664) addressed private landowners at least as much as the government of the day. But in the nineteenth century the British colonial administration in India became converted to the idea that the state embodied a higher rationality in relation to the forest. The role of the state has anyway been a central issue of forest history since the sixteenth century, and it has also come to occupy a key position in environmental policy as a whole.

3 Wood and Historical Change

The properties and use-values of different kinds of wood

When wood became an object of policy and scientific study in the early modern period, one of the first strategies was to teach people that each type of wood should as far as possible be used for things to which it was best suited, and above all that no precious wood should be wasted on uses for which inferior kinds were sufficient. As we saw in the case of 'Ötzi', this distinction has been common since time immemorial, as have others based on practical know-how. An ethnologist once recorded no fewer than twenty-seven different kinds of wood in the home of a poor peasant living in the forest, all chosen on the basis of their suitability for a particular task (Blau 1917). But how did wood become the object of scientific study and scientifically legitimated official policy?

Research into the physical and technical properties of wood made only little headway even in the nineteenth century, and its countless variants escaped being theorized for a long time. In 1860 a professor of forestry advised consulting 'basket-weavers and woodcutters' to check the tenacity of various woods; he himself had lost 'all appetite' for attempts to measure it exactly (Nördlinger 1860: 377f.). Even a hundred years later, 'trying to break wood' was 'the only tolerably secure way of establishing its strength' (Internationaler Holzhandelskongress 1976: 155). The 'destructibility test' – a key advance in assessing a material – developed later in the case of wood than in that of iron. For engineers who longed for something more exact, this remained an inherent defect of wood as a material.

But since wood is an organic and therefore always individual material, intuition also played a role in determining the strength of its elements – more than in the case of rock or iron. 'A fibrous wooden beam is comparatively easy for humans to understand. But do you know what a block of cast iron feels like before it breaks, or how and why the crystals link together inside it?' Max Eyth (1906: 493), the well-known mechanical engineer and publicist, put these words into the mouth of the chief designer of the railway bridge over the Firth of Tay, which, despite its cast-iron pillars, collapsed under the weight of a train one stormy night in December 1879. Only modern advances in material testing made iron and steel more susceptible than wood to precise calculation. But fresh advances have meant that wood has again been catching up fast.

Classification

The classification of wood is a source of vexation for those who love its diversity: 'The woodworker typically reacts to the idea of scientific classification and naming of woods with distaste and discouragement, because gaining a mastery of the subject seems impossible' (Hoadley 1980: 10). No wonder. Those who read encyclopaedic manuals of wood from cover to cover in the hope of finding practical guidance end up in despair. There is no end to the diversity of wood, and the advantages and disadvantages of this for silviculture or technical processing are a constant subject of discussion.

Supporters of a rational choice approach look for simple alternatives, and at first sight it seems easy to find them. There is a dualism of deciduous and coniferous, of hardwood and softwood, and in a global perspective there is the contrast between tropical deciduous forest and boreal coniferous forest. Very roughly speaking, there is an overlap among three pairs of oppositions, and indeed in the English language hardwood and softwood have become synonymous with deciduous and coniferous. But in specific cases the fit is far from perfect: the lightest of all woods, balsawood, is tropical deciduous, and other deciduous woods such as basswood, poplar, alder and willow are also relatively soft, while larch – the only European conifer that sheds its needles in autumn – has hard wood and is prized as 'the oak of conifers' (Hufnagel and Puzyr 1980: 53). In North America, various pines have also acquired the prestige of oak (Johnson 1973).

The terms 'hardwood' and 'softwood' originated in the timber trade, in which the most common woods really are softer than the 'three great staple hardwoods – mahogany, teak, and oak' (Latham 1957: 19). Latham, scion of a family timber business, draws on experience when he writes:

> The hardwood importer's business is considerably more intricate than that of the softwood branch, inasmuch as the former has to deal with a far greater variety of both species and qualities. To such an extent is this true that over 350 species of hardwoods have been known to be listed in customs declarations in one year. The larger importer deals through agents, as does his softwood confrere. However, as his goods are received from literally all over the world, he has to keep in touch with a much greater number of markets.

Since hardwood is more irregular than softwood, trust is here especially important; drying takes longer than for softwood and is a quality factor of greater significance (ibid.: 80f.).

Nevertheless, the average hardness of various kinds of wood is of limited significance, since real levels can vary quite considerably with location, tree age, the part of the tree from which the wood is taken, and so on. The same is true of the wood's toughness: 'It is not uncommon for one piece of wood produced in a sawmill to be five or even more times tougher than a second piece of the same kind of wood of the same dimensions' (Internationaler Holzhandelskongress 1976: 155). This casts some light on the difficulties that traders have even today in exactly calculating the technical uses to which natural wood can be put.

Anyone in search of a straightforward picture will certainly be feeling confused! But the modern timber industry has radically simplified its range of available woods and its definitions of quality, thereby giving some scope for 'rational choice'. When the sociologist Niklas Luhmann writes that the performance of systems depends on their reducing complexity, we may well doubt the general truth of his claim, given that some systems make life more complicated. Luhmann's systems theory is undoubtedly relevant to the timber trade. But the historian should not view the whole history of wood with the categories of today's timber trade.

The most striking external difference is between deciduous and coniferous woods; it also corresponds to salient differences in cell structure. Coniferous woods consist mainly of the fibrous kind of cells that not only make a tree strong but also provide it with water.

Deciduous trees, on the other hand, have a more complex and irregular cell structure, specialized in accordance with various functions. It is more difficult than in the case of conifers to draw conclusions from the external aspect of a tree trunk about what lies inside. Therefore deciduous wood continues to present greater problems for the automation of sawmills – which is another reason for the dominance of conifers in industrial age forestry. Deciduous trees appeared later than conifers in the history of the planet: the natural evolution ran from the uniform to the more diverse. In the wood culture of the modern age, however, at least until very recently, the evolutionary path has been in the opposite direction.

Until the eighteenth century, people used the forest mainly as pasture and as a source of firewood. Oaks and sometimes copper beeches were cultivated as 'fruit trees' or 'living trees'; others were considered as 'dead wood', and conifers even as 'bad trees' (Hesmer and Schroeder 1963: 225). Pinewood was disliked as a cooking fuel because of its 'very dense and unpleasant smoke' (Hartig 1804:31). Mine managers, however, had reasons to prefer it for underground galleries, where spruce, pine and larch, in particular, responded to increased pressure with a groaning sound that gave advance warning of a threatened collapse. This is why British mineworkers initially opposed the introduction of iron props. Pine forests became especially widespread in mountainous regions in the early modern age, and their rapid advance at the expense of deciduous forest in the nineteenth and twentieth centuries is the least controversial trend in modern forest history.

Hardness, thickness and strength are the three qualities most widely used in the trade for the classification of wood, although they are not always positively correlated with one another. Hardness implies resistance to penetration by foreign bodies. But this is by no means the whole story: basswood, for example, though not used for building, was appreciated long ago as a material for shields because of its lightness and its elastic cushioning of blows (Buchholz 2004: 46, 106), and artistic engravers and turners valued it for its softness and homogeneity. Although woodcarving shops often used to feature in paintings, the great German carvers around the turn of the sixteenth century did not often cover the natural wood with varnish.

The British art historian Michael Baxandall (1980) situates the golden age of south German limewood crafts between 1475 and 1525, when the soft wood had a special 'aura' that was reflected in a self-confident civic culture. If we look today at carving from that period, we find wormholes everywhere. Further to the north, in the

Figure 1.2: Hardwood rasps from the prison and paupers' home founded in Hamburg in 1620. The model for this establishment, the Amsterdam *rasphuis*, refers in its name to this wood-filing activity, which made use mainly of a red Brazil wood that yielded a costly colouring powder. In the sixteenth century, the procurement of this wood had been a major impetus behind the Portuguese colonization of Brazil. The processing of tropical woods by hand was extremely arduous work. Wood-rasping for the paper industry remained prison labour until well into the twentieth century, when it was finally mechanized. British convicts were also frequently set to work with wood. Jeremy Bentham, known as a philosopher for defining 'the greatest happiness of the greatest number' as the yardstick of morality, worked with his brother Samuel Bentham, Inspector-General of Naval Works, to introduce machinery into prisons that made it easier to employ unskilled workers. The same machines were then subsequently used in the world outside (Latham 1957: 210f.).

Hansa cities, the use of hard oak pointed to quite a different world. The city council in Lübeck, for example, ordered that 'no one shall make a spiritual work except in oak' (Flade 1979: 285).

Hardness may be an indication of high quality, but it can also make it more difficult to work with wood (see figure 1.2). A carver who likes to use oak has an attitude that is different from that of the limewood carver: the resistance of the wood positively excites him. But let us not exaggerate the extent to which certain kinds of wood go together with certain epochs and cultures. Two centuries after Tilman Riemenschneider (c.1440–1531), the great master of German limewood arts, was working in Würzburg, Grinling Gibbons (1648–1720), one of the greatest British woodcarvers, was producing limewood art as delicate 'as bone lace' (Sentance 2003: 41).

Gross density is often cited as the most important factor in characterizing a type of wood; it is calculated as the proportion of mass to volume. A historically very important quality of wood depends on its density – that is, its capacity for floating. Oak and beechwood could be floated only on a foundation of conifer logs, and this became one reason for the widespread cultivation of pine forest. The wheels of commerce called more and more for timber floating, since transportation over more than a few kilometres used to be worthwhile only on waterways. Large supplies of firewood for smelting and saltworks were most easily conveyed on water, in the form of unbundled logs.

Charcoal quality is another important factor that historically depended on density and hardness. High-density charcoal obtained from oak and beechwood traditionally had the best reputation in many quarters, but by the eighteenth century these woods were no longer enough on their own to meet the increased requirements. In Styria, 80 per cent of charcoal was then being obtained from spruce (Lackner 1984: 192).

The question of which wood gave the best coal had only theoretical significance when only certain kinds of wood were available in large quantity. By the eighteenth century this sometimes meant that fast-growing fir was better than oak; the quickening pace of the economy brought many a change in the traditional ranking of trees. The Prussian forestry expert Friedrich Pfeil, who was fond of provocative ideas, mounted a frontal attack on the timber hierarchy by declaring that fast-growing poplar had a better claim than oak to be called the 'noble' wood (1816: 203f.). He particularly complained of the 'strong old oaks in the middle of the forest', which held back the growth of other trees and were 'no more than a costly boast for foresters who wanted to appear good managers'; the 'fine poetic elegies about their loss' were 'most ridiculous' (quoted in Hasel 1982: 268). But one anonymous author complained: 'Oh, ye brave ancestors, where you laid down oaks and beeches, we plant willows and poplars, because we are able to use them in their third year

39

already. We do live in the economic century after all!' (Anonymous 1788: 77). Trees species as epoch-defining! When Prince Paphnutius brought the Enlightenment to his land in E. T. A. Hoffmann's novella *Klein Zaches* (1819), he had the forests chopped down and the fairies driven away so that he could plant straight avenues of poplars in their place.

In Italy, especially in the Po Valley, poplars were traditionally pre-ferred for cultivation. Not only could furniture be made from them; Leonardo da Vinci's *Mona Lisa* is painted on poplar wood. More than once, in times of wood shortage, poplar also experienced a boom in Germany. After 1945, contrary to all tradition, the German Poplar Society helped to spread a veritable poplar mania among foresters, and in other countries too it was then considered the 'most exciting of all woods' (Hesmer 1951: xii). It gave rise to greater international cooperation than most other kinds of wood.

In building construction, generally the most lucrative application of wood, the strength of the material was decisive; it has often been considered the most important quality of wood in modern times. A distinction is usually drawn among several kinds of strength, accord-ing to the load on the fibrous structure of the wood. Compressive strength denotes the ability of the wood to withstand the crushing or squashing of its fibres; tensile strength refers to its resistance against the (mainly lengthways) tearing of its fibres. As a building material, wood differs from stone by its higher tensile but lower compressive strength. Wood behaves quite differently according to whether the stress on its fibres is lengthways or crossways. 'Stone is a mass: but wood, by its nature, is already a structure' (Mumford 1963: 78). The tensile strength of wood could be better utilized in conjunction with iron than with old wooden joints. In this sense, iron gave wood new opportunities.

This was true not only of building but also of pianos. Until the eighteenth century, the soundbox of the harpsichord consisted entirely of wood. When Bartolomeo Cristofori invented the piano in 1709, allowing a dramatic increase in volume through the strik-ing of the keys, the new force threatened to burst the wooden soundbox. Only the iron frames introduced after 1800, together with the music of Beethoven, succeeded in releasing the dynamic of the piano and assisting its rapid rise as the characteristic instrument of nineteenth-century bourgeois musical culture (Bramwell 1976: 194).

The natural differences between trees are not considered to be as important as they were in former times. The group of woods in

Box 1.1

The beech has been an especially controversial tree in both ancient and modern times. It is 'the most aggressive of the deciduous trees' (Burschel 1979: 82), it thrives on many soils and, although its dense top hinders the growth of other trees, its foliage improves the quality of the soil. But this does not always happen. If the leaves decompose slowly, involving fungi more than bacteria, an acidic raw humus forms that inhibits the beneficial activity of creatures in the soil. The truth about beeches is soil-dependent. This explains why they are 'sometimes lauded as "nurturing mothers of the forest", but at other times condemned as the worst producers of raw humus' (Leibundgut 1983: 107).

No tree illustrates better the dilemma of ecological value judgements. In 1982, the forestry scientist Dietrich Mülder published a polemical pamphlet, *Helft unsere Buchenwälder retten!* [Help to Save our Beechwoods!], but others thought that the diversity of nature needed to be saved from beeches. Hugh Johnson, in his *International Book of Trees* (1973), described with palpable displeasure how the beech, with its 'domineering methods', was the 'final winner in a struggle for dominance in the forest'. 'Hence the long-answering echo: the echo of an empty room.' Nevertheless, 'to see the sun playing on its pale curves and hollows . . . is one of the winter pleasures' (1973: 150).

As long ago as 1664, John Evelyn's classic *Sylva* was torn this way and that when discussing the beech. First he quoted a poetic eulogy of the tree and its usefulness to housewives: 'Hence in the world's best years the humble shed, / Was happily, and fully furnished: / Beech made their chests, their beds and the joyn'd-stools, / Beech made the boards, the platters, and the bowls.' But then he complained that it was used too frequently, as it was susceptible to worm attack, and wished that 'the use of it were by law, prohibited all joyners, cabinet-makers, and such as furnish tables, chairs, bedsteads, cofers, screws, & c.' (Evelyn 1664: 181ff.). The greatest glory of mahogany, in his view, was that it was not susceptible to worm attack (Latham 1957: 155).

In large parts of Germany, as far as the Bavarian Alps, the natural conditions are better for the beech than for any other tree. It used to be thought that it needs good soil, but we now know that it thrives in low-nutrient terrain, since its own foliage produces the soil it needs. People thought they knew the beech well, but they did not understand what it was capable of doing. Alfred

Möller, an early pioneer of ecological forestry, described the claim that the beech needed good soil as 'one of the worst dogmas' of the spruce fanatics ([1922] 1992: 80). If nature were left to itself, a large part of Germany would be covered with beech or mixed beech woodland. At the time of the Thirty Years' War, when forestry came to a standstill, supporters of the oak already had experiences of the 'beech's intolerance' of other trees (Nieß 1974: 59f.). But, for friends of the beech, this belonged to the vocabulary of its opponents.

These natural conditions soon meant that foresters were faced with the need to make decisions. The beech had important pluses in traditional society: it counted as the best firewood and provided good potash for glassworks; beechnuts could serve as pig feed, which in many places was the principal use of woodland for farmers. And in the nineteenth century, when all such uses became secondary in the forest economy, the beech sank low in people's estimation. By 1920 it was being described as the 'lost tree species' (Hasel 1985: 78); the 'beechwood crisis' became a standard phrase of the day.

By then many regions had long been waging war on the beech – for example, in the southern Alpine saline forests and in Württemberg, where it was declared a nuisance in the sixteenth century and allowed to be freely cut down (Hauff 1977: 42). However useful the beech was to the local population, it did not do such a good job in filling the ruler's coffers. It was too heavy to be rafted, except in combination with coniferous wood, and so it was not very good as a tradable commodity.

Since beechwood warps badly over time, it was considered 'the worst construction timber' (Jägerschmid 1827–8: 1/82). Nor was it popular with joiners and turners because of its tendency to shrink (Rodekamp 1981; 99). 'No tree in the forest is more difficult to raise or less rewarding in its yield', forestry scientist Philipp Geyer complained in 1879, when he described pure beech forest as an 'idle aristocrat' (Schäfer and Zandonella 1993: 25). Since beech was unsuitable for barrels that contained salt, and since it also held back the growth of floatable pinewood, the Alpine salt refineries waged constant battle with it, whereas their counterparts in the Lüneburg plain, who used ships to transport their wood, prized it for its high calorific value.

The twentieth century also saw constant shifts in the evaluation of beech. In the rising tide of ecological awareness, the challenge of 'massive beech-destruction campaigns in northern Hesse' (Hubert

Weiger, in Hatzfeldt 1996: 144) in the 1970s led to calls for the beech forests to be saved (Mülder 1982). After the environmental summit in Rio in 1992, there was a new international impulse to respect the beech, and pro-beech foresters in Germany were surprised to learn how the beech forests of Central Europe were seen as unique. Friends of the beech view global warming with equanimity, if not grim satisfaction, because it seems to offer the beech a good opportunity to stop the conifer in its tracks in Central Europe.

Much of the carpenter's traditional deprecation of beechwood has turned out to be a prejudice. Ralf Pollmeier, one of the top figures in today's beech sawmill industry, trumpets that 'beech is harder than mahogany' and open to many uses. The chipboard and cellulose industry has also revalued beechwood, especially in the Lippe region, where farmers successfully defended the beech forests around the turn of the nineteenth century against orders from above to replace them with coniferous trees. Modern glue technology has turned the special properties of the beech to good advantage. 'Beech is one of the toughest and strongest woods and weighs less than a tenth of steel with the same building specifications, but it has a third of its resistance. Scarcely any other material has such a favourable ratio of tensile strength to weight' (Schäfer and Zandonella 1993: 25). And beech was always relatively inexpensive: its price in the nineteenth century, for example, shadowed the upper end of firewood prices.

In recent years – what a change! – rocketing demand for beechwood, especially in East Asia, has led to such a huge price increase that many local users in Germany who settled into its low-cost niche have had to file for bankruptcy (Schulte 2003: 1/459). Most of the German beechwood now exported to China comes back as finished or semi-finished products.

Traditionally, oak was considered the best construction timber – at least in regions where it was indigenous. Its high tensile strength and resistance to pests and unsettled weather, on account of its tannic acid, made it ideal for external walls. It had an annoying tendency to bend as it grew, but even crooked oak could be used for beams in half-timbered houses (Marstaller 2008: 67ff.). Henry David Thoreau, the prophet of the American forest, loved massive oak trees, but he also had a high regard for the little shrub oak so common in New England: 'rigid as iron, clean as the atmosphere, hardy as virtue, innocent and sweet as a maiden' (Logan 2005: 82).

43

Curiously, he thought that the oak's strength exhausted the soil, and that this had to be regenerated by pine trees (Worster 1977: 71f.). How imprecise was people's knowledge of the forest soil in the nineteenth century! So too was their knowledge of the genesis of oak groves.

In Germany, the most famous place of worship of picturesque old oaks has for the last century been the 'virgin forest' near Sababurg castle on the Upper Weser, a traditional forest pasture. On the initiative of Theodor Rocholl, a painter of battle scenes who thought he had discovered the forest of the ancient Germans, this was made a protected natural park in 1907. Foresters looked after the game, and the landscape remained unspoiled even after the forest ceased to be used for pasture – until the wild animal reserve was abolished in 1968 and natural conservation was handed over to ecologists, who left the forest entirely to its own devices. To the horror of many forest lovers, the oaks have since been overrun by beech trees and are in the course of dying out. Experiences of conservation thus taught people that the oak forest was not at all 'virgin', but had been specially cultivated as pasture. The true virgin forest in Germany is beech forest; humans have played a much larger role than formerly believed in shaping the presence of oak (Rapp and Schmidt 2006: 45, 71, 81). Recent research in England has come to similar conclusions (Rackham 1990: 31), although Latham (1957: 193) considers that the forest there originally consisted of oaks.

The oak became a national symbol in England at least as much as in Germany: 'The oak had been a symbol of strength since at least the sixteenth century. Always the king of trees, it became, with the growth of the Navy, an emblem of the British people and as much a national symbol as roast beef' (Thomas 1983: 220). 'Thousands of verses, good and bad, have extolled the "heart of oak" and its place in the wooden walls' (Albion 1926: 19) – a metaphor that the English took over from the Venetians. The first and longest tree chapter in Evelyn's *Sylva* (1664) is devoted to the oak, whereas the pine, so revered in later centuries, does not merit a chapter of its own.

Modern archaeologists have shown that the oak, not without reason, was often associated with eternity. Research at the ninth-century church of St Andrew at Greensted-juxta-Ongar, Essex, whose walls consist of halved oak trunks, brought a realization 'that oak, if allowed to do so, will survive outdoors for a thousand years', and that we still do not know any limits for 'its survival inside a building' (Hewett 1997: 29). More often than on the continent, one finds crooked oak used here for structurally useful and decorative purposes in half-timbered houses – which has encouraged speculation about the influence of shipbuilding upon house construction.

Oak was also the most highly valued construction timber in the Mediterranean. A historian writes of Central Europe: 'If we compare the incidence of oak trees and good old half-timbered houses, we find that they follow the same line in the south-east and break off equally abruptly, and that in the plains to the north and east half-timbered buildings tail off in the same gradual way as the oak' (Walbe 1979: 392). Until the eighteenth century there was a tendency to overvalue oak as construction timber; prosperous farmers showed off with oversized half-timbered oak frames at the very time when builders were generally becoming more economical in their use of wood.

In countries like Norway where tall oaks were relatively uncommon, churches were built entirely of pinewood even in the Middle Ages; the shape of many of these 'stave churches' is reminiscent of spruce trees. They were put up by rural craftsmen, without any influence from southern models. Originally it was possible to look into the open roof truss and marvel at the construction (Burger 1978: 8). In 1350 the Black Death put an end to this tradition, and later generations found these churches too dark. But today's wood lovers are in raptures: 'To approach a Norwegian stave church for the first time is to be overwhelmed by the feeling that the structure is alive' (Holan 1990: 103).

In Britain, it was only when oak became scarce during the Napoleonic wars that the Admiralty discovered that other foreign timbers were just as good, if not better, for naval construction (Albion 1926: 399). This started the brisk rise in the fortunes of teak, which became a theme of Britain's India policy. But old oak regions on the continent were also forced to look for substitutes, and there too it came to be realized that oak had disadvantages as well as advantages. Its short-fibered wood was unfavourable for spanning open spaces. Its heaviness increased the structural demands when it was used in upper floors of buildings or even bulbous domes; the total timber cost was greatly reduced when bulbous domes were made out of light fir wood. It was noticed in a number of places in the Middle Ages that the fibrous structure of conifers such as spruce and fir gave them good bending strength (Binding et al. 1977: 60); they were therefore preferred for beams and rafters for all sloping or level upper parts of buildings.

The greater 'economies' made by farmers assisted the spread of coniferous forest. Did the wide use of conifer wood in construction reflect this? Presumably it was more a question of a correlation between the two: the technical merits of conifer wood impacted on the forest economy. In the iron age, moreover, it became a source of frustration that oak's high tannin content led to corrosion in any iron elements with which it was associated (Bramwell 1976: 156).

Birchwood was popular in many regions, such as East Prussia; 'a birch forest . . . can be used a good dozen times, and no harm is done if the wood is used for many things at the same time' (Mager 1960: 2/188ff.). For these reasons, and because of their fast rate of growth, many forestry experts recommended the planting of birch trees in the eighteenth century. Later forest science, however, looked back at it scornfully as the age of 'betulomania' (from the Latin for birch: *betula*) (Bernhardt [1872–5] 1966: 2/341). Yet around the year 1800 'ships entirely built of birch' were reported from the Canadian port of Saint John (Latham 1957: 132), and in the early twentieth century birch experienced an industrial rehabilitation in such areas as plywood production and airplane construction.

Generally speaking, foresters today still dislike birch on the grounds that its branches have a 'whip-like effect' on other trees. Landscape artists love the birch, but strict conservationists who want to restore the original moor have launched 'de-birching' campaigns, complaining that it soaks up too much water. Nor is any love lost between ornithologists – the conservationist crack troops – and the birch tree, since it offers no breeding ground for birds. Alfred Möller ([1922] 1992: 81), however, condemned the 'bleak war of extermination' against the birch that he observed in many places. More recently, in the year 2000, the German Forest Conservation Society selected the 'silver birch', the 'pioneer of trees', as Tree of the Year, because of 'its beauty and high ecological value' – another stand against the old prejudice that the birch is a 'forest weed'.

routine use is anyway now limited to a few species, and their natural imperfections can be offset by varnishing and waterproofing. On the other hand, many natural properties of wood are more appreciated than they were in the past, or have been discovered at all only as a result of modern developments in technology. This is the case, for example, with the fact that the cellular structure of wood makes it a poor conductor of heat and sound; but it also applies to its bending strength and glueability, and not least to its irregularity, which hampers the mechanization of woodworking but is increasingly thought of as an attractive contrast to the monotony of synthetic materials.

Light woods had a tumultuous career in the early days of airplane construction. At first considered the 'main material for flying machines', by virtue of its unique combination of lightness, solidity and elasticity, wood became a trump card such as had never been seen before in the history of technology. Later, in the Second World War, the wooden Mosquito bomber became a legend in the US air force: 'No other bomber has such speed and concentrated fire power' (Horn 1943: 232). The history of wood in the industrial age features a long chain of surprises, and even today no end to them seems in sight. Nowadays the timber industry claims that the cellular structure of wood makes it vastly superior to other materials for heat insulation – fifteen times better than concrete, 400 times better than steel, and 1,770 times better than aluminium!

The *chemical* properties of wood were first studied and purposefully used in the nineteenth century – a trend that is still going strong. People learned to value the capacity of various kinds of wood to resist aggressive chemical substances. New industries in the twentieth century (cellulose, wood glue, other wood-based materials) made both the fibrous and the cellular structure of wood relevant to technology. The 'nature' of wood displayed properties of which no one had previously been aware.

Forms of forest economy

Historians speak of 'forest economy' or simply 'forestry' only after that extensive and systematic regulation which the princely forest authorities proclaimed in the sixteenth century, but which in most cases took effect only around the turn of the nineteenth century. There had previously been forms of woodland economy, which spawned certain typical configurations. The farm economy alone gave rise to three distinct types: 'selection forestry' (*Plenterwald*) for the extraction of timber, 'low forest' coppices for the cutting of firewood, and pasture forest for animal grazing. All three appeared both as carefully regulated formations and as products of random and harmful overuse. There were also mixed forms such as the so-called middle forest, a combination of high forest and low forest.

Selection forestry is a particularly old form, used mainly for the farmers' own needs, not for trade. It did not yield a large mass of wood in a single operation, but involved the selection of individual trees of one kind or another as and when the farmer needed them. From the sixteenth century on, this *Plenterwirtschaft* came under attack from a number of edicts issued by regional rulers; it was said to be 'disorderly' and to stand in the way of commercial utilization. Many forestry reformers claimed that the word *plentern* came from *plündern* (to plunder). The practice was actually forbidden in many parts of Germany in the eighteenth and nineteenth centuries.

In recent times, however, ecologically oriented foresters have rehabilitated selection forestry – above all in the mountainous south of Central Europe, which is threatened with erosion – and even held it up as the ideal form of forestry, which spares the forest ecosystem and provides for natural rejuvenation in keeping with local conditions; no bare patches emerge in the forest, and the soil remains protected. Since trees of all ages stand alongside one another, younger ones can grow in the spaces left by the removal of older ones. Nevertheless, the treetops usually remain so dense that only shade-tolerating species such as fir, beech and spruce, not trees like the oak that require light, can prosper in the *Plenterwald*.

A well-run *Plenterwald* requires managers with extensive local knowledge. There are no general formulas; each individual tree must be assessed for its growth potential. Selection forestry has for a long time had no place in large and bureaucratized forest economies, where the felling of trees is highly mechanized. But, under the influence of less sweeping counter-trends that aim at practices closer to nature, selection forestry has been undergoing a certain rehabilitation. Starting from the farming woodland in the Swiss Emmental, a number of experiences have won recognition from foresters too (Liebundgut 1983: 205).

The low forest (*Niederwald*) coppice – a form once very common in Central and Western Europe – has today almost disappeared even in Germany (figure 1.3). In this form, regeneration took place through natural rejuvenation from parts of trees left standing – which meant that only trees with a strong capacity for this (alder, ash, oak, hornbeam, willow, poplar), and to a lesser extent the otherwise hardy copper beech, were able to survive. Conifer woods were completely absent. Coppicing was a form of forestry that did not need to be invented; the trees created it themselves from their own shoots. It differed from *Plenterwald* and other forms of high forest by its low 'rotation time', trees often being felled when they were less than ten

Figure 1.3: Former coppice and pasture forest (beeches) in Emsland, Lower Saxony. The strange tree shapes have their attraction for today's ramblers, but foresters considered them a nuisance because they could scarcely be sold as timber. An account written in 1672 in the principality of Minden complained that 'felling operations were so bungled that the trees looked in many places like an abortion' (Hesmer and Schroeder 1963: 137). Earlier coppice and pasture forest that has for generations grown wild is often thought of today as 'virgin forest'.

years old. It was firewood forest, not timber forest. Young trees also provided much leaf fodder for livestock. The short rotation time had further advantages: thin tree trunks were easier to cut through; regeneration was strongest in young trunks; and, most important of all, people did not tend woodland for a future they would not live to see, but harvested the fruits of their labour with their own hands (Trier 1952: 11f.).

Sustainability was a simpler matter than in the case of *Plenterwald*: one had only to divide the forest area into as many 'strikes' – sectors for annual lumbering – as there were years in the rotation time. In addition to firewood and animal fodder, other uses might include the extraction of oak tannin and the pursuit of agriculture for a time. The *Haubergswirtschaft* in Siegerland was especially famous for its cyclical combination of uses.

If we leave aside the use of certain oak groves for pig fodder, *pasture forest* was not a true forest type in the eyes of foresters, since it did not serve the purpose of timber production. *Plenterwald* and coppice, too, were often spoken of disparagingly. The main trend in modern times has been towards a combination of high forest and clear-cutting. Only high forest yielded the timber qualities that made for a lucrative business. From the point of view of forest authorities, clear-cutting offered decisive advantages for timber dealers and large-scale consumers: a single operation could deliver huge quantities of timber, which could then be bundled into large rafts. Tree-felling could be conducted intensively and under supervision; and transportation – the greatest problem for the timber business – became considerably easier. The question of how the forest would grow again in the cleared areas was initially of secondary importance. Sometimes the next generation came from 'seed trees' left behind there (so-called *Laßreiser*). But the usual sequel to clear-cutting was artificial reforestation by means of seeding and planting.

'Wood defects'? Technical problems associated with the material

The technical history of wood is also a story of how people have dealt with its imperfections. But one strong reservation about its use in construction had nothing to do with any technical defects. Wood has on the whole been less appreciated in the building trade than stone, at least in regions traditionally rich in forest. If people often turned to stone for construction, it was not because timber was scarce or too expensive. On the contrary, in large parts of Central and Western Europe at least, it was because wood was cheaper than stone that people increasingly regarded buildings made of wood as unpleasant places to live in. This was not the least of the reasons why, in the eighteenth and nineteenth centuries, many timbered houses were rendered in such a way that they became unrecognizable. This brought new problems, however, since 'the moist coating deprived the timber of air, and . . . the process of decay set in all the faster' (Jägerschmid 1827–8: 2/527).

What counts as a 'wood defect' depends on what the wood is to be used for. Until the nineteenth century, nine-tenths or more of wood served as fuel, so combustibility was not a defect but an integral part of its purpose. Construction timber was another matter, of course. With the growth of towns, where houses stood cheek by jowl, the extreme reluctance to use wood for external walls was based on the danger of fire. This was in fact the origin of the urban police, which from the late Middle Ages issued countless decrees restricting the use of timber for construction that have affected how we still regard the material today. The search for a fire-resistant wood runs throughout the history of timber technology; it looks as if the goal is unachievable, as if the advantages of wood are indissolubly bound up with its combustibility.

The first prohibitions referred to massive wood-frame construction and the use of timber shingles on roofs (Lemp 1922: 6ff.). But in many regions the massive replacement of timber with stone dates only to the nineteenth century (figure 1.4), when iron appeared for a while to be the building material of the future. Alfred Krupp, the Prussian 'iron king', fearing the danger of fire, banned wood completely for the construction of his Villa Hügel in Essen. But a series of large fires eventually taught everyone that 'iron is even more dangerous than wood in the event of a fire' (Bringmann [1905–9] 1981: 2/111f.). Whereas massive oak beams can hold up for some time in a fire, since they form a charcoal layer strongly resistant to further flame penetration, it happened that iron and steel girders – once touted as 'fireproof' – suddenly lost their load-bearing capacity and collapsed. The 9/11 disaster at the World Trade Center clearly revealed that the stability of reinforced concrete is still overestimated; the steel supports of the 412-metre high towers collapsed so quickly after the aircraft set them on fire that it was impossible to rescue thousands of people in time. It has been reported that even Bin Laden was surprised by the devastating effect of the terrorist attack. The myth of concrete is one of those that fell apart on 11 September 2001.

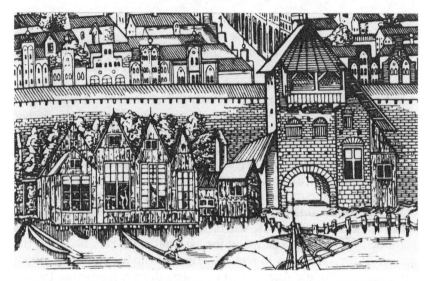

Figure 1.4: Detail from the Lübeck townscape by Elias Diebel (1552). The *Küterhäuser* (slaughterhouses) on the Wakenitz in front of the city walls are still made of wood, but the more pleasant houses behind the walls are built of stone (brick). The *Küterhäuser* show that solid wood buildings still existed alongside the half-timber style. Fire restrictions on timber construction ceased to apply outside the city walls.

The fact that wood, as an organic substance, can rot and become brittle was considered another major disadvantage in regions where builders had used it for generations. Stone therefore tended to dominate in the substructure and ground floor of houses. Often the rule of thumb for wooden objects was: 'Everything that isn't used becomes worm-eaten.' The various kinds of wood were different in terms of durability. Many lasted especially well in water; but a shift between wet and dry conditions shortened the life of all woods quite considerably. For mill wheels, it was best if they remained in constant motion and never dried out. Wooden boats also begin to rot if they stay dry for too long. The wood of the alder – a tree common in damp riverside forests – lasts an average of 800 years in water, 400 years in constantly dry conditions, but only five years if it is alternated between the two. Copper beech wood survives only ten years in water, white beech wood 750 years. Elmwood can last a thousand years in water, and for this reason was favoured for construction in Venice (figure 1.5); water pipes were still made from it in modern times (Bieler 1949: 104). All these figures can today be considerably modified by means of impregnation techniques.

Figure 1.5: Wooden piles form the substratum of Venice. Since the wood of
some tree species can last for centuries if it is constantly exposed to water,
timber has remained indispensable in modern times for anything built on earth
or water. The city of Venice rests largely upon tree trunks. Thick pile structures
of elm and larch were rammed into the marshy ground in order to extend the
inhabited area. The picture shows the baroque Santa Maria della Salute, the
largest church in Venice, which was built on 1,250,000 stakes (UNESCO 1971:
182ff.). It was an astonishing achievement for the city to acquire such a huge
quantity of suitable timber. The expansion of Amsterdam and other Dutch cities
on similar foundations gave a strong impetus to the Netherlands timber trade.

Wood warps in the course of time. 'Wood and woman never remain
the same', goes a German saying; 'a young wife, new bread, and
green wood devastate a house', goes a Flemish one (Champion [1938]
1963: 186, 19). As the pace of economic development quickened,
this characteristic of fresh wood became more irksome because of the
time required by the drying process (Piest 1954: 26). The stocks that
piled up over the years in timber yards became 'dead capital' as soon
as the transition was made to modern bookkeeping.

Artificial drying, especially of hardwood, caused many a misfortune while people were still learning from experience, and for a time
it was cursed as an 'unnatural' way of treating wood. In 1847, the
otherwise progressive technologist Heinrich Poppe groaned that,
although 'the joiner's work [had] recently increased so much in

perfection', 'the older products were as a rule more durable', since joiners had formerly shown greater patience in allowing the wood to dry (Poppe [1847] 1972: 229f.). In the case of hardwoods, there was a partial return to natural drying methods. These make it possible to dispense with toxic preservatives, which in our ecological age would be harmful to the image of wood.

Certain ambiguities of progress were soon recognized in relation to wood. The irregularities of the material became a source of considerable danger when fast-running machinery was introduced for woodworking. 'Wood defects' were more of a nuisance than before in the mechanical processing of wood and the production of standardized mass goods. Nowadays, knotholes give wood its sex appeal for lovers of the material, even in the province of mass production. As Josef Krauhausen, editor of the *Holz-Zentralblatt*, remarked: 'IKEA has made knots socially acceptable.' Redheart beech, formerly deprecated because of its irregular colour, is today more expensive than 'immaculate' light beechwood.

Twisted growth and other deviations of the tree trunk from a regular cylindrical shape could be exploited in one way or another in the range of early uses of wood. Forked trunks were sought after for shipbuilding and knotted trunks for roof trusses; yet modern manuals treat all such properties as 'wood defects'. They are generally more in evidence in deciduous trees and mixed woodland – one more reason for the favouring of conifer monoculture.

One basic property of wood bound up with its organic nature and cellular structure is its 'hygroscopicity' – that is, its tendency to absorb moisture. One always has to reckon with this aspect, whether one is talking of wood as timber or as fuel. Actually, it is not a 'defect of wood'; the pleasant indoor climate of timber houses is associated not least with the fact that they ensure a degree of moisture in the air. But the drying of wood considerably increases its calorific value; fresh wood has on average only half the value of air-dried wood, and artificial drying can raise thermal efficiency even higher. In the case of timber, drying before use plays a very important role in preventing changes to the shape of the product; the wood shrinks crossways to the fibre as much as fifteen times more than it does lengthways. As a result, major tensions, tears and deformations may arise in the body of the wood.

If the wood is dried naturally, it has to be stored for years on end. Wainwrights and cartwrights, for whom it was important that the wood should shrink only minimally, kept it for approximately five years before use; this was not the least of the reasons why they were able to obtain higher quality than in the competing products of turners and joiners (Siuts 1982: 268). But the more expensive that raw wood became, the more capital it tied up for long storage times. It used to be thought that the degree of drying could not be measured precisely but only estimated on the basis of previous experience. But artificial drying and new measuring instruments have changed the picture a great deal in this respect.

Modern technological developments have been double-edged: on the one hand, they have turned the natural properties of wood into 'defects'; on the other hand, they have created the means to overcome traditional difficulties in the handling of wood. The history of the interaction between man and wood has thus acquired new tension in the industrial age.

MIDDLE AGES AND EARLY MODERN PERIOD: MAXIMUM EXPLOITATION AND THE BEGINNINGS OF SUSTAINABILITY

House floors and barn beams or pillars were made of pine, scythe handles of Norway maple or white maple; the beech gave its wood for the making of carts, loom parts, chopper handles, door handles and the latches on antiquated front-door locks; the birch was the origin of harrows, whisk spikes and the 'birch' itself . . ., while its big sister the spruce was the perfect maid-of-all-work, providing rafters, beams and shingles for housebuilding, benches and chairs for the furnishings. . . . There was a larch box, a pine chest, a cherrywood table; the lime tree supplied the frame for the loom that stretched up to the living-room ceiling; the plum tree the little boat; the elder the shuttles. From elmwood we got spokes and hubs, from aspen the rods for the fodder basket . . ., from poplar, troughs; from oak, a quarter measure . . ., a chisel with a pearwood hilt, a hack whose handle was made from the wood of a wild apple tree, then bread baskets fastened with willow and three walking sticks from hazelnut, barberry and blackthorn.

Josef Blau (1917), on the building of a farmer's house in the Bohemian forest

1 Medieval Society and the Limits of the Forest

From random clearance to forest regulation

Forest clearance did not, as it was long thought, begin with the large-scale operations of the High Middle Ages. Neolithic farmers already burned areas of forest to gain new agricultural land and pasture. What was new about the medieval clearances was the regulation and planning: we can still identify the villages that grew up on cleared land from their planned lay-out. The movement was driven by power-ful interests, both from the top and from below. The lords extended the area under their rule, while the peasantry achieved a degree of autonomy unusual for the time: clearances created freedom. But, instead of a tempestuous struggle against the forest, it was often an operation that testified to prior awareness of the value of the forest (Lohrmann 1979: 316). Contrary to what is frequently claimed, the forest was not an enemy for the peasant but a valuable pasture, all the more vital as the share of cereals in agriculture gradually increased, partly under pressure from the landlords (Hambloch 1974: 364f.).

If at first there was sometimes a right to clear the forest as far as one could throw an axe, the peasants themselves took care to set some limits during the clearance operations. The planning called for counter-measures to preserve the forest. It was by no means the case that all forest soil was suitable for agriculture; people in many places sensibly divided forest from field in accordance with the quality of the soil (Hasel 1968: 143) – but not everywhere. Much land was ploughed for a while and then surrendered to the forest again.

England was centuries in advance of the continent in its strict royal control of the forest. After 1066 the Norman kings turned huge new domains into royal forest and threatened malefactors with 'blinding, emasculation and death'. Not surprisingly, 'the royal forest provoked more negative comments from chroniclers than any of their other acts' (Young 1979: 11, 7). That is precisely the point: the king's sway over the forest was not legitimated by the common good, by the need to guard against wood shortages, or by supply requirements for ships, mines and foundries. It served the royal hunt and nothing else. And, since the king could not hunt everywhere at once, it is doubtful whether the proclamation of royal status had universal effect. 'Forest' was not synonymous with woodland and did not necessarily protect the latter from clearances.

At the end of the Middle Ages, a major turn in large parts of Central and Western Europe, prepared by landlord decrees (originally founded upon royal forest rights) but driven by general fear of wood shortages, meant that authority over the forest came to manifest itself not so much in clearances as in conservation. Both the continent and England now witnessed a flood of lordly rhetoric about shortages and constant complaints about 'the great decay of timber and wood' (Latham 1957: 196). Using forest ordinance, the lordship that had originally had the legal status of an association of persons pushed deep into the forest and established a rigidly defined territory there. Superintendence of the forest became politics of the first order. Modern environmentalism has breathed fresh life into this concept, which has become common property all around the world. In practice, however, it is becoming clear that forest conservation as a state function does not have a long tradition behind it in most non-Western countries.

Communes and 'wood courts'

According to Oliver Rackham (1990: 146), the woodland of the British commons was 'jealously protected by the medieval courts of the manor against over-exploitation by any of their users'. In Central Europe, on the other hand, forest conservation in premodern times was not driven only from above. In many parts of Germany, special 'wood courts' (so-called *Holthinge* or *Taidinge*) regulated the use made of the forest by the communes of the day. These communes, the *Markgenossen*, have set quite a few puzzles for historians. Within them, laws were not passed down from on high but decided by the questioning of peasants who formed part of the commune – a practice that conflicts with the usual image of feudalism as a hierarchical pyramid of fiefs. Historical research in various regions has shown that feudalism was made up of communal as well as lordship structures (Wunder 1986: 143). This was true especially where the forest was concerned, for it was a basic law that effective regulation of forest use required a degree of cooperation with people living there. It is difficult to see clearly in thick forest, and an official cannot be posted by every tree.

Written communal laws and 'wood court' rulings begin to play a major role only in the late Middle Ages. They do not, however, point to a society of individuals with equal rights; the count who presided over the wood court was often appointed by the landlord or territorial lord. It was not uncommon for the court to rule that the peasants' pigs should share the forest with the mass of 'lordly pigs', to which the 'officials' pigs' were later added (Endres 1888: 171). The number of pigs that were allowed to be driven into the forest was a token of prosperity and social rank.

When communal laws and court rulings began to be recorded in writing in the late Middle Ages, it was presumably because growing tensions between peasants and landlords led to disputes over legal rights. But the communes also increasingly served to limit the use of forest and pasture by the lower orders. Participation in the *Markgenossenschaft* became the hallmark of a long-established farmer concerned to differentiate himself from those below him in the social scale.

The trend to tighter regulation applied to pig-grazing even more than the cutting of timber. In fact, this remained by far the most lucrative use of oak forest right up to the eighteenth century, despite the rising prices of oak timber. Money could be made quickly from pig-grazing, whereas it took time before timber could be sold at the going price. In the Solling hills around the year 1600, pig feed from the fruits of trees brought in twenty times as much money as the whole timber sector. Rulers struck special feeding agreements with one another – the Count of Schaumburg, for example, had his pigs driven all the way to Pomerania in the sixteenth century (Knoke 1968: 78) – and a number of regular 'swine wars' broke out over forest grazing rights. The forest yield of pig feed varied considerably from year to year, so it is hardly surprising that it featured in church prayers or that there were 'pig saints' – the most prominent being the anchorite Antonius, known in Westphalia as 'Fickel-Tünnes' (Porkling Antonius) (Bonnemann 1984: 275; Cate 1972).

Many wood court rulings are famous (or infamous) for the grisly punishments they threatened to impose on infractors, especially for any harm done to oaks, the most valuable 'fruit trees' for pig feed. 'If anyone girdles an oak [excoriating a strip of bark and causing the tree to die], what shall his punishment be?' And the Hülsede Mark in the Weser uplands handed down the brutal answer: 'His gut shall be wound around the oak.' 'If anyone beheads an oak, what shall his punishment be? His head shall be hacked off and put in that place' (Bernhardt [1872–5] 1966: 2/132f.). Such were the 'mirror penalties': he who did harm to a tree should have the same harm done to him. The tree as a living creature with equal rights! Even Ottoman sultans concerned to protect naval timber ordered that anyone who illegally felled a tree should have his head cut off!

This seems to have been the norm only for particularly valuable trees. To 'behead' blossoming trees was a common practice of farmers in 'coppice' areas. In many cases, illegal cutting of timber might be overlooked for a round of beers; wood courts also had a more jovial side. The restrictive criterion they used everywhere was the needs of the local commune; the 'abduction' of wood to other parts was strictly forbidden. Yet, as it became possible to commercialize timber over and above local needs, it became more and more difficult to regulate cutting effectively in accordance with the needs principle.

The ban on selling wood to outsiders appeared repeatedly in later territorial ordinances, but often with the ulterior motive that the prince and his favoured entrepreneurs should hold a monopoly on the timber trade. The strengthening of the territorial lords and the meteoric rise of the timber trade in the early modern period inevitably plunged the *Markgenossenschaften* into crisis, often turning them into mere instruments of the authorities.

Forest reformers contrasted long-range official thinking to the short-termism of peasant communes. But this logic – the larger and more hierarchical the institution, the more far-sighted its action – is open to question. Governments have often behaved in a short-sighted manner, and small communities frequently act more intelligently than large ones. Historically speaking, sustainable forestry is an invention of the forest communities; it was taken over only subsequently by the state administration (Stuber 2008: 22).

The struggle over ownership

To whom does the forest belong? In the Middle Ages this question would have had no meaning. It presupposes the modern concept of property, which excludes use rights for persons other than the owner; forest ownership in that sense did not exist in those days (figure 2.1). Until the nineteenth century, a view lingered on in poorer sections of the population that the forest was a gift of God or nature, which everyone had a right to use even if powerful people had wrongly prevented this. This view applied especially to firewood, which was needed for everyday life and which in many regions was of only little value (in the sense of exchange-value).

In the various regions of Germany, the rule was that 'the forest serves the peasants as far as the crowing of the village cocks can be heard' (Selter 1995: 96) – a kind of natural law from which we can see that there was not yet any talk of sharply defined rights to the forest. The medieval poet Freidank wrote in 1230: 'Dem richen walde kleine schadet / ob sich ein mann mit holze ladet' [It harms the rich forest little / If a man loads up with wood] (Bühler 1911: 11). Between the lines one reads a norm that may still be found in modern times: people may take from the forest as much as they can carry on their back. But even then the verse hints at attempts to limit the free gathering of firewood on the grounds that it might damage the forest.

Strong pressure from above was soon felt in regions where the feudal system first took shape – in Normandy, for instance. As early as 997 a large peasant revolt took place under the watchword: 'De tut ferum nos volontez: de bois, de eaux et de pres!' [Let us do as we wish with everything: the forests, the waters and the pastures] (Hausrath 1924: 186). But in many areas the forest meant a free space that the feudal lord could not fully penetrate, especially if it was thick and contained peasant 'communes'. It could then serve as a counterweight to the risk of failed harvests in agriculture. Besides, the forest offered many social 'niches' for poor people who would otherwise have been rootless. There is a theory that a region is the more deeply shaken by social unrest the less forest and moorland it contains (Fourquin 1975: 566). And, indeed, famine and everything that goes with it took hold in the wake of the great clearances.

It was customary for peasants to perform services in return for their right to use the forest: they would plant trees, remove dry wood, keep tracks clear, provide for the forester, and supply wood to their landlord. These 'servitudes' could vary enormously in character. In western and southern Germany, 'labour service' often did not

Figure 2.1: From Eike von Repgow's *Sachsenspiegel*, the most famous German medieval book of laws (1220–35). In forest law and other domains, it consists of a mixture of feudal and pre-feudal notions. The top picture is believed to show how God granted free hunting and fishing rights to the newly created (and therefore naked) human beings – a conception of law that guided many a peasant revolt. The bottom picture, on the other hand, illustrates the limitation of hunting rights. There were three royal forests in Saxony (represented by three trees), in which the king had supposedly brought peace to the game. The king's authority is thus justified in terms of a peaceful order for wild animals! The right to cut timber was not yet derived from rule over the forest.

have undertones of a feudal burden: it mainly benefited commune members and registered their use rights in the forest (Seidensticker 1896: 2/548). In eastern Germany, on the other hand, where the seigniorial system intensified over time, the 'forest corvée' – cutting timber and taking it to the lord – became a real incubus in the late Middle Ages, and was one of the main causes of the East Prussian peasant revolt of 1440 (Mager 1960: 1/197).

The more lucrative timber sales became, the greater was the temptation for landlords to increase labour services. Such a way of obtaining timber was not economically efficient, however, because the difficulty and weather-dependence of transportation gave the peasants many opportunities for passive resistance. In many areas, therefore, they were paid to fetch wood from the forest, although feudal relations often made it possible to keep the price low. Local wood shortages were often partly due to the fact that peasants did not have the necessary incentive. In 1574 in Freiberg, for example, the miners (who were otherwise no friends of the peasantry) stood up for better compensation for labour services, since the pittance previously paid for the corvée had brought the local peasants to the brink of ruin (Wilsdorf et al. 1960: 281).

In western Germany, disputes centred more on forest services than forest rights. Tensions were so great in the early sixteenth century that they triggered the famous Peasants' War of 1525. More and more peasants who had no stake in the forest were forced to buy wood, at prices that were then generally moving upward. The forest was thus a treasured source of income for the landlords, all the more so because it was difficult for them to increase the fixed feudal levies from agriculture.

At the same time, the landlords began an offensive to make more communal woodland available for the expansion of mining and foundries. Although historians have doubted that the peasants' lot worsened dramatically before the great war of 1525, their existing situation and their prospects for the future were bad enough to trigger its outbreak. One of the twelve points raised by the rebellious peasantry was that the lords had 'taken all the forest for themselves' – a claim which, though exaggerated at that time, pointed to a trend that seemed clearer in southwestern Germany (where conditions were tighter and woodland more coveted) than elsewhere. In Thuringia, the other focus of the Peasants' War, where conditions were similar to those in the southwest, one banner of the insurgents carried images of fish, fowl and wood as symbols of their lost freedoms (Lohse 1965: 21). Two-thirds of their list of complaints featured rights in relation to wood (Blickle 1977: 35).

The defeat of 1525 was not as devastating as previously thought for the social position of the peasantry. Their resistance was not totally in vain, and it may be that after 1525 fear of another revolt made the princes more circumspect in pruning peasant rights (Troßbach 1984: 90, 98). This was true not least of the forest. If local communes held together, they were often able to reclaim rights that had been whittled down over the centuries.

In the Tyrol, the heartland of mining in the early modern period, where the landlords had been particularly ruthless in trying to lay hands on communal woodland but where the mountainous terrain gave the peasantry some strong cards, the communes held their ground in a judicial 'five-hundred-year struggle'. They finally emerged victorious in 1847, when their ancient rights were recognized under property law (Oberrauch 1952: 21).

In general, the absolutist state and modern concepts of property were a greater threat than medieval feudalism to customary forest rights. Rule in the medieval sense was rule over persons; rule in the modern sense was also rule over territories. Only now could the forest fully become the object of claims to power. The legal theorists working for princes, who overrode ancient popular rights with the help of Roman law, often invoked the principle that the sovereign had ultimate dominion (*dominium eminens*) over all the forests of the land that did not belong by documented right to a seigniory. Control of the forests was defined as an ancient 'regalian right', which had passed to the noble lords with the weakening of royal power. Ordinance was therefore issued to cover all the forests in the land, not only those considered the property of the sovereign.

In fact, it was by no means clear to what extent control over the forest had been an ancient regalian right (Kaser 1929: 37), or whether the sovereign's 'forest rights' included a right to exploit the forest for economic gain. In the sixteenth century, forest rights were derived from mining rights: the massive demand of mines and foundries for wood not only allowed the sovereign to exploit the forest economically but also functioned as an instrument of rule.

Again and again, the ruler's authority over the forest was justified in terms of the need to protect it, especially against the peasantry. Ordinary people, it was said, would think only of today and tend to plunder the forest; only the wisdom of the great helmsman could preserve it for future generations (Endres 1888: 107). Even the Austrian socialist Otto Bauer, who described the 'princely plunder of the forest' as a flagrant breach of the law, came to the conclusion: 'An economic necessity asserted itself in this bloody, gruesome process' (1925: 41).

Despite everything, the prince's sway over the forest had in his eyes been necessary to preserve it for the future and therefore to ensure economic progress. This argument needs to be looked at more closely.

Were peasants the bloodsuckers, and princes the saviours of the forest?

In 1740 a Württembergian privy councillor wrote that livestock farmers were the most dangerous neighbours for a foundry – more dangerous than bears, wolves and wild boar – because they stared wantonly at fresh saplings (Thier 1965: 285f.), thought only of animal feed and had no regard for the growth of the forest. In 1773 a trained East Prussian *Oberforstmeister* referred to peasants as the 'bloodsuckers of forests', since they thoughtlessly cut down trees for domestic fuel, charcoal and tar (Mager 1960: 2/239). In 1816 the Prussian forestry expert Pfeil railed against the 'army of vultures who gnaw at the marrow of the forest' (Stuber 2008: 155). As we see, foresters tried to outdo one another in lurid imagery. Forest historians who rely on government records have often uncritically swallowed these damning judgements, although they must have been aware of the *parti pris* involved in them. Kurt Kaser, who paints a dramatic picture of the 'struggle over forest rights', speaks of the peasants' 'impulse to devastation' and counts them among the 'horde of wormwood' against which the Styrian archdukes had good reason to wage 'pitiless war' (Kaser 1929: 44, 31).

Let us look at this from the point of view of the peasant. Whether there was reason to speak of 'forest devastation' depended on what was thought of as 'good forest' and what were set as its normal limits. So long as people's need for food was greater than that for wood, it made sense to turn forest into fields and pasture. It was also sensible to convert 'high forest' into 'low forest' (coppice) if the main requirement was firewood and animal fodder. If one starts from the principle that 'forest must remain forest' – which was what most foresters subscribed to – then such conduct was indeed predatory. But if we consider that agriculture generally brought higher rewards than forestry, we might think it remarkable that so much forest survived.

The wood supply was not a big problem for many peasants. Even if there was a lack of large closed forest, the still unenclosed lands contained enough groves, riverside woods, hedges and scrub to cover the needs of local people. Underwood was far more important than tall forest for everyday purposes, and shortages of underwood did not occur so readily in pre-modern times; it was more likely to be the case that the forest grew too quickly. Supple willows and hazel bushes, which in the eyes of foresters were not real trees, had the same importance for the peasant economy as bamboo had for the peasants of Asia; so the real problem was not sustainability but the prevention of uncontrolled growth. 'Wood and sorrow / Grow bigger every morrow' (*Holz und Sorgen / Wachsen alle morgen*), 'Wood, weeds and misfortunes grow bigger overnight': one continually comes across variants of this piece of peasant wisdom.

The struggle for exclusive ownership positively forced the peasantry to make excessive use of the forest and to obstruct the growth of new forest. Traditionally, the right to collect wood was set by the usual level of need. In times when forest rights were disputed, peasants cut and consumed as much wood as possible in order to uphold their claim. The more the forest became an instrument of rule, the more dangerous it could be for a peasant to let new forest get a hold. 'When there's wood enough for the spurring knight / the peasant has lost his age-old right' (*Wenn das Holz dem Ritter reicht an den Sporn / hat der Bauer sein recht verlorn*): so runs one doleful couplet (Hasel 1968: 144). This principle, which certainly had practical application, was supposed to prevent peasant farms from going to waste, but it could also be an instrument of rule in the forest, whereby scrub and underwood became the exclusive 'domain' of the dependent peasantry.

In a similar way, as E. P. Thompson (1977: 130f.) has shown, 'timber' became a policy matter in the early modern period in the shipbuilding region of Hampshire: firewood and wood for tools and fences formed part of the farmers' subsistence economy, while the bishop laid hands on the 'timber' necessary for shipbuilding. As soon as many trees had grown to the right size, they disappeared from sight, as either 'firewood' or 'timber'; timber could be defined in an arbitrary manner. The simple fact that the government patented wood-saving ovens, to safeguard the navy's wood supply (Picard 1997: 32), shows that 'firewood' and 'timber' were partly interchangeable. It was therefore dangerous for farmers to allow trees to grow too tall.

As we know, farmers had strong and multiple interests in the forest and in forms of forest economy and conservation. A major one had to do with pig feed, which affected the quality of the much sought-after hams (figure 2.2); many an oak grove in Central Europe or the Iberian peninsula had this to thank for its existence. It naturally made farmers hostile to reforestation with pine trees.

Farmers' wood directives regularly contained provisions for the

Figure 2.2: November pig feeding in oak forest, from the fifteenth-century Venetian manuscript *Breviarium Grimani*. November also features in other picture calendars as the pig-feeding month. Swineherds did not generally make do with acorns lying on the ground, but used long sticks to knock them from the trees or even climbed onto the branches. From the sixteenth century, attempts were made to forbid this custom by means of special ordinance (Sippel 1938: 24, 32).

cultivation of oak trees, even as early as the sixteenth century, when forestry was still based on natural rejuvenation and mostly avoided expenditure on artificial methods. Oaks were planted not only by farmers but also by their pigs, which, in burrowing for acorns, buried some in the earth and ate up various pests that might otherwise have held back the growth of new trees (Schramm 1984: 105). In the course of the nineteenth century, when old battlegrounds between foresters and farmers lost much of their potency, many foresters actually learned to value the presence of pigs. In Spain, where large areas of land were cleared for sheep-farming, there are impressive contrasting examples of lush oak forest that developed as a result of pig-farming (Parsons 1978).

Whereas pigs could promote forest conservation, this was less the case with cattle, and not at all with sheep and goats. It was soon realized that sheep, and even more goats, were damaging to young deciduous forest, and they were forbidden by wood courts when they clashed with pig-feeding ('The nanny pays with her neck!'; Verhey 1935: 129). The grazing of goats was a real issue, though, because they were 'the poor man's cow'. As the stratum of peasants with little or no land increased in size, it became more and more difficult to forbid them to graze their goats; the same is true today in many developing countries. Cattle-grazing, on the other hand, another bugbear of eighteenth-century foresters, was looked on more kindly in the nineteenth century and, within limits, even considered beneficial. Whereas forest reformers had warned that grazing would eventually turn the forest into wilderness (Rapp 2002: 70), developments on the ground strikingly refuted the prophecy of doom; some forest that was used for pasture even became a conservationist El Dorado. The ideal pasture forest was airy and rich in undergrowth, not cultivated for a maximum wood yield.

In some circumstances, farmers and others were less conservation-minded. In the long run, silviculture presupposed that farmers had hereditary use rights, but for some time this had not always been the case. Communal forestry gave good results only if there was a certain cohesion among members of the commune. But they had an interest in producing more wood than they needed only if the price was high enough to make the effort of transporting it worthwhile.

Whether a farmer could make a profit on silviculture depended mainly on the size of his business and how the forest fitted into his farm in economic terms. Farmers, like princes, often used small stands of high forest as a reserve 'for a rainy day', perhaps to pay off a pressing debt burden. The large farmers of the Black Forest, well known for their exemplary forestry, sometimes boasted that it was they who taught foresters the art (Hansjakob 1922: 336f.).

In their twelve-point programme, the insurgent peasantry of 1525 declared that the return of the forests to the communes would not result in clearances, since specially appointed 'councillors' would supervise the cutting of timber. This assurance was thoroughly credible. As for the rulers' complaint that farmers were ruining the forest, this should not be taken at face value: it was a catchphrase, invoked to justify forest ordinance, on the part of court officials whose competence in the matter was disputed. Whenever they wanted to bring a new area under their control, they claimed that it had fallen into a pitiful state on account of the local farmers' ignorance and guile. But the farmers could turn the accusation round against the ruler and his officials, since it was they who gave over large swathes of forest to meet the requirements of the burgeoning mines and foundries.

Sometimes we find a farmer playing the role of forest conservationist. In 1702 there was an uprising in the Mollnertal in Upper Austria, when thousands of trees were felled to build a fortress for the war then raging with Bavaria (Grüll 1963: 257ff.). At the same time, a long series of peasant revolts began there against the overcultivation of forest game, which threatened to do irreparable damage to agriculture. The unrest spread in 1716 to become what is known as the 'Upper Austrian Hunting Revolt'. Large numbers of big game were shot, in a display of contempt for the strict poaching laws. The Peasants' War of 1525 had triggered a free-for-all in many areas, and the Revolution of 1848 would do the same a century and a half later.

From the Middle Ages until the eighteenth century, hunting was a strong, if not the strongest, passion behind the rulers' forest policy. But no other issue brought that policy into sharper conflict with local farmers, and nothing else made them more bitterly aware of the contempt that those at the top felt for their vital interests (Eckardt 1976). They had to stand by as deer and wild boar ruined their fields, and to fear gruesome punishment if they hunted game themselves; they came to feel that they counted for less than the animals. Nevertheless, historians sometimes regard hunting as the major contribution to forest conservation. What are we to make of this?

The question of whether game-hunting helped or ruined the forest is still hotly debated. In fact, its overall impact was contradictory: hunting interests helped to preserve many areas of woodland that would otherwise have been cleared, but they did not bring forth a forest culture. Hunting was essentially a passion; no rational way of relating to the forest resulted from it.

In the abstract, gamekeeping, like pig-feeding, produced an interest in 'fruit trees' such as the oak and beech. But a large stock of game blocked the growth of deciduous forest and therefore favoured the advance of conifers. Excessive hunting, so detrimental to mixed deciduous forest, contrasts with the farmers' once careful regulation of forest pasture. When forest superintendence broke down in many parts of Germany in the revolutionary year of 1848, many foresters deplored the farmers' acts of sacrilege against the forest. In the longer term, though, the hunting free-for-all had a beneficial effect: 'A large number of valuable mixed fir areas in the Black Forest owe their existence to the Revolution of 1848 and the confusion that followed it' (Hasel 1985: 14). Significance attaches to the unintended as well as the intended effects of human attacks on the forest; there is many an irony of history.

2 Timber Becomes a Commodity

Oaks for shipbuilding: the beginning of wood shortages and the timber trade

Around the year 1140 Abbot Suger of Saint Denis – one of the founders of Gothic architecture, whose heavenward thrust pushed the technique of the time to its limits – gave a dramatic account of the difficulties he had encountered in procuring 35-foot beams for the nave of the abbey church of Saint Denis. Tall oaks nearby were cut down for the purpose, and foresters could hardly refrain from laughing as Suger hunted around for the best available. He himself described it as a divine miracle when he found what he was looking for (Gimpel 1976: 76f.). We should not conclude that wood was generally in short supply at the time; Suger had to fight his way through thick forest to reach particular trees capable of providing timber of the right length and solidity. In those days shortages were only local, although that was troublesome enough in view of the underdeveloped state of the timber trade.

Scarcity of the right kind of construction timber continued over the centuries (figure 2.3); the distances over which it had to be carried kept growing, but so too did the trade in premium-quality items. Sir Christopher Wren needed a number of years to gather the 50-foot oak logs for London's St Paul's Cathedral (1675–1710) (Hudson 1978: 38), and he was 'most solicitous' until he acquired them (Latham 1957: 197). But since it anyway took decades, if not centuries, to

REGLEMENT

nach welchem künfftig die

Forst-Frevel

in denen

Fürstenthümern Oranien-Nassau

zu bestrafen.

---

1) Eichen-Holtz betreffend.

		Fl.	Alb.	Str.
1)	Wer einen Eichen Hauptstamm ohne Erlaubnis hauet - - - - - -	30	—	—
2)	Eine Eiche, so eine Schwelle giebt - - -	15	—	—
3)	Eine Eiche Balcken starck - - - - -	15	—	—
4)	Eine Eiche zu einem Sparren - - - -	6	—	—
5)	Eine Eiche Achsen starck - - - - -	6	—	—
6)	Eine junge Eiche, so zu starcken Faß-Reifen schicklich - - - - - - - -	4	—	—
7)	Eine junge Eiche, so verpflantzt werden kan, desgleichen andere verpflantzte Bäume, wer dieselbe aushebet oder beschädiget - - -	1	15	—
8)	Wer Eichen oder sonstige Stämme stümpfet, zahlt vor jeden Stamm - - - -	4	—	—
9)	Wer sonsten Eichen-Bauholtz desgleichen Werckholtz entwendet, zahlt den Werth des Holtzes doppelt, und zur Strafe - - - -	5	—	—
10)	Wer einen Wagen Abgefäll oder Stöcke entwendet - - - - - -	5	—	—

Figure 2.3: From a tariff of fines levied for forest offences in the region of Nassau, Germany. It reads like a price list and focuses on the use of wood by farmers and craftsmen. The 'going rate' varied from year to year in accordance with general price levels. The pages of entries give some idea of the widespread and routine character of forest offences, which were not even regarded as such by those who committed them. The list also shows how oak of different quality was valued according to its potential use.

71

build a cathedral, the time spent on finding the wood for it was not usually critical.

The picture was very different in shipbuilding, especially with regard to large warships. Here time was often a key factor, money calculations were more precise, and wood could never be replaced with other materials such as quarry stone or brick. It was in relation to shipbuilding that wood procurement and wood scarcity first became highly political issues, as early as fifteenth-century Venice (Lane [1934] 1992: 230–3). In many travel guides, we read that Venetian shipbuilding was to blame for bare mountainsides all the way from the Dolomites to Dalmatia and Crete. But, as Karl Appuhn has recently shown, the historical reality was the opposite: the Venetian forest regime – the *provveditori sopra boschi* and the *provveditore alle legne*, which were capable of taking really energetic measures – formed 'not only Europe's earliest fully articulated legal and institutional apparatus dedicated entirely to resource conservation, but also its most unusual' (Appuhn 2009: 289). Far-reaching official measures were taken in the early modern period to protect certain forests (though not in mountainous areas) and to organize the collection of wood especially for shipbuilding. In addition to the large warships and ocean-going vessels that became the stuff of legend, we should not forget the host of smaller ships and boats which – in purely quantitative terms – were certainly far more important for regional supplies. And in their case wood procurement was not such a dramatic affair.

Since spokesmen for the fleet invariably complained the loudest about timber shortages, it has often been thought that deforestation was mainly a result of naval construction. In reality, however, shipbuilding was the strongest political inducement to conservation. It was not ships but sheep that hindered forest regeneration in many parts of England (Rackham 1990: 206). Timber bottlenecks arose for a number of reasons. At a time when wood-bending techniques were little developed, ship curves called for oak timber that had grown naturally crooked in the desired manner; it was much stronger than sawn timber, which involved cutting into the fibres of the wood. But such growth was more likely to be found in individual trees and hedges than in closed forest. Furthermore, while shipbuilders needed oaks that were more than 120 years old, forest owners preferred to fell them earlier, since there was a risk that parts of the tree would become rotten, and such ageing was anyway not necessary for other building purposes (Albion 1926: 1).

Taking the Hanseatic cities as the model, we may say that European shipbuilding underwent a revolution in the late Middle Ages that made it possible to rule the ocean waves. Ships were no longer put together from the outside in, with a thick casing of planks, but built outward like houses around a central structure. This increased their solidity and allowed for greater storage space, but it also reduced their density. The planks were no longer nailed to one another directly, like roof shingles, but fastened to the frames. The Netherlands soon forged ahead with the new techniques, shaping up as the leading maritime power.

Whereas in the Middle Ages the whole ship was still 'made by axe' (Olechnowitz 1960: 9) – which helped to ensure the strength of the wood – saws and sawmills now began to play a role too. The ready availability of evenly cut planks gave a decisive impetus to so-called carvel boat-building, in which the planks are fixed to a frame so that they butt up against one other. This made it possible to build longer ships than before and created new scope for the art of manoeuvring. As the European powers competed on the high seas, sails became ever larger and tougher; robust high masts were the cutting edge of naval technology (Phillips-Birt 1979: 137–46). But they were more and more difficult to obtain.

Since the key issue here was elasticity – tensile rather than compressive strength – there was a preference for fir trees. But, since long tree trunks were in short supply, it was necessary to form the masts out of several logs – a makeshift solution which, in the absence of industrial glues, reduced a ship's seaworthiness. Ships with huge single masts could still travel at full sail when others with composite masts had to shorten. This is cited as one of the reasons why the British outstripped the French at sea in the eighteenth century (Bamford 1956: 208).

Nowhere was perfect density of wood as important as in water, where knotholes or decay could have fatal consequences. The purchase of timber for shipbuilding was considered a risky business, since the seller often tried to cheat by covering holes in the wood or plugging them up (Olechnowitz 1960: 108). More generally, the purchasing of wood was a matter of trust, not to be approached as an anonymous business transaction; the buyer felt most confident if he had known the supplier well for a long time. Even England hesitated as long as possible before importing ship's timber from distant forests.

In the sixteenth and seventeenth centuries, the Baltic acquired a reputation as a reliable supplier, so that there was a reluctance to draw on other sources. Even in the eighteenth century, shipbuilders had strong reservations about the vast forests of North America. Their preference was to go into the forest and select the most suitable trees, and even to take personal charge of felling operations. This was not certain to produce the right result either, since many wood defects are not visible on the outside. John Evelyn, whose *Sylva* (1664) is the most celebrated appeal for forestation in English history, coined the witty comparison: 'A timber-tree is a merchant-adventurer, you shall never know what he is worth until he be dead.' 'There is not in nature a thing more obnoxious to deceit, than the buying of trees standing, upon the reputation of their appearance to the eye' (Evelyn 1664: 158; Albion 1936: 100).

The more distant the origin of the wood, the less could ship's carpenters be sure of the quality of the material: there was no satisfactory solution to this problem in the early modern period. Even as late as 1810 a scandalous fate overtook the *Queen Charlotte*, which never saw the high seas and was completely rotten two years after launch (Albion 1952: 15). The use of poorly dried timber that had been felled outside the normal winter season was the main cause of rot damage. Many well-built wooden ships lasted a hundred years or longer, but many did not even make it to their twentieth anniversary (Bramwell 1976: 186), and others had to be rebuilt from scratch after a few years' service because the timber had become warped. Artificial kiln-drying did not yet produce successful outcomes: the wood was in danger of becoming too brittle.

Ship damage was the cause of one scandal after another, as Samuel Pepys's famous diaries testify. 'It is clear that many ships, particularly those constructed under pressure in time of war, commenced to rot almost from the day they entered the water.' Warships, moreover, often did not put to sea for years in peacetime, so it was hardly surprising that they started to rot (Latham 1957: 270, 279). And, when war came, the main priority was to build new ships as fast as possible; there was no time to dry the wood for years. Wooden ships were rarely completely watertight; they nearly always had to be pumped out at sea (Gordon 1968: 148). A preservative that could withstand the constant alternation of wet and dry had not yet been invented. Many of the technical options available to shipbuilders began to appear only in modern times. One twentieth-century expert stated that wooden ships do not necessarily leak and that many problems had to do with imperfect expertise; 'it is a mistake to exaggerate the virtues of traditional design' (ibid.: 21).

It was mainly cities and countries with a large fleet that needed top-quality timber most, but they also had greater means to procure it. Wood was not only a material used for building ships, it was also a cargo that gave a strong impetus to maritime trade, especially as there was no other practical way of conveying it over long distances. Wood was the most transport-intensive mass commodity of the early modern age; the price for the end consumer was made up almost entirely of shipping costs. Baltic timber cost twenty times as much in British shipyards as where it was felled (Albion 1926: 103). This meant big profits for timber dealers, but only if they lowered their transport costs and built ships especially for cheap bulk transport. The timber business, which experienced strong growth in the North Sea and the Baltic from the fifteenth century on – mainly because of soaring demand for shipbuilding material in the new maritime age (Soom 1961: 80) – contributed to the development of a new and more spacious vessel: the *hulk* (or *holk*).

At the same time, an effective system of timber trading came about in northern Germany. Under the supervision of publicly sworn assessors (known locally as *Bracker*), Danzig and other Baltic ports introduced forms of standardization and quality control that turned this naturally so varied material into an article of long-distance trade – still a decisive aspect in today's timber business. The different grades were 'good', 'rubbish' (*wrak*) and 'double rubbish' (*wrak-wrak*) (Stark 1973: 96ff.). In East Prussia, timber exports were under way on a large scale by the sixteenth century, and in the next century they were a major spur for the rulers of Brandenburg-Prussia to develop a forest policy. As the East Prussian oak resources started to run out (Mager 1960: 30), Riga increasingly became the metropolis of the timber trade.

From the sixteenth to the eighteenth century, colonial expansion and the beginnings of world trade brought a sharp rise in maritime transport. Technically, however, shipbuilding reached limits in the fifteenth century that would not be fully overcome until the iron revolution of the second half of the nineteenth century (figure 2.4). However far ambitious men tried to push the limits of wood as a material, the dimensions of trees continued to restrict the size of ships (Albion 1926: 5f.). The English economist and natural philosopher William Petty, who learned his shipbuilding and mathematics in Leiden, developed new forms of construction around 1670 that aimed to make the now scarce 'knee shaft' redundant (Sharp 1975: 69). In the eighteenth century, the first attempts were made to bend wood under heat. The bottleneck for certain grades of timber was forcing people to be inventive.

The growing scarcity of suitable timber induced many seafaring cities to curtail external shipbuilding orders. This contributed to the

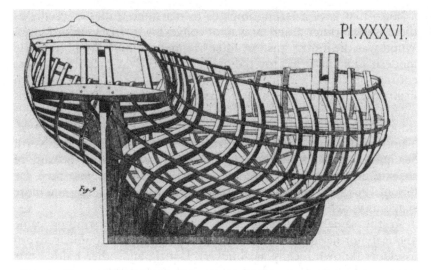

Figure 2.4: Drawing of a ship's frame by F. H. Chapman (1768), which shows the need for naturally curved logs. To have achieved this effect by combining several pieces of timber would have made the ship less strong and watertight.

dominance of small businesses well into the nineteenth century, reinforcing guild structures and a craft mentality based on tradition and experience. This was also true of England, even at the time when it was the greatest maritime power in the world (Davis 1972). Workers were still sawing by hand in the English shipyards of the eighteenth century (Holland 1971: 26f.).

Timber framing: from the art of combining wood to the art of construction

Various historical processes affected the development of timber construction: human-influenced change in the forests, a growing scarcity of certain kinds of wood (especially oak), more economical ways of handling the material, the rise of stone and brick construction, modifications in carpentry techniques and, not least, changes in housing. Once more, a turning point came in the fifteenth and sixteenth centuries.

Around the year 25 BC, the Roman architectural theorist Vitruvius mentioned half-timbering as an unstable form of building that he wished had never been invented. Even when it was filled with stone wall, the stability, water insulation and heat retention of

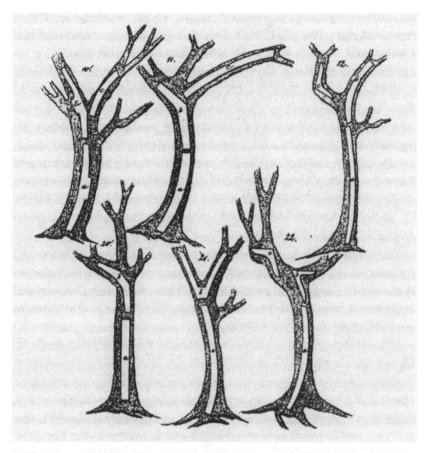

Figure 2.5: Crooked trees, which the modern timber industry does not consider utilizable, were still sought after for shipbuilding in the early nineteenth century; attempts were made to classify and standardize them in accordance with their various potential uses. The Venetians, who were experts at adapting young oaks from the forests of Istria for shipbuilding, allowed them to grow crooked (Bevilacqua 2009).

half-timbering did not represent a good halfway solution between full timber and clay or brick architecture. Its disadvantages were overcome only in combination with more modern technologies.

Massive wooden timber frames were still common in late medieval Europe (Terlau and Kaspar 1985: 473) in either 'stave' constructions or (in the South) 'block constructions', using perpendicular or horizontal timber respectively. From the beginning, half-timbering was a way of cutting down on the use of wood, and as such it was still massively used in the eighteenth century by the population of East Prussia (Mager 1960: 2/130ff.). This drive for economy also runs like a red thread through later developments in half-timbering.

Archaeologists tell us that timber houses were rebuilt every twenty to twenty-five years in medieval Danzig, so quickly did the beams rot or decay (Wyrobisz 1973: 69). This is scarcely surprising, given the use in the Middle Ages of fresh, undried timber that was easy to work with. Well-dried oak that had been stored for a long time was so hard that it could scarcely be worked on with the tools of former times. Solidly built joists that limited the penetration of ground damp and made the construction more durable became common in most places only in the fifteenth century. Without them, houses had to be replaced every fifty years, if not more often.

A kind of scissors opened up between the ambition of landlords and the dwindling number of large trees. In the sixteenth century, however, half-timbering grew to such an extent that in Germany it was adopted by the nobility, which had elevated stone to a status symbol in the age of castles (Terlau and Kaspar 1985: 481). Improvements in multi-storey construction now made it possible to achieve monumental dimensions in half-timbering.

The French restorer Viollet-le-Duc considered that the prosperous Butchers' Guildhall in the market square in Hildesheim (figure 2.6) – which had never been thought spectacular until the nineteenth century, and which the mayor thought too expensive to restore in 1852 – was the most beautiful timber house in the world: 'If you roam the entire planet, you will not find another half-timbered house that radiates as much beauty, strength and harmony as the Butchers' Guildhall in Hildesheim.' The later fate of the Butchers' Guildhall reflects the changing times and offers food for thought. On 22 March 1945 it burned to the ground in an air raid. In 1953 a poll was held in Hildesheim to decide whether the market square should be restored in the old style or enlarged and modernized; the modernizers won with a bare majority. In 1970, however, the year of the 'ecological revolution' in Germany, a 'Society for the Reconstruction of the Butchers' Guildhall' was founded. And in 1984 – by which time the modern hotel erected in its place had gone bankrupt – the city council gave in to pressure and decided not only to rebuild the hall but to restore the whole of the old market square.

This was the high point in the half-timber restoration movement. After computer calculations yielded surprisingly positive results about the strength of old buildings, the Butchers' Hall was rebuilt wholly in wood, with approximately 400 cubic metres of oak and 4,500 joins.

Fig. 83. Das Knochenhauer-Amtshaus in Hildesheim.

Figure 2.6: Butchers' Guildhall (*Knochenhaueramtshaus*) in Hildesheim
(built 1529, destroyed 1945). This centre for the prosperous and politically
influential master butchers was 'in technical terms indisputably the most
accomplished work of timber architecture not only in Hildesheim but in the
whole of Germany' (Lachner 1882: 61). But in the early nineteenth century,
when architecture lost its artistic status for those who worked in the profession,
the hall was in danger of being pulled down. The half-timbered style is here
the basis of monumental architecture. Its vitality comes not only from the
sumptuous carving but also from the protrusion of the upper storeys (by
as much as 2.7 metres). Around the year 1500, Hildesheim was the leading
member of a forest commune and vigorously and successfully fought for its
rights in the forest against the bishop. From 1526 the mayor of Hildesheim also
had administrative responsibility for the forest (Timm 1960: 44f.).

79

As there was no time to allow thick oak beams to dry for years, a lot of wood was recycled from other half-timbered houses that had fallen into disrepair. The works manager, Michael Machens, sounded triumphant: 'This structure has no precedent in recent history, all wood and no iron, rising twenty-six metres above basement level.' Hildesheim had regained its 'historic heart', the press rejoiced. 'With each metre that the Butchers' Hall rose up, so too did the expertise of past builders rise in everyone's estimation' (Petzoldt 1990: 21, 54, 60f., 123).

The transition from the jettied floor technique to multi-storeying at the end of the Middle Ages – in England as well as Germany and elsewhere – marks the sharpest break in the history of half-timbered architecture. Originally the vertical 'pillars' of the house stretched up to the roof; when higher storeys made their appearance, the supporting crossbeams were in a way slotted or 'shot' into the vertical members – hence the German expression *Geschoßbauweise*, which has persisted to this day. It had its drawbacks, though, which became more and more important over time; it originated in a world where housing was still entirely geared towards a central hall (the farmer's *Deele*), but was ill-suited to a path-breaking new age in which the living room was the central element in the house. The higher houses became, the more difficult it was to track down oaks large enough for columns that reached up to the roof. There was limited scope to build higher storeys in the existing houses, and the supporting beams were also restricted in their load-bearing capacity.

Originally, timber houses were built around pillars that had been driven into the ground like stakes, but this form of building disappeared in modern times. The half-timber structure thus came to rest only on the construction as a whole and its wooden joints. Individual wooden elements of a building, unlike stone elements, cannot be relied upon to hold themselves up alone. But, even more than stone construction, half-timbering requires comprehensive advance planning and a timber frame that provides solidity for the house. 'Carpenters must think in terms of unit length of timber, units well suited to resist every building stress known', writes Cecil A. Hewett, the historian of English carpentry, 'while masons were reduced to terms of stone, quarried and worked in the most practicable sizes and forms, and basically capable of resisting only compression.' In a sense, then, carpenters had to think and plan more than stonemasons. Yet 'carpenters' problems did not change much, if indeed they changed at all' (Hewett [1980] 1997: 100f.).

The problem of building high with timber elements of limited length was solved once and for all through the multi-storey technique

(*Stockwerkbauweise*), in which each floor was independently timbered on top of the one lying beneath it. The load-bearing capacity of the beams that supported the upper storeys could be increased by making them 'jut out'; this also made it possible to gain additional space. In the sixteenth century, even existing structures of this kind were replaced with multi-storey designs in which the pillars were cut off at the level of each storey. The protruding style became a characteristic feature of half-timbered houses, especially in closely built cities; the unique physical properties of wood allowed for this in a way that would scarcely have been possible in a stone structure. The municipal authorities campaigned against this architectural style right from the beginning, since it meant that fire would jump even more quickly across the narrow streets. But the population stubbornly resisted official prohibitions (Lemp 1922: 5, 14). Since timber-framing was visible on the outside, the overhanging upper storeys displayed the carpenter's skill in the structural design.

The change in housing construction went hand in hand with changes in carpentry. Wooden joints were the core of the carpenter's technique, and in this respect there were typical shifts in emphasis between the medieval and modern periods: so-called halving was prevalent in the former, mortising in the latter. Halving is externally visible; it requires more careful work and generally results in a more solid joint. It exists in countless different forms, depending on the stress to which it will be subjected. Mortising is more straightforward: it is looser than halving, and so it requires other ways of ensuring the strength of the building, such as triangular joints or diagonal bracing. Later it became the rule that wooden joints should be regarded as 'more or less pivotable' and that adequate strength could be achieved only by joining together at least three pieces of timber (Warth 1900: 24).

Less accurate detail in wooden joints made greater care necessary in construction, until in the end wooden joints were replaced with steel elements. This development turned construction design from a matter for carpenters into a matter for engineers and architects – and nowadays for computers. Of the many kinds of carpentry joint, including the artistic dovetail (figure 2.8), the only one that survives in modern timber construction is the primitive wedge shape.

The great rebuilding of rural England in the Elizabethan age mostly involved the use of half-timbering (Harris 1978: 50ff.). In the seventeenth and eighteenth centuries, its artistic quality declined both in England and on the continent, so that stone was now used for the construction of prestigious buildings. This breakthrough is only partly explained by wood shortages, since, even in cities where

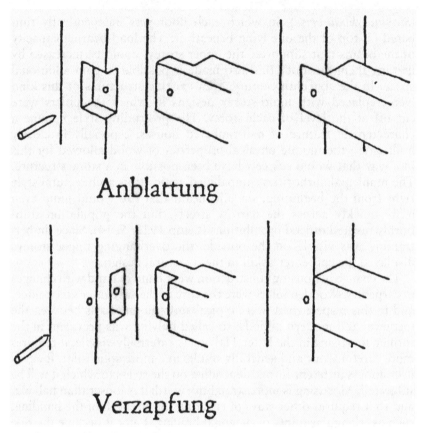

Figure 2.7: Halving (above) and mortising (below).

wood procurement was relatively expensive, half-timbering remained cheaper and more popular than stone construction into the eighteenth century (Lemp 1922: 13f.). In the age of absolutism, however, the values of the court shaped the taste of lower levels of society – and stone had greater prestige there than timber. Engelbert Kaempfer, the most famous European traveller to sixteenth-century Japan, failed to appreciate the high art of Japanese timber construction, considering it puny in comparison with European prestige architecture – although he did realize that Japanese wooden houses were 'very healthy to live in'! (Scurla 1974: 79f.).

A lot of timber was used, even in stone constructions, without appearing on the outside. People noted the parallels in the history of art: the fifteenth and sixteenth centuries, when burgher culture set the

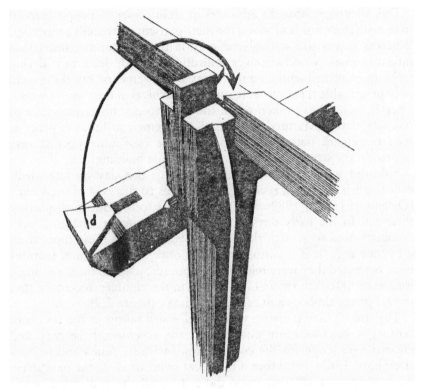

Figure 2.8: Ornate dovetail joint from the late Middle Ages, which bears stresses of various kinds and does not cease to function properly even in the event of wood shrinkage; it remains effective today. Dovetails were very popular in England until the sixteenth century, but preferences later switched to simpler joints (Hewett 1969: 190, 194). Bruce Hoadley (1980: 169, 174) noted: 'Nothing is more symbolic of the woodworking tradition than the dovetail joint', although he had no scruples about reinforcing it with nails.

tone in Germany, saw the blossoming of the wood engraver's art; this later declined into mere folk art, complete with the dwarfs and other knick-knacks that one can find in today's souvenir shops.

Everyone knew that well-built wooden houses were comfortable to live in and feared the unhealthy radiation from freshly plastered stone buildings: 'Houses with new walls are so dangerous to the health of those who live in them that it is said of such people . . . that they have built their own death' (Ackermann and Ramazzini 1780: 1/152). Police regulations and shifts in the prevailing taste played a decisive role in the acceptance of stone construction.

Oak shortages brought advances in architecture as people learned to use different kinds of wood for their particular strength properties. Whereas it was still wrongly believed in the eighteenth century that moisture made wood stronger (Nördlinger 1860: 386), new drying techniques subsequently led to quality improvements. But these were only practicable if people were more economical in their use of wood, since it would have taken much too long to dry huge quantities of oak adequately. Matured oak was also extremely arduous to process. Its replacement with lighter wood for the roof and upper storeys improved the structural analysis of the whole building.

Splendid wooden roofs have survived to this day on late medieval English churches, revealing themselves to the eyes of the visitor (Ostendorf [1908] 1982: 95ff.). Carpenters took pride in displaying their art. In the early days of scientific construction analysis, technologists used to scratch their heads over many of these roofs from a bygone age: 'It is a curious fact that once such structural features were perfected they were relegated to sporadic use and then seemingly forgotten' (Hewett 1997: 170). It was in the eighteenth century that the art of the timber vault reached a climax (figure 2.9).

The use of iron together with wood – still taboo in the sixteenth century – became more common in the seventeenth century and created new scope for the construction of roofs, vaults and bridges (Deinhard 1963: 19). From a technical point of view, the new stress on economics and 'economies' did not signal the end of the wood age. In roof construction, in particular, timber remained the optimum material in modern times, since it could only have been replaced with expensive stone vaulting.

Unity and difference in the crafts

Once, carpenters were the only professional craftsmen handling wood. In France, it was against their resistance that cabinetmakers, cartwrights, coopers and shingle-makers were recognized in 1382 as crafts in their own right (Velter and Lamothe 1976). It is true that there had always been plenty of wooden objects in everyday use, but they were unsophisticated and have survived in such small numbers that their existence is often forgotten.

Wooden containers – chests, bowls, coffins, small boats ('dugouts') – were originally made by hollowing out tree trunks, a wasteful method from a later viewpoint. Craft differentiation involved more economical, more purposeful ways of dealing with wood. The carpenter, with his relatively crude labour, retreated more and more in

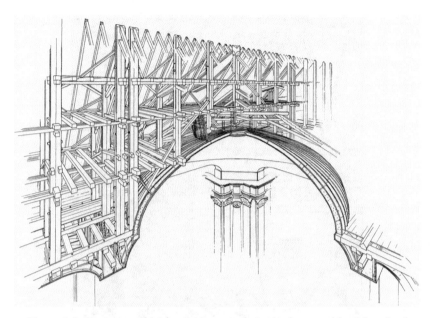

Figure 2.9: Timber roof with crossing cupola in the former abbey church of Wiblingen (near Ulm), built in the late eighteenth century. It is considered the 'highpoint of late baroque carpentry in southern Germany' and a 'structure already tending in the direction of civil engineering' (Sachse 1975: 96f.). In the modern age, carpenters learned better and better how to use the natural properties of wood alongside stone cupolas and vaults, and to manage with timber of ever lower strength. This led to structures which in many respects make us think of modern glued wood constructions. In the seventeenth and eighteenth centuries, iron joints were already opening up new possibilities. Trusses were developed that would also have a bright future ahead of them in bridge construction, where it became possible to achieve spans of 50 metres, unheard of in the Middle Ages.

the face of other crafts (figure 2.10). Around the year 1800, an author surveying the crafts 'for young people' wrote: 'In the life of the community, the carpenter is looked upon as a humble craftsman, because he processes wood with the very simple means of axe, hatchet, saw and other familiar tools' (Voit 1804: 1/219). The cabinetmaker, turner and cartwright were capable of greater development and could attain a far higher degree of sophistication. But 'ebonists', the artistic cabinetmakers of the eighteenth century, still preferred to work as much as possible with simple wooden tools (Stürmer 1982: 85).

The range of tools in the timber crafts was endless, but the underlying principles remained remarkably constant until the major advances

Figure 2.10: Carpenters at work: copperplate by Peter Troschel, in Johann
Wielm, *Architectura civilis* (Nuremberg 1668), the first woodwork manual
in the German language. The ground floor and tower-like stairwell are
already built of stone, while the upper floor and roof are in the half-timbered
and timbered style. The supervisor with the cane in the foreground is
giving instructions to a carpenter with a set square; the composition, as in
other pictures, gives prominence to the measuring instrument. The use of
prefabricated elements gave timber a promising future in comparison with
stone. In pure timber-framing, most of the actual work was done in the timber
yard. It took only a few days to assemble the parts, although this required
several people to work on it together.

86

of twentieth-century mechanization. Equipment costs were relatively low; craftsmen could carry their tools around with them and use them as a badge of their status. Manual dexterity counted for more than any start-up spending. Woodworking, a thoroughly male domain, offered models of craft mentality, manual self-confidence and trust in the experience handed down by previous generations.

The craft mentality included differentiation from kindred trades, and in many towns there was frequent quarrelling among them. Since their tools were quite similar and easy to obtain, and since work techniques made it difficult to draw sharp dividing lines between areas of responsibility, boundary disputes were a routine occurrence. One craft would accuse another of encroaching on its territory. Furthermore, there was growing competition from rural craftsmen, who often lived closer to the forest.

Cabinetmakers had to fight on several fronts: they were latecomers on the scene, but they soon outnumbered other craftsmen and placed the greatest emphasis on their distinctness. They developed into a fully fledged trade only in modern times, when furniture became 'mobile' and prestigious, cabinets and chairs moved away from fixed positions by walls, and, at least in the upper classes, a more individualistic lifestyle began to take shape. John Evelyn still felt nostalgic for the age of his ancestors, when 'sturdy oaken bedstead and furniture of the house lasted one whole century; . . . long tables both in Hall and Parlour were as fixed as the freehold; nothing was moveable save joint-stools' (Picard 1997: 49).

It now became advantageous to use lighter woods than oak for domestic furniture. There were certain parallels in the construction of houses and cabinets: both had applied timber-framing since the sixteenth century, although statics problems were much greater in the case of houses. Carpenters still occasionally taunt cabinetmakers today that they instal domestic fittings as if they were pieces of furniture, without bothering about structural design issues, while cabinetmakers jibe that furniture made with the carpenter's axe is just a heap of logs.

'The cabinetmaker can glue things together, the carpenter must use the mortise and tenon': this adage is still around today. But originally cabinetmakers also dealt in tenons, and for the English Arts and Crafts movement of the nineteenth century an 'honest' piece of furniture was recognizable by its joints. Pre-modern bone glues dissolved in moisture and could therefore be used only inside houses.

In fact, gluing and veneering (an up-and-coming technique from the seventeenth century on) became the province of cabinetmakers and generated new areas of expertise within it. The new cultural importance of furniture meant that the rise of the cabinetmaker's art was unstoppable. In the baroque and rococo periods, master cabinetmakers even had a decisive influence in architecture, 'without growing into that function' (Hellwag 1924: appendix, 72), since, with the art of gluing and veneering, joinery now developed out of the closely related art of cabinetmaking. In the twentieth century, to be sure, wood-frame construction was revolutionized precisely by new bonding technology.

Veneering techniques came to Central and Western Europe from Italy in the sixteenth century and were further developed over the following centuries. They originated in a drive to employ high-grade wood from often exotic places – which was prohibitively expensive to use on a large scale – for individual items of furniture. Thus wood veneer, which involved high transport costs, brought forth both a global timber trade and early mass production of furniture. 'A mass market for bourgeois furniture could now develop for the first time among the *classes respectées*' (Stürmer 1982: 99). Thin slices of high-grade wood were typically glued onto less costly wood, making it 'invisible'. The wood joints were also covered by the veneer, so that 'the unity of construction language and pictorial language was lost' (Flade 1979: 181). But, thanks to more sophisticated planing techniques, the result was completely even surfaces.

Advances in the art of sawing and planing could yield paper-thin veneer (figure 2.11), but even the most refined techniques produced too much waste. In the nineteenth century, therefore, knives began to be used to peel off costly wood veneer (Stürmer 1982: 97) – a logical conclusion to an economy drive that had previously replaced the axe with the saw.

Veneering techniques made it possible to respond flexibly to a shortage of high-grade wood, especially as the art of imitating certain exotic woods – the coveted mahogany or ebony, for example – became more widespread at the same time. In eighteenth-century Britain, mahogany was by far the most sought-after wood for both furniture and boats; a definite interrelationship established itself between colonialism and furniture-making. In 1803 Thomas Sheraton wrote in *The Cabinet Dictionary*: 'Of all woods, mahogany is the best suited to furniture where strength is demanded. It works up easily, has a beautiful figure and polishes so well that it is an asset to any room in which it may be placed. Other woods for cabinetwork are quite laid by since the introduction of mahogany.' By 1860 'mahogany was truly king in Liverpool' (Latham 1957: 160, 56). The period from

Figure 2.11: Veneer sawing: French illustration from 1774. Never before in the history of woodworking had the art of sawing been so delicate and precise, and never before had such hard (tropical) and costly woods been processed in such great quantity. Highly specialized sawyers, active only in such great metropolises as Paris, London and Amsterdam, had an 'unheard-of ability in the art of slicing thin wood veneer' (Stürmer 1982: 100), as thin as 1 millimetre.

1770 until the end of the nineteenth century is known in the British furniture history as the 'mahogany age'. The outcome was a global depletion of the precious wood, so great that today naval engineers complain of no longer being able to find any suitable mahogany. But we are beginning to run too far ahead . . .

Techniques of gluing, veneering, staining and imitation made cabinetmaking more and more independent of the natural properties of wood. This was not the case with turners, however, who, like other traditional woodcraftsmen, retained a close link to the forest. Not so long ago a turner in Germany still reported that he 'awfully enjoyed buying wood in the forest' (Rodekamp 1981: 97).

In olden as well as modern times, any huge demand for wood has come from the construction sector. Next in importance have been coopers, the producers of barrels and other such containers. To the anger of other tradesmen, carpenters and coopers were sometimes active in the purchasing and selling of wood (Hellwag 1924: 290f.).

The significance of the cooper's craft grew *pari passu* with trade in general, since barrels and the like were needed to transport many goods. 'I do not know of consumption of oak greater than that of coopers', declared a witness before a British parliamentary commission in 1792 (McCracken 1971: 60).

Whereas other craftsmen produced individual items to order, coopers were already turning out standardized mass goods. Since water-tightness was an important factor, they preferred oak and ash – which meant that they had many competitors for the wood. Coopers were selective, even in the case of oak, since the timber had to be free of branches but also not excessively hard. Tough ash was especially coveted for barrel rings. In the saline forest near Salzburg, coopers habitually took samples from their chosen firs and spruces and even, after felling them, discarded a large amount of wood as unsuitable: 'Both involved huge wastage of wood' (Koller 1970: 235). Wandering dunes in Sweden have been traced back to deforestation that once served the production of herring barrels for the Hanseatic cities.

Already in the sixteenth century, the oak required by coopers was in shorter supply than oak used in construction (Bonnemann 1984: 371). In 1768, Frederick the Great urged in his testament that saltworks should make use of sacks in order to cut down on the consumption of cask wood. And in the early nineteenth century France 'no longer even had high-quality oak to keep its wine in barrels' (Rubner 1967: 102). White oak, which provided the best cask wood, became the 'first important commercial tree of New England' (Charles F. Carroll, in Hindle 1975: 25).

As we have seen, since the most ancient times humanity has acquired extensive knowledge of the properties of particular woods. It is therefore scarcely surprising that many woodworkers thought they had a natural right to the wood suitable for their purposes, or that they were imperious towards the foresters in charge of timber allocation. But natural law is ambiguous, in the forest as well as outside. A number of crafts required the same properties in the wood they used. The more dynamic the economy became, the more the various demands on wood came into conflict with one another.

Wainwrights or cartwrights also required high-quality oak and ash (figure 2.12). The wood for axles, hubs and spokes had to withstand extreme pressure, most of all where carriage-making was a technology in the service of rulers – as it was in the case of war chariots in antiquity or coaches in the baroque period (when wheels climbed higher and higher) (Treue 1965: 214, 228). Carriage-makers were then self-assertive and demanding. One senior forestry official

Figure 2.12: Wheel-making in the eighteenth century, from the *Encyclopédie* of Diderot and d'Alembert. It is no longer a handicraft in the traditional sense, but a manufacturing activity based on a strict division of labour. On the left, a worker drives spoke holes with a four-cornered gouge; in the centre, spokes are fitted into a hub; on the right and at the back, rims and spokes are adjusted. It is largely a matter of assembling ready-made parts: neither the inputs (wood) nor the end product (the carriage) are visible.

complained that the allocation of wood to cartwrights was 'anything but pleasant, because the finest trunks must be selected, and the forest repeatedly combed to find the required quality' (Jägerschmid 1827–8: 1/147). Wheel rims were still hewn into shape in the forest in the eighteenth century, since on top of everything else it was necessary to have branches with the right kind of bends (Duhamel du Monceau 1766–7: 2/76). Around the turn of the nineteenth century, however, steam began to be used to produce suitable bends for such things as ships' planks and barrel staves.

Most 'machines' in the pre-industrial age – windmills and water-mills, water-driven hammer mills and scoops, wine and printing presses – consisted largely of wood; the same was true of gear mechanisms, for which hard common beechwood was needed. Only seldom was special equipment used to produce such machines; it was more typical of the Wood Age that workers produced their implements, when these were themselves made of wood.

Only millwrights, who also knew how to make water wheels and gearing mechanisms for mines and forges, emerged as independent, often ambulatory, craftsmen (Dubler 1978; Bedal 1984). But repairs were so often necessary in wooden mills that even millers had to have some of the skills involved. A Munich ordinance of 1487 stipulated that, in order to qualify as a master craftsman, a miller must be able to produce new paddles and new cogs for the mill wheels (Kohl 1969: 5). The development of a new machine industry in the nineteenth century marked the end of this Wood Age in tool design and construction.

3 Large-Scale Firewood Consumption and the First Wave of Forest Ordinance

Wood and the 'fire trades'

Until the nineteenth century, wood was used most of all as domestic fuel. Municipal policy concerned itself mainly with this aspect, and the literature on the economical use of wood liked to dwell on the design of tiled living-room stoves and cooking ovens. However, certain industries had a spectacular appetite for wood. A blast-furnace master in the eighteenth century claimed that a single furnace consumed more wood than two small towns. One observer was even more astounded by the huge charcoal stocks he saw in foundry warehouses than by the quantities of charcoal sent every day to Paris (Duhamel du Monceau 1762: 12).

Old illustrations show even more impressive woodpiles in saltworks, which sometimes stood a little higher than the boiling house (figure 2.13). Saltworks and ironworks were the great 'wood gluttons' of the early modern age. Foundries used wood in the form of charcoal, reduced to approximately a quarter of the original volume, whereas saltworks nearly always used wood in its raw state.

Transport problems were much greater in the case of firewood than in that of wood used for construction and other purposes. Firewood and charcoal were used in much greater quantity, so the cost of transporting them (and the resulting profits) were much less than for construction and other timber, which fetched a much higher price. Often the existence of a salt- or ironworks was secure only if it could raft or drift logs there by water and if it had exclusive purchase rights in a particular forest region. Ancient sources refer to ironworks as 'forest works' and to metalworkers as 'forest people' (*silvani*) (Neuberg 1901:3), so close was the link between them and the forest.

For all the iron- and saltworks that obtained their own wood from the forest, the supply problem was mainly one of manpower

Figure 2.13: The salt spring (*Haalquell*) in Schwäbisch Hall, with its ten 'ladle booms' and its neatly stacked piles of logs. The salt spring built in 1590 can be seen in the left foreground; the copper engraving of 1715 is meant to demonstrate more recent technological advances in excavation. The booms, from which buckets are suspended, are operated by human muscle power. The huge woodpiles created major space problems. In 1682 it was forbidden to pile wood in the town streets because of the fire danger.

organization. In the eastern Alps, where large stretches of forest were 'given over' to them until the end of the eighteenth century, they drew the great bulk of their labour from forest workers and charcoal-burners (Mitterauer 1974: 238f.). As the drive for uninterrupted

93

production intensified, it became more difficult to be sure of a constant supply of wood and more necessary to stockpile large reserves. This was a major problem for saltworks. In eastern Alpine ironworks, charcoal warehouses (*Kohlbarren*) are documented as early as the fifteenth century (Wehdorn 1982: 97). They recommended themselves all the more because people had begun to recognize how much the quality of charcoal depended on a dry place of storage. The walls protecting the charcoal depot were indeed sometimes more carefully put together than the works itself.

The weight of the supply problem varied greatly with the kind of metal produced. Wood input rose proportionately with the melting point, but it was also true that 'poorer' ores contained less metal in the state in which they were found. Iron has the highest melting point (1,528 degrees Celsius), but brittle cast iron melts at 1,150 degrees, a temperature already attainable in primitive smelting works (Sperl 1984: 90). Next come copper (1,083 degrees), gold (1,063 degrees) and silver (961 degrees), and far behind them zinc (420 degrees), lead (327 degrees) and tin (232 degrees). Lead works therefore put up with almost any price for wood, especially as lead had been experiencing a boom since the fifteenth century, as a new means of separating off silver and later for use in firearm rounds. The extent to which metal production depended on wood prices was determined not only by fuel requirements but also by the value of the final product. Thus, the price of wood was a much less important factor for silver output than for the production of less valuable zinc.

The coal and steel industry needed not only firewood and charcoal for its foundries, but also mine timber for the excavation of deposits. On Rammelsberg Mountain near Goslar, for example, more construction timber was used than in the whole of the town (Suhling 1983: 111); and the demand increased still further in the nineteenth century, when coal mining went deep underground and the threat of a cave-in became more acute. Until early modern times, wood was also needed as a fuel in mining, since explosives were not yet available and fire was used to loosen rocks.

It was not only for metal and salt extraction that large quantities of firewood were required. In many places, the list of large users also included blacksmiths, brewers, bakers, potters, glass-makers, lime-burners and brick-makers. Wood consumption was a problem that varied enormously among these different trades. Complaints were often heard among the citizenry of Nuremberg that 'brewers, bakers, dyers, launderers and others' illegally bought up wood before it came onto the market, thereby causing shortages. The Frankfurt city council also blamed dyers and brewers, in particular, for the rising price of wood (Bothe 1913: 379). Bakers and brewers had their fixed place in urban society; they produced staples and therefore had a rightful claim to firewood. But in some places – the Nuremberg region, for instance – brewing was becoming a powerful export business, whose fuel requirements were a disturbance to the traditional timber trade.

Potters represented the oldest 'fire craft', but their high consumption of wood made them unpopular in the cities. Lime ovens and brickworks greatly increased their use of wood in the modern age; indeed, as early as the fifteenth century, the city brick-maker in Zurich was by far the largest craft consumer of wood. In late medieval Hamburg, people blamed brick-makers for the retreat of the forest. But, since those at the top preached the virtues of the brick – whether as a defence against fire or as a way of saving on costly construction timber – it was not easy to object to these 'wood gluttons'.

The firewood trade was a world apart from the construction and household timber sector. It used and dealt in wood differently; it absorbed much larger quantities, almost all from the nearby area, and often not via the market but from 'dedicated forest areas'. The limited character of forest resources first made itself felt in relation to construction timber, but it was subsequently more blatant and more worrisome for people living at the time. They needed wood to avoid freezing in winter, and in the Little Ice Age, which stretched from the sixteenth to the early nineteenth century, cold winters came one on top of the other. 'Economy drives' run like a red thread through the history not only of household wood usage but also of the early modern firewood and charcoal industry.

How high was wood consumption in ironworks? If one wishes, one can extrapolate horrific figures that make the situation of the forests look hopeless. But the iron industry did not go under. For the question of total wood consumption is wrongly posed for the time in question: it assumes that the metalworks had to be of a certain normal or minimum size to be competitive, and that there was an economic compulsion for the works to operate continually. However, until the eighteenth century, the metalworking industry ranged all the way from archaic forges operating within farms to blast furnaces with early industrial features (figure 2.14). A seasonal trade with long interruptions was quite normal. These basic facts mean that all grand calculations about pre-industrial firewood consumption are inevitably spurious.

Figure 2.14: Drawing of a Swedish 'farm forge' – a primitive furnace for smelting iron, enclosed with strips of wood on the outside (1732). Women were also worked to the limit, both operating the bellows and spinning. Alongside the blast furnaces, tall as a house, that became established in the early modern period, smaller furnaces allowed farms to continue producing iron for a long time. To the right (off image) a smelter uses an axe to split a ball of iron obtained from the furnace; the ore (left) is still burning inside it.

It is more meaningful to look for relative quantities, for the consumption of wood or charcoal per unit of iron output. But here too the figures for the eighteenth century are divergent, and their reliability is not infrequently open to doubt. Furnace masters who held traditional forest rights had to declare a high demand for wood in order to continue enjoying them. Furnace employees were interested in doing the same, if they wanted to disguise the fact that they were surreptitiously producing extra iron for their own benefit. One comes across the suspiciously round ratio of 10:1 – ten weight units of wood to one weight unit of iron (Johannsen 1953: 129). Since carbonized wood shrank by approximately a quarter, this would correspond to a charcoal–iron ratio of 2.5:1. But ratios of 5:1 also appear – and in the eighteenth century even something close to 1:1 (Handtmann 1982: 55). Such figures reflect differences not only in furnace technology but also in ore quality.

Similar difficulties arise in determining the input–output ratio in saltworks. When the salt masters in Schwäbisch Hall were asked in 1738 'how much wood was consumed per week', they refused to give a definite answer: 'It varies: some weeks more than others. It also depends on time differences, whether it's summer or winter, whether the wood is light or heavy, and so on' (Radkau 1986a: 16).

Wood consumption varied with fluctuations in the salt content of the brine and also with changes in the weather and temperature. Sometimes a ratio of 100:1 was reported between a kilogram of salt and a cubic metre of wood, although this figure, again suspiciously round, set wood consumption too high and was applicable only to weak brines (Hägermann and Ludwig 1984: 170). As early as the sixteenth century, twice as much salt was being produced per unit of wood in the Aussee mines; in Lüneburg, with its 23 per cent brine, the figure was nearly four times as much (Witthöft 1976). Ten times more wood was required to boil away a 5 per cent brine than for a 25 per cent brine (Emons and Walter 1984: 128). The prices that boilers had to pay for wood also varied in the eighteenth century from one salt works to another, sometimes ranging from one to ten. Demand and costs were therefore by no means fixed quantities – a fact that set up an impetus to rationalization and technical innovation.

Expansion frenzy and the 'wood brake' in the coal and ore industry

The sixteenth century saw a leap in the exploitation of forest resources, especially in regions rich in coal, mineral ore and salt. This affected large parts of Central Europe, where the coal and metal industry was much more widely dispersed than in the nineteenth and twentieth centuries, and where salt was also extracted in a large number of places. The expansion was truly explosive around the year 1500 in the Ore Mountains (now straddling Germany and the Czech Republic) and the Tyrol, where a 'mining fever' gripped the offices of business magnates and princes alike. Several impulses combined to drive the boom: the rise of the modern state and its insatiable need for money, the dynamic of early capitalism, the stream of silver from the Americas, and advances in water technology that made it possible to mine at greater depths. Duke Julius of Brunswick (1528–89) confessed that, whereas other princes had the 'hunting devil' inside them, he was possessed by the 'mining devil' (Baumgarten 1933: 25); Emperor Maximilian (1459–1519) might have said of himself that he was possessed by both. Sometimes the hunting devil and the mining devil got in each other's way. In 1550 Landgrave Philip of Hesse prohibited the search for mineral resources, because he did not want 'the forest and game to be corrupted by iron, lead or copper ores' (Bonnemann 1984: 323).

Both devils pushed for dominion over the forest. In an age when taxation systems were still little developed, mining was for many princes the only way of coming into money. It was recalled that mining was an old *Regal* – a sovereign right of the king, later passed down to princes – and everywhere territorial lords now asserted this claim in order to make as much money as possible. They often did this by pledging mines to the financially strongest entrepreneur, as Maximilian did to the Fuggers in the Tyrol. The princely need for money was the driving force behind the tempestuous expansion of early capitalism. But this did not add up to a solid foundation, since it was by no means always possible to rely upon the capacity or the willingness of princely debtors to pay up.

The mining and metal industry was entirely dependent upon large supplies of wood. In the late Middle Ages, when the expansion of this sector began, the population decline and agrarian retreat following the Black Death meant that wood was available in abundance. In the sixteenth century, however, when population pressure made itself felt in many areas (Abel 1986: 99ff.), the situation in the forest grew acute. The forest rights of landlords and territorial rulers were now a power factor like never before. It was not unusual for wood to serve as part of a princely ploy to gain control over a metal- or saltworks: the Duke of Brunswick, for example, in his decades-long dispute with the city of Goslar, won back his mining *Regal* over the Rammelsberg after 1525 (Rosenhainer 1968: 91ff.).

It was generally more difficult for a ruler to enforce his supreme property rights in the case of iron than in that of non-ferrous and precious metals. For iron deposits were widely dispersed, often lay close to the surface, and did not need skilled miners to extract them. In such conditions the mining *Regal* had little force. At the beginning of the modern age, iron ore extraction was in many cases a sideline for farmers. But the fact that smelting required large quantities of wood gave the ruler scope to intervene. In 1625, for example, the government in Vienna included iron production in the Ore Mountain of Styria among the prerogatives of a special enterprise, the Innerberger Hauptgewerkschaft, and endowed it with extensive forest rights. Yet, despite this state sponsorship and control, the mines had to contend with the competition of 'forest iron' produced by farmers and landowners in the same region.

Saltworks were not a typical field of operations in early capitalism (Tremel 1954: 62f.); they were traditionally owned by long-established families, and monasteries also often had a stake in them. In the sixteenth century, however, many rulers attempted to gain possession of them – with particular success in places like Hallein (Alps), Hall (Tyrol), Hallstatt and Aussee, where salt was gained from the mountain and the ruler could more easily assert his ancient rights (Palme 1983: 508ff.).

In these Austrian regions, salt was released into water by means of a so-called *Sinkwerk*, and the resulting brine was then drawn into boiling houses. On the other hand, most saltworks in Germany were able to access the source of salt overground or through an accessible spring. Here the main investment was in sometimes lavish pumps, which drew the brine into boiling houses. In these conditions, it was more common to retain the traditional form of economy, in which ownership of the saltworks was shared among many citizens. Nevertheless, quite a few salt springs became dependent on the local ruler if they were forced to use wood from his forests and were subject to his marketing monopoly.

The Alpine saltworks, with their more concentrated ownership, had huge boileries that stretched over several hundred square metres. In older German saltworks such as those at Lüneburg, Halle or Schwäbisch Hall, however, the brine was 'evaporated' in many small boileries, and the constitution of the saltworks ensured that this practice continued. Theoretically, much less heat must have been lost in large boileries than in smaller ones, but their size would also have made them liable to be repaired more frequently.

The princes profited from salt not only by directly appropriating saltworks but also by controlling the salt trade and taxing consumption. In 1541 the French king claimed a salt monopoly for the whole country (Hocquet 1984: 305); this resulted in huge conflicts, and the struggle over the *gabelle*, the salt tax, persisted all the way down to the French Revolution. The imposition of a salt monopoly was a sign of victorious absolutism in other countries (Hroch and Petráň 1981: 151f.). One of the first measures taken by Peter the Great to strengthen himself financially was the transfer of the salt monopoly from the monasteries to the tsar. One can also clearly see this connection between salt and political power in Mahatma Gandhi's campaign against the British salt monopoly in the Indian Raj.

The salt industry was by far the largest consumer of wood in many regions, and it was in the interest of governments that they should be the main provider. This too intensified the pressure on the forests. In the sixteenth century, forest resources were in many places stretched to their limit. As early as 1348 a number of hammers fell silent in the region of Vilseck in the Upper Palatinate 'because charcoal burners there had completely consumed the forest' (Fritsch 1974: 25). In the Siegerland, Europe's largest iron-producing region around the year 1500, the period during which ironmakers kept their furnaces in constant operation was cut in 1528 from twelve to eight weeks (Becher [1789] 1980: 520), and by the seventeenth century it had been reduced still further. Charcoal shortages, as well as inadequate deliveries from farmers, were given as the reason for the number of furnaces out of operation in the Harz around the year 1600 (Rosenhainer 1968: 121). Already in the sixteenth century, straw was often used to heat saltworks in the Halle/Saale region.

It is hard to conclude from all this that wood shortages resulted in an economic crisis. The crisis symptoms gathering in the mining sector since the mid-sixteenth century had more to do with competition from silver pouring in from the Americas and with the ruthless plunder of the mines. Only the best lodes were mined, low-value ores were thrown onto the waste tip, and miners therefore soon reached depths where the water could no longer be adequately scooped out. Many such bad experiences were necessary before mining eventually reached its optimum level.

If wood shortages repeatedly interrupted the operation of forges and smithies, this did not necessarily point to a crisis. In the sixteenth century, furnaces were often not yet lavish enterprises: they fitted into the farmyard scene, and their most expensive element was the water-driven bellows. For this reason they were known as 'bellows houses' (Blähhäuser) in the eastern Alps. Most were not very solidly built, and even in the eighteenth century a smelting period of eight or fourteen days was considered on the high side. The idea that high investment costs required continual operation did not carry much weight. A more common approach was that the operation of these rural works, often supplied with ore and charcoal as a sideline on the part of farmers, should fit into the rhythm of the yearly agricultural cycle, especially as quite a few of those employed in them had a piece of land or some livestock of their own.

In these conditions, it was not a 'wood brake' but unrestricted growth that tended to result in crisis. Wherever this happened, it had a devastating impact on farming: the provision of ore and wood took place at the expense of agriculture and livestock-breeding; and the demands of proliferating mines and furnaces caused acute difficulties. This was especially the case in remote, inhospitable regions. A shortage of lard was often a greater problem than a shortage of wood in the Ore Mountain region of Styria (Radkau 1983: 525). For all these reasons, a first phase of outright plunder gave way to a realization that the coal and metal industry had to be kept within the limits of sustainable forestry.

Then, as now, the big issue was what practical consequences this realization would have. It depended on whether there was an interest, and a capacity, to act with a long-term view of things. By and large, such an attitude was far more prevalent in saltworks than in the mining and smelting sector. Many saltworks displayed a greater sense of social solidarity, and a less adventurous business spirit, than was generally the case in early modern mines; people thought of them as enterprises that had remained much the same for generations, with little or no change in their ownership structure.

The principle of sustainable forestry, which was at the heart of later developments, can already be found in the sixteenth-century dispositions of the Reichenhall saltworks and their reference to the 'eternal' forest. This term was further explained in 1661: 'God has created the forests for the salt spring, so that, like it, they may continue for ever. So must men keep it: before the old runs out, the young should already have grown again for felling' (Bülow 1962: 159f.). Sustainable forestry meant acting in accordance with the God-given order – 330 years before the Rio conference on the environment!

The fate of many mines was very insecure: 'No enterprise decays or dies as rapidly as mines do', we read in the illuminated *Schwazer Bergbuch* manuscript of 1556 (Suhling 1983: 108). It was scarcely surprising, therefore, that people in the forest did not pay much heed to the future. But not all mine masters shared this attitude, and over time learning processes had their effect. In 1720, a four-furnace enterprise in the Harz Mountains was discontinued 'until the woods have recovered' (Riehl 1968: 80). Moreover, clear felling was often not so radical or extensive as to prevent the natural regeneration of the forest. Where furnaces obtained their wood from coppices, as they did in England, sustainability was more or less built into the art of forestry, since the trees in question grew again spontaneously in the absence of rigorous measures to support them. Not by chance did long-range planned sustainability originate in Central European mining regions that obtained their wood from high forest. Sustainability arises as a project in places where it is in danger.

Whose wood emergency?

Karl Bücher, a leading light in the German Historical School of political economy, wrote of forest history: 'Perhaps a historian can be found to treat the true history of the forest together with the history of mining, recognizing both for what they really are: a plundering of the people for the benefit of the few' (1918: 58). Many mines in the early modern period obtained their wood almost for free. In the

101

sources, we find numerous complaints by mines and furnaces about a 'wood shortage'; the supply crisis did not hit these privileged industries, however, but rather those who suffered as a result of their exorbitant wood consumption.

Representatives of the coal and metal industry liked to say that the population as a whole lived off them. But the truth is that people in the early modern period lived overwhelmingly from agriculture. The mining frenzy of the sixteenth century worried many at the time, since its main consequence was a rising cost of living. Saltworks and the coal and metal industry were often considered a misfortune because of their insatiable appetite for wood – except when earnings from the supply of wood weighed more heavily in the minds of the nearby population.

One night in 1628, farmers angry at the destruction of the local forest set fire to an ironworks in the Hasli region of Switzerland. The government in Berne took responsibility for rebuilding it, but in 1770 all the inhabitants of the valley refused to cooperate in providing timber for the construction work (Stuber 2008: 63f.). Switzerland, with its population of small farmers, gave the iron producers a harder time than they had in the Habsburg-ruled eastern Alps. In the so-called Ore Mountain there, whose forests were placed at the service of the 'mine factories', the Hundshübel commune complained in 1695 'that, after the previous times of hunger, we have been tormented with a dire shortage of wood that has been almost as bad'. The strong growth of the French iron industry in the eighteenth century triggered a wave of popular protests against the 'wood-gobbling' furnaces (*les gouffres dévorants*) (Woronoff 1984: 227f.). For the society as a whole, as far as the forest was concerned, cutbacks in the coal and metal industry were conducive more to stability than to crisis.

One significant effect of wood shortages for economic history was that, from the sixteenth century, large wood consumers tended to locate themselves in peripheral areas. Enterprises were under instructions to seek out and follow forest resources; metal production and metal processing could not be advantageously concentrated in the same district. If the 'wood brake' impeded the formation of large conglomerates in the 'fire crafts', this certainly did no harm either to society or to the environment.

Hammer mills and smithies migrated north and south from the Ore Mountain in Styria, spreading out along the River Enns and the tributaries of the Mur. They also migrated northward from the Siegerland. After 1460 Nuremberg, one of the major metalworking centres, moved its *Seigerhütten* processes for the separation of copper and silver to the forests of Thuringia and started tin production in the Ore Mountains. Whereas, in the nineteenth century, coal-mining led to the formation of giant industrial conglomerates, early forms of industrialization were drawn to the countryside and the forest by the availability of wood. The growing importance of water as a motive force strengthened this trend. The greater the scarcity of wood and water power, the more these production factors became location-dependent. A whole period of economic history, from the late Middle Ages to the early nineteenth century, was marked by this decentralizing tendency in pursuit of wood and water. The beauty of many old towns rests not least on the fact that the natural resources situation kept their quantitative growth within limits and left open only the option of qualitative growth. The Wood Age looks promising today from this 'progressive' point of view.

Forest ordinance and mining interests

When princely councils used to extol the value of the forests for mining, they could wax quite lyrical at times. In 1583, a commission reported back from the Harz to the Duke of Brunswick: 'The forests are the hearts of mines and the treasure of princes; when no forest is at hand, mines are like a bell without a clapper or a lute without strings' (Baumgarten 1933: 4). The forests as the 'heart', 'soul', 'jewel' and 'treasure' of the iron industry: these also appear as stock expressions in the state records in Styria.

Many early regulations applying to the forest actually come under mountain ordinance. Rulers began to issue forestry rules in the High Middle Ages, and a veritable stream of ordinance appeared in large areas of Central Europe in the sixteenth century. In this respect, the Harz, the Alpine mining regions and parts of Saxony and Hesse with mining interests took the lead. Historians of the German forest speak of a dawning 'age of forest ordinance' in the sixteenth century. Decrees issued in the seventeenth and early eighteenth centuries often do no more than repeat provisions laid down in the sixteenth.

Forest ordinance was keen to stress that, in areas set aside for the yearly 'cull', all trees – and not only the best or the most convenient – should be cleared. *Gute Arbeit ist ganze Arbeit* [a job well done is a job perfectly done] was the motto. This clearance instruction, stemming from the coal and metal industry, was repeated 'wherever mining interests came into play' (Oberrauch 1952: 49), although its effects were devastating in the high mountains, where it caused soil erosion and landslides on steep slopes.

103

The forest ordinance of the sixteenth century mainly regulated the felling of trees; it scarcely concerned itself with reforestation. In any case, the governments of the day lacked the necessary organization, and there were not even any reasonably precise forest maps. What they could do was to ban farmers from driving their livestock into young woodland. Sometimes it was envisaged that, after the clear felling, individual trees (so-called *Überhälter* or *Laßreiser*) would remain for reseeding.

Emotional laments about the destruction of the forest and the supposedly imminent danger of wood shortages were considered good form in sixteenth-century forest ordinance (Endres 1888: 106f.); such complaints were needed to legitimate the intervention of the authorities in forest affairs. Subjects of the ruler found them less convincing, however, since the tree-felling directed by the mining industry, and covered up by the ordinance, put all previous deforestation in the shade.

In many regions, there was a wood shortage only from the point of view of governments hell-bent on economic growth. Even the official chronicler of Landgrave Philip of Hesse (1504–67) expressed amazement that the *Hofmeister* Hans von Dornberg – the court tutor and master of ceremonies, who showed great fervour in forest policies – was fond of saying that 'oak and wise people will be lacking in the land of Hesse': this from a man who, according to the chronicler, was unable to tell whether or not there was a shortage of oaks or judicious men (Zimmermann 1954–5: 92). The *Hofmeister*'s fervour paid off, however. On his watch, forest revenue rose from zero to the equivalent of a fifth of the Landgrave's yearly income. Revenue from the saltworks was even higher; it too ultimately derived from the wood in the forest (Krüger 1980: 292).

The plethora of forest ordinance from the sixteenth century onwards is attributable not only to mining interests but also to the ambition of governments, which were eager to absorb all the special rights handed down from the Middle Ages into a single authority covering the whole territory of the state. There is a close connection between the genesis of the modern state and the intervention of rulers in the forest. The need of mines for wood served as a means for the sovereign to derive forest rights from age-old mountain rights (Künßberg 1904: 204f.); the forest *Regal* served in turn for the construction of territorial dominion. In regions with good transport, both mining and wood sales made the forest an important source of money as early as the sixteenth century.

Whereas the earliest forest ordinance had applied only to the prince's personal property or to areas in the immediate vicinity of mines, the regulations of the sixteenth century increasingly covered whole territories. This led to conflicts, however, some of which simmered on for centuries. In the opposing camp were not only farmers' marketing cooperatives but also powerful noble landowners who wished to dispose freely of their forest land.

Forest allocation for the iron industry around the Ore Mountain in Styria, whereby high and 'black' forest was declared crown estate, hit the Admont monastery especially hard. Bitterly resisting these exactions, the abbot appealed to the interests of his farmers and did not shrink from social demagogy: 'Under the cry "crown estate, crown estate"', he said, the wood chiefs of the iron barons were intruding on monastery land in a blind frenzy, squandering wood, taking the bread from the farmers' mouths and ruining the whole land (Kaser 1932: 152f.). The imposition of a general forest ordinance in Styria, Karnten and Krain was postponed from the sixteenth to the eighteenth century, thanks to the resistance of the assemblies representing the regional landed nobility.

The practical effect of this early modern ordinance remains an open question. The rush of princely decrees looks impressive on paper, but until the nineteenth century there were not usually enough suitable people to translate the fine words into action. In many cases, the foresters themselves had the strongest interest in unlimited exploitation of resources, since they lived on the relevant fees, or *Akzidentien*. Around the year 1530, the Württemberg town of Böblingen rightly claimed that it could look after its forest better than the ruler's forester, since 'the matter concerns us and our descendants rather more than it does others' (Hauff 1977: 31). The town historian of Minden, Heinrich Tribbe, accused its wood custodians of using 'all their brain on boozing', instead of watching over the 'public property'.

In the early modern period, small woods within the field of vision of those with the right to use them were generally a better business proposition than large expanses of forest. Scarcely a single forest was measured or mapped in the sixteenth century; the rulers did not know the forests they claimed to protect (Corvol 1984: 5). Even in the nineteenth century, a well-known Austrian forester could complain that it was 'unbelievably difficult to guard the boundaries of the great forest estates' (Wessely 1853: 1/508). Whereas many authors of the time demanded closed forests as the necessary condition for good forestry, the Prussian theorist Wilhelm Pfeil realistically observed that many official decrees had to be read critically and that the true history of the forest often lay hidden behind such sources.

Nuremberg conifer-seeding, Zurich's Sihlwald regime and the Hauberg system in the Siegerland

The sowing of pinewood in Nuremberg and the Hauberg system in the Siegerland are the best-known examples of late medieval forestry that went beyond mere supervision towards active reshaping of the forest. The initiative for them came not from princely forest departments but (in Nuremberg) from a wealthy patrician entrepreneur and (in the Siegerland) from farmers, charcoal-burners and ironmakers' guilds. The interests of the iron industry came into play in both cases, but the social and geographical conditions were different. The result was two quite distinct forms of forest economy.

In most regions, artificial conifer forestation began only in the nineteenth century. This makes it all the more remarkable that it was introduced as early as the fourteenth century in the imperial forest in Nuremberg. Nuremberg conifer-seeding appeared in history 'with the suddenness of a meteor', writes one forest historian (Mantel 1981: 666). This is an exaggeration: there had already been reports of similar experiments in the Heide forest in the city of Dresden (Hausrath 1982: 62). But the initiator and the date are precisely known in the case of Nuremberg. Peter Stromer began sowing in the Lorenzer Reichswald at Easter 1368, writes his half-brother Ulman Stromer in their family chronicle (Sporhan and Stromer 1969: 79) – mostly pines and firs, but also some birches.

The conifer-seeding was a real 'invention', since it was not easy to obtain and prepare the seeds, and success came only after a number of trials.

> The winged, rather diminutive seeds flew out of fir or pine cones that had fallen from trees or were damaged by pests. The cones therefore had to be harvested from the trees before they were fully ripe. Today, as in the past, plucky men swing skilfully from treetop to treetop to do this. Then the fruit must be subjected to mild heat treatment, so that it neither dries out nor goes mouldy; the cone scales open up and release the seeds, which then continue to ripen. . . . Only through long and costly effort was the right soil depth established at which the little plants could bud and actually sprout forth. (Sperber 1968: 28)

Such seeding techniques could not develop out of the activity of farmers in the forest. Being mainly interested in 'fruit trees', they would have had no time for the conifer forestation that turned the forest into a mere source of wood and interfered with its function in providing fodder or foliage. For a long time, even forest officials were sceptical about artificial seeding. In 1540, draft forest ordinance

Figure 2.15: Nuremberg, surrounded by its two imperial forests (front Sebaldi, rear Lorenzi): picture card, 1516. This famous illustration expresses the claim of Nuremberg to have been 'founded with the forests' and to be inseparably bound up with them. In reality, the city had to struggle for centuries to gain control over the forests, which the Hohenzollern margraves owned and used for hunting.

for the Joachimstal in Bohemia noted that 'no household wood or firewood' results from hand-sowing (Koch 1963: 131). Yet by the fifteenth century Nuremberg was doing a roaring trade in conifer seeds (Hauser 1972: 57) and sending sowers along with them who knew exactly what to do. Noë Meurer, a counsellor to the Elector of the Palatinate, whose *Jagd- und Forstrecht* (1561) was one of the first works of German forest literature, published what he knew from Nuremberg about conifer-seeding (Mantel 1981).

If the Reichswald in Nuremberg (figure 2.15) had been an old pine forest, Stromer's feat would have been less astounding. In fact, the conifer forest there was long considered indigenous, but all the

greater was the surprise when soil analysis after 1945 led to the conclusion that by far the largest part of it had originally been deciduous
woodland. This discovery underlines the novelty of Stromer's conifer-
seeding, but it also casts what happened in a more questionable light;
his achievement appears a path-breaking advance only if conifer
monoculture is regarded as the ideal type of forestry. As it turned out,
the Nuremberg Reichswald showed dramatically the vulnerability
of artificial coniferous forest, since in the 1890s a third of the area
was wiped out by rapidly spreading pine worm infestation, and the
devastation was worst precisely in parts of the forest where Stromer
had begun his seeding in 1368 (Sperber 1968: 124)! It has been seen
repeatedly that naturally rejuvenated forest is ecologically more
stable than artificially planted areas – a lesson that also leads to a new
interpretation of forest history.

Peter Stromer was one of the great businessmen of his day: he was
employed in the coal and metal industry of the Upper Palatinate and
planted the coniferous forest in his own interest. He used timber for
his mine props, charcoal for his ironworks and smithies, and potash
for his glassworks. The city of Nuremberg initially had nothing to do
with the forestation, but in the end it achieved superintendence of the
surrounding forest, albeit in constant dispute with the neighbouring
margraves of Ansbach-Bayreuth.

Cities and territorial rulers differed in their forest policies.
Subordination to coal and iron interests conflicted with the principle that citizens should first be provided with the necessities of
life (figure 2.16). This attitude seemed reactionary in the eyes of
later forestry theorists, for whom the main priority was the maximization of output. In fact, Nuremberg was a stronghold of the
metal-processing industry, but the domestic needs of citizens had
taken precedence in wood deliveries from the Reichswald. As early
as 1340, at the request of the city of Nuremberg, Emperor Ludwig
the Bavarian withdrew the forest rights of charcoal-burners, glass-
blowers and pitch-burners and forbade wainwrights and coopers
to fell trees (Jegel 1932: 137). In 1544 the Nuremberg council
ordered that anyone who 'uses brass or wire hammers, smelting
works or other great fires' should no longer receive wood from the
Reichswald. In 1490, Augsburg banned the construction of smelting works within a radius of 6 miles, so as not to jeopardize the
wood supply for its citizens. Later, in the charcoal age, many cities
gambled on the growth of industries that consumed large quantities
of energy. But such ambition would have seemed absurd in the logic
of the Wood Age.

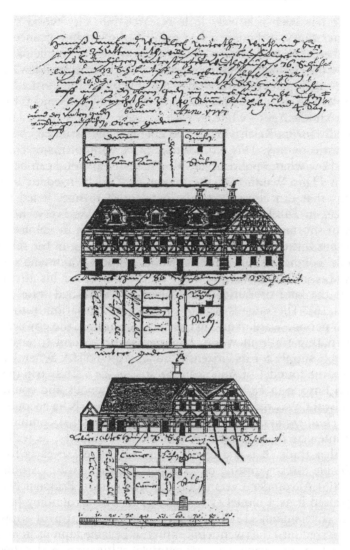

Figure 2.16: From an application for construction timber to the Sebaldi forest office in Nuremberg (1717). The brewer and innkeeper Hans Deinhard wanted to renovate his 'quite dilapidated' inn and to use the same opportunity to expand it; he therefore requested that 140 tree trunks should be allocated to him. He enclosed sketches of the existing (below) and planned (above) house. This shows how a building project might develop around the management of valuable construction timber. Sketches contained in the Nuremberg forest records, which go back to the late sixteenth century, are among the earliest known construction plans (Großmann 1986: 13).

There has been relatively little research into city wood supplies in former times, although it is a subject of great importance. After Nuremberg, the best-known example of far-sighted municipal forest policy in the German-speaking world is that of the Sihlwald in Zurich. The recorded history of the Zurich forest is by far the most extensive available. The city gained exclusive rights over the Sihlwald as early as the late Middle Ages – while, as we have seen, Nuremberg had to fight repeatedly for its Reichswald – and energetically assumed control of the forest economy. This did not take place without major conflicts, which show what a politically explosive material wood can be.

When Hans Waldmann, the mayor of Zurich, tried to ban old customs that ran contrary to the new forest regime, it led to disturbances in 1489 that ended in his execution. As everywhere, the threat of shortages was used to justify intervention in the use of the forest, but this could not have been very convincing in the relatively enviable conditions of Zurich's wood supply. Waldmann's forest policy was in fact power politics – an instrument for his attempt to convert the land of Zurich 'into a centrally governed state' (Weisz 1983: 1/16). The same is true of most forest legislation in the early modern period. Waldmann's demise was a warning: the city certainly did a roaring trade in wood, but it was also careful to ensure an affordable supply for its citizens (Radkau 1997: 51f.). When Gifford Pinchot, the founder of American forestry, made a study trip through Central Europe in 1890, 'the mixture of hardwoods and conifers in the Sihlwald' was the highlight among all the models he encountered.

The *Hauberg* system in the Siegerland (figure 2.17) combined the forest interests of local farmers and the iron industry, as well as of the leather trade. It is the best-known example of an early form of sustainable forestry resting on a cooperative foundation. Around the year 1800 Alexander Eversmann, the well-known Prussian Bergrat, still praised it as a model system 'that puts all surrounding lands to shame' (Eversmann [1804] 1982: 15). It was a form of coppicing that survived into the twentieth century; it became famous in modern times, when coppicing and cooperative cultivation had otherwise largely disappeared from the scene.

The Haubergs in the Siegerland were mountain forests consisting mainly of oaks and birches, but also of alders, hornbeams and hazelnut trees. The forest was worked within a cycle that lasted a maximum of twenty years; the second growth – typically for premodern forest – took place through coppicing and the retention of seed trees. The Haubergs belonged to cooperatives that regulated tree-felling. Depending on the length of the rotation cycle, there were

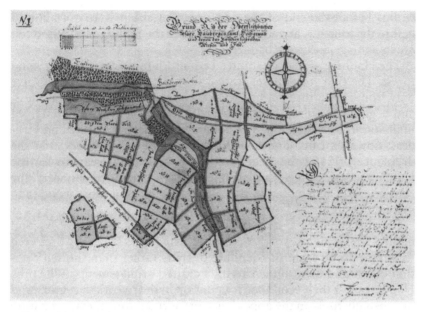

Figure 2.17: Land register map of 'Haubergs' in the parish of Oberfischbach (west of Siegen), 1774. The Haubergs, unlike the high forest (top left), are not represented as forests but rather as agricultural land. They did in fact serve *inter alia* as agricultural land, within a cycle similar to that of a multi-field system. The numbering of the Hauberg areas runs from 1 to 16, which points to a sixteen-year rotation cycle.

sixteen, eighteen or twenty fellings – a very high number in comparison with many other instances of coppicing.

The work on each felling began in spring with the 'clearing away'. All trunks and bushes (but only branches in the case of oak trees) were chopped off as firewood. In May, when the sap was rising, the oaks were stripped of their bark and sold to tanners for their tan – a lucrative and increasingly important part of forestry, not only in the Siegerland. Then the bare trunks were felled with an axe, destined for use as charcoal. In midsummer the remaining 'grass' was slashed with heavy Hauberg hoes and then burned; the ashes served as fertilizer. In the autumn, rye was sown among the stumps and roots and ploughed in with a light instrument specially designed to avoid damaging the young spikes; the rye had to be cut the next year with a sickle, so that the next growth of trees would not be in danger. The 'young copse' was then protected from livestock 'until the young wood outgrew the animals' mouths' (Schenck 1820: 191). Pigs could be driven into the woods before the end of the first year, but sheep were not allowed before the fourth year and cows not before the fifth. Goats caused too much damage and were banned.

The Hauberg system guaranteed equilibrium between industry and forest. The two social bases were a farming class that could not live only from agriculture but had to branch out into the timber business, and a guild-organized iron industry which, in its own interests, set limits on iron production. The equilibrium between nature and business, however, came under severe strain. Only a few years after the ordinance of 1562 the Siegerland began to supply weapons for the Dutch freedom struggle, and iron production expanded despite all the restrictions. The temptation was always there to cut more wood than sustainable forestry allowed.

But the Hauberg system became a way of life, a kind of 'second nature' for local farmers (Ranke and Korff 1980: 28). They preferred to import wood from surrounding districts rather than shorten rotation cycles and disturb the carefully crafted arrangements. When the Haubergs lost their economic foundation in the twentieth century and increasingly took on the appearance of 'normal' forest, many a nature lover regretted it. Some of the earliest conservationist laws passed by the North-Rhine Westphalia government were designed to preserve the Siegerland's Hauberg system (Schulte 2003: 2/594f.).

Rafting and drifting: water transport as impetus for the timber trade

A close correlation developed in modern times between forestry and river floating, and generally between official policies on wood and rafting. If one wishes to gauge the wood supply situation and the state of the timber trade in a particular city or region, it is best to look first of all at the prevalence of rafting and drifting. Economically active regions with little wood of their own could be well supplied if the conditions for rafting were favourable; poor forest regions lying on floatable rivers gave up their wood to distant customers. In pre-industrial times, transport expenditure was higher for wood than for any other bulk commodity, but wood, with its ability to float, was also the cargo most easily transported by water. In fact, the quality of wood was actually improved by rafting and drifting, since it later dried faster and was less vulnerable to pests.

Rafting is an age-old practice, but it really gained an impetus in the sixteenth century, when it spread to watercourses that were not naturally suited to it but had first to be specially developed for the purpose. In 1578 work started on the Elstergraben in Saxony, which eventually reached a length of 93 kilometres and supplied Leipzig with timber (Wilsdorf 1960: 71). Rafting penetrated deeper and deeper into the Black Forest, the Harz region and the Ore Mountains, and cargoes were floated up from the Tyrol to the Black Forest. Many mountain streams were also made 'floatable', through the building of special locks that enabled logs to be lowered in water to valley level. Lock construction, as well as watercourse development and channelling, required a lot of skill and experience. It was a working environment that people of the plains knew nothing about, and which came to be appreciated only in the nineteenth century, when engineers began to feel their way around in it.

When a region was made accessible for drifting and rafting, this heralded a transport revolution comparable only to the later development of the railways. At a stroke, transport costs were reduced to a fraction of their former level – indeed, in many cases transport became possible in the region for the first time. The technology soon developed a dynamic of its own, which it acquired elsewhere only in the industrial age. The existence of watercourses suitable for rafting or drifting often decided whether major commercial consumers of wood could set up in a district; it determined the forest economy of whole regions.

Rafting and drifting were thus a unique driving force in the economic and technical history of wood, above all because the prior hydrological work to make them possible involved a level of expenditure that paid off only if large quantities of timber were constantly shipped from forest areas to market outlets. The dynamic here, more than for many large consumers of wood, was already one of capital in search of profits. This being so, it was more difficult to maintain a regional equilibrium between forest and economy than in cases where the natural growth of wood was not geographically remote from its consumption. Since conifer wood could be drifted and rafted more easily than many deciduous woods, water transport was one reason for the development of coniferous forest.

The *Holzriesen* – 'giant' wooden chutes used to carry wood down from mountain to valley – were also part of the system of rafting and drifting. The wood from which they were made up was often equivalent to a third of the total wood they conveyed, and they could be used only for a few years. They positively demanded tree-felling on a large scale, since only that could provide the mass of sellable timber that made the construction of 'wood giants' worthwhile.

The importance of rafting went well beyond the timber industry. 'The rafters must have been of a quite uncanny agility', wrote one historian about early modern rafters in Styria (Kaser 1929: 29). 'They bought up not only wood, but also foodstuff, hairs, linen, loden and countless other commodities; smuggled them past toll posts on the Mur, no doubt dumped goods if they were caught.' Rafting probably lay at the origins of river trade. In modern times, too, it stimulated commerce and transport, even if it made things more difficult for river boats.

Rafting obviously had its limitations, since its success generally depended on access to flowing water. Rafters could move only with difficulty across lakes and bodies of standing water, and a log that sank was irretrievably lost. Lake Titi in the Black Forest, once much used for rafting, was still 'full of sunken timber' in 1808 (Stoll 1954: 261). A river with a low gradient was also a problem: for example, Venetians complained in the fifteenth century that rivers on the nearby mainland were clogged with drifting wood. Only in the twentieth century did the introduction of towboats make it possible to float wood even on the high seas.

Formerly, log rafts were taken apart and sold at their river destination. Unlike ship travel, it was a form of trade that did not require freight for a return journey; commodities were exchanged not for other commodities but for money. In fact, rafting gave a spur to the money economy. Water transport turned wood early on into a commodity on a grand scale. If it could be easily carried to lands where it fetched a high price, wood might become expensive and run short even in densely wooded regions.

Forestry became politics as a result of water transport. The rivers were controlled by cities or territorial rulers; river trade was subject to tolls at many points along the way. Since rafting, and especially drifting, often damaged river banks, weirs and bridges, and since it interfered with fishing and required special hydraulic projects, official regulation became necessary and gave rulers the opportunity to intervene (Geistefeldt 1963: 8ff.).

In his short story 'Floßfahrt', Hermann Hesse reports from his childhood that 'there was perpetual warfare between millers and rafters'. Log rafts damaged the mills, and the millers hit back by letting off the dammed-up water and leaving the rafts high and dry. Lüneburg city council had to buy up watermills on the River Ilmenau in order to secure the wood supply for its saltworks (Wagner 1930: 13).

In the towns along a river, the purchase of rafted wood was often a public responsibility that also included allocation and price regulation. In Vienna, in accordance with an imperial decree of 1559, only the central government had the right to purchase wood from a raft on the first day after its arrival; the city administration had the next pick on

Figure 2.18: Winding ropes in the Black Forest; in the background is the *Bähofen* shed for heating the tree trunks. The principle of shaping wood by heating, already applied here in early modern times, would revolutionize furniture production in the nineteenth century (Michael Thonet!). The 'hardest part' was the winding, when the bark came off and sap gushed from the trunks (Schoch 1985: 161). The massive use of young trees for rope was 'sometimes a major nuisance' for foresters (Jägerschmid 1827–8: 1/182).

the second day, ordinary citizens on the third day, and only then timber dealers (Sazenhofen 1980: 79). In Frankfurt, Jews had to wait their turn after fully entitled citizens. However, Goethe's father and two other prosperous burghers were denied permission when they wanted to bring in a whole boatload of wood at their own expense in 1761.

Rafting involved three major technical problems: securing the logs, steering, and controlling speed. Often several floats queued up behind one another, forming a 'giant chain' (Hafner 1983: 218): the fastening therefore had to be at once extremely solid and elastic, so that the rafts could follow the bends. For this purpose rafters used wooden ropes called *Wieden* (figure 2.18), in fact, young tree trunks that had been heated in special ovens and wound round a rotary bar (Keweloh 1985: 67) – one of the earliest examples of wood-bending under heat. The rafts were steered with various kinds of rudders, and the braking device consisted of logs that could be driven into the river bottom (figure 2.19).

Figure 2.19: Raft, consisting of bundled logs, on the River Enz (Black Forest) around 1900. The length can be seen from the rafters at the front. The picture shows that quite large rafts navigated even small rivers. The logs had to be connected elastically in order to negotiate river bends, but over longer routes many bends were straightened or modified.

The type of raft varied widely with the breadth, depth and dangers of the river, but also with local tradition and the kind of wood being transported. But, since the maximum width and weight were limited on smaller watercourses, standards had to be set as the space on available rivers was used up. The growth of legislation covering rafts also resulted in new norms. In the Black Forest, a *Floß* (raft) was also the name for a unit of wood.

In many regions, floating was a seasonal business: the preferred time was spring, when the water in rivers and streams was at its highest. Cold water was also better than warm, and summer drifting led to greater losses in 'sunken timber'. On many watercourses, floating was possible on only a very limited number of days each year. Where it was more or less continuous, as in the Alps and the Black Forest or on the great rivers, rafting became a self-assured occupation in its own right. The objective prerequisites – above all, maintenance of the waterways in good condition – led to cooperative forms of labour (Gothein 1889: 454). In the Black Forest and the Alpine

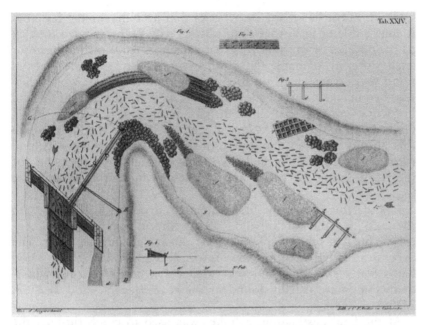

Figure 2.20: Driving logs through a weir and on a mill canal. On the right is a trap designed to hold firewood back from the millrace without blocking the water supply to the mill. The millrace is further protected against runaway driftwood by another trap and a 'mill rake', which 'is all the more necessary . . . because pieces of firewood that get through with the intake water cause great damage to the mill blades and arms' (Jägerschmid 1827–8: 2/285). Complex arrangements were therefore needed to defuse the chronic warfare between millers and rafters.

foothills, the timber trade was dominated by rafting cooperatives. In 1575–6 a strike of 'rafters and forest workers', who felt exploited and victimized by the Zwickau municipality, brought the whole sector to a standstill (Wilsdorf et al. 1960: 75f.).

If timber rafting was based on wage labour, an incentive arose to cut down on steerage personnel by making the rafts bigger and longer. But this trend reached full force only in the eighteenth century. Following its first surge in the sixteenth century, the sector ran up against a number of natural, technical and legal obstacles; its further advance was closely bound up with developments in hydrologic technology, water-tightness and trade.

Log driving – that is, the drifting of unassembled logs (figure 2.20) – was used mainly for the transportation of firewood in bulk over short distances. It would appear to be the simplest

117

method, but it has many drawbacks that account for the fact that it emerged later in history than rafting. The timber tended to stick to river banks or in shallow water, causing environmental harm or itself suffering damage. On small mountain streams, an artificial pond was created high up to collect the drifting logs, which then raced en masse into the valley when the weir was opened. If this did not work – as was sometimes the case in narrow valleys – workers might be mobilized into a special team to dislodge them, although this always involved dangers from the logs rushing down behind them. In the Black Forest whole villages might be called out for the work, lining the banks and repeatedly attempting to shift the logs.

Log driving generally first appeared in Central Europe with the mass demand for firewood of the fifteenth and sixteenth centuries; only in many Alpine regions did it date further back. The process already sorted out the firewood: 'Lighter, well-dried wood floats faster and represents the vanguard, whereas . . . the worst-quality logs are usually found in the rear' (Jägerschmid 1827–8: 2/306).

At the final destination, a 'rake' was used to comb through the water and haul the drifting logs to the shore. This had to be capable of resisting the pressure of the logs, as well of spring meltwater. Such devices incurred high costs and bordered on the limits of what was technically feasible at the time. In 1549, despite being warned against it by rafters, people from Augsburg built a rake on the River Lech; but it broke on its first impact with a log. Even rakes that resisted longer had to be frequently repaired. As late as 1828, Jägerschmid warned of the 'enormous costs' of the 'giant wood traps', and recommended log driving only when rafting proved impossible (1827–8: 2/234). In the eastern Alps, iron smelting centres grew up around raking points (Hieflau, Großreifling).

High costs and the risks of loss generally meant that only sizeable businesses could make a profit on log driving (Köstler 1934: 76). It always raised legal issues and was possible only with official approval. Without support from the government, it always succumbed at the millers' weirs, or as a result of theft or demands for compensation from people living along the river. In the early twentieth century it lingered on in southern Germany as a 'capitalist business' (Kroiß 1928: 28). And in sparsely inhabited forest regions, where it does not interfere with boat transport, it survives to this day.

Twilight trades: potash-boilers, pitch-burners, glass-makers, charcoal-burners

Until well into the modern age, many local people made money from the forest not directly, by selling timber, but by the indirect means of practising a craft. Their place in the forest economy was disputed, however, and it grew worse over the centuries. The more the forest was thought of as a mere supplier of timber, the more the traditional forest crafts came under fire. But, whether or not they had the support of the forest authorities, they remained among the main consumers of wood until the nineteenth century, especially in remote regions.

The growth of iron production put charcoal-burning at the top of the forest crafts in early modern times (Rubner 1975: 98). In the sixteenth century, forests in the Eifel region were valued mainly for their charcoal yield. At the same time, the glass-making trade rose to become the third largest consumer of wood after metal and salt production. Many forests were being used by glassblowers even before the mining industry arrived there. Glass production required either beechwood or charcoal for fuel and large quantities of potash as flux for the glass. The addition of potash reduced the melting point of the glass mass from 1,800 degrees to 1,200 degrees Celsius, which was attainable even in less solidly built kilns. Large quantities of the best firewood were used for this purpose too.

Potash production was itself one of the most important forest crafts, needed not only for glass-making but also for boiling soap and bleaching. The rise of the textile industry, together with improved purity standards, hugely increased the demand for potash (figure 2.21). Tar and pitch distilleries experienced a boom in connection with shipbuilding. They could be combined with charcoal-burning, when tar was distilled from resinous conifers and collected in a ditch around the charcoal pile.

Official policy in early modern times had an ambiguous relationship to all these uses of the forest; they were considered less valuable since they caused wood to lose its natural properties and reduced it to a fraction of its original substance. In charcoal-burning, wood lost three-quarters of its substance, but this paled beside the ratio in potash production, where roughly 1,000 kilos of wood were needed for an output of 1 kilo (2,000 kilos in the case of spruce wood, but only 700 in that of beech) (Blau 1917–18: 1/102).

Wood was burned, the ashes were leached with water, and the solution was evaporated (with the use of more wood). Technically speaking, it involved the most lavish expenditure of wood. Things were not

Figure 2.21: Potash boilery around the year 1800. By early modern standards it was a large works – which was not yet generally the case in the potash industry. In forest regions, glass-makers produced their own potash supply. There was resistance in the towns to the arrival of potash-boilers, who, according to a decree of the Nuremberg council in 1697, caused harm to the public because of their large wood consumption and because potash gave rise to 'foul smells and stenches'.

much better with pitch production, where only the resin was used and the substance of the wood was treated as waste material. But, since this huge volume shrinkage meant that transport was no longer such a problem, the craft was an ideal way of using the forest in remote parts of the country and opening it up to trade. It also suited the hunting-obsessed forest authorities, who resisted the building of pathways that might disturb the game.

Already in the late Middle Ages, pitch, tar and potash were important articles in the East–West trade of the North Sea and the Baltic (Stark 1973: 113ff.). By the late sixteenth century, Danzig merchants were making higher profits on potash than on grain (Maczak and Parker 1978: 8), and the Polish nobility was also benefiting from the trade (Bogucka 1984). Pitch was the only commodity exported from the Gulf of Finland until the seventeenth century (Åström 1975: 2f.), and it became, like potash (Miller 1980), one of the first goods exported from North America. The boom in shipbuilding was a major component of the increased demand for pitch and tar in the modern age.

When efforts to maximize the use of the forest began in the sixteenth century, the forest crafts might be encouraged because they promised to open up new remote areas. But, if more intensive exploitation was planned, they might be increasingly discouraged. Around the year 1720 it was even suggested in Württemberg that ash-burners yielded higher profits than the rafting of the Dutch wood. A forest superintendent, incensed by this claim, countered that ash-burners were 'extremely damaging' and were ruining the forests.

The kind of wood required by the forest crafts allowed plenty of scope for them to be integrated into the broader economy. Tar- and pitch-burners could use otherwise unserviceable stumps, roots and branches of trees (figure 2.22); a treatise on tar-burning actually recommends it as a means of keeping the forest tidy (Cancrin 1805: 13). The burners themselves, however, often shied away from the effort of digging up stumps and preferred to use good wood, even if it meant starting forest fires. A leading German economist of the eighteenth century advised 'leaving it to the Muscovites', since it 'brought great ruin on the forest' (Justi [1760] 1965: 96). In many parts of the Bavarian forest, pitch-burners were outlawed as 'the worst parasites', and foresters were permitted to gun them down (Blau 1917–18: 1/117ff.). They formed themselves into armed gangs, and in eighteenth-century Bavaria there was even a special guild that tried to monopolize pitch-burning (Schwappach 1886–8: 1/373).

Ash-burners were able to use waste wood and ash waste, and so potash production could be combined with the collection of wood

Figure 2.22: Tar production in Österbotten (Sweden), as depicted in 1749. The wood – preferably conifer roots – is placed in a disc-shaped ditch, covered with grass and pounded together with special equipment. Then the heap is lit and carbonized at a low temperature, as in a charcoal kiln. The tar is sweated out and drained through a pipe into a barrel, which can then be promptly shipped off.

Figure 2.23: Late medieval glass kiln, from Jan Mandeville's travel report around the year 1420. The contraption still looks quite primitive, but the cooling oven (left) is already linked to the smelting furnace in order to make maximum use of the heat.

and the consumption of firewood. Branches were especially useful because of their high calcium content, which is important in the production of potash (calcium carbonate) (Hohenstein 1856: 35). However, ash-burners often did not keep within their limits, and even damaged the forest by reducing the floor to ashes and starting forest fires; for this reason they were sometimes prosecuted for wrong-doing. A medieval judgement relating to the Dreeich *Reichsforst* near Frankfurt ordered that an ash-burner should have the soles of his feet burned (Endres 1888: 55).

As large consumers of potash, glass-makers also had to defend the legitimacy of their activity (figure 2.23). The first German manual of the trade stated that beech, alder and birch were more suitable than oak for glass kilns (figure 2.24) (Kunckel [1689] 1972: 314).

Figure 2.24: Seventeenth-century glass kiln system (*Deutscher Ofen*), modern and economical by the standards of the time, but costing so much to build that it was scarcely compatible with the traditional character of glass-making as an itinerant trade. Its main improvement was in raising the heat of the furnace to the temperature required for glass smelting. But the exhaust gases escaped into the working area through the openings for removal of the molten glass, and from there through the roof into the open air (Gleitsmann 1985: 52).

Yet blowers often used the best oak, producing heated quarrels with timber merchants who supplied the shipbuilding industry. Beech trees, also much coveted by glass-makers, yielded good charcoal for the iron industry.

Glass-making was one of the expanding trades of the sixteenth century. Glass windows soon became 'status symbols' for the well-off, changing lifestyles and acquiring an importance unprecedented in the history of architecture (Mumford [1934] 1963: 125). In 1537 a glass-makers' association was founded at Großalmerode in the Kaufung Forest, under the patronage of the Landgrave of Hesse; it was unique in reaching north all the way to Denmark. But in 1538 the Landgrave insisted on taking a share in the Sooden saltworks (Henkel 1908: 13), and, since mining in general held first place in Hesse's forest policy, most of the glassworks in the region had to be abandoned. From then on, glass-makers were able to use 'wood pining after the axe' only in remote areas of the forest (Bonnemann 1984: 312). Elsewhere, too, mining and metal interests took precedence over glass in the allocation of wood supplies.

This craft hierarchy also took hold in England. In 1615 James I issued a strict ban on the use of wood for glass production, since 'the great waste of timber in making glass is a matter of serious concern', especially as 'timber hath been of all times truly esteemed as a principal patrimony of this our realm of England.' On these grounds, he concluded, 'it were the less evil' to return to the 'ancient manner of drinking in stone and of lattice windows' (Perlin 2005: 193f.). It may be doubted whether this was meant altogether seriously, since coal was already available for use in British glassworks.

Were the forest crafts discriminated against simply because of their wastefulness? Writers who condemned glassworks as forest pests certainly made their voices heard more than glass-blowers. But, as the cost of building a glassworks steadily increased, it became more and more difficult for blowers simply to plunder the surrounding forest and then move on; self-interest alone dictated a degree of sustainable forestry, and in some cases they seem to have developed a well thought-out planting system (Sellner 1988: 22ff.). In fact, one of the main reasons for the discrimination against forest craftsmen was that they were difficult to check on and tax. Whereas the mining and metal industry was a key source of revenue for many early modern governments, glass-making was overwhelmingly conducted away from the public glare. Tar- and pitch-burning was often a sideline for farmers, and the Swedish government, for example, failed in an attempt to make it a state monopoly around the year 1700 (Lindqvist 1984: 45).

Potash production was also a farmer's sideline in forest areas. Glass-blowers, on the other hand, lived separate lives and often had violent clashes with local farmers. They married among themselves and, in the best guild manner, passed their craft on from father to son. If an area of forest became exhausted, or if their user rights expired, they packed their bags and moved on. Their kilns mostly had a life of six months – one summer season (Bonnemann 1984: 304). They were a mobile element that could easily be brought in to develop a new area of forest, and then sent away when more profitable opportunities presented themselves.

Charcoal-burning enjoyed special protection when it served the mining and metal industry. The authorities of the early modern period tried to gain tighter control over it – which proved easiest in regions such as Styria, where it depended on log driving and could be concentrated at places on a river where the timber was raked in. Here burners were forced to sell their charcoal to ironworks at a price that was kept artificially low (Ast and Katzer 1970: 14f.).

In the Siegerland, by contrast, the charcoal trade was pursued at times under freely competitive conditions and was 'a constant source of dispute' among the ironworks (Kruse 1909: 107). In 1598 the iron-makers accused the hammersmiths of treating charcoal-burners to free drinks in the tavern in order to buy up their wares. In general, charcoal was traded freely earlier than firewood, since it could be transported overland to more distant places. However, the longer it was carried on bumpy roads, the more it crumbled and lost its value (figure 2.25). A primitive form of charcoal-burning was carried out in ditches in the ground. But, as quality became more important, the material was laid out in roughly layered piles; charcoal-burning then developed into a skilled trade that could not easily be performed by farmers as a sideline. Medieval iron-makers already believed that the type of charcoal influenced the quality of their product (Duhamel du Monceau 1762: 11ff.).

The rise of metallurgy placed charcoal-burners in a key position in many regions. In the Siegerland, where they were sometimes considered 'too powerful' (Irle 1964: 24), a works bill from 1553 specifies that charcoal accounted for three-quarters of total costs, against a mere twelfth for the iron ore (Becher [1789] 1980: 526). In 1615 a Saxon ironworks administrator complained that it was easier to find a silk embroiderer or a goldsmith than a capable charcoal-burner (Ress 1957: 21), and good ones were much more difficult than miners to replace with people from outside the area.

Charcoal-burners preferred coppices for the solid, high-grade

126

Figure 2.25: A cart carrying charcoal and ore to a hammer mill: picture from
the *Hausbuch der Mendelschen Zwölfbrüderstiftung* in Nuremberg (*c*.1390).
The pictured Leupolt Karrenman – that is, 'Carter' – would probably have done
this as his main occupation. In the sixteenth century, there were complaints
in the Upper Palatinate that charcoal and ore transport was distracting many
farmers from their work on the land. A two-wheeled cart was also a unit
measure for charcoal, so it must have been of a more or less standard size.
Wood, too, was measured by the cartload, but in units of *Klafter* (cords).
Charcoal carts were fitted with a wattled basket to absorb shocks.

Figure 2.26: Charcoal kiln in the foundry at Mariazell, northeast of the Ore
Mountain in Styria, *c.*1880. In the thickly forested eastern Alps, the iron
industry continued to operate with charcoal fuel at a time when this had been
replaced elsewhere with coke.

material they provided; one historian described them as the 'inventors of the Hauberg system' (Kruse 1909: 71). The carbon content of the wood mass, which was roughly 50 per cent in the natural state, rose to approximately 80 per cent in the charcoal product. The construction of charcoal kilns varied from region to region; often they were built around a kind of shaft, which was used to light them. The burner's art consisted mainly in ensuring that the kiln – which in later times exceeded a man's height and could only be reached by a ladder – would heat thoroughly, without bursting into flames and 'bolting'. The kiln was therefore covered with earth to limit the intake of air, while holes that the burner poked and closed in it enabled him to observe and regulate the fire.

The burner had to check the kiln intermittently by day and night (figures 2.26 and 2.27). Blue steam coming out of the holes was a sign of trouble; it was not uncommon for the kiln process to fail and cause a major loss. Reports suggest that a charcoal-burner's existence was marked by lack of sleep and 'constant anxiety' (Ast and Katzer 1970: 59). And the higher the kilns grew, the more dangerous it became to climb them; 'all charcoal burners were scarred with burn marks' (ibid.: 58). It even happened that a build-up of steam caused the kiln

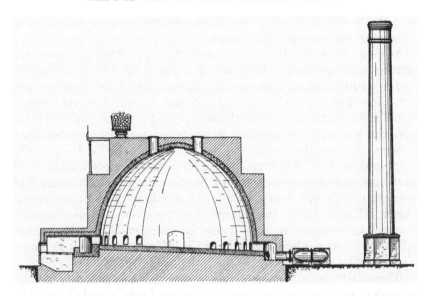

Figure 2.27: Charcoal kiln built in Sweden around 1820. The burning and
distillation process also gave off other products (tar, wood vinegar).
The construction, which follows the rounded contours of the open kiln
and is externally reminiscent of a nuclear power station (or 'atomic kiln',
as it was known in the early days!), shows that the transition from open to
walled-in charcoal-burning marked a considerable leap forward. It not
only reduced the number of personnel required but also used less costly
wood that had been unsuitable for open kilns. On the other hand, the
resulting 'chemical charcoal' was less solid than charcoal produced in
open kilns (Hinz 1977: 98f.).

to explode. To outsiders at least, charcoal-burning seemed a gloomy,
solitary and perilous trade.

In early modern times, however, thanks to the sharply rising
demand for charcoal, burners could achieve a degree of prosperity. At
least in mountainous regions, they were the best-paid forest workers
and often traded the charcoal on their own behalf. Though so solitary
in appearance, they sometimes established self-confident cooperatives; one is mentioned as early as 1327 in the Bohemian mining town
of Kuttenberg, a century before the founding of a miners' association
(Heilfurth 1981: 100). In the Styrian Ore Mountain region, some
noblemen even joined the charcoal-burners' fraternity (Jontes 1984:
451). Some of the Alpine charcoal-burners' associations had a rebellious spirit: the 'Carbonari', in the Italian Alps, and the 'Charbonnie',

over the border in France, were revolutionary secret societies of the eighteenth and nineteenth centuries.

Around the year 1800, a Nuremberg writer painted an impressive picture of the prudence and experience that a good charcoal-burner had to exhibit; nearly every master craftsman had 'his own maxims for controlling the fire', and 'one certainly cannot deny the professional sophistication of most of our charcoal-burners, since they are not exactly among the humblest or poorest classes that go about their business in a purely mechanical manner' (Späth 1800: 440). In the nineteenth century, however, charcoal-burners were often thought of as the poorest of the poor: farming people who 'could no longer find work at Candlemas were forced into tree-felling or charcoal works' (Ast and Katzer 1970: 56); women, too, took on work as charcoal-burners. In the eastern Alps, it was an occupation for older, more inflexible forest workers (Wessely 1853: 1/458f.), and in the Pyrenees it was carried on by lepers and their offspring (Rubner 1975: 99).

When charcoal-burners worked on their own account, they usually depended on an advance payment, for it could take months before the wood on which they had to pay the forest tax was dried out, carbonized and delivered to the customer (Hardach 1969: 25). Like many other tradesmen, they fell into a financial dependence that was more oppressive than wage labour. On the customer's side, the need for advance payments fostered the growth of large, financially powerful corporations. Thus, charcoal-burning led to the deeper penetration of capitalist elements into both the forest economy and the iron industry.

Saving wood as the aim of new inventions

Luther's comrade-in-arms Philipp Melanchthon predicted several times that 'the world will run short of three things: good coins, wood and good friends' – a saying later attributed to Luther himself, in a century when such prophecies were popular. It was a kind of learned piece of wisdom, a riposte to the peasant maxim: 'Wood and sorrow / Grow bigger every morrow'. For many farmers, the procurement of wood required considerable effort, but it was not in itself a problem that posed any threat. What was threatening was the fact that wood supplies did not suffice for the ambitions of the salt and metal industries.

Fear of wood shortages was already a 'spectre' haunting salt regions in the sixteenth century (Srbik 1917: 64). As commerce advanced, individual producers were increasingly exposed to outside competition and less and less able to shift the rising costs of wood onto the price of their own product. If the wood supply had traditionally rested on a monopoly in the hands of customers and resulted in artificially low prices, then it was directly threatened precisely by the appearance of competitors who could offer better terms to forest farmers.

Wood supply worries were not confined to privileged large consumers, however, but also affected the poorest layers of the population, who had no rights in relation to wood or the forest and had to rely upon leftovers remaining in the forest. By the late sixteenth century, it was reported in Württemberg that poor people were more worried about where they would get their wood from than about their daily bread (Hauff 1977: 131).

'Wood-saving' was an endlessly repeated objective between the sixteenth and nineteenth centuries, just as fuel economies are in our own time. Forest ordinance often contained regulations that limited the consumption of wood. The Saxon *Holzordnung* of 1560, for instance, pedantically laid down how much wood each subject might consume and the way in which he was supposed to obtain it (Wilsdorf et al. 1960: 30f.); it even stipulated that new houses must be built of stone (Schwappach 1886–8: 1/359).

'Perhaps the most far-reaching provision' in the Siegerland forest ordinance of 1562 was the clause which stated that public baking ovens should be built in each village (Irle 1964: 73); it was an idea that would often reappear in forest ordinance up to the nineteenth century. Public ovens could be kept running more constantly than private ones; they avoided the repeated hours of heating-up time; and they made it possible to cut wood consumption to a fifth of its previous level (Papius 1840: 13). Of course, it presupposed a degree of cooperation among villagers that was not always present.

With the onset of modernity, economies also became a matter of technological innovation. The sixteenth century was the first great age of inventors, and from mid-century on wood-saving inventors sometimes received prizes and imperial privileges – a full third, in fact, of the total number of imperial privileges bestowed on inventors between 1530 and 1600 (twenty-six out of seventy-eight) (Gleitsmann 1985: 73f.). In 1554 the Nuremberg municipal council spent 600 gulden on the acquisition of a wood-saving patent (Sporhan and Stromer 1969: 80), and in 1575 Frankfurt set aside 500 gulden for the same purpose (Schnapper-Arndt 1915: 173f.). These were considerable sums of money – enough to buy a house. Unfortunately, we seldom have the technical details that would tell us exactly what was involved.

The technology of wood-saving from the sixteenth to the eighteenth

131

century concentrated on two main areas: domestic stoves for cooking and heating, and salt works. There are several reasons for this. The real or ostensible inventor was often a dilettante, who did not pursue a wood-consuming trade and could most easily conduct experiments with his own household oven. At a time when much of the heating and cooking was done by means of open fires, and when oven technology was still in its infancy, it was relatively easy to identify more economical ways of using wood.

In many saltworks, business success depended largely on fuel consumption if the firewood had to be paid for. 'The secret of the saltworks rests upon wood economies', wrote Frederick the Great in his political testament of 1768. It is true that the wood dependence of ironworks was comparable in scale, but there it was more difficult to reduce fuel consumption (and scarcely possible for an outsider to propose innovative measures); the whole business of smelting and forging was shrouded in secrecy. In ironworks, flames came into direct contact with the product; what went on there was obscure and long remained the preserve of alchemical speculation. Some ascribed a cleansing power to the fire and argued that the quality of the product would suffer if wood consumption was reduced. Similar reservations were to be found among glass-blowers. But saltworks, on the other hand, used the long-familiar process of boiling, which could be the object of experiment in one's own home.

There was a further reason why rulers turned their attention to domestic stoves and saltworks: the fact was that not everyone shared their interest in wood-saving measures; higher fuel consumption was indeed good for forest revenue. But domestic firewood was in many cases obtained not from the market but upon presentation of a permit; so the more fuel-efficient the household oven, the less would be the claim for wood allocation. Moreover, lower wood consumption in salt boilers also helped the princely classes to line their pockets, since in the early modern age they usually had a stake in saltworks.

The best-known German wood-saver of the sixteenth century was Pastor Rhenanus, who in 1559 was appointed by the Landgrave of Hesse to supervise and improve the saltworks in his Sooden parish, and who until his death in 1589 was regarded as a salt expert even outside Hesse. At the Landgrave's behest, he wrote a *Neues Salzbuch* that ran to more than 2,000 pages; he called it his 'salt bible', and it earned him the title of 'the salt pastor'. Rhenanus later won special fame as an early pioneer of coal, having conducted not unsuccessful experiments with brown coal in salt- and glassworks, though without any path-breaking results.

The 'salt pastor' became the most hated man in Sooden – hated both by master boilers and by the *Holzvogt*, the forest superintendent (Killing 1927: 67). This was not necessarily because they rejected innovation in principle: many boilers actually experimented with wood-saving in their own interests. But the introduction of coal raised labour costs and necessitated a redesign of the boileries, especially a system of closed fires with chimneys (Emons and Walter 1984: 79, 103). The 'salt pastor' was also accused of falsely taking all the credit and, during the boiling tests, of not putting in an appearance at the brewing house; instead, it seems, he 'got blind drunk in the city of wine until midnight, broke the windows in the penny parlour, knocked the gate open in Sooden, and wanted to bind the poor watchmen like a thief' (Radkau 2006: 80ff.). One invention that he boasted about – the enrichment of brine with *Poys* (sea salt) bought in Bremen – only appeared to have the effect of reducing wood consumption.

Two other late sixteenth-century inventions were more important for the salt industry: the graduation works which – on the model of natural salt formation on the coasts – used solar and wind energy to enrich brine; and the preheating of ladles with the waste heat from boileries. As far as we know, Europe's first graduation works was built in Nauheim in 1579, but it developed into a mature technology only in the eighteenth century.

A few basic principles may be identified for wood-saving techniques in the sixteenth to eighteenth century: closed, walled-in furnaces, no larger in size than necessary; ovens that prevented heat from escaping too quickly; the use of waste heat to preheat or dry material; and greater continuity in the production process, to reduce the number of periods when a furnace was left burning for no purpose. Most of these economy measures were perfected only in the eighteenth and nineteenth centuries. They often required larger production units, higher capital investment and tighter labour discipline. But, as far back as Agricola's time, waste heat from smelting was used to preheat the lehrs in which glass products were allowed to cool slowly so that they did not crack.

It should not be forgotten in all this that, until the eighteenth century, technical innovation was by no means the normal response to wood shortages. The real answer to Sooden's wood problems came not from the fancies of Rhenanus the 'wood pastor', but from the development of log rafting between the Black Forest and the River Werra (Krüger 1980: 1790). Even the large saltworks at Halle and Lüneburg reacted to wood shortages mainly with reorganization rather than technological innovation (Wagner 1930: 129, 224). The

133

most common measure was to limit production: shortages of wood, as of anything else, were a fact of everyday life, not a 'problem' to be solved or a 'crisis' to be overcome.

An early wood substitution measure was the use of explosives instead of fire in mining operations. This novelty, sometimes overblown as an 'industrial revolution' in mining, was first reported from Venice in the year 1573, then introduced in Schemnitz (Slovakia) and Freiberg in the seventeenth century; it finally became the norm in the nineteenth century. Fire-setting used a great deal of wood, but for a long time blasting was even more expensive and, because of the unpredictability of early explosives, not without danger for mining personnel.

We know from a whole series of saltworks that most of the 'wood-saving' inventions touted in the sixteenth and seventeenth centuries were mere bluff. One man with long experience in Schwäbisch Hall reported that the 'wood economy guys' were a real 'pest', in most cases no more than 'adventurers and swindlers', and nowhere more brazen 'than in dealing with people from saltworks' (Bühler c.1850: 2/477). The philosopher Blaise Pascal was repeating a common view among educated people when he complained in 1670 that a majority of supposed inventors, particularly the smoothest talkers, were char-latans (Sombart 1928: 2/463f.). Whereas the sixteenth century, under the impact of inventions such as the printing press, the compass and gunpowder, had witnessed a craze for technology and a blind faith in its miraculous powers, the next few centuries displayed a scepti-cism that was based not simply on prejudice but on a host of negative experiences (Papius 1840: 12). 'Project-maker' became a synonym for 'conman'. But, in the wake of industrialization, 'project' again became a magic word. Since then, economic history has been characterized by an ever faster succession of euphoria ('hype') and disillusion.

For the nineteenth century, the previous era dominated by craft experience was one in which the dull force of habit had stifled all innovation. But that past has two faces. The age of practical knowl-edge and craft skill was also an age of great technical diversity and flexibility. The conception, planning and production of tools were not taken away from the worker: each tool or kiln turned out differently, and techniques varied from one region to another. Work with wood as a material required constant testing and adjustment to its natural properties. And even periodic shortages were a dynamic factor in work techniques that can be followed all the way through the history of the craft consumption of wood.

— 3 —

FROM THE APOGEE OF THE 'WOOD AGE' TO THE INDUSTRIAL REVOLUTION

Historians like to present the eighteenth century as the prelude to modernity, focusing especially on its incipient industrialization, the French Revolution and the rise of civil society. The course of events in relation to wood, however, can be properly understood only if it is followed back to the sixteenth century. Many of the efforts to handle wood more 'economically' did no more than repeat or develop earlier beginnings. The history of wood in the early modern period executed a cyclical movement in Central Europe and bordering regions: the first attempts to maximize the exploitation of forest resources gave way to a backward movement caused by population decline in the Thirty Years' War and the commercial and economic 'crisis of the seventeenth century' (Hroch and Petráň 1981). In the eighteenth century, however, wood experienced a new surge of economic growth. Many older measures to save on wood consumption and to ensure supplies were now brushed up and perfected, making the eighteenth and even the early nineteenth century the apogee of the Wood Age.

At the same time, spreading out from England, a growth dynamic and general speeding-up of the economy was bound up with the use of coal as a fuel and of iron as an industrial material. The two phenomena are often seen as part of a single development, in which the rise of coal is explicable by critical shortages of wood. But wood shortages per se do not contain an impetus to growth. There were also forms of rationalization and technological progress that did not lead from wood to coal but brought improvements in the 'wood economy'. The history of wood and the forest is closely linked to the great breakthroughs of that time, but these pointed in several directions.

1 Reform, Revolution and the Wood Economy

Commercial revolution, timber boom, Dutch log rafting and the American War of Independence

The 'Industrial Revolution' that began in England in the eighteenth century was preceded by a major expansion of world trade – a 'commercial revolution' that created the markets and capital sums without which industrialization would not have been possible. The timber trade was one of the driving forces of this commercial revolution (especially in the North, from the Gulf of Finland to the coast of New England), and its impetus came in turn from the general growth of trade. A very long boom in construction timber began in the late seventeenth century and lasted until well into the nineteenth. It seemed

136

as if timber prices could not but creep up and up for evermore. In late eighteenth-century Germany it was considered such a reliable trend that people began to convert firewood forest into high forest, even though the full income benefits would take a hundred years or more to materialize.

It seems natural to begin the history of wood in the nineteenth century, as in the sixteenth century, with a look at shipbuilding and ship travel. As soon as a country rose to become a maritime power, the supply of timber became a political issue of the first order. In the fifteenth and sixteenth centuries, Venice, Spain and Portugal had to confront the growing shortage of this commodity; in the seventeenth and eighteenth centuries, it was the turn of Holland, England and France. In the struggle for the oceans – from the sixteenth century to the Napoleonic wars – the quality of ship's timber was of strategic importance.

The most famous plea for reforestation in British history, John Evelyn's *Sylva* (1664) – written by a friend of the navy minister, Samuel Pepys – responded first of all to the interests of the Admiralty; the same was true of the warning issued by Louis XIV's finance minister, Colbert – 'France will perish for want of timber' (Albion 1926: 47). As a general assertion, this was exaggerated: France lagged behind England mainly in the supply of tall conifer trunks for ship's masts; and, in fact, the Royal Navy too had its problems in obtaining enough. Until the Elizabethan age, however, England had acquired its ships from Hamburg and Lübeck, Genoa and Venice (Perlin 2005: 171), and so such problems were relatively new in London in the seventeenth century.

Colbert's warning came from the mouth of a mercantilist, who conceived of trade through the prism of power politics. The fact that champions of the navy everywhere sounded the alarm over timber shortages should not make us conclude that shipbuilding regularly suffered from them – on the contrary. The one who shouts the loudest is often the one who can be sure of being heard. In 1739 the natural scientist and ironworks owner Comte de Buffon warned of an imminent danger of timber shortage (Bamford 1956: 70). In the seventeenth century, such voices had been more typical among opponents of the iron industry, both in Britain and on the continent. But as soon as iron came to be seen as a pillar of state power, 'timber shortages' could serve as an argument for the government of the day to secure the fuel supply of the iron industry. In the eighteenth and early nineteenth centuries, more than ever before, iron gave a lasting impetus to the wood economy.

The forests of Norway, Finland, Russia and the Baltic gave new dimensions to the timber trade and demonstrated the value of conifers. Even in a classical 'oak region' such as northwest Germany, farmers took advantage of favourable economic conditions to buy conifer wood for their homes from the Baltic and Scandinavia (Meiners, in Fansa and Vorlauf 2007: 171f.). Amsterdam imported large quantities of long timber – including much oak from the Spessart region – for the pile structures on which its houses are built (Gothein 1889: 453). And in the eighteenth century England too began to import construction timber from the Baltic on a large scale. Construction was the driving force of trade for the English economist Nicholas Barbon, who was himself highly active in this sector after the Great Fire of London in 1666 (Klein 1973: 90). In the eighteenth century, a half of Britain's imports by volume – though only 3 per cent by value – consisted of timber (Davis 1972: 176).

One of the main historical sources for early modern trade in the North Sea and the Baltic are the Sound Dues registers, which show that the quantity of westward-moving timber increased no less than eightyfold between the end of the sixteenth century and the first half of the eighteenth. The transport of iron rose seventeenfold, whereas that of cereals (in which Western Europe became self-sufficient) declined by nearly a half (Bogucka 1980: 20).

Oliver Cromwell stepped up imports of timber from the Baltic, and from the late seventeenth century the Crown tried to secure the Royal Navy's supply of timber (especially white pine trees for its ship's masts) from the forests of New England. In 1729 Parliament passed a law that 'no white pine trees are to be cut without licence', thus reserving mainly for the navy 'all the Masts . . . exceeding Twenty four Inches Diameter, All Trees that exceed Fifty-four Feet in length in the Stem, All young thriving Pine Trees that seem promising to grow to Masts'. These were all designated as 'king's trees' (Green 2007: 166).

As the colonists grew increasingly restive, the enforcement of forest conservation against the wishes of local people had the same effect as elsewhere in the world: it encouraged them to cut down trees intended for the rulers as early as possible, or to prevent their growth in the first place. 'The first trees woodsmen cut were those specifically marked to be saved for the Crown. As the surveyor put the royal sign – the broad arrow – on only the best timber, he inadvertently helped the lumberjack's search for trees most suited for cutting' (Perlin 2005: 292). A law passed in 1729 led to an endless chain of confrontations between woodsmen and Crown officials. Colonel David Dunbar, who

138

high-handedly tried to demolish the Maine sawmill blades that processed white pine trees, barely escaped with his life when local people
dressed as Indians set upon him in 1732; he no longer ventured into
the forest after that experience (ibid.: 299ff.).

The acts of rebellion culminated in the Pine Tree Riot of 1772 in
New Hampshire, which, though less well known than the Boston
Tea Party – the backwoodsmen were less skilled at publicizing their
activity – was also a key event in the run-up to the American War
of Independence. Since the New England states needed tall pines for
their own ships – Salem in those days had a flourishing trade with
China, and Boston with the West Indies – the struggle over mast
timber affected far more vital interests than did the protest against
tea taxes. The roots of the military conflict should be sought more in
tree-felling than in tea-drinking, especially if we accept the famous
argument of Frederick Turner, the 'vanguard of American ecologists'
(Worster 1977: 218f.), that 'American democracy came from the
forests', from the combative sense of freedom of self-reliant backwoodsmen. 'This forest philosophy is the philosophy of American
democracy' (Turner 1920: 154, 207). It is an idea familiar to everyone
from Hollywood movies.

The victory of the American independents made Britain even more
dependent on the Baltic for its timber supply (Lower 1973: 123ff.).
Imports from Canada also rose sharply, so that by 1825 Quebec was
'the greatest timber port the world had ever known' (Latham 1957:
138). No doubt Boston would have liked to achieve that position.
Timber conflicts with the American settlers could probably have been
easily avoided if they had been allocated the trade in white pine trees
or even some shipbuilding; they anyway earned a lot of money by
shipping timber to England. But the white pine trees for ships' masts
had become the symbol of British rule. Like any other government
eager to insist on its forest supremacy, Whitehall stepped up its talk
of timber shortages, its appeals to the public good and its complaints
against self-seeking indigenous people (Perlin 2005: 291). Lumbermen
were not impressed, and the conflict continued to escalate.

The white oak tree also developed into a symbol of American
freedom and sea power. In 1798, when war threatened with France,
a shipbuilder in Salem launched a patriotic appeal: 'Let every man
in possession of a White Oak Tree, be ambitious to be foremost in
hurrying down the timber to Salem, and fill the complement wanting,
where the noble structure is to be fabricated, to maintain your rights
upon the Seas, and make the name of America respected among the
nations of the world' (Latham 1957: 111). From 1807, however,

the shipyards of Salem were ruined by the embargo that Jefferson imposed on the warring powers.

The imaginative inventor and businessman John Wilkinson (1728–1808) found a way of his own to reduce Britain's dependence on Baltic timber imports, by driving the bellows of his Shropshire furnaces with steam engines that used the more combustible coke instead of charcoal. A song of praise to Wilkinson contains the verse: 'That the wood of old England would fail, did appear / And tough iron was scarce because charcoal was dear, / by puddling and stamping he cured that evil, / So the Swedes and Russians may go to the devil' (Radkau 1983: 515f.). Here we see the origins of the myth, vigorously denounced by Oliver Rackham, that the shift to coal made necessary by timber shortages was the salvation of the forests. Of course, what the verse shows is that the charcoal supply was simply a question of price. Charcoal was usually obtained from coppices, not high forest, but it is certainly true that without coal the tempestuous growth of the British iron industry would have driven up timber prices and reinforced the dependence on the Baltic states.

What impact did the timber trade have on the supply countries? Then as now, some argued that countries which specialized in exporting raw materials fell behind in development. In the eighteenth century, in an attempt to hold back the growth of sawmills in timber-exporting countries, to the profit of their own sawing industry, the Dutch gave preferential treatment to roundwood and slapped high import duties on cut timber. One critic wrote in 1784 that Dutch trading companies were 'extracting indescribable sums of money from Germany' (Ebeling 1987: 9). And in 1837 an author who argued that a local timber-processing industry should replace exports from the Spessart region claimed that 'no one can point to a land that has grown rich by trading its own timber' (Müller 1837: 112).

The export of raw materials can indeed hinder the development of a country's processing industry while promoting industrial growth in the recipient country and reinforcing international inequality. The timber trade too had this effect. On the other hand, it not only brought money into forested areas but also led to improved river transport and a more 'economical' use of wood – both of which in turn promoted the development of trade and industry within the timber-exporting countries. In the Saar region, timber exports to Holland in the eighteenth century encouraged the opening up of hard coal deposits (Sieferle 2001: 161f.). Baltic trade gave the first spur to Russian industrialization. Both Russia and the USA, the two world powers of the twentieth century, first made their entry into the world market as suppliers of timber and forest products.

The dynamic of the American economy was driven first by large-scale trade in timber, then by regional exhaustion of forest resources and the transfer of timber capital into new branches of industry. Frederick Turner, who came from Wisconsin, observed there how the timber men turned sawmill towns into industrial cities once nothing but 'stumps of the pine forests' were left around them (Turner 1920: 235). One after the other, Boston, Cincinnati, Memphis and Chicago changed from timber centres into great industrial cities. Wood gave new opportunities to peripheral regions, as well as to the vanquished states of the South. Stanley F. Horn and Bryan Latham find it significant that Scarlett O'Hara in *Gone with the Wind* eventually founds a sawmill and achieves prosperity. For it was precisely after the defeat of the South that the southern pine reached the height of its fame and the 'distinction of providing a larger proportion of the country's total lumber production than any other species' (Horn 1943: 97ff.; Latham 1957: 121).

Hamburg acquired a key function in the timber trade between the Baltic and Western Europe, just as, in the eighteenth century, the timber port of still Danish Altona became the economic centre of the city. The Hansa city was also the great entrepôt for the timber that the Elbe carried up from Bohemia, Saxony and Brandenburg. In 1798, an envoy from the Leipzig woodcrafts watched with impotent rage how, 'in Torgau alone, in the space of half an hour, four ships laden with pole wood, each of which could have held at least a hundred cart loads', were sent on their way up the Elbe to the vast storehouses of Hamburg, while the Leipzig crafts were left in the cold. The Prussian government profited from the timber trade, however, even as it urged its citizens to be economical in their use of wood (Pfeil 1839: 135). For large swathes of northern and eastern Germany, from Thuringia to Silesia, wood was 'a richly flowing source of sustenance' in the late eighteenth and early nineteenth centuries (Gülich [1830–45] 1972: 2/313). The iron industry had its wings clipped in the eighteenth century, since timber exports were more lucrative. But, on the whole, the timber trade of Central Europe continued to be shaped more by local and regional demand than by exports to other lands.

The interaction between forestry and log rafting became especially striking with the onset of modernity. 'The rafting trade would have been as unthinkable without a rational forest economy as forestry would have been without the large-scale rafting necessary to transport forest produce to the most distant regions' (John 1934: 55).

141

Figure 3.1: Log rafting on the Rhine, near Unkel: copper engraving from 1798. The so-called Dutch rafts consisted of several units and resembled 'floating villages'. The rudders were up to 14 metres long, and seven men were required to operate them. The navigator sat on a special platform, visible on the right of the picture, which was raised more than 3 metres above the deck (Keweloh 1985: 90ff.).

The 'Dutch' timber trade on the Rhine and the Black Forest rivers became legendary in the eighteenth century (figure 3.1). Before then, Norway had been the ideal supplier for the Netherlands: its high forest stretched right down to the deep fjords, which, thanks to the Gulf Stream, remained ice-free all year round, and its timber could be shipped to Amsterdam without the encumbrance of tolling stations. But in the eighteenth century large-sized 'Dutch balks' were ever harder to obtain from Norway, as the timber trade became more geared to southwestern Germany (Latham 1957: 90). The Dutch trade was the most spectacular in Germany at that time, since the Netherlands had little forest of its own but an insatiable appetite for timber; the wealth of the Dutch merchant princes was proverbial, and the Rhine was the perfect route for their trade. In the eighteenth century, it covered as much as a half of Dutch timber requirements (Ebeling, in Keweloh and Carle 1988: 87).

The origins of 'Dutch rafting' went back to the sixteenth century, but it first shot up in importance in the late seventeenth century, when the Dutch faced growing competition from English timber merchants in Scandinavia and the Baltic lands. 'Dutch' became a standard term for fir trees more than 20 metres high and approximately 40 centimetres in diameter. But even oaks could be rafted if they were combined with lighter coniferous timber; the retreat of oak in the Black Forest, where it once reached high up the mountainsides, is attributable to the Dutch trade (Keweloh 1985: 90ff.). In fact, this had an epochal impact on the Black Forest economy, by opening up streams and rivers for the carrying of timber from previously untouched areas.

At first, Black Forest timber was shipped to Holland in stages via Mainz and Cologne, but in the eighteenth century a direct link was established along the length of the Rhine. This was a leap into the unknown, and in Wilhelm Hauff's fairy tale *Das kalte Herz* (1827) the devil himself had a hand in it. Rafters used to write their will before undertaking the voyage to the Netherlands, and often they would return only in the following year. Accidents were not uncommon when a raft had to negotiate a narrow part of the river.

By Victor Hugo's time these giant rafts were on their way out. He thought that the art of navigating them was a secret possessed by only one man in each generation, and that the whole trade would die out with the last bearer of the secret (Badré 1983: 134). The trade certainly promised rich pickings, but it also involved a risk of huge losses that only a big businessman could afford to take. It could happen that low water levels on the Rhine would keep a large raft immobile for two whole years, so that the whole operation would inevitably record a loss when the consignment was finally sold at Dordrecht (Ebeling, in Keweloh and Carle 1988: 89). In the Netherlands, there was also competition to face from the Baltic lands. Oak was the one wood they could not supply, but they gradually learned how to replace it with conifers.

Rafting became a big capitalist business; the Rhine allowed a huge expansion of the trade, especially as ships still posed few obstacles to navigation. In the late eighteenth century, the size of many Dutch rafts was almost beyond belief; the main section alone measured up to 400 metres in length and 80 metres in width, and on top of that there were two add-ons or 'knees'. It was manned by several hundred oarsmen and could also carry hundreds of passengers. Both crew and passengers were lodged in huts on the raft, segregated by social position, one of which was even designated the 'manor house'; the whole vessel was like a floating village. There was a 'sharply defined hierarchy' among the crew (Mohr 1897: 14): orders were passed down from the top – 'France!' or 'Hesse!' – according to whether the raft should steer more to the left or the right bank. Rowing boats had to go on ahead, to warn ships lying at berth and water mills of the approaching colossus. A lot of navigational skill was required to navigate it through the narrow section after Bingen and to dock it at the stopping place. Once in Holland, the owner of the raft needed all his wiles and patience to cover his expenses. 'The selling of a raft often takes one or two years, and a master who is not completely familiar with the usual tricks and commercial practices in Holland . . . will be constantly exposed to major losses.' The conclusion: 'Without sums of capital, no branch of commerce offers less hope than the timber trade of making a pure trading profit' (Müller 1837: 88, 145).

Until the seventeenth century, rafting was a mere sideline for farmers in the Black Forest; the Dutch trade turned it into an occupation in its own right, while making the felling and carrying of timber a form of wage labour increasingly performed by people from outside the region. Whereas members of the old rafting fraternities had also been farmers, and in their own interest had often made exemplary use of the forest, 'Dutch rafting' was partly in the hands of large foreign businesses that cared little about the fate of the forest. In many cases, the result was unrestrained plunder of the forest.

Yet the clear-cutting was not so thorough that the 'hoped-for happy new generation' failed to arrive (Jägerschmid 1827–8: 2/18f.). Bye-laws in Schiltach, in the Black Forest, limited felling in order to keep prices high. And the cooperative forest of the *Murgschifferschaft* – an association of farmers and rafters first mentioned around the year 1400, which in the 1770s a senior forestry official called a 'free-thinking autonomous republic' (Scheifele 2001) – had by the 1930s become the forest with the largest proportion of old wood in the whole of Germany (Hasel 1985: 88).

In the *Schifferschaft* forest, unlike many other woodlands around the turn of the nineteenth century, the use of high forest for construction timber had clear priority over the firewood trade. In the early nineteenth century, the *Schifferschaft* opposed the 'blanket felling' ordered by the forest authorities and reintroduced the shelterwood selection system (*Femelwirtschaft*), which was akin to traditional *Plenterschlag* selective felling. Nor is it only in the Black Forest that we have to thank resistance to 'progress' for the survival of magnificent expanses of forest. Around the year 1910 Bavarian rafters campaigned against the plan to build a power station on the Alpine Lake Walchen, which threatened to eliminate the flow of water. Count Toerring, an advocate of modernization, caused 'great mirth' in the Bavarian parliament when he denounced them as a bunch of degenerate alcoholics for whom no one should have any regrets (Gribl 2002: 52). It was the railway age; such contempt for rafters would have been unimaginable in earlier times.

Capitalism and protectionism

Krünitz's *Oeconomische Encyclopädie* gushed with emotion when it reached the entry on *Holz* (wood) in the revolutionary year of 1789:

> None of our possessions is so little exposed to danger, to storm and other damage, as wood is; none of our products is . . . as assured as wood is of annual increases in both quantity and price . . .; none of our plots of land has such long – I would even say, such constant – use going back to the beginning of time as wood does, since what we fell today is often there again, better and more plentiful, in 15, 30, 60, 80, 100 and often even more years; in short, no safer means of placing money can be found than using it to buy up tracts of forest. (Krünitz 1789: 796)

Wood is needed for an endless number of things, but for that reason it becomes ever scarcer and more expensive: this already seemed common knowledge in the late eighteenth century. But quite diverse conclusions were drawn from it. Some held that the allocation and consumption of wood should be strictly controlled, to ensure that this scarce good, so necessary to human life, should be available to all citizens; but others argued from the same facts that the forests should be opened up as much as possible to free trade. It was possible to conclude that valuable timber should be kept inside the country, but also that the forests offered a golden opportunity to participate in the growth of international trade. One might be led to the view that tree-felling should be forcibly curbed, but also strengthened in the belief that the forest should be spared for the future. Certainly enough material for argument!

Much as early modern legal rulings often prohibited the selling of wood to foreigners, the timber trade – and especially the selling of firewood abroad – was considered somehow disreputable until well into the nineteenth century (*Das Proletariat* 1851: 35f.). The economist Johann Justi taught (about 1760) that the export of timber never worked to a country's advantage (Krünitz 1789: 733). The population complained that it led to shortages and high prices; economists believed that it impeded industrial growth; and foresters saw it as an inducement to misconduct and 'poaching'. All these complaints, however, were no more than rearguard protests against the rapid commercialization of wood. In 1768, Frederick the Great proudly noted in his testament that Prussia exported timber to the value of 300,000 thalers.

From the Middle Ages on, city councils combated the 'advance purchase' of wood before it came onto the local market. But the longer the distance between forest and consumer, the greater were the opportunities for middlemen. Again and again it was forbidden to buy wood in quantities above one's own yearly needs, but anyone who had enough space and did not need the ready cash could store wood for a long time – longer than in the case of grain or textiles. Indeed, the quality of wood improved through storage. As soon as wood began to run short, it became an object of speculation.

The timber trade was subject to many restrictions, but shrewd businessmen knew how to get round them if high profits beckoned. The transport of wood over long distances was hugely expensive, but it promised good business to entrepreneurs who operated on a large scale (that is, who built mountain slipways, developed streams for rafting, and came to an arrangement with foresters and customs officials). Precisely because many barriers to the timber trade had existed for centuries, it underwent a veritable explosion once a certain threshold was crossed. This was the case in the eighteenth century, and it was also reflected in many contemporary complaints about 'wood shortages'.

As we have seen, the conditions of the timber trade favoured large businesses, but they did not necessarily favour free trade. Since much depended on connections in high places – forest departments, customs authorities, navy officials – and since trust was an important factor in the buying of wood, certain large dealers easily acquired a monopoly position. At the turn of the seventeenth century, Jakob Kast – 'one of the earliest and most significant figures in the capitalist form of economy' – already controlled all rafting on the Rhine downstream from Strasbourg (Gothein 1892: 40f.). The Dutch trade also elevated men into 'timber kings' in the Black Forest region. Another opportunity for big businessmen was the supply of wood to saltworks and the metal industry. When in 1747 the Swabian ironworks hired the dynamic, unscrupulous Johann Georg Blezinger as its supplier, it suddenly had more charcoal than it could handle, but also a flood of complaints from local people and officials; for Blezinger it was a springboard for further industrial activities (Thier 1965: 282–323). Around the same time, the Hirn brothers took over the wood supply for the saltworks in Hall (Tyrol), built their gigantic 'Hirn chute' from the Leutasch to the Inn valley, and pillaged remote Alpine forest for decades (Heis 1975: 16ff.). Timber dealers who supplied the British Navy in the eighteenth century became especially rich and powerful, since its need for high-quality timber was growing by leaps and bounds. By means of an artificially induced shortage of wood, they managed to keep the Navy Board in a constant state of anxiety (Albion 1926: 58ff., 316–45).

The timber policy of many eighteenth-century governments involved two opposite aims: on the one hand, in keeping with the patriarchal self-image of the state at that time, they liked to claim that they were providing the poor with a cheap source of wood; on the other hand, they wanted to make as much money as possible out of the sovereign forests. Not infrequently, the first objective was pleaded as an excuse, while the second corresponded to the reality on the ground. Concern for poorer subjects was used to justify a state monopoly that helped to fill the princely coffers (Endres 1888: 147).

Equally ambiguous were the firewood depots ('wood yards' or 'wood gardens') run by the municipal and regional governments of the day. The usual justification for them was that they supplied poor people who could only buy wood in small quantities, whereas rafters preferred large customers. However, it was possible for the wood gardens to attain a monopoly position in the timber business. The public wood yards found themselves caught between fiscal and social-political objectives, often achieving neither the one nor the other, but simply running up losses without noticeably improving the wood supply for the poor. Sometimes they encountered stubbornness on the rafters' part. In 1746, for instance, the 'whole shipping fraternity' of Württemberg displayed 'great obstructiveness' when the government set a price for timber that they considered too low; they refused to supply wood, however much the duke's officials raged at the boycott (Radkau 1988: 38). Rafting was a rough trade; rafters were not as easy to discipline as railway employees. After 1800 states and munici-palities generally lost interest in timber monopolies, and fewer and fewer obstacles were placed in the way of trade.

The growing popularity of auctions among forest authorities worked in the same direction. These were already required by law in seventeenth-century France and were introduced into Prussian domain forests in the early eighteenth century; elsewhere they were actually prohibited, until they finally became the norm in the nine-teenth century. Sale by auction corresponded to the fact that, because of its individual properties, timber had to be inspected beforehand and was difficult to trade at commodity exchanges, and that general price levels were of limited value when it came to setting a target price in particular instances. The properties of wood were simply too diverse, and the price too tied to local factors. Auctions thus reflected a situation in which timber dealers were pressing for the forests to disgorge their increasingly scarce commodity, and the timber market – to put it in modern terms – was turning from a buyer's into a seller's market. Auctions became lucrative for the forest authorities only when a number of timber purchasers were competing with one another.

Timber auctions strengthened the tendency to liberalization in the trade. The old struggle against 'advance purchasing' was waged less and less in earnest. Of course, free competition came as a shock to those who were used to buying cheap, and it struck them as a scandalous breach of traditional allocation priorities. Purchasers who needed timber for highly productive purposes, and who were able to pay any sum for it, drove the price to unpredictable heights before snapping it up from under their competitors' noses.

In a well-known article, E. P. Thompson (1970: 96) uncovered the 'moral economy' behind many revolts of the lower classes that earlier historians had classified as plebeian unrest in defiance of the law; its core belief was that every human being had a right to a livelihood, so that the stormiest protests were typically directed against the export of vital necessities in times of great need. This moral economy of subsistence is also apparent in the traditional ways in which villagers have related to the forest and wood. For wood was certainly considered one of life's necessities, however violent the disputes over issues of both quantity and quality.

In 1848, the cultural historian Wilhelm Heinrich Riehl gave an account of how farmers in the Middle Rhine region had debased the auctions officially prescribed for the sale of timber. When 'bidders showed up from outside the area, they drove them out of the forest with flails and pitchforks, then auctioned their own wood among themselves at ridiculously low prices' (Jantke and Hilger 1965: 402). Riehl told this story as an example of the farmers' levity and lack of understanding of economics, but they were only following a basic principle of the old legal rulings – namely, that wood from common woodland should be set aside for the needs of local people.

Free competition led to a redistribution of timber resources and fuelled the compulsion to use them as productively as possible. Economic life adjusted to the new conditions only gradually, with many anxieties along the way. There was a wave of violent reactions to the liberalization of the timber trade. At the end of the eighteenth century, this whole sector of the economy appeared to be in feverish movement; the situation was hard to comprehend for a while and set many alarm bells ringing. The soaring timber trade kept crashing into newly imposed restrictions. And where these contained loopholes, the competition for timber grew all the fiercer and filled the weaker players with dread.

A polemical tract published in 1802 noted the 'extremely well-known fact' that 'in nearly all the German provinces timber bans have been in place for several years', and that recently these trade barriers have been to blame for the wood shortages that are complained about in many places (Zanthier 1802: 34f.). From time to time, a wood shortage would provide grounds for the extension of old systems of protection and allocation. By the turn of the century, however, these systems were visibly overstretched and had lost legitimacy in most people's eyes.

The age of liberalism also announced itself in the timber trade. 'So, in with these vast stretches of forest – in they go into the competitive circle of private activity and speculation!!!' (Hazzi 1804: 769). So much the better if, as a result, wood became scarce and expensive, since then there would finally be an economic incentive to proper silviculture. And if it proved more profitable to turn forest into agricultural land, that too would do no harm – after all, there was wood in abundance in the wilds of America, and it did not matter at all 'whether the wood is chopped on boats plying the river Oder or in Ohio' (Pfeil 1816: 23). Tree trunks seemed to have lost their leaden weight and to be travelling the world at random, driven on by the laws of the market. These were fantasies, of course, far outstripping the reality of Germany at that time.

State reform and forest reform

Not only the rise of trade and capitalism, but also war, public debt and the state's urge to assert its power gave a new impetus to the timber trade in the eighteenth century. Whereas in the sixteenth century state interference in timber matters originated mainly in southern and central Germany, it was Prussia, the new leading power in Germany, that set the pace in the eighteenth century. The 'soldier king' Friedrich Wilhelm I had left instructions for his successor, Friedrich II (Frederick the Great), to introduce 'better regulations for the purchase of timber', so that 'merchants from Holland and Hamburg pay more and better than they do now', and that the 'swindling' by forest wardens is ended. There was 'still much to be done' in these respects (Dietrich 1981: 109).

Especially after the Seven Years' War (1756–63), which ruined

Germany, Friedrich II tried hard to achieve a more efficient and lucrative organization of the forest economy and the timber trade. In 1763 he set a price that would encourage 'as little wood as possible to be used in domestic stoves' (Usemann 1980: 63ff.). In 1764 he gave orders (with little immediate effect) for domain forests to practise single-age tree cultivation (*Schlagbetrieb*) and prohibited the plantation economy. In 1765–6 he authorized state concessions allowing companies to operate the timber trade and to provide Berlin's firewood. In 1769 he ordered the break-up of common lands and therefore also the partitioning of communal forest, in the expectation that private interests would bring about improvements in silviculture. In the following period, both Prussia and Saxony (which Prussia had defeated militarily) forged ahead with tree-planting and the reorganization of forestry.

The convulsions of the Napoleonic wars, which gave an impetus to reform in many areas, cleared the way for far-reaching measures in forestry. In 1811 Georg Ludwig Hartig, the most eminent forest scientist of his day, was appointed head of the Prussian forestry department. His 'general regulations', which some officials followed with doctrinaire rigidity, gave a 'Prussian' boost to the forestation movement, as the forest was brought under something akin to military discipline.

Around the turn of the nineteenth century, however, many doubted whether it was desirable for the state to own extensive areas of forest. Liberal thought, which was gaining ground at the time, considered state monopolies over forest or wood to be harmful and 'bureaucracy' in general to be an evil. Liberal authors regularly directed their fire at the incompetence and corruption of forestry officials, and doubts grew within the administration itself when the state's forest ownership expanded through the abolition of ecclesiastical territories in the Napoleonic period. As a modern tax system was introduced, the ruler's domains in general became less important for the state coffers, and it was tempting to sell off woodland to repay debts incurred as a result of war. This became a highly controversial issue in most parts of Germany in the early years of the nineteenth century.

The sell-off was another inducement to reform, since foresters had to demonstrate that they were capable of efficient management. But, as the century wore on, it again became the established view in Germany that the state had a special mission with regard to the forest. 'Only the state manages things for eternity', taught Heinrich Cotta (1763–1844), one of the founders of forest science. And by mid-century a political economist such as Wilhelm Roscher could argue that the 'eternal personality of the state' was most fitting for the long growth periods of trees (Roscher 1854: 22). Of course, there was something typically German about this trust in the state; it was far from universally shared, and it presupposed a reform of the civil service and a higher professional ethos. In Britain, by contrast, the general view was that politicians thought only of their time in office, whereas private individuals had one eye on those who would come after them. The idea that the state was the best forest manager also rested on the assumption – again typical of early nineteenth-century Germany – that high forest exploitation was the only real form of forest economy; coppices did not require any officialdom to run them. Today the utility of state-owned forests is once again a controversial issue in Germany.

In the eighteenth century and later, people commonly drew a link between how the forest was treated and the level of public and private debt. Woodland was thought of as a 'money box' by farmers and as a 'treasure trove' by princes – that is, it was not for regular use, but was to be kept for hard times, and then systematically cleared. The nature of woodland meant that the supply side (to use a modern term) was very elastic in the timber trade. Many other goods stagnated or fell in value if they were stored for a long time; but trees continued to grow if they were left standing. Of course, this elasticity was of little benefit to woodland owners who urgently needed to raise some cash.

Victorious armies were also in the habit of using the forest to cover expenditure (Hasel 1985: 53). In the eighteenth-century age of fortresses and standing armies, soaring levels of debt threatened to destabilize state budgets or even to shake the whole system; the French Revolution broke out in the midst of such a financial crisis. However powerful the absolutist rulers were, they remained subject to the power of money and credit. Wars and financial crises put the forest under increased pressure, but even then it was ultimately preferable to exercise restraint and, by good management, to raise the value of the forest and hence the creditworthiness of a state threatened with bankruptcy.

In France, the first post-revolutionary decade and the revolutionary wars placed the forests in a critical situation: while the Jacobins held sway in Paris, goats – the 'cows of the poor' – wandered freely among the trees. The twists and turns of the Revolution were also reflected in the forest. In the early years of the new century, however, the consolidation of the Napoleonic monarchy again brought strict supervision of the forest (Woronoff 1979: 4ff.).

Forest policy in France and Germany developed in quite different

151

directions. Whereas forestry in Prussia acquired a large degree of autonomy and – amid an international boom for construction timber – specialized in the cultivation of high forest, the interests that prevailed in France were overwhelmingly those of the iron industry and firewood consumers; rotation times were reduced, and in some cases high forest was even converted to coppices (Rubner 1967: 91ff.). The high forest system became known as 'German theory', against which nature and French silviculture had to be defended. Yet the German model gained ground internationally as the demand for firewood declined with the triumph of hard coal, giving way to the dominance of construction and industrial timber.

However much class interests and ideological factors stood behind the great forest reform that spread out from Germany, the forestation movement was one of the great accomplishments of history. Although in later times it often led to afforestation with purely coniferous stands, this corresponded only partly to what the reformers had intended. A vision narrowly linked to short-term profit was alien to forest scientists such as Hartig and Cotta, whose broad and far-sighted thinking paved the way for the later inclusion of ecological aspects into forestry.

The 'agrarian revolution' and the boundaries of forest and field

The Hohenlohe pastor and agrarian reformer Johann Friedrich Mayer, whose propaganda for gypsum fertilizer earned him the nickname 'Gypsum Apostle', once described his idea of a badly organized landscape:

> Here I see pasture, then again scrub, over there a field and again woodland, all jumbled up, all a bear garden: lake, forest, fields, bushes, meadows, pastures and gardens constantly alternating; the country looks wild and sinister, a wasteland, filled with marshes, cold, windy, bleak, poor and utterly infertile. Game is lord here and the farmers are poverty-stricken, as weighed down by misery as slaves.

And his concluding appeal: 'Open up the fields to be impregnated by the warmth of the sun. Chop down the widely scattered woods, give everything its rightful place: let pasture and field lie beside each other in the plains and valleys! Saw the forest on mountains, fence it in, seal up the noxious wild animals' (Mayer [1773] 1980: 216f.). The 'Gypsum Apostle' painted a picture which today's hiker would probably find attractive, but which was an abomination for agrarian reformers of his day.

In the eighteenth century, the improvement of agriculture was one of the liveliest public issues, more so than the incipient industrialization, and incomparably more than the fate of the forest. Agrarian reform was like a magic charm: it promised at one and the same time to banish the constant spectre of hunger, to raise the income of landowners, and to overcome the age-old conflicts that had come to a head in the century of revolution.

The ideal of agrarian reformers in the eighteenth and nineteenth centuries was an interlocking system that would make agriculture more intensive and radically transform the conditions under which farmers lived. The first step was a change to the traditional three-field rotation, whereby feed crops (clover, lupin) were grown on land in the years when it used to lie fallow. But this seemingly minor modification unleashed a chain reaction. Old collective pasturage rights in fallow land had to be given up, and the way was open to complete privatization of the peasant economy. Fallow became a place for experimenting with new edible plants. The development of high-value feed crops made it possible to switch to feeding cattle in their stalls. Former pastureland could be used for agriculture, and dung collected from stalls all year round multiplied the amount of fertilizer available, especially if urine was also trapped and used. Alongside clover, potatoes became the emblem of agrarian reform, their higher calorie content reducing by a third the amount of land necessary to feed a person. At a time when 'fruit trees' were becoming ever scarcer, the potato offered a virtually inexhaustible resource for the lucrative fattening of pigs.

All the innovations fitted together with amazing logic, at least in the model. The programme excited its supporters and sustained a new faith in progress. The fact that it would make the farmer's daily life more arduous, and women's labour in particular more severe, did not trouble the apostles of reform, and in some cases was even welcomed by them. For their ideal was an industriousness that never flagged (Sandgruber 1982a: 114f.). One begins to see why the reforms took generations to complete.

What effects did the 'agrarian revolution' have on the forest? Since it was no longer used for animal fattening and pasture, it could be turned into a pure supplier of timber (figure 3.2). The common woodland that had until then been taken for granted as an indispensable part of the farming economy became an object of contempt for the reformers. In their eyes it yielded only the fruits of nature, which men did not have to work harder to obtain. One agrarian reformer from Westphalia fulminated: 'I have never come across anything that encourages indolence more, or that is more obstructive to agriculture,

153

Figure 3.2: Ploughed fields near Fürth in Bavaria, c.1770 (copper engraving). Clearly visible is the sharp separation between agricultural land and the closed economic space of the sovereign forest.

more pernicious to landowners and inherently less lucrative, than wide expanses of common pasture and woodland' (Schwerz 1836: 319).

This new situation had two sides for forestry. On the one hand, it offered a chance of autonomy, since the forest could now be exploited without regard for local farmers; a goal pursued in vain since the beginning of the modern age finally came within reach. On the other hand, agriculture was much more important than silviculture for most of the agrarian reformers; they could see no reason not to clear the whole forest for agriculture, even if this would require huge amounts of fertilizer.

The princely passion for hunting had disturbed the peaceful coexistence of forest and field: game caused considerable damage to agriculture, which farmers had had to suffer with impotent rage. But now their time had come, as the pioneers of agrarian progress began to advocate a strict demarcation between agriculture and forestry. 'Hostility between the two branches of the economy soon developed out of the campaign to separate them' (Bernhardt [1872–5] 1966: 2/233). At first this threw forest people onto the defensive.

Higher agricultural output led to a population increase, which in turn added to the pressure on the forest. The question was not only whether forest should be cleared and converted into farmland;

agriculture was anyway crossing its traditional boundaries. The agrarian reforms, which only gradually took effect, did not always or immediately result in a balanced system. Flocks of sheep that had previously grazed on fallow land were pushed into the forest, but above all else the practice of stall feeding created a growing demand for woodland litter.

The shift to more intensive farming triggered a real race for fertilizer. 'Farmers do anything to get quantities of dung', Mayer wrote. 'If they could, they would certainly strip all firs, spruces and pines of their foliage and scatter it in their cowsheds' ([1773] 1980: 78). For one nineteenth-century forest scientist, sheep pasture and the use of floor litter were the 'gravediggers of delightful forest vegetation' (Liebich 1844: 1/187). The agricultural lobby tried to prove that the collection of organic material from the forest floor did no damage, but forest scientists, who were now beginning to spread their wings, counter-attacked all the more effectively, the more the value of humus soil for forest growth was recognized. The struggle over forest litter continued to rage well into the nineteenth century.

The fighting on such fronts, together with the consolidation of agronomy and forest science as independent disciplines, tended to obstruct more integrated approaches. Only Heinrich Cotta, under the impact of the food shortages of 1816 and 1817, proposed reopening the forest for agriculture and moving to a combined *Baumfeldwirtschaft*.

In the tracks of 'Father Cotta', the Prague-based forest scientist Christoph Liebich propagated the idea of agroforestry with missionary zeal. Nature itself, he enthused, strives towards a mixing of forest and field: 'It is well known that nature employs the grandest means to achieve its goals. But it could find nothing grander than trees to cover the floor with fertile earth, defending it against strong winds and the sun's wasting rays' (1844: 1/89). Bubbling over with unconventional ideas, he argued that forestry as it had existed until then had been a cancer and a crime against humanity, and that it was possible to combine the highest degree of economic and ecological perfection (Bernhardt [1872–5] 1966: 3/225). In Switzerland, Karl Kasthofer also advocated Cotta-like principles of agroforestry (Stuber 2008: 169ff.). He considered the alarm over wood shortages to be greatly exaggerated, and in republican Switzerland even foresters thought it advisable to reach an accommodation with farmers' interests.

For the forest science establishment, a man like Liebich was an eccentric whose ideas were not worth discussing. Nevertheless, the few attempts that were made to combine tree and field cultivation had encouraging results (Hausrath 1982: 197ff.). Since agroforestry resulted in highly labour-intensive agriculture, in which ploughs were replaced with hoes and spades, it had no chance in Europe. But the situation is very different in today's developing countries, where cheap labour is plentiful, technology is backward and solar parching ruins the soil in open farmland; the old idea of Cotta and Liebich is in their case an ultra-modern approach learned through bitter experience, even though its implementation meets resistance on the part of commercial timber interests. The real problem here is not technological but social: the political weakness of small farmers in large areas of the modern world, and the remoteness of modern forest administrations from traditional farming.

2 The 'Spectre of Shortage': Did the Timber Trade Face Catastrophe?

Historians and eighteenth-century alarms

In the eighteenth century, complaints about wood shortage rang out not only in the preamble to forest ordinance but among the population at large. In 1763 in Frankfurt, for example, speeches were made in the city council expressing alarm at 'the general discontent over the wood shortage', and a large quantity of wood was distributed to the poor as a precautionary measure (Scharff 1868: 295). In the 1780s, an average working-class family in Berlin was for the first time spending more money on firewood than on bread (Krüger 1958: 353). In France wood riots occurred on top of the well-known bread riots, and the tone was at its most strident and alarmist in the revolutionary year of 1789, preceded by one of the coldest winters of the century.

The *Forst-Archiv* (VI/3: 163) warned in 1790 that wastefulness and pilfering would become more and more of a problem; 'considering that these forest ravages are already associated with open acts of violence and will in future inevitably end in bloodshed', another hard winter would mean that the worst was to be feared. One prizewinning essay prophesied that 'life, trade and work will be made more difficult in every way for those who come after us, and that our destructive acts will make them think of us with horror' (Franz 1795: x). An inventor of an economical oven declared: 'If the wood shortage grows worse over the next twenty years at the same rate as in the past twenty, then may God have mercy on us!' Most people would have to spend the greater part of their income on wood, and the further brutalization of morals, already in shreds as a result of war, would mean that 'no fruit tree and no garden fence or gate was safe' (Bus 1797). 'Not enough wood! High wood prices! is the general complaint in nearly all the large and small towns of Germany': so began the 'frank thoughts on the wood shortage' of one forest author (Laurop 1798).

These warning cries sank into oblivion in the nineteenth century. During the First World War, however, when people in Germany suffered from hunger and lack of firewood, Werner Sombart – one of the luminaries of the economic and social sciences – recalled these fears from a bygone age. His thesis was that in the eighteenth century the 'end of capitalism' had seemed impending as a result of deforestation; wood shortages had been the deeper reason for many crisis phenomena; but coal had rescued capitalism and the advance of civilization in Europe (Sombart 1928: 2/1137ff.).

Historians of various persuasions, as well as popular literature, made Sombart's thesis their own (Radkau 1983: 514). Conservatives, liberals and Marxists were agreed that the fiendish dynamic of capitalism would inevitably break the bounds of the lethargic timber economy – that progress had led towards coal and coke, and that without these the economy would have fallen into a severe crisis. The concept of progress prevalent in the history of the economy and technology did indeed force the conclusion that the Wood Age had been doomed.

Wood shortage, ecological or institutional crisis, and the 'moral economy'

The scarcity of wood in the late eighteenth century was not a new phenomenon; complaints about it were an 'age-old story going back more than two hundred years', as the manager of the Schwäbisch Hall saltworks remarked in 1738 (Radkau 1986a). Half a millennium earlier the great clearances had run up against the limits of the forest, and the art of preparing for the finitude of wood had centuries of experience to draw upon. Many social institutions – from village communes to the output restrictions of municipal guilds – rested on the scarcity of wood and other goods and derived legitimacy from the periodic shortages.

There were certainly crisis symptoms in the eighteenth century, but these did not necessarily point to catastrophic deforestation. Rather, they were bound up with the reduced efficiency of traditional allocation systems: forest user rights, communes, distribution hierarchies and municipal officialdom. The decline of these institutions was caused not by deforestation but by a change in the dominant interests and economic doctrines. The growing diversity of commercial timber consumers put a great strain on officials responsible for the allocation of wood from the forest; the free market increasingly covered not only construction timber but also the firewood sector. What looks at first like an ecological crisis was in essence an institutional crisis.

In the 1740s, municipal deputies in Frankfurt complained that 'wood matters were in a state of indescribable disorder' and that 'unutterably great confusion' reigned in the Wood Office. In the revolutionary year of 1789, Frankfurt city council decreed – quite in the spirit of the old 'moral economy' – that the Wood Office should 'as far as possible take account of everyone's real need' in its allocation decisions. But what was 'real need' in revolutionary times? In the same year, the Frankfurt Wood Office threw in the towel in the face of this task (Radkau 1997: 69). One might say it anticipated the collapse of the communist planned economies: the more it tried to build a total state in relation to wood, the greater the confusion became.

There were two kinds of difficulties: those of traditionally privileged persons, who had to turn to the free market, and those of poor sections of the population. Previously the forest had offered many social niches where customary rights allowed wood to be obtained almost for nothing. But, as soon as wood acquired a market price and had to be measured more precisely, the costs to consumers shot up with alarming rapidity. The situation seemed hopeless if extrapolated into the future – and that was the attitude that spread through society towards the end of the eighteenth century (Radkau 1983: 535f.).

New ways of evaluating the forest also changed the picture. A large part of the woodland that had more or less sufficed for local needs, essentially as forest pasture and a source of firewood, looked pitifully run down in the eyes of timber dealers. Moreover, the revolutionary wars, like all wars, did great damage to the forest, thwarting any attempts by foresters to maintain a balance between felling and tree growth.

To be sure, around the year 1800 wood shortages imposed heavy burdens on the lower classes in many cities and regions, especially in the freezing cold of winter. Even if forest reforms and wood-saving measures were justified by reference to the plight of the poor, their main benefit was to privileged consumers of wood, such as rulers' residences, export industries and trading companies. Indeed, the full assertion of private property rights in the forest worsened the wood supply situation of the poor. We should note the terminological camouflage: forest reforms were justified in the language of the old moral economy, but their actual effect was to roll back that moral economy.

We should look at the traditional complaints about wood shortages more critically than earlier historians of the forest were wont to do. Oliver Rackham made this point again and again in relation to England, where spokesmen for the navy – from John Evelyn's time down to the Napoleonic wars – repeatedly shouted at the top of their voices about a wood supply crisis, when in reality only special kinds of timber were affected. We must distinguish between vocal and silent wood deprivation: those who shouted the loudest were usually the ones who could expect their complaints to have an effect, whereas the rest of the population, who had no privileged user rights, would only have driven prices higher by their protests. As everywhere, true need is often mute.

There is much to indicate that not the least of the reasons why the moral economy could be vanquished from without was that it was also hollowed out from within. The moral economy became based more and more on double standards. With the growth of landless and 'jobless' layers in society, long-established citizens gave an increasingly exclusive character to 'ancient rights': the forest no longer belonged to all in the same way. Household needs, the basis of the old economic morality, expanded to the point where they no longer offered a solid foundation for the moral economy. Many farmers also became caught up in the commercialization of timber and forest pig-fattening, so that forest wardens could now point a 'moral economy' finger at them for 'betraying' wood with strangers and driving outsiders' animals into the forest. Furthermore, many farmers in the eighteenth century could no longer be sure that their forest commune would endure in the future, since there was a growing temptation for its members to grab as much as they could for themselves. Garrett Hardin's thesis of the 'tragedy of the commons', in which the various users of the forest are as dumbly egoistical and isolated from one another as the wretches of the 'prisoner's dilemma', shows no knowledge of the old communal wood courts, the *Holthinge*, but is accurate enough in relation to the crisis of the communes.

Transport bottlenecks

In the late eighteenth century, the wood supply was still chiefly a question of transportation, especially along watercourses. Even amid the general complaints about inflation at the turn of the century, firewood prices were in few regions so high that it was worth transporting it by land for more than one day. A Bavarian report from 1790 noted that in some places the price of wood was changing 'almost every quarter of an hour', mainly owing to the poor state of the roads. While prices were rising in Landshut, 'wood was all but rotting at a distance of two or three hours from there' because of the impassable roads (Köstler 1934: 65). Much depended on whether the local farmers had an interest in the matter: it was reported from the Bohemian forest that wood transports were 'hell for animals and men' and deleterious to local agriculture (Blau 1917–18: 1/53).

Transport bottlenecks might also occur outside the forest because of developments in the economy. As trade grew faster than transport capacity – a general trend before the railway age – so too did the costs of conveyance, especially for transport-intensive goods such as timber. Overland routes had their 'oats limits': it was not possible to keep increasing the number of horses in a region. The timber trade could therefore operate only where suitable rivers and streams were present. In Canada, 'five miles was the maximum distance which horses or oxen could haul the great sleighs over the specially prepared iced roads' (Latham 1957: 142) – and it was much more difficult to carry wood over muddy surfaces. But water transport too had its limits, at least in densely populated regions, where shipping and newly expanding water-power systems often tried to use every stream and every metre of downward slopes.

In early modern times, commerce displayed a decentralizing tendency that corresponded to the spread of natural resources and the difficulties of transport. But there was also a centralizing counter-tendency in the rise of capital cities and large commercial and financial centres, where politics and public opinion were shaped and the wood supply was a major issue. On the other hand, the high levels of consumption there tended to favour special wood transport systems that ensured a regular long-term supply.

From 1789, the building of the Schwemmkanal near Schwarzenberg connected the River Vltava with the Danube catchment basin, making 'virgin' areas deep inside the great Bohemian forest available for Vienna's wood supply. It was the first artificial waterway to pierce the divide between the North Sea and the Black Sea, and was still used for rafting as late as 1966. The forest engineer Josef Rosenauer, who planned and supervised the canal, was famous for his 'precision of a scientist and fanaticism of a man possessed' (Kogler 1993: 7).

Even more celebrated was Georg Huebmer, the 'Rax king', who began his career chopping wood in the Ore Mountain region in Styria and learning the art of timber floating, yet, quite unlike Rosenauer – who had studied mathematics and physics – remained illiterate all his life. From 1822 to 1827 he directed work on a 450-metre timber-floating tunnel through a mountain ridge in the Rax range southwest of Vienna, in order to supply the capital with firewood from the hitherto virgin forest (Ingoviz 1909). At the time it was the longest tunnel in Austria!

The scale of the transport problem leads one to conclude that absolute wood shortages could not often have been due to complete deforestation. In pre-industrial conditions, it was no simple matter to exploit timber resources to the point of exhaustion. There were plenty of famines, but no hailstorm or crop failure would result in a sudden shortage of wood. A retreat of the forest and ensuing shortages made themselves felt in the form of rising transport costs, even where no free market operated. There was thus an economic counterforce acting against limitless plunder of the forest. It was weakest where timber could be easily rafted and local consumers of wood were powerless to resist shipments out of the area. It is still the case today in Third World countries that the best protection for the forest is a lack of roads. In modern times, too, road-building is a critical issue in forestry.

Decentralized industrialization in the eighteenth century

From a modern point of view, it seems plausible to assume that a timber-centred economy would sooner or later have been throttled by resource scarcity and a lack of growth opportunities. Yet no real evidence has yet been produced that a major economic crisis was caused by a shortage of wood. Rather, one has the impression that many trades were capable of reacting flexibly to shortages; the demand for wood was not as rigid as people claimed in order to protect their user rights. If the situation grew serious, there were many ways of economizing and many measures that could be taken to protect existing forest or to cultivate more. People did not need modern science to know how to keep forest in good condition – if that was what they really wanted.

Of course, the forest set limits to the growth of a large timber consumer such as the iron industry. But did that mean crisis? Certainly not in the sixteenth century. The answer may not be quite so straightforward for the eighteenth century, but there is plenty of evidence to show that, even in the iron industry, it was thought quite normal to limit production out of a concern for the forest.

Disputes arose over the limits that should be respected in particular cases. In the 1750s, for example, a heated argument raged over the Elector of Bavaria's ironworks in Bodenwöhr, which had been expanding rapidly and was then the largest industrial complex in the Upper Palatinate. The forest director responsible for the area, with the support of officials in Amberg, accused the Bodenwöhr mining department of illegal output increases and destruction of the forest. 'New furnaces' were being lit 'almost daily' and 'operated with such intensity' that no wood was left for other forges in a wide surrounding area. The director of the Bodenwöhr mine department was furious and accused the forester of being a malicious liar, who in fact had himself been illegally rafting the best timber to Austria and allowing Amberg hammersmiths to lay waste to the forest. For all the shouting, however, it was taken for granted that mines and ironworks ought to be run 'in proportion to the state of the forest' and, if necessary, 'be cut back' to allow the 'communal landscape to remain lastingly wooded' (Amberg municipal archive). It never occurred to the mining director to gloat about successful growth; he pointed, rather, to the allegedly low and discontinuous level of iron production.

In 1766 the imperial government in Vienna enquired whether it would not be advisable to procure 'as much iron as possible'. But the mines director himself declared that it was 'one of the greatest evils to procure iron in excessive quantity'; it was certainly an 'indispensable metal', but one that should 'not be enjoyed like bread' but consumed for specific purposes (Radkau 1986a). This was still a long way from the idea that iron was the key to economic growth. If there was monopoly control of a sales outlet, it was in the interests of the iron producer himself to limit production and keep prices high. To be sure, not everyone in Vienna shared this view in 1766; growth propaganda was already doing the rounds.

For centuries the Siegerland iron industry limited output as a way of keeping iron prices high and charcoal prices low. In the 1770s the economist and Pietist Johann Jung-Stilling wanted to help Siegerlanders to seek 'profit in the quantity of goods, not in the high level of prices'; the businessman's trust in God was supposed to lie in the principle: 'one produces as much as one can, unmindful that the means to do so might ever fail' (Kellenbenz and Schawacht 1974: 78). But the government of the principality of Nassau-Dillenburg considered it 'much too petty to answer such twaddle' (Kruse 1909: 129).

Friedrich Anton von Heynitz, whom Frederick the Great appointed head of the Prussian Mining and Foundries Department in 1776, believed that a 'military state' such as Prussia could not afford to

162

restrict its iron industry (Radkau 1983: 529). In France, in 1782–5, the government oversaw the building of Le Creusot's coal- and coke-based ironworks in order to break the link with the forest, but this last great industrial project of the Ancien Régime would remain for decades an economic albatross.

Growth of the iron industry in the eighteenth century had much to do with power ambitions and war: 'war was pretty certainly the greatest consumer of iron' (Hobsbawm 1968: 50). It is hard to see the limits to its growth as a crisis factor. For the rest, agriculture was then the largest consumer of iron products, but horseshoes, scythes and ploughshares did not call for sharply rising mass production. The dominant type of economic growth in the eighteenth century corresponded to the foundations of wood and water-power: it was local, mainly based on manual labour, and often geared to quality more than quantity (Sieferle 1984a: 42ff.).

A kind of mass production of homogeneous wood products spread in forested regions in the eighteenth and nineteenth centuries, but this occurred mainly in the sector of handicrafts and homeworking (clocks in Switzerland, toys in the Ore Mountain area, picture frames in South Tyrol's Grödner valley). Before the machine age, mass production could bring a degree of prosperity to homeworkers (Müller 1837: 236ff.).

Decentralized industrialization partly corresponded to what is now heralded as the 'soft path' to growth: the scarcity of wood prevented heavy industry from becoming the leading sector of the economy. A tendency could already be seen towards urban concentration and a core–periphery polarization, but it was held back by the basically local energy resources. As energy-intensive industries expanded, they were increasingly attracted to forests where timber did not incur high transport costs. There was a broad consensus that economic development had to be adapted to the resources available in a particular region.

Many people saw the explosive industrial growth of the nineteenth century as more of a crisis. As Barrington Moore (1967: 506) pointed out, 'there is no evidence that the mass of the population anywhere has wanted an industrial society, and plenty of evidence that they did not.' The historian Franz Schnabel (1965: 243), who had a keener eye than most for the technological side of history, even suspected that, if democracy had survived at the beginning of the nineteenth century, 'it would have made modern technology impossible. Artisans, workers and farmers would have voted together in parliament against machinery.' For Schnabel, a liberal from southwestern Germany, this was not necessarily an argument against democracy. And it is one further argument in support of the view that the 'wood brake' did not necessarily imply a wood crisis.

Who had an interest in complaining of wood shortages? Which were the contrary voices?

It is often hard to judge how seriously one should take the complaints about wood shortage at that time: they were almost as diverse as wood itself. An alleged shortage of wood might be used to claim traditional rights. The wire-drawers of Altena, for instance, fiercely invoked a wood shortage to keep other trades out of their customary woodland, yet in 1768 they opposed the establishment of a rafting business that would have relieved it (Betzhold 1986). So long as the demand for wood could justify special rights, complaints about shortages were part of the system. It was precisely when those rights seemed under threat that they had to be strengthened through more frequent and more forceful assertion – and, naturally, wood could become scarcer for other people as a result. Anyone who depended on the market and was really hit by higher prices did not necessarily have an interest in raising a public alarm, since this might simply drive prices higher and encourage speculation.

The conversion of firewood into a commodity with a market price always provoked a flood of complaints, but these subsided once buying and selling had become a matter of course. After governments handed over wood supply responsibilities to the market, they too lost interest in any literature concerning shortages and economy measures, especially since state-owned forests profited from rising prices. It is striking how quickly the warning cries disappeared at the beginning of the nineteenth century, without a dramatic improvement in the supply situation.

Indeed, voices could more often be heard pouring scorn on alarmist talk and asserting that there was still far too much woodland, or that wood prices needed to be even higher to make sustainable forestry a worthwhile proposition. The champions of the free market were especially keen on this argument. 'The Scarcity of Timber ought never to be regretted, for it is a certain proof of National Improvement', declared Thomas Preston, a former Suffolk county official, in 1791 (Albion 1926: 119). Joseph von Hazzi, a celebrated councillor in the Bavarian State Directorate, likewise maintained that, the more expensive wood became in a country, the higher was its level of industry and culture and the more productive its exploitation of wood;

shortages raised prices and were therefore an inducement to increase the production and supply of wood; the 'frightful ado about impending shortages' was a way for 'forest charlatans' to impress the government and public opinion; and from time to time they did indeed manage to whip up a wild hysteria.

The 'spectre of wood shortage' became a proverbial bugbear for those who ridiculed such fears. Karl Kasthofer, a liberal Swiss forest reformer who believed in regulation by the market, wrote in 1828 in his popular pamphlet *Der Lehrer im Walde*: 'As regards the spectre of wood shortage, you will already have noticed that, however chilling it looks, it does not scare me much. Complaints about wood shortage are so old, and the predicted horrors have so rarely come to pass, that they do not even cause much concern.' In Switzerland, as in America, optimists could still believe in the inexhaustibility of the forest. But that was not all there was to it. Behind the dispute over wood shortages, Kasthofer rightly discerned 'two opposing systems that have long been fighting it out in Germany too': the liberal system of thought, and another that started from the necessity of official intervention (Stuber 2008: 37, 149f., 153).

Friedrich Pfeil, head of the Prussian State Forest Administration, declared with his usual acerbity that 'the constantly approaching monster of the direst wood shortage' was 'a chimera that many forest people and other writers want to frighten us with, as Africans frighten their women with mumbo jumbo' (Radkau 1986a). And in 1821, in a speech at the opening of the Berlin Forest Academy (which later moved to Eberswalde), he thundered against foresters who could not get enough woodland, and for whom the forest was an end in itself, in a polemical style not unlike that which the early Karl Marx used to denounce the Prussian Law on Thefts of Wood (see the section 'Wood Talk' at the end of this book):

> They continually fight with the nation over the forest, because they do not know how to reconcile the interests of the two. Locked in everlasting combat with agriculture, hating any useful domesticated animal more than the fiercest predator, the plough more than the plague, regarding any new house or settlement as the opening of an abyss, the bad forester wages an eternal struggle against increased national prosperity and a rising population. He heedlessly tramples on people for the sake of trees. He fights with success, because he makes the spectre of wood shortage his ally against those who waver. (Hasel 1982: 193)

In a recent study of forest conflicts in Bavaria between 1760 and 1860, Richard Hölzl reached a conclusion that is applicable to many other parts of the world: 'The position of the rural population in the modern bureaucratic state was also being negotiated in the law courts and official departments' (2010: 494). And the results were not usually favourable to the rural population. As Fernand Braudel realized, the process of greatest world-historical importance in the nineteenth and twentieth centuries was the decline of a peasant culture that had existed since Neolithic times. This process is precisely reflected in the history of the forest and wood – from forest use rights to half-timbered houses.

Commercial users of wood, too, often did not correspond to the destructive image that foresters painted of them. Adding his voice to the scorn, Oliver Rackham wrote that any economic historian who makes the industrial wood consumption of earlier ages responsible for the destruction of the forest is forgetting not only that trees grow again but that large timber consumers were not in the habit of committing suicide. The forest survived precisely when it was used; it disappeared when no one exploited it (Rackham 1980: 102f., 153). Whereas historians traditionally focused on high forest, Rackham reminded everyone how widespread coppices used to be.

Even John Evelyn may testify as a witness for the revisionist view of forest history. The author of *Sylva* did, it is true, complain about the 'prodigious waste which these voracious iron and glass works has formerly made', but elsewhere he maintained that his father's forge and mills 'were a means of maintaining and improving his woods, I suppose by increasing the industry of planting' (Williams 2006: 172). In his *Fumifugium* (1661), he campaigned against the smell of coal in London and vigorously pleaded for a return to firewood, so little did he believe that it inevitably destroyed the forest.

Criticism of the wood shortage alarms is well founded. But the assumption that crises could never happen in principle goes to the opposite extreme and is scarcely realistic; it is far from always the case that people act with the future in mind. In mountainous regions, or in areas prone to karstification, forest regrowth did not happen so easily and wood shortage was a real possibility (Hauser 1972: 231f.). The same was true where wood was rafted to faraway destinations or consumers with high purchasing power appeared on the scene. If people had neither the power nor the money to pay higher prices or to restock local forest, then a shortage of wood did not create an impetus for forestry to develop. Also, when the wood price was kept artificially low, the incentive to take care of the forest was lacking.

But fear of a wood crisis, most acute when one threatened to occur but had not yet broken out, was itself a force regulating supply. It would seem that people tended more to underestimate than overestimate the resources of the forest: deforestation was most apparent around settlements or along forest paths; regeneration, on the other hand, went almost unnoticed. The glaring contrast between the slowness of tree growth and the speed with which wood goes up in smoke has always made a strong impression. Concerned foresight contributed at least as much as the market – which functioned imperfectly in the timber trade and often disappointed liberal hopes – to stabilization of the wood supply.

As the 'spectre of wood shortage' lost its terrors for the public, foresters liked more and more to use proto-ecological arguments for forest conservation – in particular, reminders that the forest regulates the hydrologic balance and serves to counter both drought and flooding (Radkau 2008c: 220). This line of argument first appeared in the early nineteenth century in Switzerland and France, typically represented by critics of liberalism, but it subsequently spread more widely, from the United States to British India. In 1825 Alexandre Moreau de Jonnès, a guiding intellectual force of the Restoration in France as John Evelyn had once been in England, declared: 'The first tree felled for the building of a country may be the beginning of its civilization, but the last tree felled is its end.'

The Swiss forest policy expert Xavier Marchand, an opponent of the liberal Kasthofer, saw the frequent floods of the nineteenth century as a result of deforestation in mountainous areas and coined the term 'Alpine plague' to refer to them. Acting like the punitive God of the Old Testament, nature took its revenge for man's sins in the forest by unleashing 'the Alpine plague, whose destructive effects [were] increasingly uncontrollable in the wake of deforestation' (Stuber 2008: 219f., 225). As a matter of fact, the causal link between deforestation and flooding is questionable for that period in Switzerland. But the idea of 'nature's revenge' became a cornerstone of modern environmentalism.

Forest reform and ecological crisis

The self-confident German forest reformers who championed regulated exploitation of the high forest took it upon themselves to heal the 'festering wounds' of the previously 'depraved and irregular' forest economy – as the Amberg Forest Administration put it in 1800. A torrent of scorn poured over traditional attitudes to the forest, and the literature of the late eighteenth century was awash with complaints about its pitifully run-down state. But if the condition of many forests appeared critical in the light of new economic goals, this should not be confused with an ecological crisis.

It should not be imagined, of course, that ecological harmony prevailed everywhere in nature in pre-modern times. Agriculture and pasturing had long given rise to volatile ecosystems, and the struggle against soil exhaustion ran like a red thread through the history of farming. Sheep-grazing had turned large parts of the forest in northwestern Germany into heathland; and, in many areas, extensive removal of forest and moorland soil as agricultural fertilizer had finished things off and left dunes and wasteland behind (Schwerz 1836: 122).

In sparsely populated areas, in particular – where peat could easily cover fuel needs, large industrial timber consumers were lacking and sheep had become more important than swine (an especially marked tendency around the year 1800) – the forest had little or no protection. In the nineteenth century, parts of the Emsland district in Lower Saxony were described as a 'Libyan desert' (Bruns 1981: 50). Wind-borne sand already threatened fields and villages in early modern times; only slowly did people pull themselves together and begin to combat the 'sands of woe' with forestation (Hausrath 1982: 179ff.).

Nevertheless, major elements of the pre-modern economy served to maintain an ecological balance in the forest. The diversity of local needs favoured mixed deciduous and coniferous forest with a large amount of undergrowth. Outright invasion of nature was uncommon, and the conversion of forest as a result of changed needs usually took place only gradually. Selection forest and coppice, typical forms in farming areas, were both relatively stable from an ecological point of view, and they were less of a threat than clear-cutting or coniferous monoculture to the quality of the soil. Even forest pasturing was beneficial to the soil if it was properly regulated.

Owners of forest land tried to ensure that all the branches, rootstock and wood waste left behind after clear-cutting were removed. Local people sometimes refused to comply, however, on the grounds that the litter would continue to fertilize the forest. Although this may sometimes have been a pretext, it appears right on target from a modern point of view; the unserviceable wood from tree branches, whose mineral content is three to nine times higher than that of trunk wood, is especially valuable for fertilizing the forest floor (Hesmer 1966–70: 1/128). It seemed obvious to farmers that they should also take care of the forest soil, whereas soil experts abstained from a scientific approach until the nineteenth century. Farmers fertilized the soil on which they planted oaks; forest reformers tended to neglect the soil altogether.

In the Black Forest, the state forest inspectorate in Waldkirch, drawing on new 'scientific' theories, tried to impose its view of things on the town of Villingen (which had the largest areas of forest for miles around). But when the Villingen administration was accused of being idle and incompetent in forest matters, it responded with rightful indignation that the conifer seed bought from the forestry department was no good, since it came from regions with a milder climate, 'often became rotten and lifeless in times of drought, did not thrive in the bitterly cold local soil, but was at the same time very expensive'. As we know today, the experienced people of Villingen were more aware of the location-dependence of conifer seed than were foresters applying general rules (Rodenwaldt 1977: 54, 139).

In many cases, it was precisely the reforms that began around the turn of the nineteenth century that led to ecologically unstable forest formations. The special susceptibility of conifer stands to insect pests very soon became apparent. People must have been really frightened and disoriented as they watched whole tracts of north German woodland being ravaged in this way (Bernhardt [1872–5] 1966: 2/377ff.) – and it was only the beginning of a long series of catastrophes in the coniferous forest. Even Pfeil, otherwise so scornful of panic-mongering, realized that bark beetles in the Harz had done so much damage to spruce forests that mining would have to be abandoned in many places.

Despite the nature cult of the time, 'nature' was not an ideal for the founding fathers of forest science – on the contrary. Many reformers actually combated the view that the forest was a gift of nature: they thought it should be a product of, and draw its value from, man's labour. Insistence on long years of experience with the natural peculiarities of a region was more typical of conservative foresters, who tended to be sceptical about the role of science in their profession and, as far as the reformers were concerned, merely defended their old idle ways. The new forestry was to distinguish itself by a guiding theory, a logical system and general rules that could be derived from it. Yet methods devised in lowland areas often had destructive effects in the mountains, and had to be imposed against the well-founded resistance of local people. In the Black Forest, a return to plantation forestry was one of the demands raised in the revolutionary year of 1848.

In 1838 extensive clear-cutting in the Gail valley region of Carinthia led to unrest, as farmers feared economic damage especially as a result of high water levels. 'Only military assistance quietened things down' (Wießner 1951: 131). In the 1830s and 1840s, a series of disastrous floods in the Alps and southern France led the Swiss government to impose a ban on clear-cutting that is still in force today. In lowland areas, people mostly blamed forest crimes on the part of mountain farmers, with whom foresters were constantly locked in a 'secret war', as Kasthofer complained in 1822 (Hauser 1972: 290). Yet such explanations are scarcely credible, since the floods were a result partly of climatic factors, and partly of the commercially driven clear-cutting that pushed back the traditional plantation system. Even a champion of forest reforms had to concede that a 'terrible lesson' had been delivered to the 'sophisticated butchery of goods' that had 'razed' woodland areas (Bernhardt 1869: 139). A *Plenterwirtschaft*, involving the felling of trees as occasion demanded, was first rehabilitated in Switzerland.

The climate argument from Columbus to Hitler: a stopgap and the foresters' new trump card

Forest and climate: what a source of confusion! Columbus already believed that forests attract rain clouds, and concluded that the Azores and Canary Isles had become arid following deforestation by the Portuguese (Levin 2009: 476). It was always evident that some link existed between forest and humidity, since any traveller could see that, regardless of precipitation, it was often damper in the forest than in open land. But the precise causal link between the two was anything but clear. Originally, it was widely believed in Central and Western Europe that the climate was harsh in thickly forested countries – Russia and Scandinavia were mostly in mind – and that forest clearance brought milder and more human-friendly conditions. Even John Evelyn agreed with this popular view, although it contradicted his plea for reforestation. It was evident that forests retained water and therefore fed springs. But, since Central and Western Europe used to be rainier than they are today, and since people living there not only cleared forest for cultivation but also waged a struggle with water, this capacity for water retention was considered only a limited advantage. Besides, trees also *consume* huge quantities of water – the connection between forest and water was not easy to fathom. In former times, people commonly believed that the tree-tops held clouds back. Only when the water cycle between sky and earth was discovered did they draw the opposite conclusion: that, since trees consume huge quantities of water and draw up moisture through their roots from deep underground, their high levels of evaporation must contribute to the formation of rain clouds. The disastrous floods of the nineteenth century, especially in the Alps, finally taught people to value the forest's regulation of the hydrologic balance, while a new way of looking at the Mediterranean region interpreted its aridity as the result of deforestation. Precisely when the triumph of coal meant that foresters could no longer deploy the old 'wood shortage' argument, they turned to the water and climate argument as their new trump card, in the dry South and mountainous regions even more than in the low mountain ranges of Central and Western Europe.

For George Perkins Marsh (*Man and Nature*, 1864), the climatic importance of the forest weighed more heavily than all the arguments of the timber trade for forest conservation; the bare mountains of the Mediterranean were a graphic warning of how deforestation could dry out whole regions. Alert American journalists soon drew the reverse conclusion: reforestation would bring rain to the American deserts and make them suitable for agriculture. 'Perversely, it was Marsh's *Man and Nature* that proved to be the real catalyst to the upsurge of writing by the rainmakers after the Civil War' (Williams 1989: 381). It took an amazingly long time for the senselessness of such projects to be realized, so attractive was the idea of climate management. The forestry department in British India also relied more on the climate argument than on timber supply issues to justify its strict regime (Barton 2002: 29ff.); although its main concern would have been the extraction of teak, the climate argument was better suited in the coal age to play up the public utility of forest conservation. Man-made climate change here became a major issue for the first time, albeit in a way that today sounds dubious.

In fact, the history of ideas relating to man-made climate change is dubious. Adolf Hitler's table talk wanders eerily into confused speculation about the link between forest and climate and – typically for him – about a future climate war. On 11 May 1942, in his Wolf's Lair headquarters on the Eastern front, the Führer declared that the Reich would quite possibly have to wage war on Italy – his fascist ally – in a hundred years' time. Why? Just the first stage of Il Duce's forestation programme provided for the planting of 35 million trees, and if it went on like that it would 'inevitably result in major climatic changes for us. Italy would then no longer be the roasting plate that passes the warmth of its sun on to us and brings us warm rain. There would even be a danger of our going back to a rainy, misty climate, like there is in Russia today' (Picker 1963: 328).

171

3 The Forest: From Living Space to Capital

Silence gradually fell on the forest that had rung out for centuries with barking and horn-blowing from the princely chase, with cowherds' shouts, the lowing, whinnying, mooing, bleating and grunting of animals, the axe blows of cartwrights and plank-makers and the pounding of forge hammers, and where on all sides furnaces had smouldered and smoke risen from charcoal piles and tar or ash pits. It was no longer a living space, as before, but the site of systematically planned timber production, whose only aim was to deliver as much valuable wood as possible. (Mitscherlich 1963: 14f.)

The forest as artificial product and as simple arithmetic

The seventeenth century, which witnessed the Thirty Years' War, was an age of neglect for the forests of Central Europe, but also one of reduced stress. The economic growth of the next century, however, put greater demands on it than ever before. Economic 'rationality' was everywhere the order of the day, and 'forest economics' was ostensibly raised to the level of a science (figure 3.3).

But what did it mean to deal with the forest 'economically'? What kind of science was the theory of the forest supposed to become? As soon as one got down to brass tacks, it became clear how difficult it was to answer these questions unambiguously; considerable differences of opinion persist to this day. As ever, the basic problem for a science of the forest is that, although experiments on the ground go back for generations, their results have always been tied to a particular location. Forest history therefore emerged in the place of experiment, but it was often written dogmatically without a critical examination of its sources. Dogmas have been reaffirmed over and over again, but just as regularly they have foundered on the diversity of local conditions. An aged forester can today still sum up his lifetime's experience by repeating after Socrates: 'I know that I know nothing, and that is the extent of my wisdom.'

From the eighteenth century on, 'sustainability' was proclaimed as the guiding objective of forestry – that is, the principle that each year only as much wood should be cut as grows in the space of a year. This left many questions open, however. It corresponded to the original Greek etymology of *oikonomia* ('household management'), but it said nothing about how forestry departments should react to trade cycles or how the forest to be sustained should actually look. Only gradually was it realized that the sustainability principle was not simply a question of mathematics but involved 'preserving the productive

Figure 3.3: Title page of *Sylvicultura oeconomica* (1713), by Chief Mining Superintendent Hans Carl von Carlowitz, one of the pioneering works of German forest science. The page lists the contents of the book in baroque detail. Some of the German terminology is interesting: the older *hauswirthliche* is used at the top instead of *oeconomica*, but at the bottom *Nationalökonomie* already appears in its modern sense of political economy. Reforestation is justified – how else? – by the 'great scarcity of wood'. It was Carlowitz who first introduced the term 'sustainability' (*Nachhaltigkeit*) into forestry (Peters 1984:261). But we should not make too much of this: it does not mean he was the first to have the idea, and it was anyway for him only one aspect among others. In reality we owe sustainable forestry to the mining and iron industry. The word first appeared where sustainability was most under threat.

power of the soil' (Köstler 1954: 13). Today's public requires that sustainability should apply not only to wood harvesting but also to the general ecology of the forest and its recreational value (Peters 1984). 'Sustainability' was always more a theme of forest literature than a guiding principle in the practice of forestry, where no one ever managed to spell out what it meant simply and straightforwardly. The modern ecological concept of sustainability represents a scientific step forward, but its increasing complexity still places considerable difficulties in the way of practical application.

From the Middle Ages until the eighteenth century, state forestry offices with significant powers usually came under the relevant mining, foundry and saltworks department. By the turn of the nineteenth century, forestry was seeking to assert its autonomy. But what place did theory have in this? In a first 'Essay on the History of German Forestry' (1795), we read: 'Forestry came into the hands of scholars and economists in the course of this century; attempts were made to associate it with the study of nature, botany and mathematics, and to elevate forestry itself to the dignity of a science' (Moser 1795: 201). Since that time, the study of the forest has repeatedly shifted backwards and forwards between economics and biology (and, later, ecology). The attempted link with economics has produced no lasting success; not even the most up-to-date economic theory has helped any forest cultivator to foresee what the timber market will be like when his trees are ready for felling.

The first task of the new forest science was to take stock of the forests – that is, to calculate the wood matter contained in them and the yearly increase. Only then could it be precisely ascertained what rate of wood clearing was consistent with sustainable forestry. However, these estimates – ranging over centuries in the case of annual growth figures – were 'a thoroughly awkward problem' that left many foresters helpless. Paths did not yet exist in large areas of forest, and even a head forester became 'grey and old, lethargic and querulous' before he knew his forest inside out (Pitz 1965: 29, 32). Advances in statistics and cartography since the late eighteenth century enabled a closer appraisal to be made, thereby clearing up many disputes over the state of the forest and allaying many concerns. People still did not know what the forests were worth, though.

Forest mathematicians had a particularly hard time when the trees were of different ages and species (figure 3.4). The ambition to measure the wood and value of a forest was itself a factor that encouraged clear-cutting and the development of single-species stands.

Figure 3.4: Illustration from the German edition of Duhamel du Monceau's ground-breaking work on forest labour (1766–7), showing the calculation of tree volume. The straight tree on the left can be measured with simple geometric figures; the crooked one on the right with many branches forms a frightening contrast. Crooked trees were a nightmare for forest mathematicians, although they could be useful in shipbuilding.

Clear-cutting was considered 'the most transparent economically' (Bernhardt [1872–5] 1966: 1/238) – the statistician's point of view. The author of a manual entitled *Waldwirtschaft und Forstpolizei* (1798) fulminated that those in favour of a return to unregulated

175

plantation forestry should be thought of as madmen or countryside pests (Pacher 1964: 54).

Artificial cultivation developed slowly around this time, often with a preference for conifers based on centuries of experience, but a lot of seed was wasted along the way. Major successes began to appear only in the 1830s, thanks to improved planting techniques, but again it was mainly pines that profited from them. Soon afterwards, many foresters were recording an ominous advance of coniferous woodland.

Forest science played an ambiguous role in this process, which little by little changed the face of the forest in Central Europe. The quest for higher profits and pure stands gave an impetus to 'coniferization', but mixed forest was also valued highly in theory. A favourite ploy was to cultivate pines as a traditional measure, on the grounds that the soil was too run down for finer woodland and that forest personnel were not yet sufficiently well trained for higher tasks (Pfeil 1839: 273). The stereotyped character of this argument, in quite varied soil conditions, should make us take it with more than a pinch of salt.

Another motive was often plain to see, and it filled farmers with a sense of outrage. The cultivation of coniferous woodland was a cold-blooded means used by foresters to undermine the customary rights of farmers, especially in relation to pasturing and foliage collection. What was initially conceived as a temporary arrangement became a lasting trend. Even Pfeil, who more than any other 'forest classic' promoted clear-cutting and pine cultivation (Schwappach 1886–8: 2/704f.), eventually complained of 'today's speculative and coldly calculating age', which was replacing 'genial deciduous trees' with the 'endless uniformity' of coniferous woodland (ibid.: 2/70).

Which kind of felling was compatible with 'sustainable' forestry depended on the length of the tree rotation time – one of the main bones of contention from the eighteenth to the twentieth century. In traditional forestry, this time varied enormously – from five years in coppices (which foresters thought of as little more than brushwood) up to 250 years in highly regarded oak forests. According to one French historian, the 'cult of high forest' was the 'state religion of the Ancien Régime', rooted in an ultimately irrational 'ancestor worship' (Corvol 1984: 178, 117). No wonder, then, that the Revolution dramatically reduced rotation times. German foresters, on the other hand, became 'increasingly fanatical champions of high forest systems' after 1800, with rotation times up to 120 or even 180 years (Bernhardt [1872–5] 1966: 2/336).

But what kind of rationality lay behind this preference? Only in high forest was there an opportunity to sell logs as expensive construction timber; but the largest proportion of wood was still used as fuel until far into the nineteenth century. Pfeil, thinking laterally as he so often did, asked in 1833 in his Kritischen Blättern: 'But do we really need so much construction timber and lumber that we have to nurture all stands everywhere for this purpose?' (Hasel 1982: 291). Indeed, was it rational to pursue a high forest policy, which speculated on construction timber prices a hundred years into the future, when good prices were being paid there and then for firewood and charcoal? It was even frequently argued that firewood, with its lower rotation time, earned the highest profits, since 'all deciduous wood grows fastest in the first twenty years' (Helfrich 1807: 10). Tanners and charcoal-burners valued oak most highly at eighteen years. In general, a demand for lower rotation times could be justified by reference to the growing pace of economic life. In the late nineteenth century, the phrase 'lazy workers' (faule Gesellen) was in use as an insult for old trees whose growth had slowed down (Hilf and Röhrig 1938: 258). It was discovered that the age at which the growth of forest stands peaked was much lower than people had previously believed: around thirty for pine and larch, but over a hundred for beech.

If long rotation times were nevertheless the norm in nineteenth-century Germany, this had much to do with the professional interests of foresters. At a time when the purpose of state forestry officials and large state-owned forests was being called into question, only the long time perspective of high forest systems justified the existence of lifetime employment in the service. Often decried in the past, and now faced with doubts about their very existence in a bourgeois society, they sought to embody the concern for the future that high forests seemed to involve.

Friedrich Schiller, who at first treated foresters as mere hunters, came to hold them in high esteem when he heard that Hartig had drawn up forest enterprise plans for 120 years and more (Meyer 1966: 234). 'Clear-cutting with subsequent planting' was characterized, not inappropriately, as 'economic bureaucratism' (Beamtenwirtschaft) (Preßler 1865: 5). But even forestry departments could not entirely escape the pressure to lower rotation times, and they tended to favour fast-growing conifers as the way to make these compatible with high forest systems.

Most of what farmers regarded as the main utility of the forest – pasturing, pig-fattening, foliage consumption, use of floor litter – was now listed by forestry departments as 'secondary uses', if not outright misuse, of the forest. Nor is it even certain that this radical shift in

177

forest management everywhere reflected the interest in maximizing financial yields. Around the year 1830, pasturing in many areas still earned a higher return than all other uses of the forest (Hundeshagen 1830: 103), so that for forest owners in the Münsterland it was still an open question whether it was more profitable to sell oak stands as shipbuilding timber or to keep them for pig-fattening (Heymer 1934: 61). Since, however, pasturing and pig-fattening required strongly lit forest, they jarred with the new forestry plans.

Tanbark brought confusion to the forest economy in the early nineteenth century. Oak coppices, which were maintained purely for this purpose, brought in high profits at the time, but many foresters were 'so taken with the high forest idea' that they 'scorned any thought of comparing the profitability of coppicing with that of high forest' and in 1837 even forced communes on the Bergstraße to pass from the one to the other (Bernhardt [1872–5] 1966: 3/236). Prussian tanners vigorously agitated for oak coppices in the revolutionary year of 1848, and, despite the hostility of forest officials, they won the backing of the government in Berlin, since leather tanning was then one of the leading branches of industry in Prussia.

One champion of high forest wrote that, if it was 'demoted' to mixed forest or coppice, it would diminish the 'capital invested in the timber trade' (Papius 1840: 24). In this view of wood as capital, the high forest policy represented the best accumulation of capital, so long as the growth of the trees continued. But what if the soil was considered as capital, and the forest only as interest on it? This is how the Saxon forest scientist Max Robert Preßler proposed to look at things: a series of five brochures that he published in the 1850s and 1860s, under the collective title *Rational Forestry*, were a direct challenge to the forestry of his day. On the premise that the aim of silviculture was to maximize the return on land capital, he devised a mathematization of forestry that turned it into pure business management (figure 3.5). With a superior show of irony, he revealed that up to then forestry had not been as rational and economical as it claimed to be.

But could forestry ever be exact in the economic sense? Preßler's polemic led to a split in forest science whose consequences are still with us today. Many of his opponents tried to turn his 'return on capital' argument against him, taking forest instead of soil as the capital on which the return is made. Preßler's sharply provocative position led many foresters to give thought to the previously unexpressed principles of their profession, and in the end it was the theory of a 'return on the forest', with its high rotation times, that prevailed in Germany. In the middle of the nineteenth century, 'nature' as a

178

Aber nur bei und unter angemessen technischer Messungs-
und Rechnungspraxis, und angemessen fortgesetzter Selbst-
thätigkeit und Selbsterfahrung auf diesen Gebieten, kann
es eine wirklich forstliche Bedeutung haben jenes nette Pfeil'sche
Wort:

„Fraget die Bäume....!"

Denn die Ultima Ratio aller Wirthschaft ist und bleibt:

Die Zahl!

Figure 3.5: Conclusion of the fifth in a series of polemical pamphlets by Max
Robert Preßler, *Der rationelle Waldwirt*. The way in which the title 'Die Zahl'
stands out illustrates his fetishization of 'figures'; it is counterposed to the motto
'Fraget die Bäume' [Ask the Trees], which already points in the direction of
environmentalism.

category established a place in forest science (figure 3.6); more and
more voices called for a forestry that was closer to nature and were
increasingly able to cite the results of biology and earth sciences. Up
to now, mixed deciduous forest has survived better in southern than
northern Germany – a result of natural conditions, but also of old
traditions of forest maintenance.

Scarcity decreed

The following complaint appears around the turn of the nineteenth
century in the forest byelaws of the Lippe region: 'Poor people used
to go with an axe into the forest early in the morning, chop some
wood for themselves – which the forest ordinance allowed them to
do – and then go off happy and carefree to a hard day's work.' Now,
however, they could go into the forest only three days a week. Again
and again, the sources of that period display a temporality shaped
by wood and the forest: the good old times, when it was a joy to be
alive, were the times of forest plenty and free access to the forest. As
a British rhymer wrote: 'No lack of timber then was felt or fear'd / In
Albion's happy isle.' But was not Lippe still rich in forest around the
year 1800? Was there not enough wood to go round in many other
regions too?

Es fällt durch der Sägen und Aerte Gewalt,
Der frische, fröhliche freie Wald;
Was Wunder, wenn endlich der Baum sich rächt
Und seinen Mörder in Stücken sägt.
Verkehrt ist die Welt!

Figure 3.6: 'Fresh forest happy and free / Falls to the blows of saw and axe.
/ No wonder the tree finally takes revenge / and saws its killer into pieces.
'Tis a topsy-turvy world!' From the *Fliegende Blätter* (1852), one of the best-
known satirical magazines of its time. Forest conservation, which until the late
eighteenth century had mainly been something that the authorities demanded
of people, became a popular cause in the nineteenth century. The forest was
increasingly seen not as an economic factor but as a recreational space and a
symbol of the eternity of nature. The idea also began to appear that nature
would take revenge for what humans did to it.

180

But this is precisely the point. Wood became scarce during the eighteenth century not least because it was *intended* to become scarce; only then did it seem 'natural' that wood should fetch a high price, which as far as possible should apply to all wood, including firewood. What looked like scarcity to consumers of wood – and therefore, in the pre-modern 'moral economy', would have been blamed on the state forestry department – now became a matter of business cycles. Until then, often low firewood prices had been a sign of a country's prosperity and just system of rule, indicating that the authorities cared for the poor as well as for business consumers of wood. But a new logic came forth in the age of forest reform, mounting state debt and advances of liberalism. Now high wood prices were a good thing, since they laid the financial basis for improved forest management, boosted the creditworthiness of public and private owners of forest land, testified that the forest was being intensively worked, created an incentive for more sparing use of wood, and spurred people on to technological advances. In the traditional view, rising wood prices were reason to complain of a 'shortage'; in the new way of thinking, they were the best safeguard against wood shortages.

The old wood economy segmented into different sectors. There was, to be sure, already a free market, but it often played no more than a supplementary role in the wood supply. There were also special entitlements of various kinds: a number of groups of people received some wood for nothing, while others paid a single lump sum, and yet others paid a range of prices for logs or chopped wood. Restrictions now operated more and more between sectors. Rising timber prices also had a knock-on effect in other branches of the economy. If a forest owner used some of his wood commercially, he demonstrated that the rest also had a monetary value. When Count von der Leyen founded an ironworks in 1732 at St Ingbert in the Saar, in order to use up 'surplus wood that was damaging the forest', he also required local people to pay for their wood and triggered a legal dispute that went on for nearly a hundred years (Lenk 1974: 206ff.).

In olden times, people often paid a straightforward tax to cover their wood requirements, or else they bought standing wood and cut it down themselves. The introduction of pricing by quantity then made two important changes necessary: the wood had to be cut down by men working for the forest administration, and it had to be measured. The first decrees to this effect date back to the sixteenth century (Endres 1888: 74), but it was only around the turn of the nineteenth that it became normal for firewood to be measured and for the purchaser to be prevented from doing his own felling. When it was cut and processed by hewers working under official supervision, it could be immediately packed in *Klafter* measures (see below), and 'many pieces of wood that would otherwise end up in fires [could] be used as lumber instead' (Krünitz 1789: 769).

Commercialization led to arguments over measurement, from very early on in the English case. 'It is obvious that timber merchants and their customers must, from medieval times, have been much preoccupied with the problems of both trees and squared timbers.' At a time when tree species and their various uses were by no means as standardized as in the modern age, measurement was a much more complicated business. John Evelyn wrote in *Sylva*:

> Every person who can measure timber thinks himself qualified to value standing trees; but such men are often deceived in their estimates. It is the perfect knowledge of the application of the different shaped trees that enables a man to be correct in his valuation. A foot of wood may be of little value to one trade, but of great value to another. This is the grand secret which enriches the purchasers of standing timber. (Latham 1957: 33, 38)

As timber became scarcer and more valuable, the task of measuring it grew in importance. In Frankfurt, where it was originally women's work, it was decided in 1623 that 'female persons who are in future caught measuring wood [shall be] taken to the madhouse' (Schnapper-Arndt 1915: 177). By the 1800s, the most common firewood measure was the *Klafter*, originally a measure of length, which denoted the span of a man's outstretched arms; it also served as a surface measure for a man's height (figure 3.7). As an exact spatial measure, it came into frequent use only in the nineteenth century. According to how scarce wood was at the time, the pieces were quite simply cut longer or shorter; older measures in klafters are therefore often not reliable. When an exact cubic klafter was established (approximately 3 m³), it brought considerable disadvantages for the purchaser of wood, who often bristled against it. The ironworks administration in the Ore Mountain region in Styria protested in 1816 that, whereas it had formerly paid an 'insignificant flat-rate tax' for wood in church-owned property, the price had, believe it or not, risen 450-fold since the tax began to be calculated in cubic klafters (Radkau 1986a).

Setting the economically correct price for wood remained an unsolved puzzle for forest science, which even in modern times 'failed to determine the cost price of various species and types of wood' (Weck and Wiebecke 1961: 171). Forestry was required to adopt a cost–benefit approach, but without proper clarification of the input data.

Figure 3.7: Measuring wood in 'klafters' with a special stick. Logs are being drifted on the river in the background. At the top right is a piece of a rake for capturing logs. From *Der Vollkommene teutsche Jäger* by J. F. von Flemming, one-time lieutenant-colonel in the service of Augustus II of Saxony (1719–24).

'Freedom' in the forest: private property and 'wood crimes'

Economic liberalism, which shaped public opinion and government policy from the late eighteenth century on, was based on the conviction that people develop maximum energies leading to the common good only when they acted in their own personal interest. According to this logic, it was fundamentally wrong to expect good forest management to result from state ordinance and supervision: indeed, these destroyed 'the natural foundation of forestry, which is a crisp delight in business activity shot through with a consciousness of ownership' (Bernhardt [1872–5] 1966: 2/59). 'Free property and free culture are the two powerful magic words which, like an electric shock, can transform any country from an impoverished wasteland into paradise.' This profession of faith comes from the pen of Joseph von Hazzi (1804: 144), the Bavarian reformer of forestry and agriculture.

The practical implications of this creed were various. 'Free property' certainly meant abolition of the 'servitudes', the traditional use rights of individuals other than the landowner, whom Pfeil (1816: 44) compared to 'an army of vultures pecking at the marrow of the forest'. For many poor peasants and cottagers, however, such rights were essential to survival, whereas exclusive property rights locked them out of the forest (Grewe 2004). 'Free property' could mean the carving up of common woodland and the abolition of the communes.

183

Many reformers got worked up about the dilapidation of the commons and equated common woodland with 'common whores' (Bauer 1925: 87). But it might also happen that a forest was made the property of a whole commune or even of the state.

Hazzi's talk of 'free property' was also a dig against the state administration and the landowning nobility. His liberal creed conflicted with state control of private forest and with hunting rights in forest that was not the ruler's private possession. In cases where the state owned large areas of forest, 'free property' was also advantageous to the state administration. Depending on local conditions, more weight attached to one or another aspect of liberalization, and various alliances of interests took shape behind the demand for unrestricted property.

The enforcement of full property rights in the forest, to the exclusion of other users, was a process whose origins stretched back centuries before the age of liberalism. It was already a factor in the Peasants' War of 1525; and one has the impression that it was later considered too hot to handle and left to lie dormant. When farmers opposed curbs on their customary forest rights, they had a definite chance of success in the courts; they might also resist with force if their right to gather wood was taken away on the pretext of 'rising prices'. From time to time, the planting of conifers was a way of getting round the old 'servitudes': pig-fattening and the gathering of forest litter were not possible in coniferous forest, and the conditions were worse for pasturing.

Throughout the eighteenth century, the statelet of Wied-Neuwied was the scene of violent conflicts between landowners and farmers. Things took an unexpected turn in 1791, when the new government of Prince Friedrich Karl accepted an accord that gave the farmers roughly two-thirds of the forest. It came under fire from state officials and manufacturers, however, who saw it as a threat to their wood purchases: it was no coincidence that Germany's largest furniture factory (Roentgen) and largest plate mill (Remy) were both situated in Wied-Neuwied. In 1792, the anti-farmer alliance went straight to the imperial court and secured the prince's abdication on grounds of mental illness (Troßbach 1985: 29ff.).

These events show that the farmers' traditional user rights were opposed not only by rulers and landowners, but also by the rising industrial bourgeoisie and the state bureaucracy. Yet an agreement was often possible if some woodland property was allocated to them, or if they received financial compensation for loss of their customary rights. In the eighteenth century, it was sometimes even fellow commune members who sought to divide up the common woodland and to turn it into private property, so that they could deal in timber unhindered and keep the growing numbers of small farmers and landless out of the forest.

The state itself exerted pressure for the dividing up of land – from 1769 in Prussia, a generation later in Bavaria. In many areas the landowning nobility were the great beneficiaries; the lower orders mostly came out of it empty-handed. 'Thus, the divisions represented a class struggle of the large proprietors against small farmers and those even further down the ladder' (Mager 1982: 467).

When woodland became free property, it could be bought and sold. Later, many stories did the rounds in villages about how farmers or whole communes had been cheated of their woodland for a derisory sum. Nor was it uncommon for forest to be cleared and converted into arable land. Foresters who had initially urged the division of common woodland as a way of improving forestry often had their hopes dashed. Scepticism about economic liberalism became vocal, and the old communes were sometimes romanticized. People recalled how the communal wood courts (*Holthinge*) had once severely punished thieves, whereas the courts of their own time showed little inclination to do the same (Pfeil 1839: 188). But, when farmers owned a piece of woodland and discovered that it could be a source of profit, they sometimes defended it more brutally than the police had ever been able to do. In Ravensberg, for instance, where local farmers obtained rich pickings from wood, lynchings of wood thieves were reported around the year 1800 (Mooser 1984).

Complaints about wood thieves were already recorded in the eighteenth century. But it would seem that the 'thieves' in question – who, from their own point of view, were simply asserting age-old rights – observed certain rules of the game, such as leaving construction timber and ready-split logs untouched, and that up to a point the courts turned a blind eye to pilfering. There was a saying that 'no gallows has been built for a wood thief' (Krünitz 1789: 684), or, in Russia, that 'for timber, not even a parson is a thief' (Champion [1938] 1963: 270). If God had created the forest, it belonged to all human beings.

We find repeated references to the fact that 'wood theft' was an essential aspect of the timber trade and that the prohibition of such practices had interfered with the wood supply of whole towns. Since 'wood crimes are one of the sources of food', 'the forest office' ought to 'proceed with caution' (Jung [1788] 1970: 336). In 1816 a Saxon official wrote of the Ore Mountains: 'Higher timber prices force

Zur Erinnerung an den 9ten März 1848.

Figure 3.8: March by Nuremberg residents with forest entitlements outside the Sebadli Forest Office in 1848. The revolutionary mood of the time encouraged such protests against the curbing of age-old rights to use forest litter (Sperber 1968: 94). The marchers evidently included some venerable citizens who had long had a tense relationship with forestry officials. Those with forest rights were unwilling to respect the various byelaws, while forestry officials were angered by the 'almost inborn pilfering of wood by members of the forest cooperative' (Radkau 1986a: 12).

the common man here into wood theft, or so stunt his wretched life that, as one often sees in small mountain towns and factory villages, four and more families have to live together in one heated room' (Staatsarchiv Dresden). In the middle of the nineteenth century, the memory of times 'when wood could be had for next to nothing' remained alive in the population (figure 3.8) (Roscher 1854: 14).

The disputes centred not only on firewood but also on the use of forest litter. Since women often performed the work of collecting both, they were especially prominent in defending the associated rights in many regions. In 1723 women descended on forestry officials near Laasphe who had denied them access to leaf mould (Troßbach 1985: 69f.), and in France women were in the van of woodland disturbances

186

in the first half of the nineteenth century (Perrot 1981: 84). In the 1860s poor farmers in southern Germany asserted that 'forest litter' was 'the centre around which our whole economy turns'. 'Rather no bread on the table than no straw in the stall, we say. If the foresters take this away from us we shall have to sell our only cow, which is our source of food and fertilizer' (Nördlinger 1869: 59).

In the nineteenth century, however, with the help of science, faith in progress and a strong police force, the forest administration was better able to conduct its fight against 'servitudes' and 'sidelines'. Whereas much earlier ordinance never went further than the paper on which it was written, enforcement now began to be taken seriously. It is true that the early modern feudal-absolutist state had been all-powerful ideologically, but its lack of effective organization had left a lot of room for local autonomy. The modern state, on the other hand, was liberal in its ideology but practised a degree of centralism of which earlier rulers could only dream. These new conditions also gave a new character to forest policy.

In 1821 a general law on wood theft was enacted in Prussia, and the government subsequently concluded agreements with nearly all neighbouring states for the joint prosecution of 'forest criminals' (Bernhardt [1872–5] 1966: 3/142ff.). The courts were soon inundated with wood-related cases. In many areas, a considerable part of the population became 'delinquents': in Prussia in 1850 there were approximately 35,000 cases of 'common theft' but 265,000 of 'wood theft' (Mooser 1984: 43). If we are to believe Annette von Droste-Hülshoff's much-read novella *The Jew's Beech* (1842), this created an abyss of contempt for the law. But it also reflects the way of thinking of the landed nobility, which demonized 'forest criminals' and used the law to defend its forest property in full against encroachment by poor farmers. Heinrich Hansjakob, one of the most popular novelists of life in the Black Forest, wrote in 1897:

I do not know who first came up with those ugly words 'forest crime' [*Forstfrevel*] and 'forest criminal' [*Forstfrevler*]. It was a hard man who made it so that the fetching of brushwood and firewood – which is what the poor do to warm themselves and to cook their frugal meal – appeared a crime. But the word is still thriving in the courts. (Hansjakob [1897] 1984: 55)

This was social criticism in the spirit of the old moral economy!

The unremitting conflict in the early nineteenth century between a modernized forest administration and large parts of the population bears the clear hallmarks of a social crisis. 'In the period from 1815 to 1848, wood thefts chipped away at the image of the "well-policed" Prussian state' (Blasius 1978: 58). The debates in the Rhineland parliament about the wood theft law gave the 24-year-old Karl Marx his first impetus to grapple with economics and the whole problem of the bourgeois concept of property; he fulminated that wood had become the 'Rhinelanders' fetish' and was more important than human beings to the modern state (Marx 1975: 262).

The situation was contradictory, however, since many farmers too were lusting after full property rights. In the decades before 1848 the nobility mounted one last defence of its hunting rights, 'with incomparable energy' (Reif 1979: 196); modern property law was the farmer's best weapon against this worst of all irritations. As before in 1525, farmers began hunting down the despised game in the forest and took out firewood and litter in huge quantities, until the Prussian king had no option but to pass an amnesty decree for forest crimes. Complaints about 'destruction of the forest' by 'underlings' reached a final climax, but in fact the reduction of game stocks in 1848 gave the German forest the luckiest break it had had in a long time.

Although forest conflict contributed so much to the revolutionary mood in the run up to 1848, the forest was not a major issue in the bourgeois revolution itself. However much the rising bourgeoisie felt for the hungry rural poor, it had no sympathy for 'forest criminals' and stood at the forefront of those fighting for 'freedom of property'. Farmers who enjoyed full ownership of their land as a result of emancipation also ardently defended the right to dispose freely of private property.

In the forest, this 'freedom' meant that the landowner had every power to bar town-dwellers from access, and so the bourgeois mood on forest issues began to waver. It was a time when the forest was becoming the favourite recreational area for the German bourgeoisie – a refuge from the noise and smoke of the industrial age. This change of mood, combined with a sceptical attitude to liberalism, was given striking early expression in 1854 by Wilhelm Heinrich Riehl, who saw free access to the forest and the remnants of cooperative use as one of the most valuable German traditions. The forest was for him a free space that German society could not do without: 'Lay the axe to the forest and you demolish civil society as historically constituted' (Riehl [1934] 1990: 49). Unlike England and other countries, Germany was embracing the view that everyone had a right to enter the forest for recreational purposes. The economic consequences of bourgeois society clashed with nostalgia for the forest as a living space; it is a tension that is still with us today.

Foresters and woodcutters: forest labour turns professional

That a forester should be knowledgeable about forest management has not always been self-evident; in former times many were first and foremost hunters. The roots of the ruler's hold on the forest varied from region to region, and might include hunting, the mining and metal industry, the finance and domains department, rafting and the timber trade. This variation was reflected in the early forest authorities. Only in the seventeenth to eighteenth century did they develop into a system with a clear hierarchy. Often it was the chief huntsman who stood at the top, since hunting had greater prestige than any other forest activity in courtly society. The forester may have had to be 'well versed in wood' (*holzgerecht*), but he was mainly expected to be 'well versed in deer' (*hirschgerecht*) – all the more so in the case of top forestry officials.

According to an imperial directive issued in 1701, only hunters were entitled to wear the green costume (Hafner 1983: 231); they bore weapons and therefore, in the eyes of the lower orders of society, had the emblems of a free nobleman. For many princes and nobles, hunting was the epitome of *joie de vivre*, a world to itself with its own special aura; the jargon of the hunt had something of a 'secret language', while the terms for forest labour were merely farmer's talk (Kehr 1964: 224). Well into the nineteenth century, the top jobs in forestry were with rare exceptions reserved for members of the nobility.

But the further one went down the hierarchy, the less reputable the milieu became. Forestry jobs tended to be given to people who, for one reason or another, had to be found something, or anyway got out of the way; a typical example would be a subordinate who deigned to marry the former mistress of a superior who was causing difficulties at court (Endres 1888: 95). By contrast, Friedrich II of Prussia established a close link between forestry and military service: members of his *Feldjägerkorps* – a kind of military police, which survived until 1919 – could claim a position in the forestry department after their retirement from the army.

Forestry officials were an irksome breed in the eyes of many townsmen and farmers, and their position – a dream job for later Germans – became all the more unpopular the more high-handedly they behaved. 'At the end of the eighteenth century, no state institution was more detested than the forest police, no post held in such contempt by the public as those of lower forest and hunt officials' (Endres 1905: 214).

The norms of society changed in the second half of the eighteenth century. A preference for hunting was ridiculed as 'canine philosophy'

(Logau, cited in Endres 1888: 89); 'economics' became the buzzword of the time. Even docile government economists spoke harsh words about the princely passion for hunting and denounced the damage that game did to agriculture (see box 3.1). Hunting also interfered with business, since foresters 'well versed in deer' banned the clearing of forest paths so that game would not be disturbed by the sound of falling trees. Friedrich II and Empress Maria Theresa – the two most powerful rulers in the Germanic world of that time – were enlightened opponents of hunting and provided cover for those working to curtail it. The forester well versed in deer would give way to one well versed in wood: a different human type, a cool-headed calculator.

Yet Carl Maria von Weber's *Der Freischütz*, which turned the forester into an operatic hero, and whose huge success did more than all songs and stories combined to popularize a German romanticism of the forest, still assumed as a matter of course that prospective foresters should be skilled in armed security and shooting. This was precisely the type of forester that the reformers wanted to do away with! In the end, however, they have still not achieved their goal; many foresters today remain at heart more 'versed in deer' and loathe those for whom the forest is more important than game and the damage done by wild animals is a scandal.

Friedrich II was deeply distrustful of his foresters and treated their reports of success as so many lies. 'I know what those in the forestry service get up to. They make some effort on the paths they know I will travel on, and there you can find some trees for a few hundred paces, but then all is stripped bare and nothing is being done about it' (Gleitsmann 1985c: 490). Senior officials who saw the forest only from the 'chief forester's route' were similarly duped by their subordinates (Mager 1960: 1/178). Traditionally, silviculture was not one of the forester's responsibilities; rather, forest ordinance urged local farmers to plant oaks and beeches, much as commune directives had done in the past; sometimes the issuing of a marriage licence would depend on whether the work had been carried out. But such means did not achieve the ends of the new forestry. A far-reaching change was necessary in the forester's job description.

Whereas, in the past, foresters had sometimes been paid less than labourers, they gained skilled status in the late eighteenth century, and 'the raising of trees' became a respected profession sometimes held up as a model for the newly emerging science of pedagogy, the 'raising of children'. Beginning in northern Germany, a whole wave of establishments was founded to educate the new-style forester, upright and correct, observant of the letter of the law, equipped with theoretical

190

Box 3.1

Wer bist du, Fürst? daß über mich
Herrollen frei dein Wagenrad,
Dein Roß mich stampfen darf?
Wer bist du, Fürst? daß in mein Fleisch
Dein Freund, dein Jagdhund, ungebläut
Darf Klau' und Rachen haun?
Wer bist du? daß durch Saat und Forst
Das Hurra deiner Jagd mich treibt,
Entatmet wie das Wild?

Der Bauer an seinen Fürsten (1773)

Who are you, prince, that over me
Your waggon-wheel can freely roll
And your steed freely trample?
Who are you, prince, that into my flesh
Your friend the hunting-dog can sink
Its claws and teeth unpunished?
Who are you, that through field and wood
The hurrah of your chase drives me
Panting like the game?

* * * * * * * * * * *

Ihr Jäger nehmt nun eure Hunde,
Und heult mit ihnn aus Herzens-Grunde,
Die Wälder sind nun alle leer,
Ihr habt nun gar kein Wildpret mehr,
Wie wollt ihr nun zur Jagd gelangen,
Ihr müßt den Jungfern die Flöhe fangen,
Da, da gefällt euch stets die Jagd,
Nach der Besoldung ihr nicht fragt.

Trost-Schrift an die sächsische Jägerey (1790)

Hunters, take now your hounds
And howl with them from the heart,
The forests are all empty,
You have no more game left.
When now you would a-hunting go,
'Tis a maiden's fleas you must catch,
Since such hunting is still your fancy,
Do not ask what your reward will be.

Anti-hunting verses: the first by the *Sturm und Drang* poet Gottfried August Bürger, the second from a satirical poem on princely hunters written at the time of the Saxon peasants' revolt in 1790, when the hated game were driven from the forest.

knowledge, who saw it as his task to develop the maximum wood yield. The sharp break with the traditional type of forester led to tensions within the profession whose fall-out is still present today.

Chief Forester Heinrich Calaminus, who earned the title 'despot' for his attempts to apply strict economics in the Sauerland forests towards the end of the eighteenth century, mocked that his predecessors had run 'a wretched forest economy, since what was done in a year was not even enough to wear out a forester's shoes' (Selter 1995: 71, 214). Eduard Zaminer, the chief forester of Kronstadt (Braşov) in Transylvania, at the southeastern edges of the empire, described his predecessors as 'voracious monsters', who, in the grip of a perverse greed, had lined their own pockets by egging local people on to 'feverish' or 'pest-like' destruction of the forest (Zaminer 1891: 77, 257). On his own watch, wood was exported to Romania on a large scale: it was serious business, not criminal 'desecration'.

Pre-modern traditions did not die out. In his novel of life in the Black Forest, *Waldleute* (1897), Heinrich Hansjakob contrasted the old forester from Teufelstein – a splendid man with a heart and experience of life – with colourless modern office-workers. Around 1920 in Württemberg, it came to a so-called foresters' war against academically trained forestry officials (Rubner 1985: 17). And still today people sometimes choose a forest career more out of a love for hunting than a penchant for forestry. Unofficially, hunting has retained a high prestige; a conference in Munich in 1975 thought it a 'scandal in our country' that quantity was being placed above quality in relation to game stocks (Weibecke 1975: 41).

Until the eighteenth century, and even later in a region such as Mecklenburg, corruption was endemic in forestry as well as other civil service departments; the pay was low, and officials depended on the 'fees' they charged for authorizing various practices. Many prohibitions in the forest ordinance merely allowed foresters to line their own pockets by turning a blind eye to a forbidden practice.

The modern bureaucratic state that took shape in Central and Western Europe in the 1800s radically altered this picture. The new forester, living on his civil service salary, exercised effective control over woodcutting, especially as the task was now performed not by local farmers but by wage-labourers in the employ of the forestry department. German foresters made a powerful impression on one of the most knowledgeable British writers on Bismarckian Germany: they were 'a very different type of person from the English game-keeper, whom we are expected to "tip" when invited to English country-houses.' 'Forest culture [in the German Reich] is at the same time a means of rearing one of the hardiest and most useful elements of the population.' Trained in the use of firearms, the many thousands of German foresters 'form the main contingent of the sharp-shooters of the German army' (Whitman 1912: 72f.).

Bernhard Danckelmann, a leading Prussian forester in the Bismarck period, who, though found unfit for military service, used to pose for photos as a full-bearded warrior type, would mock foresters who went out with an umbrella instead of a gun (Milnik and Danckelmann 1999). The proud combination of forester and soldier, underlined by the wearing of a uniform, marked the social position of this profession until 1945.

Forestry workers

Technically speaking, the cutting and carrying of wood in mountainous areas was more difficult than many a skilled craft, especially when workers had to ensure that as little as possible was lost along the way. One need only think of the giant trees in the forests of North America, where lumberjacks swung their axes to head height and brought a tree crashing down onto a stake driven into the ground. To perform this art, they had to grow up with the work and to have muscles perfectly attuned to it. There is an intelligence of the body as well as of the mind.

'The woodcutter needs a sharp mind more than physical strength', Homer already knew (*Iliad* 23: 315). It was because of their position on the periphery that forestry workers counted as unskilled and were unable to organize in guilds. Before the nineteenth century, they constituted a distinct trade (*Holzerschaft*), mainly in iron- and saltworks, which consumed large quantities of wood. Above all in remote mountainous regions, where transport was difficult and farmers thin on the ground, forestry workers were left to their own devices and had to show real ability in coping with many different tasks. The most difficult and dangerous part was not the tree-felling itself but the transportation of the wood afterwards (Waß 1985: 137).

Precisely because transport was so expensive, it was advantageous to have as much of the preparation as possible done in the forest: not only disengaging the wood and stripping the bark, but also making it the right length and cutting it into boards or logs. Attention also had to be paid to the intended final use: there was often a division of labour for lumber, construction timber, firewood and charcoal (Schwappach 1886–8: 1/474). Since the woodcutting affected the quality of construction timber, in particular, carpenters often lent a hand themselves. A *Manual of Rafting* published in 1825 notes: 'It is very important to have competent men, especially for the felling of Dutch wood. An unskilled worker can inflict damage both on the forest and on the entrepreneur' (Keweloh 1985: 59). Oak and other expensive wood did not allow of any waste: the Dutch traders of the early nineteenth century, who were eager to use 'every bit of wood up to the top of the trunk', made sure that 'experienced forest carpenters' were hired (Müller 1837: 59).

When the aim was to rationalize the whole timber trade, it made sense to begin in the forest. In the second half of the eighteenth century, the natural scientist and inspector of the French fleet Duhamel du Monceau – again the navy's needs at the origin of things! – published epoch-making treatises on the 'physics of trees', tree-planting, woodcutting, transport and charcoal-burning. In his work on woodcutting, which also covered the uses of wood, he recognized that forestry workers had been his first teachers (Bernhardt [1872–5] 1966: 2/143). Woodcutters were the people who knew the forest inside out in former times, and so they were also needed for the work of assessing wood stocks and evaluating them prior to purchase. Krünitz (1789: 768) too asserted that 'old and experienced woodcutters [were] often much more skilled' at these things. Woodcutters and their wives therefore sometimes acted as timber brokers with a good head for business. A directive adopted by the Frankfurt council in 1793 tried to put a stop to this 'piece of nonsense'. But Pfeil, going his own way as ever, advised foresters to listen to forestry workers in matters relating to the purchase of wood (Hasel 1982: 37f.). Success did not lie merely with a top-down 'scientization' of forestry.

Mountain loggers were far more than simple woodcutters: they also had to know how to build wood chutes (figure 3.9) and slides and weirs for the rafting of timber. The riskiest job, which left its mark on the men and boosted their self-confidence, was the sledging of heavy logs down to the valley in winter (figure 3.10). In the Alps, according to Wessely (1853: 1/459), 'lumber and charcoal workers' were 'kings on the dance floor and with the lasses'; they 'set the tone at festivities, coming up with the songs that worked best and well-timed flashes of wit'. The song 'We are the merry woodchopper boys', set to music by the Viennese 'march king' Josef Franz Wagner in 1900

Figure 3.9: An old wood chute in the Eng, Austria. A watchman's hut is visible at the back left, typically placed at a bend, where logjams could be dealt with before too much timber piled up. The chutes were moistened with water to make the wood pass more smoothly. Logs kept moving even at tight corners on ice-covered chutes, and so for Wessely (1853: 406) these were 'the best of all chutes'. The wood shot 'fleet as an arrow' to the valley below (Hauser 1972: 233), where a narrowing of the chute slowed it down. 'Chute-building is the mountain woodcutter's point of honour'; a lot of experience was needed to master the task.

and continually revised up to the 'Holzhacker Twist', is still popular today at parties in the Alps.

The lumberjacks of the American West were more cut off from villages and local festivities, but they had much more meat and apple pie on their plates than their counterparts had in the Alps (Horn 1943: 75). In the American forests, where the trees towered higher and the rivers flowed more wildly, the 'riverman' who rode his logs like a cowboy on his horse became even more of a legendary hero than the lumberjack (Pike 1984: 344). The transportation of wood was quite an adventure in the Alps too. But, in terms of material conditions, the lives of Alpine forestry workers were wretched and not always merry. A traveller in 1804 who saw their barrack-like quarters in one lonely region thought them 'a sad dwelling for even sadder men' (Sandgruber 1982a: 344). Perhaps a sentimental, melancholy ballad

Figure 3.10: Log-sledging in the Austrian Alps, *c*.1900. Wessely (1853: 412) writes that sledging appeared 'especially in modern times', when high timber prices made it desirable to avoid spending large sums of money on wooden chutes. Sledgers used their arms as brake levers and steered with their legs. Accidents were a common occurrence.

like the Canadian 'The Jam on Garry's Rock' better conveys how they saw their lives: 'I'll sing you of a shanty boy, so noble, true and brave / Who broke the jam on Garry's Rock and filled a watery grave' (Latham 1957: 116). The average life expectancy of American lumberjacks was less than ten years from the time they started their job.

Woodcutting, which was also performed by farmers as a sideline, counted not as a trade but as unskilled labour. But people would have accepted that it should be valued more highly and, as far as possible, perfected, in order to make optimum use of forest resources. Krünitz (1789: 594) recommended honouring woodcutters as 'lead players in the forest economy' and establishing woodcutters' guilds. Forest work could generate its own craft pride and even be an inspiration for forest science. Experienced woodcutters knew their forest much better than foresters straight out of college. The great Prussian forest reformer Georg Ludwig Hartig admits as much in his memoirs, although his rules for the forest later came to epitomize a rigidly schematic approach. Writing of his early years in Hesse, he says that he once instructed his woodcutters to carry away a thirty- to forty-year-old beechwood as if it was coppice. This caused a great stir among the whole 'company of woodcutters': they thought it a sin and a scandal 'that such a young beechwood should be butchered almost before it could stand on its feet'.

As we see, woodcutters had their own ethos and a special way of loving the forest. Hartig eventually agreed that only the trees that were growing poorly should be cut down – a compromise that founded the practice of 'thinning', which 'all [his] woodcutters took a great liking to' (Radkau 2006: 96). They too had a sense of professional honour. Even in the twentieth century, we learn, 'woodcutters set fire to a tree trunk on which a sawing job had been thoroughly botched, in order to erase the traces of the mishap and to avoid ridicule from colleagues' (Steinlin 1970: 335). But before 1900 woodcutters had often been occasional or itinerant workers; in the nineteenth century it was not the forestry worker but the forest warden who became 'professionalized', and therefore promoted to the status of a skilled trade.

The social position of forestry workers could be highly varied. In mountainous regions, the masters had to make many concessions to woodcutters, who in the fourteenth century, for example, had the right at the Hall saltworks to impound wood in the case of late payment of wages (Oberrauch 1952: 40). Around the year 1500 Kaiser Maximilian put them on the same level as miners; for mining depended on inputs of wood, and many men active in it doubled as forestry workers. The great majority of forestry workers, however, probably came from the sub-farmer strata of the population who were unable to live from agriculture alone.

Winter was the traditional time for woodcutting. The quality of construction timber, in particular, crucially depended on felling trees when the flow of sap was at a halt and pests were unable to survive. But the fuel value of firewood was also higher if it was cut in winter. Forestry work was therefore suited as a sideline for farmers at a time of the year when the fields lay dormant.

This picture changed in the age of agrarian reforms and stall-feeding; fetching wood did not fit into the new system. One reformer taught that 'farmers with a head for business' should not engage in such activity, since it ruined their horses and oxen; only those who 'hate work in the fields, like to laze around in taverns ... and are very close to mischief' would get involved in it (Mayer [1773] 1980: 130). The separation between agriculture and forestry was one reason why the latter became an independent profession even in non-mountainous regions. At the same time, forestry workers became subject to closer supervision; the story of how the saw was imposed is an indication of how tight the control could be.

Resistance to the saw

At first sight, the saw looks like a tool whose purpose could scarcely be clearer. It was known since antiquity in the carpenter's trade, but only in the nineteenth century did it become commonly used everywhere for woodcutting, a full four hundred years after it was first introduced into forestry work. It was 'the technological revolution, the essential novelty in woodwork' (Koller 1970: 303). Its rejection by woodcutters was the main factor holding it back for centuries – a refractoriness that from a distance seems rather narrow-minded.

In 1752 Empress Maria Theresa ordered that trees should not be felled 'with axes, according to the pernicious old customs, but sawn off close to the roots', since axe blows led to too much waste (figure 3.11). Sawing could reduce waste by 20 per cent for hardwood and 15 per cent for soft wood. Moreover, fine sawdust was a better fertilizer than thick wood chips for the forest floor (Koller 1975: 27).

Saving wood – often time as well – is the leitmotif of directives for the introduction of saws. In some cases, compliance was rewarded with financial benefits. Yet, around the turn of the nineteenth century, saws were still little used in Alpine forests. In the eighteenth century only thieves preferred them, because they could not be heard as far away as axes (Corvol 1984: 96ff.). Wood theft with a saw was therefore punished more severely than wood theft with an axe (Hafner 1983: 189).

Volume 24 of Johann Georg Krünitz's *Oeconomische Encyclopädie*, which appeared in 1789, contains an entry on wood that runs to no fewer than five hundred pages and reveals what an important topic it had become in those days. According to Krünitz, use of the saw in woodcutting was 'beneficial and necessary to the general well-being of the state' and should therefore be made compulsory under 'the law of the land'; 'no attention should be paid to the supposed complaints of any subjects'. Otherwise, any attempt to break woodcutters from their 'old habits' was futile and ran the risk of embroiling one in court cases that one might well lose.

The martyr Simon, who according to legend was sawed to death, featured in eighteenth-century Austrian churches as the patron saint of woodcutters. Did they choose him themselves? As late as 1834, forestry workers wished 'a pain in the neck' on officials who tried to force the saw on them, since in their view it was 'an instrument

Figure 3.11: Sawing a tree in Styria, from instructions written by hand in 1821 on 'the use of wood saws in felling and slicing trees'. The kneeling posture, designed to raise productivity, is quite different from that used in wielding an axe. The author, forester Alois Josef Kofler, writes in the introduction that expenditure on saws is 'a thousand times worthwhile' because of the higher timber yield and 'lower wages'.

fit only for carpenters and cabinetmakers that caused them unnecessary toil and trouble' (Killian 1982: 119). Workers accustomed to
the lean axe felt contempt for the lumpish saw, describing it as a
'tyrant's blade' or 'martyr's blade' (Matzek 1992: 52). Even woodcutters in the American West, untouched by European traditions,
still preferred the axe well into the nineteenth century, since they
could not saw through the giant trees there with the strength of
their arm alone. People in the United States also discovered that the
age-old and seemingly so simple axe, which had come to symbolize
the pioneering spirit, was susceptible of many improvements: 'The
American ax evolved from European models into an elegant instrument, so well balanced and finely designed that with it a man could
fell three times as many trees in the same time as with its English
counterpart' (Hindle 1975: 6). The wood waste produced by axes
was a matter of little or no concern in nineteenth-century America.
Not without reason did railwaymen consider that sleepers were
more resilient if made with chopped rather than sawn wood (Fogel
1964: 137).

Was it just force of habit that made woodcutters so stubborn? On
closer inspection, their seemingly irrational opposition proves to be
well founded, since the economies gained from sawing appeared only
if trees were sawn at the lowest possible point. Moreover, the new
kneeling posture meant that novices 'complained of painful sensitivity in their backs and hands' (Killian 1982: 122); the work no longer
had the even, body-friendly rhythm of axe blows. The economist Karl
Bücher recalled just how important it had been for the men's joy in
work that they could sing along to the rhythm of their axe. Only later,
when cast steel blades were developed with a curved line of teeth, did
sawing acquire 'more of a rocking movement that left workers feeling
less tired' (Großmann 1916: 28f.).

As if all this were not enough, the sawing down of trees often took
longer than chipping away at them with an axe; a lot of practical
experience and technical improvement was necessary before it had a
conspicuous time-saving effect. Poor performance in the early days of
sawing was at the forestry worker's expense, while later productivity
increases led to a lowering of piece rates (Killian 1982: 133).

Woodcutters using saws had to work in pairs and to interact with
each other. Tool maintenance also took longer than with an axe, since
it was necessary to spend at least an hour a day keeping a saw sharp.
Even more time-consuming was the work of making a new saw sharp
enough for use or repairing one that had become bent from use. A
special 'saw adjuster' was needed for this, and they were not so easy

to come by in the forest. The saw thus made the woodcutter markedly less autonomous.

Finally, a saw cost roughly six times more than an axe to purchase. As government officials admitted, forest sawing was too expensive for the 'common man' around the turn of the nineteenth century. If a forestry worker was provided with a saw by the person who hired him, it meant that he was no longer in possession of his means of production; he fell to the position of a mere wage-labourer, whereas he had previously had some of the hallmarks of an independent craftsman. The introduction of saws only really accelerated when the foundry masters in the Styrian Ore Mountain region began to distribute them to workers free of charge in 1802.

Saws were used much earlier for cutting up wood than for felling trees; the process was already mechanized by sawmills in the Middle Ages. Here began the distinctive work culture of carpenters, very different from that of woodcutters. Yet even in the twentieth century axes were still preferred to saws for working on such things as load-bearing beams, ship's planks, barrel staves and wheel spokes – whenever the wood had to be especially watertight and solid. For the fibrous structure of wood that ensured these properties was better preserved under the axe than under the saw. Hermann Phleps (1928: 75), a modern classic in the art of woodwork, called the saw the 'most dreadful of tools', in whose growing popularity we could see how the 'attachment to wood' had begun to unravel.

The history of the saw shows that the widespread implementation of a new technique may be much more significant than its original invention (about which we know nothing in this case). Often it is unclear whether it represents 'progress' for the people in the front line, since it may be more difficult than before for them to determine the rhythm at which they work; the innovation may make them more dependent and complicate the task of maintaining their tool in working condition.

The rise of sawmills

When we consider how tenaciously woodcutters fought against the saw in the nineteenth century, it may seem surprising that not only saws but even water-powered sawmills were already in use in the late Middle Ages. The first mills were recorded in southern Germany, in the early years of the fourteenth century. The mentions become more frequent after 1500, there being a clear link between the spread of sawmills and the first great boom of the timber trade. The sawmill created an incentive to exploit the forest more intensively, not only on the part of nearby iron- and saltworks, but also for distant consumers of lumber and construction timber. Mass production of boards and beams gave new scope for woodwork and the construction of half-timbered houses. Sawmills encouraged the spread of joinery as a specialized trade, no longer burdened with the hard labour of sawing.

In the eighteenth century, however, mills had not yet completely replaced sawing by hand. English workers fought against their introduction, because they made foreign hardwood (which was difficult to saw) cheaper than indigenous woods (Hammersley 1957: 151). Until the nineteenth century, however, the simple farm sawmills of southwestern Germany were suitable only for coniferous wood, not for the harder oak. The literature rarely refers to the dangers of early sawmills, but Bryan Latham, a scion of hardwood traders who must know what he is talking about, tells us: 'The early sawmilling machinery must have been very, very dangerous: practically no guards were provided, and the mills were a mass of unprotected shafting and belting' (1957: 222). Moreover, they operated so slowly that sawyers often had a break of a quarter of an hour while the saw gates worked their way through a log (Horn 1943: 22).

Sawmills were often combined with grain mills (figure 3.12) and could be inserted into the traditional rural economy. In the eighteenth century, when the 'Dutch wood' trade encompassed large tracts of the Black Forest, many large farms there had a sawmill of their own; but 'sawing collectives' were also formed to carry out the work in common. It was advantageous to have the mill inside the forest, since cut wood was easier to transport. Many 'saw millers' were also active in the timber trade (Hellwag 1924: 302ff.).

The oldest and simplest type of sawmill was the 'knock saw' or 'drop saw', which used the same principle as a water-driven hammer. The 'wave tree' – the elongated axis of the mill wheel – had a number of projecting cams that forced the saw gate upward, so that the cutting action occurred as it fell back down. The characteristic loud knocking sound as cam struck gate was what gave this kind of saw its name, but it was also its main drawback. For it required thick blades, which produced large amounts of sawdust, and the vibrations could easily result in an uneven cut. The quality of the product in this early phase of mechanization was lower than in hand-sawing. Curved saws, which transferred the circular movement of the water wheel to the vertical plane of the saw gate, reduced the vibration effect. But, before the introduction of the transmission belt in the nineteenth

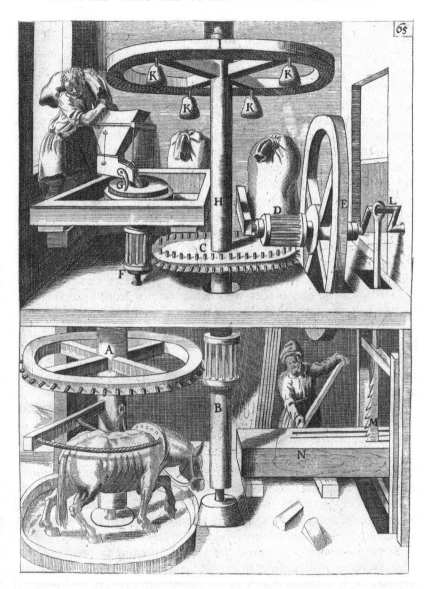

Figure 3.12: A sawmill around the year 1700. It is combined with a grain mill – quite a common practice at the time. The horse gin is a reminder that animal traction was one of the main 'energy sources' in pre-industrial times. The saw gate has only one blade, which is serrated in such a way that it can cut only if it is pointing downwards. The saw miller makes sure that the cutting is straight: it is still a long way from full mechanization.

century, the gear wheels (as long as they were made of wood) operated with a great deal of wear and friction loss.

It was fairly easy to build a sawmill; one traveller to the United States noted around the year 1810 that it was usually 'the first building to go up in the wilderness' (Perlin 2005: 335). But, even in preindustrial times, sawmills had a considerable technical potential for development. A water wheel could be used to activate the log-feeding conveyor and its retraction movement, although this did not mean full mechanization; the sawyer still had to be 'devilishly alert to ensure that the cutting was even' (Heller 1980: 71). It was also possible to increase the number of blades in the saw gate, so that a tree trunk could be sawn in one pass. This innovation was first introduced in Holland in the seventeenth century and was then adopted in the eighteenth by large Dutch timber dealers, as well as the Scandinavian countries and the Baltic lands (Åström 1975). At the same time, saw blades became thinner and less productive of waste, making it possible to boost productivity and to reduce expenditure on squaring.

So long as the saw blades were made of cast iron, however, they had to be constantly sharpened. Only the steel blades that became widely available through industrial mass production allowed the mill to be run more or less continuously, since they did not need to be sharpened so often. Advances in technique – especially non-stop rotation, circular sawing and band sawing – were closely bound up with improvements in steel quality. But even today, in a mill that processes tropical hardwood, the saw blades have to be changed every three hours!

These innovations had little resonance in the Black Forest, where they would have blown the farming economy apart. Village smithies could not produce finer saw blades; and 'Dutch' sawmills required considerable greater investment, improved transmission and the enlistment of specialists from outside the area. Where innovation did win through, it marked a change in production relations comparable to that effected by the 'commercial revolution' of the seventeenth and eighteenth centuries. For their part, in an attempt to dissuade supplier countries from developing sawmills of their own, the Dutch still imposed high customs duties in the nineteenth century on imported cut wood (Müller 1837: 249).

What sawmills can mean is apparent from nineteenth-century America, where they were the commonest industrial plant and were seen as the 'pioneering machine of civilization' (Hunter 1979: 16ff.). That would not have sounded right in early modern Europe, where manual labour was still cheap, but even there sawmills became the cornerstone of the timber trade in the nineteenth century. Although forestry departments tried to extend their control to the use of wood in the early 1800s, this goal was thwarted in the subsequent period of economic and technological development. There was a tendency for sawmills to take over the processing of raw wood traditionally done in the forester's stomping ground.

In the forests of North America, sawmills led to a qualitative leap in housing and the beginnings of a new kind of home décor. 'So wide was the difference in comfort and convenience between the pioneer's hand-hewn log-hut and the dwelling built from the sawmill's lumber . . ., that the first frame house in the community was remarked as often in local histories as the establishment of the first school, church or store' (Louis C. Hunter, in Hindle 1975: 176). The epochal nature of the shift rested not only on the fact that home décor was starting from scratch in those parts, but also on the synergy with another unprepossessing yet hugely important innovation: the industrial mass production of iron nails in the new era of great coke furnaces. In 1807 a machine was patented that turned out 60,000 nails a day (Giedion 1967) – an extreme of mass production unique at that time.

Nails had previously been taboo for European carpenters, whose art and pride had consisted in wooden joints. But houses built entirely of wood became too expensive in large parts of Europe, as well as conflicting with the new concern for solidity and the growth of urban fire regulations. Things were very different in North America: there wood was in abundance, but neither guild pressures nor municipal fire regulations were a problem. Houses were not built to last forever; what counted most was that they should be cheap and quick to put together, without any need for trained craftsmen. That was the American way: to produce houses like boxes, with wooden walls and beams hurriedly nailed to a frame. European carpenters would have thrown up their hands in horror at such 'balloon frames' – a scornful term that soon entered common parlance. A balloon-frame house could 'be erected more quickly by two men than the heavy timber frame by twenty'. It became the standard technique of mass housing construction in nineteenth-century America (Foley 1981: 152).

4 Wood Consumers: Economies in the Home and Outside

In the second half of the eighteenth century, 'saving wood' became a political and public issue like never before. The word 'to save' here underwent a change in meaning. It originally meant to lay something

205

up in good times to keep it intact for times of need, with the aim of ensuring that one's life could remain unchanged. 'Saving wood' meant managing with as little wood as possible for some activity and keeping as much as possible in the forest for the future.

In the eighteenth century, however, 'saving wood' took on yet another meaning: to use a certain amount of wood as efficiently as possible; or to secure as much forest as possible, creating the scope for a growth of production. Whereas saving in the old sense of keeping a household store had been a female virtue (Münch 1984), saving in the new, extended sense of improving efficiency was an art that belonged to the inventor and organizer.

This new attitude is evident in the reformers' anger over the 'system of ignorant thrift' in Frankfurt, which treated the city forest as a 'money box' and hesitated to cut old wood even when it was hindering the growth of young (Fellner 1895: 86); instead of preserving treasures and favouring ancient oaks, an efficient business should constantly provide for maximum growth in the forest.

The semantic shift originated in a general change of attitudes to business. As we have seen, economics (from the Greek *oikos* = house) was a matter of household management until the eighteenth century, when its principles were applied to the state and formed the basis of 'political economy'. The norms of domestic thrift were thus turned against extravagant governments that were landing countries in ever deeper debt. Especially after a military conflict – the Thirty Years' War, the French revolutionary wars – whole campaigns were waged for 'economies'. But the meaning this had at the level of the state was not the same as in the domestic household. It took on the 'meaning of clever planning and rational management' (Brunner 1949: 242); economics acquired active, dynamic features.

The disenchantment of fire: the economics of wood and time

The new rationality underlying the expanded sense of 'wood economies' also expressed itself in two key areas for thermal efficiency: fire and time.

Vannoccio Biringuccio's *Pirotechnia* (1540), which centres on fire and all the techniques associated with it, ends with a chapter on the fire of love. In fact, we are told, the book should have begun with it, since love is the hottest fire of all and there is a lot to say about its instruments. The author wanted to end on a genial note, of course, yet analogies between the fire of love and the smithy's furnace were not mere wordplay. People in prehistoric times already felt the fructifying power of fire. From antiquity right up to the eighteenth century, it was regarded as one of the four cosmic elements, itself a living thing or indeed the epitome of the vital force (Radkau 2001: 110ff.). Since fire could unite the divided and bring forth the new, it was readily believed to have an essential affinity with sexuality (Eliade 1978; Bachelard 1964). But a purifying power has been ascribed to fire from time immemorial, since it can also be used to cleanse substances of impurities (Frazer 1978: 848ff.).

Speculations about the nature of fire did not necessarily lead to false practical teachings. If it was assumed that fire had 'a furious, volatile spirit within it, which tended by nature towards flight, towards rising and flying' (Linstedt 1723: 6), the conclusion might be that furnaces should be built in such a way that the heat did not escape too quickly up the chimney. But in trades that used fire directly for the processing of their materials, it tended to be thought – if only as an excuse for making free with fuel – that a hotter fire would improve the quality of the product.

Attitudes began to change in the eighteenth century, when so many things were stripped of their magical powers. The newly invented thermometer served not merely to satisfy people's curiosity, but also to explore ways of making room temperatures more even. It even led to the idea of automatic temperature regulation. The first pyrometers were produced for the measuring of temperatures in fires and furnaces. Scholars began to grow used to the idea that heat and fire were quantifiable.

Shortly after 1700, the first theory of combustion made its appearance, based on an imaginary substance, 'phlogiston', that was supposed to be present in all combustible materials. False though it was, it contributed to a rational analysis of the phenomenon of fire (Ströker 1982: 93ff.). It also had considerable practical implications, for, if combustion always involved the same process, then it was not so important which fuel was used: one kind of wood could be replaced with another, and perhaps wood itself with other materials.

James Watt was guided by the phlogiston theory when he used coal to heat his pioneering steam engine. Clearly the conclusion was possible that it was generally wasteful to burn wood. 'Is it not a shame that people massacre the Good Lord's oak and beech to obtain a little phlogiston extract, and . . . live in perpetual war with the forest?' asked the philosopher Lichtenberg, who himself owned a wood-saving stove (Usemann 1980: 67f.).

After 1790 the forest scientist Hartig (1804) tried to measure the calorific value of different kinds of wood, and wondered that no one

207

had ever studied it before. From 1800 on, there was more and more talk of 'fuel' in general: it mattered little whether it was wood, peat or coal; the economic and scientific attitude to wood became abstract. In 1779 Lavoisier analysed combustion as a process involving the binding of oxygen. The whole world of perception was turned upside down. Such antithetic phenomena as water, air and fire, which had been considered the basic elements of the cosmos, contained one and the same component: oxygen. Sense impressions were deceptive; only analytic dissection penetrated to the heart of things. It was a new type of science that emerged victorious in the nineteenth century.

What it meant in practice was not immediately obvious, however, and many remained unconvinced until the twentieth century. The search for 'smoke-consuming' ovens, which went back to the days before science, actually intensified during the nineteenth century, and belief in the purifying power of fire culminated in modern refuse-burning systems (Halliday 1964: 160). Iron production long remained overwhelmingly a matter of practical experience, which scientists confined themselves to reproducing. The same was true of charcoal-burning, despite efforts in the eighteenth century to give it a scientific foundation; 'only experience can make a charcoal-burner perfect' (Späth 1800: 44). The daunting and unpredictable character of fire meant that in many places 'fire workers' retained quite a high degree of autonomy throughout the nineteenth century – including the freedom to quench their thirst with copious supplies of alcohol. In large-scale industry too, the combustion chamber long remained a 'black box' peopled with sooty shapes, which escaped the attentions of the fuel-saving strategists (Radkau 2001: 115f.).

Economic rationality posed even more of a problem in relation to time. But here too the declared goal from the eighteenth century onward was that behaviour should be more 'economical'. The agrarian reformer Johann Schwerz taught: 'Time is undoubtedly the greatest capital that nature has given to man, and it melts away if he does not use it or allows a moment to be lost' (Schwerz 1836: 78). Saving on wages was readily mentioned in the same breath as economies of wood and time. When a large fire devoured expensive fuel, time really was money; to work fast without interruptions saved wood or, in other words, increased the efficiency of the wood in use. Like the wood shortage around the turn of the nineteenth century, the modern obsession with time shortage stemmed from the goal of extracting the maximum efficiency from each unit.

When non-stop furnaces (*Floßöfen*) made their debut in the Styrian Ore Mountain region around 1760, the workers there opposed the simultaneous introduction of Sunday shifts, pointing to the scarcity of water as well as wood. Night work was also motivated by the need to make constant use of limited water power from local streams. Gottfried Keller saw 'a stunted race of people wherever flowing water is used to drive wheels' (Hauser 1961: 340f.).

If the new economics saved 'time', it also often shortened the workers' lifetime. A blazing furnace environment was in the long term extremely damaging to the health. Bernardino Ramazzini's original book on occupational diseases (1700) gave relatively little space to furnacemen, but volume 2 of a new German edition published in 1780–3 painted a gruesome picture of their lot (Ackermann and Ramazzini 1780: 2/226ff.). It repeated Ramazzini's judgement that glass-makers were the smartest, 'since they have a celebratory break when they have worked for six months long, and give up their craft when they reach the age of forty'; otherwise 'such damaging labour' would completely ruin their health (ibid.: 236f.). Glass-blowing was then often still a forest craft, pursued only in winter and spring. But the rationality expressed in such lines is not that of the industrial age.

Saving wood and saving time were by no means always the same. Slow charcoal-burning, for example, was more productive than fast, and a small kiln more productive than a large one. Yet large kilns became 'more or less characteristic of a well-off farmer' who wanted to produce as much as possible in a short time (Späth 1800: 116). Salt-boiling consumed more wood if it was 'done hastily, with the finish always vividly in mind' (Schremmer 1971: 295); the use of solar and wind energy in graduation works reduced wood consumption but increased the expenditure of time. A similar tension between time and fuel existed in bleaching.

All in all, the acceleration associated with the industrial age increased energy use so much that an *idée fixe* persisted until the 1970s that economic growth and higher fuel consumption were indivisible from each other – a misconception, as we have since come to realize. Saving wood and saving time ran in parallel for only a short distance, although it might have appeared that it was a single path of rationalization.

Is necessity the mother of invention? 'Wood management' and technological change

At a little noticed point in *Economy and Society* (I, 2, §3), in the context of deforestation, Max Weber draws a subtle distinction between absolute and relative scarcity, referring to earlier times or to the supply situation of other population groups. Absolute poverty, he argues, leads to a life of worry and population decline, whereas people tend to react to relative scarcity with a 'great increase in the rationalization of economic enterprise'. Many alarmist voices equated the wood shortage with a famine – that is, with scarcity of the first type. But in fact it was scarcity of the second type – the kind of necessity that could be the mother of invention.

Along with other advantages, many inventions in the course of industrialization lowered fuel use per unit of production. Since, however, it was often worth deploying them only if there was a simultaneous expansion of plant, they contributed in the end to an absolute rise in fuel consumption. The wood shortage of the eighteenth century has tended to be seen as a major spur to technological innovation, not only by modern historians but also by people living in the early days of industrialization. 'Necessity is the mother of invention' was already a popular saying in the eighteenth century (Becher [1789] 1980: 573).

But inventions born of necessity generally had more to do with labour techniques than with fundamental changes in production systems. As to their wood-saving effect – from waste gas use in furnaces to rolling mills – this was mostly a question of increased efficiency, not of self-restraint or resource conservation. This kind of 'saving' was not due to an absolute lack of resources, but resulted from the 'dynamic scarcity' that went hand in hand with industrial growth. In 1914 Thorstein Veblen inverted the proverb and gave it a new twist: 'Here and now, as always and everywhere, invention is the mother of necessity' ([1914] 1964: 314).

In the eighteenth century, traditional recipes for the saving of wood were back in business, for the simple reason that they were quicker and more effective than the revolutionary new solutions on offer. Two centuries earlier 'saving wood' had been a promise of secretive projects, but now it became a popular theme in literature as the rising bourgeoisie raised thrift and 'economies' from a private to a public norm. Benjamin Franklin, one of the great spokesmen of bourgeois enlightenment, invented a wood-saving oven even in forested America; thrift was a matter of principle, not of necessity. Proposals on how to save wood came thick and fast, applicable to all walks of life, since wood was used in one way or another in nearly everything. In the West Indies, whose forests succumbed to plantations, people began to fuel boiling stoves with ground sugar cane (Freyre 1990: 431); it remains today one of the most effective industrial energy-saving methods in the tropics.

Quite often economies involved a change in lifestyle. Reform-minded authors did not make a song and dance about this, because it was a widespread ideal in the eighteenth century to put one's whole life on rational foundations without any concern for venerable traditions. It was therefore possible to advocate doing away with maypoles – as some did in Vienna under Emperor Joseph II – or making reusable coffins.

But many ideas were less strange than they seem today. For example, directives to replace 'dead' with 'living' fences kept recurring (Pfeil 1839: 146f.), since fences were one of the most important consumers of wood in the countryside, and a lot could be saved at a stroke if they were made into major producers of wood instead. When American settlers pushed westward from the forests of New England to the treeless prairies, their main investment was in fences to protect their fields against herds of cattle that had not been present before (Perlin 2005: 253).

In the late eighteenth and early nineteenth centuries, the Economy Deputation of the Elector of Saxony repeatedly offered rewards – first 100 thalers, then 200 – for the replacement of private with communal ovens (Ebeling 1925), as a way of reducing wood consumption to a fraction of the previous level. In villages in Franconia, communal ovens were a hub of sociability for women and young people. Opportunities to save wood depend on the popular culture.

In many cases, the building of wood-saving furnaces followed principles known in the sixteenth century, but now, towards the end of the eighteenth, they were applied more consistently than before. In theory it was easy to see that a lot of wood could be saved if smithies or brandy distilleries reduced the number of times their product was heated and cooled, but in general radical solutions had to wait until the nineteenth century. First a more hard-headed quantitative view of fire and heat had to gain acceptance.

In the past, like today, the energy-saving objective clashed with people's desire not only for warmth and comfort but also for fresh air. Especially when a fire was burning in the room in which they lived, sensitive people longed for the ventilation that medical theories of the eighteenth and nineteenth century considered essential for good health. The picture changed only with the arrival of central heating. The possibility of circulating heat had been known since the baths and under-floor heating of antiquity, and the use of a single fire connected to a hot water system seemed to make sense as a way of cutting down on wood consumption. But the full implications of this were apparent only when houses, machines, factories and whole towns

211

came to be seen as conduit systems. Even today it is far from the case that the full potential of waste heat has been realized.

Major economies also seemed likely in the 'forest crafts', which were tempted to be prodigal in their use of wood. The obscure trades of charcoal-, potash- and tar-burners were particularly open to technological improvements: it was out of them that the chemical industry and coking and distillation techniques developed. But this was also where a more economical use of wood required a huge leap in capital investment and technological competence. The move towards non-stop operation was a move towards the factory and large-scale engineering construction, but it remained inconceivable so long as the trades in question could be pursued by 'forest people'. Wood shortage alone by no means provided a sufficient impetus for innovation; fundamental changes in the economic structure were also necessary.

The advance of industrialization finally opened up new ways of dramatically lowering fuel costs. In the nineteenth century it became theoretically possible to calculate the maximum heat from a mass of wood, so that people began to set ambitious targets for efficiency improvement. Since combustion released some 60 to 70 per cent of the combustible part of wood in the form of gases – even more than for coal or charcoal – the maximum thermal efficiency of a piece of wood could now be estimated on the basis of gas analysis.

In 1838 Robert Bunsen reported the sensational finding that, in the charcoal furnaces of Veckerhagen an der Weser, 40 per cent of the fuel potential was being lost (Plumpe 1982: 215). It was discovered that the efficiency of furnaces as well as ovens greatly depended on the combustion of gases, which in turn required a source of 'secondary ventilation'. Domestic ovens remained a favourite topic in the literature on wood economies, and the 'wood-saving oven' became a term in common currency (figure 3.13). Up to the eighteenth century, oven construction had paid little attention to fuel use, and even around the turn of the nineteenth it was still possible to make savings as high as 80 per cent with the help of relatively simple innovations (Faber 1950). One of these, the iron grate, allowed major improvements to be made in fire control and fuel use. It was thought in the nineteenth century that the fuel requirement per household was only a tenth of the eighteenth-century estimates (Hauck 1866: 48).

Although the 'economy literature' of the eighteenth century contains a number of important technological insights, it is much hazier when it comes to their precise application. Even without an oxidation

212

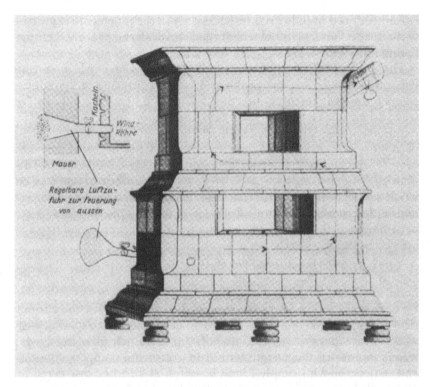

Figure 3.13: This tiled stove won Johann Paul Baumer the Friedrich II prize in 1764 for 'a stove that uses as little wood as possible'. Unlike many other designs, it was extremely practical and 'later became the perfect example of the "Berlin tiled stove"' (Usemann 1980: 63). Baumer's model featured controllable air intake and a flue gas flap, and well-matched grating size, fire capacity and external surfaces. The sketch at the top left shows that the combustion air is fed from outdoors, not from the room.

theory, everyone knew that air intake could control the fire in a closed stove, but the best means of doing this could not be ascertained, or the problem itself clearly formulated, without progress in regulation technology and gas analysis. It was known that a stove must have an adequate flue, but not how much heat should be allowed to escape through the chimney. As a result, people were torn this way and that, unable to determine the optimum temperature gradient towards the outside that still ensured the removal of the smoke. It was also known that a wood-saving stove did not need to be very big, but not how the best dimensions for a particular space should be calculated. On the other hand, the advantage of preheating the air fed into a fire – which

213

was introduced in industrial furnaces only in the nineteenth century – was already familiar to owners of tiled stoves in the previous century (Lehmann 1735: 1/17f.).

The theoretical contribution of the 'economical stove' literature was rather moderate; the problem was too confusing and complex to open up clear research directions. What the literature did achieve was to help make the spirit of experimentation more popular. The requirement that all knowledge should be grounded in experience had been more of a programme than an actual practice in the seventeenth century. But in the eighteenth Benjamin Franklin could write: 'This is an age of experiments' (1909: 164). And the author of one text on wood-saving devices gushed that experiments with them had afforded him 'indescribable pleasure' (Roth 1802: 2). The pleasure may have been heightened by the fact that many of them were conducted in breweries and distilleries.

What was the practical effect of this literature? Its own character already tells us much about the difficulties of introducing more economical stoves. For the lavishly illustrated books were too expensive for craftsmen to buy and long remained a 'plaything for the curious rich' (Jachtmann 1786: 11), who had no need to be more sparing with wood. Stove design was traditionally the province of potters, who were soon out of their depth with iron grates and complex conduits and outlets, or who simply found it no fun at all to be instructed by know-alls from outside their trade. Besides, wood-saving stoves were for a long time unpopular because of their limited capacity: one had to cut the logs more thinly and to pile the fire up more often.

So long as open hearths were the centre of home life, the more economical stove had no chance. Only a change in the whole of domestic culture made their introduction possible; in particular, the prosperous strata of society who decided the taste of the age first had to develop an interest in them. This did happen in Central Europe in the eighteenth century, more in the town than the country. The showpiece function of the tiled stove declined in relation to other fixtures and fittings: the growing requirement for cleanliness meant that smoke was no longer acceptable indoors; and, above all, a taste for highly individual domestic interiors began to percolate down from the upper classes.

So long as the whole household could come together around an open hearth, the rising price of wood was not a problem that called for technical solutions. But things were different when several family members had a stove of their own and the domestic servants also lived apart. An Austrian government report complained in 1740

– no doubt with some exaggeration – that the trend to living separately had increased wood consumption tenfold (Sandgruber 1982a: 334). By the end of the eighteenth century, there were more and more references to the fact that wood-saving stoves were not only under consideration but in actual use. Yet around the year 1800 a doctor from Cloppenburg in Lower Saxony could still write: 'The innkeeper who does not have a nice big fire can be sure gradually to lose his guests, even if his bedrooms are beautifully warm' (Kaiser 1980: 17).

The rise of coal in the nineteenth century tended to slow the spread of fuel-efficient combustion systems; lower energy use became less important than tight sealing, good ventilation and strong flues to calm the horror of smoke and the fear of gas poisoning. Cylindrical iron stoves were well suited for these purposes.

Apart from domestic stoves, all kinds of other fires – from laundry houses to chick-hatching boxes – came in for advice on how to improve wood economy. Of course, it was not always easy to make the leap from a domestic to an industrial context. Where fire and heat were needed to manufacture a product, it was more difficult than in a stove to keep the furnace compact and contained or to minimize the heat loss. Even the domestic oven took longer to introduce than the sealed heating stove.

Saltworks

Most boiling houses in saltworks first acquired a chimney when they began to operate with coal; open boiling-pans, which wasted as much as 75 per cent of heat energy, survived even into the twentieth century (Emons and Walter 1984). Yet eighteenth-century German saltworks, under competitive pressure from English coal-heated boiling processes, developed very much in the spirit of the drive to cut down on wood consumption. Typical projects of the age were brine circuits in new saltworks built in forested regions and the construction of salt graduators. These followed old models. In much the same way that a 33-kilometre brine conduit had been built way back in 1619 to ease the pressure on the Reichenhall forest after the opening of a subsidiary saltworks at Traunstein (Schremmer 1980: 33), the royal French saltworks of Chaux (in Arc-et-Senans) – already well known for its architecture (figure 3.14) – was linked in 1774 by a 15-kilometre conduit to the great Forêt de Chaux, because it lacked an adequate local supply of wood and even sufficient space for graduation houses (Hocquet 1984: 154f.).

Figure 3.14: Claude-Nicolas Ledoux's plan for the royal French saltworks at Chaux (Arc-et-Senans, Jura), of which only the front semicircle was ever built (1774–8). It was one of the last grand projects of the Ancien Régime and already contained elements of the architecture of the revolutionary period. Aesthetic and prestige factors played a greater role than functional considerations in the circular, fortress-like arrangement. When the works was in operation, the aesthetic effect was spoiled by the dense smoke rising from all the boiling houses (across the diameter of the circle) and by the woodpile in the semicircular space. The buildings, still considered a spectacular sight, point to the political significance of salt production. The project also shows how much expense was lavished on these huge industrial consumers of wood, at a time when supplies were running short in the forest.

Graduation reached technical maturity with the development of thorn graduation. Many saltworks began building graduation houses in the eighteenth century; these were huge structures by the standards of the time, and not only construction but also repair and maintenance (because of exposure to wind and severe weather) were very costly. At the Großensalza works (near Schönebeck on the Elbe), which in the 1770s had Europe's longest graduation house but little water power because of its low-lying position, 350 men and thirty-two horse-drawn vehicles were deployed on tread wheels just to pump brine into the graduation system (Multhauf 1978: 91).

216

In the 1740s boiler workers at Schwäbisch Hall opposed the construction of a graduation works, ridiculing it as 'for summer and for children', since it could not be used at colder times of the year; they also thought it much too expensive, suspecting, not without reason, that the real point behind it was that the town council, which had the necessary capital, wanted to increase its stake in the saltworks (Radkau 1986a). In any case, there were technological alternatives to such a massive project. Better ways of enriching brine were already known in the eighteenth century (Heynitz 1786), but graduation became superfluous only when deep-drilling opened up highly enriched brine in the early nineteenth century.

The iron industry

For a long time the iron industry went its own merry way, but in the late eighteenth century it too came under the scrutiny of wood economy experts. In many regions, mining and metallurgy were so used to their forest privileges that they had little incentive to cut down on their wood consumption, but, the more that economic liberalism became the spirit of the age, the more the foundries had to compete with other consumers. One milestone was the decision by the liberal Joseph II in 1783 to cancel the special forest areas set aside for the iron industry in the Austrian Alps. Only coal saved and strengthened heavy industry in the face of threats to its pre-eminence. But coal and free competition also posed the problem of fuel costs more sharply than ever before in history, and from the early nineteenth century the calculations of the charcoal-based iron industry centred entirely on the raising of thermal efficiency.

In the eighteenth century, furnaces with continuous production were by no means the rule in all iron-producing areas. There were still bloomery furnaces in the Upper Palatinate and *Stücköfen* (precursors of the blast furnace) in Styria, which had to be put out each time the iron was extracted. Only under pressure from the government in Vienna were the 'coal-devouring *Stücköfen*' finally replaced after 1750 with continuous furnaces (*Floßöfen*) in the Styrian Ore Mountain region. Historians of technology often regard this as a self-evident advance, but unlike the bloomery furnace and the *Stücköfen*, which produced malleable iron ('direct process'), the cast iron with a high carbon content that was obtained from *Floßöfen* and blast furnaces first had to be made malleable through so-called refinement ('indirect process').

For a long time refinement took place in open furnaces, where

217

the use of special charcoal was higher than in the actual smelting. In fact, with refinement taken into account, the indirect process might consume twice as much charcoal as the direct process (Johannsen 1953: 258). Only the further improvement of blast furnaces, the direct application of cast iron and the replacement of refinement with more efficient processes in the nineteenth century brought a significant advantage in fuel consumption. In the eighteenth century, blast furnaces only appeared to 'save wood'; the main reason for their introduction was to raise production and to allow continuous operation.

An area of metallurgy that typically interested fuel economizers in the eighteenth century was 'iron-roasting' (figure 3.15). This was a technically simple process, which until then had been carried out in open furnaces with the use of brushwood fuel. The purpose of the roasting was to prepare iron ore for the smelting furnace, by loosening it and removing the water and many other volatile components. The advantages of roasting were hotly debated: more and more people in the eighteenth century thought it pointless, but it came in the nineteenth to be highly valued again (Köstler 1984: 119f.). It was easy to obtain dramatic improvements simply by replacing open with closed furnaces, and in the Styrian Ore Mountain region a further idea was to reposition the roasting process on the blast furnace top in such a way as to use the heat from its gases. This naturally required the furnace top to be walled in, exposing the workers employed there to the danger of gas poisoning.

The use of furnace-top gases marked an epochal shift. After the turn of the nineteenth century, wood economizers identified the flames pouring out of blast furnaces as a sign of massive fuel waste, and it came to be taught that gas was a refined fuel that could be used in many different ways. The invention of the hot-blast stove – which preheated the air drawn into blast furnaces by bellows – brought a spectacular advance in regulation and thermal efficiency, especially when furnace-top gases were used for this purpose. This innovation, first applied in 1834 at Wasseralfingen in Württemberg, spread with amazing speed (Paulinyi 1983: 131); charcoal-fuelled blast furnaces, whose fate at the time depended entirely on improvements in thermal efficiency, led the way in this. Resource-saving innovations were a more urgent requirement when wood rather than coal was involved. There were also wooden paths to modernity – and, from today's vantage point, they may provide more of a base for the future than can the path of fossil resources.

218

Figure 3.15: Iron-roasting in the open (above) and in kilns (1690). Roasting, which served not least to evaporate arsenic ('foundry smoke'), was known early on to be damaging to the environment; the territory of Salzburg complained in 1495 that 'cattle [were dying] from the foundry smoke' (Ludwig 1979: 139). Whether roasting was in any way necessary was a controversial issue in the eighteenth century.

The construction sector, industrialization and wood

The changing times at the turn of the nineteenth century also brought a new turn in German construction techniques. Whereas brick structures had until then been confined largely to regions with little natural stone – in the Hanse area they produced their own building style, known as Brick Gothic – they spread everywhere as the century progressed (Bedal 1978: 75). Often stone construction was touted in order to save wood, but brick-making also consumed huge quantities of wood; it simply shifted the requirement from construction timber to firewood. Bricks were 'wood-saving' only in so far as they allowed low-grade wood and wood waste – around 1800, even 'straw, fern and bilberry shrubs' (Rupp n.d.: 51) – to be employed in their production. However, temperatures as high as 1,000 degrees Celsius were needed to 'cook' bricks properly, and that called for better-quality fuels. Bricks therefore fetched 'daily higher prices as wood became more scarce' (Mayer [1773] 1980: 194). Here and there unfired bricks were tried out, following the example of regions in the south.

In the nineteenth century, bricks were still often produced 'in the fields' – that is, in primitive stone and clay kilns built by the brick-maker himself, open at the top and only good for one batch of bricks (which for a long time he also shaped by hand) (Siuts 1982: 340ff.). The ring kiln, invented in 1856 in Germany, was a big step towards a factory system and engineering constructions. Praised as 'economical' by Theodor Fontane in his *Wanderungen durch die Mark Brandenburg* (1862–82), it really did reduce fuel costs to a fraction of their previous level, thanks to its application of fairly simple, long-known principles such as all-round chimney enclosure and an improved combination of heating and cooling processes, in which the fire shifted from chamber to chamber. Only later did the 'tunnel kiln' (in which the product rather than the heat source shifted around) gain general acceptance. As Fontane recognized, the ring kiln was not choosy about fuel: 'It gobbles anything up' – even brown coal or peat. It was therefore more than an 'economical oven': it enabled the building industry to expand without inhibition. The shape of bricks was also mechanized in the second half of the nineteenth century.

Construction was one of the major growth sectors in the industrialization process, and it has continued to be seen as a barometer of the wider economy. But building work retained its craft character, being among the largest consumers of wood even in the age of stone construction. In the nineteenth century, wood already showed its propensity for a higher level of industrialization in the building industry – that is, for prefabrication. Prefabricated wooden houses were first built in large numbers for the Crimean War (1853–6), by British firms and Styrian craftsmen. 'The speed of construction was incredible' (Herbert 1978: 77). This was nothing new to the Russians on the enemy side: Engelbert Kaempfer was amazed to find in 1683 that, because the wooden houses in Moscow frequently caught fire, 'houses were back up ready for sale on the second or third day after a fire, at first without clay, lime and nails' (Scurla 1974: 197).

In the nineteenth century, 'public opinion was systematically stirred up against the use of wood for building': architects and engineers, for whom the natural irregularity of wood was a thorn in their side, eager to make their profession more scientific, gave the impression that 'building in wood was a custom of barbarians and half-civilized peoples' (Bringmann [1905–9] 1981: 109). But even London's Crystal Palace, erected for the Great Exhibition of 1851 and thought to embody the most daring architecture of the future, contained a wooden construction in its gigantic vault (Evans 1982: 44). Its iron frame was inspired by half-timbered buildings, and its architect, Joseph Paxton, was said to have been 'more familiar with wood than with iron' (Herbert 1978: 91). The more precisely people learned to calculate the statics of a building, the more economical they could be with the wood. There was an 'enormous difference between what counted as construction timber in the nineteenth century and the sixteenth century; grades of wood that could not have been sold as timber in the past were now also used in building' (Pfeil 1839: 177).

Carpenters were among the craftsmen who asserted their tradition and social position quite successfully in the nineteenth century. They did not experience the 'decline of the crafts' that many thought was taking place, and in their case far more customary practices have been passed down from the eighteenth and nineteenth centuries than from earlier times (figure 3.16).

It is true that carpenters were threatened by outside control and the faster pace of work. Adam Smith, who otherwise regarded their trade as a model of healthy activity, already warned that it was a perfect example of how piece rates were ruining workmen's health in London (Smith [1776] 1961: 91). But carpenters who continued to own their means of production were able to retain a comparatively high degree of autonomy. They took the lead in the unionization of building workers in Berlin in the 1860s, and they were prominent in the ranks of French building workers, who had the highest strike-rate in the nineteenth century after miners and textile workers.

221

Figure 3.16: A gathering of Parisian carpenters (*Compagnons du devoir*) beside an exotic, quasi-historical model of fantasy architecture, *c*.1910. Critics in the eighteenth century already said that guilds were commissioning works without any practical value. The object featured here, a 'masterwork' created on the men's own initiative, was a conscious rebellion against the spirit of the modern age – 'a last protest against the usurpation of part of their work by the metal industry' (Moles 1949: 109).

Wooden shipbuilding

Craft pride held up until quite late in trades that dealt with wood, most especially in the world of shipbuilding. Not only was the nine-teenth century the great age of the steamship; it also witnessed the highpoint of sailing. Wooden shipbuilding thus lasted into the second half of the century and preserved the traditional position of carpen-ters in the industry. In Hamburg, long after their historic guild had dissolved (1839), carpenters retained a similar kind of organization that ensured them of a 'position of exceptional power'. 'A division of labour was as alien to them as a division between planning and execu-tion'; their versatility was favoured by the fact that 'the irregularity of wood makes it unsuitable for the application of general, objective rules of construction' (Cattaruzza 1984: 607f.).

The transition from wooden to iron ships went together with a change in the social history of work, since it promoted the replacement of old guild-like associations with modern industrial unions. In these too, however, skilled workers with a craft awareness were predominant. Iron also brought a new growth in ship size, which had a spin-off in the shape of new docks and harbours outside the traditional city structures. 'The new-style port became a world unto itself' (Osterhammel 2009: 406).

The building of the first great iron ships – the *Great Britain* (1845) and the *Great Eastern* (1857) – ended in a technical and economical fiasco (Weber 1982: 285f.; Broelmann 1983: 31ff.). In 1880 the president of the German Shipbuilders Association was sure that 'the age of iron troughs' – an allusion to the ungainly shape of the early iron ships – would 'soon be over': 'we shall be building wooden sailing-ships again in future' (Dau 1979: 250). But in reality iron had already triumphed over wood in the shipyards. The strongest impetus came from naval construction – and the resulting alliance between the navy and heavy industry also spelled the victory of the high-capitalist mode of production over handicrafts. Shipbuilding is paradigmatic of the turning point in the history of work that came with the transition from wood to iron.

Coal: from wood-saving to the driving force of industrial expansion

When the word 'coal' [Kohle] appeared in German literature up to the eighteenth century, what was meant was nearly always charcoal. But mineral coal was also well known, and the word itself shows that people saw it as similar to charcoal and a potential substitute for it. Before coal became the basis for explosive industrial growth, it had already served for centuries as a local substitute for wood and charcoal. Its field of application expanded in the early modern age, but it was still confined to certain sectors and regions. It could be used to heat domestic stoves, but only with the addition of a grate to improve the air intake – an innovation that sounds trifling today, but not insignificant at a time when metals were used more sparingly.

Typical trades that used coal in seventeenth-century England, though only after 1800 in Germany, were brewing and glass-making, as well as salt-boiling. The introduction of coal was technically unproblematic when the product did not come into contact with the fire, and it was particularly important in trades such as glass-making that fell behind in the competition for wood. In many areas, smiths were forced to use coal by the fact that the powerful masters of iron works and hammer mills cornered nearly all the 'charcoal' for themselves.

Coal is often mentioned in eighteenth-century literature as one means of saving wood, but it had already given rise to many disagreeable and disappointing experiences. In a city such as London, which had used coal for heating since the Middle Ages, the unpleasantness of coal smoke was well known. John Evelyn, the pioneer of reforestation, considered it the cause of many of London's ills and would have liked to see it banned from the city (*Fumifugium*, 1661).

Coal was still extracted in open-cast mining until well into the nineteenth century, but the quality of deposits lying close to the surface was poor and uneven: they could not be relied upon as a standard fuel. One expert noted that quality varied much more with peat than with wood, but that coal 'presented an incomparably greater diversity than the various kinds of peats' (Tunner 1846: 26ff.). The champions of coal used to mock the prejudices against it, much as the pioneers of the railway later spread horror stories about the stupidity of those who opposed it (Sieferle 1984a: 87ff.). Yet one cannot but wonder at the early praise heaped on coal, at a time when its economic significance was still slight.

In the eighteenth century, economists were already as sold on coal as they were on the potato: while the latter solved the food problem by reducing the grain requirement, the 'subterraneous forest of coal' was supposed to settle the fuel problem for all time. Blind prejudice against coal was no longer very substantial in the eighteenth century. But the remaining scepticism about the fossil fuel sometimes appears more well founded than the propaganda in its favour. Samuel Hahnemann, the physician who founded homeopathy, went so far as to claim in 1780, in his *Abhandlung über die Vorurteile gegen die Steinkohlenfeuerung* [Treatise on the Prejudices against Coal Fires], that coal fumes were good for the health. In 1780 another coal supporter, Pfeiffer, thought it 'outrageous' that anyone should think it could not be found in many regions (Gleitsmann 1985a: 119).

It is now recognized that the mass shift to coal was a fateful watershed in the history of man's relationship with the environment, since its sulphur content is very much higher than that of wood. It also gave quite a new dimension to the carbon dioxide problem. A purely wood-based economy would have regulated itself over time, as the carbon released through combustion was bound again in growing forest. Today we may think it a disaster that the 'wood brake' ceased to function.

224

Figure 3.17: The *Morgenröthe* ironworks in the Ore Mountains region, one of the most important in Saxony at the time, with one furnace, five coolers and four hammer mills, *c.*1830; the first hot-blast furnace in Saxony would be built there in 1834. The complex fully belonged to the new industrial age, but its links with the forest are still in evidence. In an article he wrote in 1830, the works manager Neubert discussed the coke option, but emphatically pointed to the price and quality advantages of charcoal (Forberger 1982: 365).

Abraham Darby first used coke to smelt iron around 1710, at Coalbrookdale, but no one copied his example until the middle of the century. This hesitancy was not, as many once assumed, due to irrational anti-coal prejudice, but simply expressed the fact that charcoal remained cheaper and burned better, and that the famous wood shortage did not exist (Hyde 1977: 23ff.).

In Frankfurt, where the price of wood was relatively high and coal could be obtained from the Saar, the city council began to campaign for coal after 1789 – successfully at first, because it did not arouse anyone's suspicions and had the attraction of something new. In 1790, however, questions were asked about why the city charcoal depot had 'stored up ten times more coal than was necessary' (Radkau 1986a). And by 1795 the use of coal had shrunk back and there was scarcely any real demand for it. In Saxony, coal cost more than wood around the turn of the century (figure 3.17), so that even the Economy and Commerce Deputation, which was supposed to lead by example, showed no inclination to heat its rooms with coal. After a survey of

225

'fire workers' came up with devastating results, Styrian brown coal was no longer used for anything but the extraction of alum from its ashes (Lackner 1984).

The first ironworks in the Ruhr were fired with charcoal, even though they stood on the largest deposits of mineral coal in mainland Europe. If coal became the foundation of economic life, this was not a reaction to wood shortages but a part of new expansion strategies (often enjoying state support) (Brose 1985). The growth in coal consumption did not proceed automatically, nor did it reflect technological constraints. Indeed, early industrial regions that did not have large reserves in their immediate vicinity showed a tendency for some time to limit the use of coal to certain sectors (Fremdling 1986).

Among commercial users, the introduction of coal typically went together with a transition to high-capitalist forms of enterprise, and often with a replacement of local resources and lifestyles and insertion into a transregional economic system. Many localities geared to wood or water energy – in the Harz, the Saxon Ore Mountains, the Upper Palatinate or Styria – became remote and transport-deprived in the age of coal and the railways. In the case of the Styrian glassworks, coal use did not demand any fundamental technological changes, but it did require drastic repositioning. And when the glass-maker climbed the wooded slopes down into the valley, he also 'descended into a new world of profit' (Roth 1976: 182).

For the economic historian David Landes (1969: 54), it is 'clear that the readiness to accept coal was itself indicative of a deeper rationality'. And the introduction of coal did presuppose a more rational attitude to fire and business location than the traditional mentality had involved. The switch to coal was not necessarily bound up with major technological innovations – the coke blast furnace did not differ in principle from the charcoal furnace – but it did promote a general climate of innovation. Steam engines and locomotives could also be driven with wood or charcoal, but they would have found it harder to gain acceptance in Europe. The conversion of heat into kinetic energy made no sense in a society in which sources of heat energy were as scarce as horse or water power. It became a revolutionary invention only when an abundance of heat energy came on stream. Max Weber was right to emphasize that 'rationality' is a polyvalent concept. The Wood Age had a rationality of its own.

For Andrew Ure ([1835] 1967: 29), the ideologue of England's industrialization, it was an advantage of the steam engine that it used a lot of fuel, since this stimulated coal production at the same time; such reasoning would have been absurd before the switch to coal.

During the same period in Germany, however, it was still common practice to list anticipated fuel economies when seeking authorization to open a new business. The new rationality that triumphed along with coal suppressed another that had been no less rational. A trend towards product refinement discernible in the economy before the nineteenth century – a trend involving a higher labour input in comparison with specific energy – now turned into its opposite. From today's point of view, this was 'progress' of a not unproblematic kind.

If we consider the extent to which fossil fuels have changed the whole of modern life, it is surprising how little resistance stirred against them. In the eighteenth century it was claimed that fuels lay beneath the ground everywhere; only gradually did people realize what a huge change in locational factors was coming in the wake of coal. The first literature to speak of a 'battle' between charcoal smelteries and coke blast furnaces dates from the mid-nineteenth century (Schübler 1852; Le Play 1854). The engineer and social Romantic Frédéric Le Play asserted (1854: 137f.) that iron produced with charcoal would always be better than iron produced with mineral coal, but all he could propose to save charcoal furnaces was the concentration of large businesses. The economic forms originally associated with wood could no longer be defended.

How aware were people that the switch to fossil fuels was a switch from renewable to non-renewable resources? It was only in the nineteenth century that it became possible to have a clear understanding of the origins of fossil fuels; a view of history based on the biblical account of the creation did not have space for the millions of years during which mineral coal was formed. Until the eighteenth century there was a belief that the treasures beneath the earth kept growing like trees.

Around the year 1800, when foresters were trying to present the forest as an artificial product, it was popular to praise fossil fuels as a 'gift from Nature' to man (Radkau 1986b). Other voices were raised here and there: the zoologist Bechstein, for instance, warned that a land that took its fuel from mines was eating up its capital, whereas one that drew it from sustainable forestry was living on the interest and preserving its capital for posterity.

But many landowners and forest reformers were quite happy for coal consumption to increase, since it helped them to shake off firewood obligations and to move towards a high forest economy. Opponents would no longer be able to invoke the old 'moral economy' or to protest that they would freeze in winter without free access to firewood from the forest. Pfeil played down Bechstein's

227

argument, asserting that, in the view of many vulcanologists, 'the whole of the inner earth consists of combustible materials' (1816: 166). (One is reminded of today's publicity for heat pump systems, which points out that '99 per cent of the earth is hotter than 1,000 degrees'!) Only in the course of the nineteenth century, when coal was extracted deep underground rather than in open cast mining, did it become impossible to escape the bitter fact that it was as finite in nature as the once plentiful 'mountain blessing', the ores. But by then it was too late to draw the logical conclusions from this insight.

5 Rollback

Tools and machines: the end of the Wood Age

The rollback of wood as a fuel and a material for tools and machines was a long process, connected throughout with industrialization and stretching into the twentieth century. The first stages were dominated by machine tools and the railway. But the end of the Wood Age does not coincide with the beginning of the Industrial Revolution – quite the contrary. Early industrialization was a highpoint for technology associated with wood (figure 3.18).

The first spinning machines were made largely of wood: their inventors, Wyatt and Hargreaves, were carpenters. Millwrights were also active as machine-builders. Fernand Braudel (1902–85), considered by many the greatest historian of his time, was astounded when he saw the wooden machinery at the Deutsches Museum in Munich. He thought it showed the extent to which industrial production in olden times was 'vulnerable to the wear and tear of equipment' (Braudel 1985a: 247). But that point of view depends on our looking back with the yardstick of modern times. For Braudel, wood was part of what he called the 'biological old regime', which coal and steel dissolved in the wake of industrialization. Wooden machinery confounded that periodization of world history, as it did Sombart's sequence of 'organic' and 'inorganic' ages. The industrial age too could not dispense with organic nature.

The importance of iron for the pre-industrial and early industrial periods has often been exaggerated (Landes 1969: 88f.). The wealth of experience of the Wood Age was still at hand, and a surprisingly large number of things were still made out of wood. This was true of most pipes, for example; the technique of drilling wooden ducts stood

Figure 3.18: Wooden carding machine at Cromford, the first German textile factory, founded near Ratingen in 1783, which was named after its English model, Arkwright's Cromford Mill in the Peak District. Carding – the preparation of cotton fibres for spinning – was one of the first processes in the textile industry to be mechanized; Arkwright's carding machine, also made of wood, was a key innovation. The Industrial Revolution by no means always meant the replacement of wood.

at a high level in the eighteenth century; conduit systems became a characteristic element in the development of civilization. The material-forming techniques that are still most important today, and which were eventually taken over by machine tools, first developed in relation to wood.

Industrialization did not necessarily imply that wood ceased to be associated with traditionalist production methods. In the USA, the Wood Age lasted well into the nineteenth century – the best evidence that the rise of the West was linked not only with iron and coal but also with wood and water power. As late as 1870 it was said of American sawmills: 'Almost the whole mill machinery must be improvised of wood on the spot. Timber, water power and space being of little value, while *iron* is a precious metal. . . . Mills are sometimes built almost entirely of wood, without bands or bolts, or even nails, with scarcely anything metallic except the saw' (Hunter 1979: 91).

Wood was even used in the development of serial production techniques – early forms of the 'American system of manufacture' – for such things as wooden clocks (figure 3.19) (Mayr and Post 1981: 14f.). Machines in the nineteenth century could process wood much faster than metal (Rosenberg 1976: 36), so in this respect wood use did not conflict with the demand for higher speeds. Indeed, the famous British machine-tool manufacturer Joseph Whitworth asserted in 1853 in his report on the New York Crystal Palace exhibition: 'In no branch of manufacture does the application of labour-saving machinery produce by simple means more important results than in the working of wood' (Hounshell 1984: 125).

The economic historian Alfred D. Chandler argued that the nature of wood held back the dynamic of mass production and 'economies of scale': 'There was no Henry Ford of the furniture industry.' But David A. Hounshell (1984: 127, 143ff. 151) has shown from the example of Singer sewing-machines that standardized mass production was quite possible in cabinetmaking too: it was in general not technology but fashions and customers' tastes that restricted mass production in this area (IKEA being one notable exception!).

Since wood was available in such plenty in America, lightning advances there were due mainly to mechanized timber-processing techniques, not to thriftiness or to technical and artistic refinement of wood products; here lay the difference between the American way and the European way. When firewood was there for the taking, it was not necessary to make houses scrupulously draught-proof. Europeans used to joke that American timber houses were less solid than garden sheds in Europe. As President Obama recently stressed, the simple expedient of home insulation could save America an enormous amount of energy. But, despite the icy winters in mountainous regions, much scope for insulation has been wasted even there.

A leading American wood technologist, Bruce Hoadley (1980: 137), teaches that timber is more than seven times more effective than concrete for insulation purposes, and 1,400 times more effective than aluminium of the same thickness. Yet up to now this vast potential has been only marginally tapped. The technological trailblazers worked mostly with other materials – which explains why timber receded as a construction material in the industrial age. 'Wood is a natural high-tech product, but twentieth-century man was/is often using it in

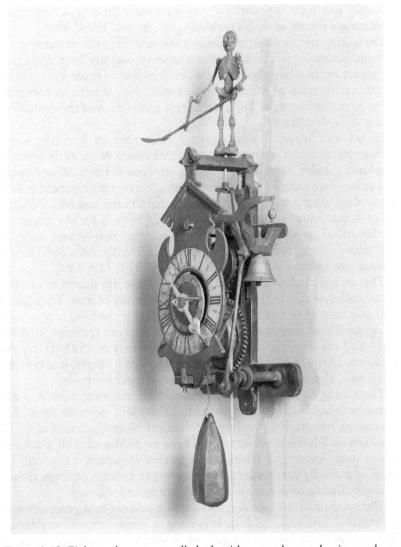

Figure 3.19: Eighteenth-century wall clock with a wooden mechanism and an alarm in the shape of Death and a pair of scales (*Tödlein Uhr*). The American Eli Terry (1772–1852) began serial production of wooden clocks early in the nineteenth century, becoming one of the pioneers of the 'American system of manufacture'. Homeworkers had been producing wooden clocks in the Black Forest since the late seventeenth century. Until then clocks had mostly been luxury and prestige items, but as they became wooden they developed into useful objects, increasingly important among wide sections of the population for the precise measurement of time in everyday life.

typically low-tech applications', complained Alfred Teischinger, one of Austria's foremost wood technologists (Bobek 1994: 386).

For a long time industrialization gave new impetus to many a traditional technology. The nineteenth century was not only the age of the steam engine, but also a time when freedom of trade gave a boost to the construction of wind and water mills. Nor should we forget the horse-gins that were the most important innovation of the century on farms in Lower Saxony.

Wood is a material that changes over time as it comes under various stresses and strains; this was also evident in the early spinning machines ('mules') and in the workers' attitude to them. 'Every operative spinner was firmly of the opinion that no two mules could ever be made alike. As a consequence he proceeded to tune and adjust each of his own particular pair of mules with little respect for the intentions of the maker or the principles of engineering. Before very long, no two mules ever were alike.' It was therefore usually not a good idea to replace one spinner with another (Catling 1970: 118, 149).

This situation changed in the 1820s with the development of automatic mules, which in the end were made entirely of iron. They meant that workers were much more interchangeable. In fact, it was often recognized that they were a response to the great spinners' strike of 1824 and the legalization of British trade unions in 1825 (Derry and Williams 1970: 563f.). Their inventor, Richard Roberts, had collaborated with Henry Maudslay, the pioneer of machine tools.

The switch to iron for the production of machine tools was also of momentous historical importance: it made it possible to achieve maximum precision by purely mechanical means, regardless of the worker's skill level; machines could now be produced with machines. There were fewer and fewer limits to this application of iron. The ideal of a totally mechanized industry began to emerge, even though in reality handicrafts remained dominant for a long time.

The production of wooden tools and machines had generally been a marginal business, seldom involving a single specific craftsman. Wooden aids for various kinds of work were normally made by the craftsman who used them. Even the wooden elements in early textile machines were produced by the textile factory itself (Catling 1970: 46). Millwrights came closest to being an exception, since not a few machine builders came from their ranks. But, given that wooden mechanisms were subject to a lot of wear, those who worked with them had to know something about repairs. According to a nineteenth-century source from Franconia, mill wheels (figure 3.20) had to have all their parts replaced every twenty to forty years; an

Figure 3.20: Wooden transmission mechanism of a nineteenth-century American watermill. Whereas the cog wheel (right) that transmitted movement from the water wheel (or from the sails in a windmill) kept its wooden shaft until well into the nineteenth century, the smaller and faster lantern gear that turned the millstone already had an iron shaft in pre-industrial times (Bedal 1984: 45). Especially hard wood (white beech, for example) was needed for the actual cogs in the cog wheel. But the wear and friction loss were still considerable.

American source puts the figure at every five years (Bedal 1984: 38; Hunter 1979: 89).

Only the breakthrough of iron sealed the rise of the machine builder and engineer. Iron machines could not be produced by the workers who used them. They offered novel scope for precision, power operation and power transmission, for mechanical serial production, faster speeds and greater efficiency. For the worker, however, the decline of wood as a material meant a loss of skills, versatility and autonomy.

The railway: a new type of technology

Massive iron use, faster production speeds, interconnected processes, changed attitudes: all these were spurred on by the railway and dramatically embodied in the experience of people living at the time.

233

More than any other innovation, the railway helped iron to become a mass product and put the iron industry on a large-scale footing. It was mainly this change in transport technology that established the superiority of mineral coal over charcoal once and for all. The railway was itself a large consumer of coal, and it provided a cheap means of transport for coal to penetrate new regions, often causing the downfall of the firewood and charcoal business. 'Free trade' had wider implications in the railway age than it had had in the eighteenth century, when, despite the growth in long-distance trade, most countries still had lived off regional resources. Only the railway made it possible for the whole of economic life to be driven by transregional systems of commerce. The lifting of all British wood tariffs in 1886 had an obvious impact on the country's ports, but also promptly led to expansion of the whole timber trade (Latham 1957: 56).

The railway brought forth a new type of technology that had existed at best in hydraulic engineering (but otherwise only in rudimentary form) during the Wood Age: technology as a complex system bound together by a logic of its own. Iron replaced wood in one part after another, beginning with boilers, wheels and rods and ending with the whole locomotive and even the wagons (which had initially been built like coaches). The wooden rails that had existed for centuries in mining also had to give way to iron, bringing the victory of mills over forges. Soon wooden bridges were a danger area in the railway system (figure 3.21), crying out to be replaced with ferrous structures. For a while station halls stuck with wood, but there too fear of sparks from passing locomotives eventually gave victory to iron.

None of this entailed a sharp fall in the demand for wood. Coal mines needed more timber than ore mining had done, and reforestation programmes continued in the Ruhr until metal stamp mills finally pushed out wooden ones after the First World War. Railway sleepers, which had to be replaced every five to seven years, hugely increased the demand for cheap construction timber, and in that department, at least, wood survived the competition from steel and pre-stressed concrete until the middle of the twentieth century. Timber for pit props and sleepers dictated the value of the forest in many regions during the great surge of railway construction and deep-face coalmining; telegraph masts determined the length of the felling cycle for spruce trees.

The use of wood for railway sleepers initiated the systematic development of impregnation agents (Pfannenschmidt 1848) and ways of calculating the strength properties of wood (Nördlinger 1860). Beech,

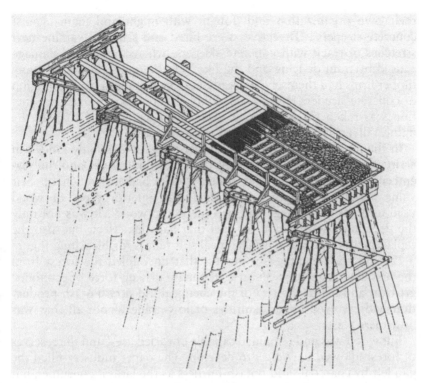

Figure 3.21: Sketch for the 17-kilometre wooden railway bridge over the Great Salt Lake (Utah, USA), 'one of the largest wooden structures in the world' when it was built in 1902–3 (Sande 1978: 98). The United States, with its vast forests, went on building wooden bridges longer than most parts of Europe. The sketch shows how much wood was needed to bear the stress of a railway bridge.
Daring, elegant structures were ruled out, and only a very short space was allowed between the pillars, which had to be as strong as possible. All in all, the railway pushed wooden bridge construction to its limits.

no longer used for firewood or charcoal, was impregnated with tar oil and given a new lease of life on the railways. Better impregnation techniques raised the life expectancy of sleepers from five to fifty years by the end of the century. Only in 1984 did the German public learn of the health dangers associated with such agents, although cases were reported way back in 1854 in which bakers had unwittingly 'poisoned' bread by using discarded sleepers as heating fuel (Pappenheim 1858: 223f.).

Anyway, by the 1980s wooden sleepers had long been in retreat. Decades earlier, the German firms that produced them had founded their own organization and 'fought with might and main against concrete sleepers'. 'Detectives were hired and sent to examine new stretches of track with concrete sleepers, where they noted damage caused by train de-icing and the like.' On the quiet, however, many timber firms had themselves already been switching to the production of concrete sleepers (Katz 2005: 996). Where modern mass production was taken to extremes, it was no longer possible to play the natural diversity of wood as one's trump card.

In the nineteenth century, the timber trade occasionally landed in a situation comparable to that of the late Middle Ages and the seventeenth century, when large timber stocks had lost much of their value because of population decline, and inferior types of wood used in times of shortage had become 'scrap wood'. It was not only the declining use of wood for fuel that had this effect, but also the replacement of potash with chemical substances for bleaching (figure 3.22) and glass-making – a process that uncoupled the forest from the textile industry (for centuries the main driving force of economic growth) and led to the rise of the chemical industry. Potash production had involved huge quantities of low-grade wood: all that was now mere waste.

But wood was and remained capable of varied uses, and the reserves of forest allowed new ones to develop. The paper industry filled the gap left by charcoal- and potash-burners as the largest consumer, but that was only the beginning of a new technological dynamic associated with 'scrap wood'.

Henry Maudslay not only helped iron on its way to victory, but also made a name for himself during the Napoleonic wars as a producer of wood-processing machinery for the shipbuilding industry. In fact, he used a whole set of thirteen steam-driven machines in a conveyor-like process that cut tackle blocks to shape (Cooper 1984). It was the beginning of the history of the modern sawmill. Circular saws (1793), bandsaws (1807) and an early veneer guillotine (1806) were also invented in England around this time, although they came into general use only in the late nineteenth century. Timber exploitation profited greatly from cheap railway transport, which in many cases made costly investments in technology worthwhile for the first time and opened the way for sawmills to develop into large businesses. Under such conditions, wood waste too could be collected and processed on a large scale.

Can we speak then of an 'end of the Wood Age'? Yes, we can, because from now on the natural properties of wood played less and less of a role in shaping workmen's skills, business locations and the

Figure 3.22: English yarn-bleaching in the eighteenth century. Bleaching made the textile industry – the most dynamic in pre-industrial and early industrial times – dependent on wood as a fuel and a leaching agent (wood-derived potash). Bleachers, like other large consumers of wood, therefore tended to migrate into mountainous regions, away from the centres of industrial concentration. The cost and quality of various kinds of potash were very important in bleaching, which an English author described in 1754 as 'the most important' but also the most 'dangerous part of our linen manufacture' (Home 1754: 202).

pace of economic life; the great innovators in technology and architecture paid less and less attention to wood. The huge new demand for wood in the early stages of industrialization – railway sleepers, pit props, electricity poles – called for standardized grades and anyway did not hold up for long. The narrow range of surviving uses also gave out in the end. Until then man's demand for wood had not preserved the original forest conditions, but at least in temperate zones it had led to mixed forest that was reasonably stable in ecological terms. Now, however, this was less and less the case. 'Sustainability' was no longer intrinsic to the industrial age; it could be recovered, if at all, only by policies that planned for the future.

— 4 —

WOOD IN THE HIGH INDUSTRIAL AGE: DEGRADATION AND REBIRTH

1 The Forest as an Economic Factor

'Forest slaughter' or sustainable silviculture and wood-saving technology? The New and the Old World

It was only in the twentieth century, and to some extent only in its final decades, that industrialization fully gripped the forest economy and the timber trade. Whereas until then mechanization had only really affected sawmills, it now also embraced logging and the processing of finished products. Different countries developed in different directions: the technology tended towards either extensive or intensive use of wood according to the size of forest resources.

A typical contrast developed here between Central Europe and North America. In Europe the processing of wood was traditionally a craft domain; in the United States the fact that wood was easy to process gave a strong impetus to mechanization. In the nineteenth century, the forest-rich regions of North America took the world lead in all such technologies, which brought advances in the quick and cheap processing of wood on a massive scale, but only at the price of high levels of waste (Rosenberg 1976: 32ff.). One expert in woodworking machinery complained in 1870: 'Lumber manufacture, from the log to the finished state, is, in America, characterized by a waste that can truly be called criminal'(Hindle 1975: 202). It was for this reason that the circular saw, supposedly invented in the Netherlands, first entered general use in densely forested regions of North America, Scandinavia and the Baltic; its early models were said to produce as much waste as timber, and sawmills that used them were in reality 'sawdust factories, with a by-product of lumber' (Latham 1957: 207, 217f.; Horn 1943: 141). Nor could it be claimed that they cut straight.

Even in 1945, forest conservation in the United States had 'scarcely reached the level of Germany more than 150 years before' (Strehlke 1961: 217). Significantly, the word 'lumber' originally meant 'junk': for the Yankee farmer pushing westward, the forest was no more than an obstacle to be overcome. Of course, this hostile attitude came in for criticism even in the days of the founding fathers. In 1818 President Madison declared to the Albemarle Agricultural Society that, of all the errors of American agriculture, none was 'so much to be regretted, perhaps because none is so difficult to repair, as the injurious and excessive destruction of timber and firewood' (Williams 1989: 144). 'The cunning foresight of the Yankee', Emerson complained, 'seems to desert him when he takes the axe in hand' (Worster 1977:

69). Perspicacious observers realized early on that the limitlessness of the American forest was an illusion – and certainly not one shared beyond the Mississippi, in the open prairies.

In 1852 Congressman Henry Hastings Sibley, later to become governor of Minnesota, exalted the 'hardy lumberman', 'who has dared to break the silence of the primeval forests by the blows of the American ax' (the ax as pioneer's emblem!); his ire fell on politicians who treated lumbermen as wood thieves because they did not bother to ask whether they were logging on public land (Turner 1920: 272f.). Anyhow, there were some contrary voices, and their numbers swelled in subsequent years.

Man and Nature (1864) by George Perkins Marsh was more impressive than any of the European appeals for forest conservation. Marsh praised in superlatives the significance of wood and the forest for the United States; Fredrick Starr was so impressed that in 1865 he calculated that wood and its derivatives paid 'more than one-half of the entire internal revenue of the United States' (Williams 1989: 331). Since that time American politicians and journalists have called ever more insistently for a sustainable forestry – particularly early and with exceptional passion in the case of Carl Schurz (Pisani 1985: 340ff.), the most famous German-American politician. Arbor Day began to be celebrated in 1872, first on 10 April, then on 22 April (which became Earth Day in 1970). In 1876 the *Scientific American* published an editorial entitled 'Timber Waste a National Suicide' (Radkau 2008a: 233). But it would take several generations for sustainable forestry to become established in practice.

The railway opened up many areas of forest for the first time in nineteenth-century America. Until the Civil War, locomotives were fired with wood (Perlin 2005: 347), and even afterwards the railway used huge quantities for track beds, sleepers, bridges and signal masts – much more than in Europe; it accounted for 20 to 25 per cent of logging in the country (Pisani 1985: 344). By the end of the century, a chorus of voices like the one in Europe a hundred years earlier was raising the alarm about an impending dearth of wood.

The railroad companies that criss-crossed the continent became the nation's largest landholders and stripped their forests with a ruthlessness that aroused public disgust. Although they also helped coal to push firewood out, 'it was gradually realized that the amount of timber needed for general railway purposes, such as buildings, stations, telegraph poles, fencing, and crossties in particular, would reach astronomical proportions if the length of track continued to expand at the rate it had in the past' (Williams 1989: 345f.).

In their rush to fell giant trees, loggers often cut into them several metres above ground level, where the trunks would normally regenerate. But when the alarm bells started ringing about shortages in the United States, as they had done a century before in Europe, the timber bosses called for the trunks to be cut further down. 'Cut 'em low, boys, cut 'em low!' Frederick Weyerhaeuser, the 'great timber baron', is supposed to have said on his death bed in 1914 (Williams 1976: 212).

In the early twentieth century, when heavy logging transporters arrived in increasing numbers to clear new areas of forest, the danger of overexploitation grew even more blatant. The warnings reached a crescendo in the United States between 1900 and 1929 (Williams 1989: 317, 440). The development of armoured vehicles in the two world wars boosted the use of caterpillar tractors, which churned up the ground as they pushed into areas of forest without proper paths.

The most important conservation measure was taken in 1900 to combat the spread of forest fires – an evil which Gifford Pinchot (1865–1946) had compared in 1898 to nothing other than slavery (Pyne 1984: 69). When Pinchot, the congenial friend of President Theodore Roosevelt, was appointed the first head of the US Forest Service in 1905, American forestry acquired the kind of charismatic figure that the Old World used to look for in vain. But in the United States, where nine-tenths of forest was in private hands, a public official had to fight harder than in a country like Germany that had a strong complement of state foresters. For a long time it was impossible to control logging in the far West, and even the Forest Reserves, established in 1891, initially had no idea of what should be done.

Although resource exhaustion was a growing worry in the timber sector itself, Pinchot came to lose all hope that the industry would adopt more responsible practices on its own initiative. In the West, logging companies were used to felling wherever they wished, with no concern for the law. The pugnacious Pinchot, who believed he was leading a war of good against evil, considered the whole timber trade to be short-sighted and corrupt (Williams 1989: 443); only tough laws and vigorous forest rangers could stop the rot. German forestry was not a model either: it seemed to him too pedantic, 'too much striving for detailed perfection' (Pinchot [1947] 1998: 17).

Feelings ran high in American as well as German forests. Taking a sober view of things, we can say that Pinchot probably underestimated the opportunity for a forest consensus; his concerns overlapped more than he realized with those of the timber industry (Williams 1989: 409, 416, 440). The small, primitive sawmills of the early days could have been moved around as and when the forest became exhausted – unless they were already fit for the scrap heap ('The ideal would be for the sawmill to fall down, after we cut the last log'); but the larger and costlier sawmills became, the more tied they were to a particular place, and the more their owners had an interest in preserving the local forest. From the 1920s on, a highly concentrated timber industry, with Weyerhaeuser at the top, acquired large tracts of forest and developed a strong interest in limiting supply to keep prices high; even Henry Ford saw wood-saving at the time as part of a rationalization strategy. This pressure to take sustainable forestry seriously then received a major boost with America's entry into the world war in 1941 (ibid.: 310ff.).

Nevertheless, in most of the USA, forestry still meant simply felling trees, not growing new ones. In German eyes, the Americans pursued 'economic butchery of the forest' far into the twentieth century. In the nineteenth century, Germany became the world pioneer of reforestation and sustainable forestry, and at times in the twentieth century – mainly in the difficult wartime and postwar periods and during the Nazi policy of autarky – it also took the lead in intensive use of the forest. In general, however, the mechanization of logging and timber-processing became widely accepted in Central and Western Europe only in the 1950s and after. We can speak of a technological revolution in timber even more important than that which occurred during the Industrial Revolution – and in line with what Christian Pfister calls 'the 1950s syndrome', which recent research has identified as a watershed in economic and environmental history.

Competing visions of a new 'age of wood' in the orbit of National Socialism

A carnival song heard in Cologne in 1948 had the lines: 'Coal is running out everywhere / Even in heaven they freeze to death' (*Überall ist große Kohlennot / Selbst im Himmel frieren sie sich tot*). In the midst of the coal age, during and after the war, Germans and other nations affected by the war had a bitter foretaste of a time when fossil fuels would run short. That coal supplies are limited and no subterranean forest keeps renewing them (as some enthusiasts had claimed) was known by the nineteenth century at the latest. It was also reckoned that oil reserves would start to run out after a few decades. Yet so long as this remained theory, without implications for everyday life, the exhaustibility of fossil fuels was not an issue that provoked much in the way of intensive thought or practical policies.

Things changed in Germany especially during and after the two world wars. Old scenarios reappeared as accessible areas of forest were cleared of every scrap of dead wood, and foresters checked people on the way in and out to make sure they were not carrying an axe under their jacket or some valuable wood on a trolley. Timber deliveries were one item on the long list of war reparations required of Germany in the Versailles treaty of 1919, and its failure to keep these up was used by Poincaré as a pretext for the French occupation of the Ruhr in 1923.

'Heat economy' was the order of the day in Germany after the First World War. What this meant first of all was using the waste heat from large industrial plant in local energy networks; the coupling of energy and heat became a rallying cry, as it would much later amid the oil crises of the 1970s. But, when better times returned in the 1920s, people began to make fun of the heat-savers as 'calorie hunters'. Investment to lower energy costs was no longer more than one policy among others, and often not a very important one.

After the Nazi takeover in 1933, Hermann Goering – who adorned himself with the titles of *Reichsforstmeister* and *Reichsjägermeister* and declared everything green to be part of his dominion – gave forestry a strikingly important place in the self-image of the new regime. The fate of the forest became emphatically an affair of the Reich. A participant in the Congress of the German Forest Federation, held shortly before the outbreak of war in 1939, recalls how it 'opened with unheard-of glitz and luxury at the Kroll opera house in Berlin'; and at the Carinhall, Goering's manor house in the forest outside Berlin, 'a whole ox was roast on a spit, and people dressed in old German sleeved clothes and practised shooting with a bow and arrow' (Steinsiek 2008: 209).

Nor was it all show. Forest and wood research was conducted as never before during the Nazi period; a spirit of euphoria spread not only among foresters but also in the timber industry. The percentage of foresters who belonged to the Nazi Party rose to 90 per cent. There was a mood of triumph in timber circles – all too premature, as it turned out – and wood acquired equal rights alongside coal and iron in the technology league (Steinsiek 2008: 19). Goering, the hunting fanatic, nevertheless pushed through a *Reichsjagdgesetz* in 1934 that removed the right to hunt on one's own land (a *cause célèbre* for nineteenth-century liberals) and imposed strict regulations that raised game stocks to a damagingly high level. Many foresters were passionate hunters, however, and so 'game damage' remained a taboo subject (Bode and Emmert 1998: 134ff.).

Strapped for foreign currency, Hitler declared maximum autarky as the goal of the Four Year Plan proclaimed in 1936; as many products as possible were to be produced with the country's own resources. The national planning authority acquired a special 'wood department' as the forest was given a prominent role in the self-sufficiency project. Popular literature began to speak of a new 'wood age', insisting that German chemistry had started out in the forest and would return there to make the Reich independent of other countries. Rhetoric centred on wood as in the eighteenth century: it was the perfect all-rounder, a natural material that kept renewing itself and never ran out.

The most widely read scientific bestseller of the Nazi period, which sold 600,000 copies, circulated in the hierarchy and was required reading in many schools, was Anton Zischka's *Wissenschaft bricht Monopole* (1936). Like so many popular books of its kind, it blithely mingled fact and speculation, predicting the 'triumph of wood' amid a burst of wild enthusiasm. 'While oak logs processed for furniture are worth fifteen times more than the raw material, chemical processing techniques increase the value of our forests a thousand times over' (Zischka 1936: 100). However, this kind of triumphalism tended to transfer wood from the hands of craftsmen to the realm of chemicals.

A first objective was to use wood waste and tree species that had had little place in the previous stages of industrialization. Synthetic fibres were produced out of wood pulp: 'vistra' was heralded as 'Germany's white gold', while 'Rayon triumphant!' was another slogan of the time. But jokes also circulated among the public, casting doubt on whether pleasant clothing really could be produced from German forests (Steinsiek 2008: 165). The development of plywood board, which made use of German beech forest in a process that involved gluing, goes back to that time (Schäfer and Zandonella 1993: 119ff.). Wood liquefaction, wood gasification, wood saccharification, wood vinegarization: these were typical projects of the autarky period, which fell into oblivion after 1945 – except in a GDR short of foreign currency – and partly emerged again only under the impact of soaring oil prices.

But what did the promised new age of wood mean for the forest? The difference of opinion that developed about this recalls today's arguments over ecological objectives: on the one side, calls for maximum use of renewable resources; on the other, demands for natural forestry. In 1934 a landowner from east of the Elbe, Walter von Keudell, who championed mixed deciduous forest and opposed clear-felling, was appointed head of the new Reich Forestry Department, under the patronage of his fellow huntsman in the forests near Berlin, Hermann

Goering. Under the watchword 'continuous forest' (*'Dauerwald'*), he pushed his model of natural forestry so rigorously that many foresters felt 'cut up' and ended by publicly rebelling against him (Radkau 2008a: 262).

The Nazis glorified the 'German forest', like everything else German, but there were arguments about what it should look like. A new rhetoric celebrated the 'eternal forest' as the living space of the 'eternal nation' (Imort 2005), but it remained controversial how the forest would be 'eternal' (read: sustainable). The forest scientist Alfred Dengler, whose home in Eberswalde was not far from Goering's manor in the Schorfheide forest, advocated 'silviculture on an ecological foundation' but *opposed* the 'continuous forest' doctrine; he sought to prove that pure coniferous stands were also adapted for northern Germany, and praised their hardiness in the northern winter climate (Dengler 1935: 542ff.). Ecology was already becoming a fighting concept!

Keudell's 'continuous forest' strategy collided with the heavy demands that the Four Year Plan made on German forests. In 1937 he had to yield to the SS fanatic Friedrich Alpers, who unconditionally backed the production goals of the Nazi leadership. With no concern for the 'German forest' – which Nazi ideologue Alfred Rosenberg had just glorified in the film *Der ewige Wald* (1936) – even the eucalyptus, the most hated of forest pests, was now given a place of honour for the sake of maximizing the timber harvest as quickly as possible (Steinsiek 2008: 179f.). The 'continuous forest' strategy was not going to satisfy the growing demand for wood. The policy of national autarky ran up against its limits in relation to forest resources sooner than any other. Self-sufficiency was imaginable, if at all, only in a much larger Reich; the crisis of autarky offered an economic justification for military expansion.

Conquests in the East took some of the pressure off the German forest. In 1941 an initiative within the Deutscher Heimatbund, the recently renamed conservation organization, aimed at saving the country's deciduous forest by means of a challenging public exposé – in the middle of a war, in a totalitarian state! – which had wide reverberations. One of its poetasters complained: 'O German forest, o beech green / And power of mighty oaks / O German forest, you fall down there / From the blows of your slayer!' (*O deutscher Wald, o Buchengrün / Und Kraft der starken Eichen / o deutscher Wald, du sinkst dahin / Von deines Würgers Streichen!*) (Radkau 2002: 264). The 'slayers', we should note, were those who complied with the high felling levels allowed by the Nazi economic planners.

The Nazi film *Der ewige Wald* showed how war destroys not only people but also the forest. In fact, amazing though it may seem, a kind of anti-imperialist tendency might have been expected from the German forestry of the time; the much cited 'iron law of the local' had become accepted doctrine only a short time before, in the 1920s. The location-dependence of forestry was proclaimed in the nineteenth century, with little scientific underpinning, but now research progress had given the idea support from the soil sciences. Many foresters were quite happy to sign up to the 'iron law', since it legitimated their autonomy from rules and regulations passed down from on high. But, by the same token, could the future of Ukrainian forests be planned from Berlin?

In reality, of course, it was imperial forest strategies that flourished in the wartime sequel to autarky. A leading actor in this was a man with wide experience, Franz Heske, whose father had administered the Black Mountain forests in Bohemia; he himself had studied at the Imperial Forestry Institute in Oxford in 1925, and in 1928–9 had been forest inspector for the Maharajah of Tehri Garhwal on the edge of the Himalayas, where he is still remembered today as a pioneer of sustainable natural forestry (Rawat, in Schuler 1985: 207ff.). It was partly on his initiative that a Comité International de Sylviculture was established in Berlin in 1937, as a rival to the Comité International du Bois founded in 1932–3 within the framework of the League of Nations.

Heske was at heart a forest romantic who cherished the conviction that the 'divine harmony of nature' would some day be restored through a bonfire of human artifice (Heske 1937: 123). For him this was reason to hope for a greater German Reich: the native German forest had become so 'tame' and unnatural that it could no longer bring forth strong and vigorous humans; expansion into wild forest areas was necessary to revive the wild energy of the German people. When the war began he thought his time had come. He wanted to make the safeguarding of Europe's wood supply a German war aim – which meant conquering Russia's northern forests, not only its southern agrarian steppes (Steinsiek 2008: 112ff.). More ambitious even than Hitler, he was not satisfied with 'living space' in the East, but dreamed of ruling vast tropical forests in an African colonial empire.

Heske had an international opponent, however, in the shape of the German emigré Egon Glesinger, who had been born into a family of timber dealers from Bohemia (also the land of Heske's birth) and was one of the driving forces behind the League of Nations Wood Committee and, later, the forestry department of the FAO, the UN

Food and Agriculture Organization. The Second World War was also fought at the level of forest strategies! Glesinger kept a close watch on Nazi autarky policy and its timber exploitation projects, and in 1947 he published *The Coming Age of Wood*, in which he rejected the then rampant resource pessimism and enthusiastically described 'what a great contribution our forests [could] make to the building of a world of plenty' (Glesinger 1949: vi) – if, that is, they were managed sustainably.

Similar ideas found resonance in the United States during the New Deal era, when, much as in Nazi Germany, the conservation and improved use of natural resources was a prime political objective. A leading British historian of the forest, Michael Williams, dates to 1933 a 'rebirth of the forest' in the United States (1989: 466ff.). The NRA codes of fair practice, whose blue eagles presaged today's certificates (and presented similar problems), also covered forestry. Meanwhile, the Timber Development Association became active in Britain and presented its first demonstration timber house at Dome Hill, Caterham, in 1938. A broad green alliance of forestry and the timber industry seemed to be shaping up (Latham 1957: 261, 85).

Glesinger was not worried that sustainable forestry might ever result in wood shortages: he was convinced that with good management the potential of the world's forests was infinite. He thought that the creation of 'integrated forest industries' would be decisive – that is, industrial complexes located in the forest and closely collaborating with the forestry service, which exploited resources so prudently that no waste would result and timber products would be able to capture many different kinds of markets. His vision of the future had some affinity with Nazi autarky projects, but it also points towards today's agendas of 'forest and wood cluster projects' and 'timber with short transport routes'. Recently, however, in both timber and industry in general, there has been a counter-tendency to focus on core expertise and to outsource other sectors.

Since transport costs are very high for mass-processed timber, regional sourcing may be seen as a rational economic strategy. A regional forest and wood cluster is also the best way to ensure a sustainable timber supply – a valuable objective for the timber sector, which even in good times is plagued by fears of future shortage. As industrial plants become more expensive, the costs of relocation rise and reliable sourcing from the local region becomes correspondingly more attractive. Autarkic thinking had a more rational, future-oriented side in the timber industry than in other sectors of the economy, but in those days such projects usually foundered on the division between forest and timber interests and were anyway over-whelmed by the oil boom of the 1950s. Up to now the main effort has gone into increasing mobility. Today it is more doubtful than ever whether large-scale industry is capable of planning several genera-tions ahead and providing for sustainable forestry.

Forestry and the profitability question

After the triumph of coal and steel in the nineteenth century, little public attention was paid to wood as an economic factor. Yet wood consumption was constantly rising. Although forest management led to considerably increased yields, Germany turned in the 1860s from a wood-exporting to a wood-importing country. The Zollverein in 1865 suspended customs duties on imported wood. Then wood prices went through the floor in the 'Great Depression' of the 1870s, and owners of forest land joined the front of those calling for protective tariffs. In contrast to the agrarians, however, they had little success either then or later.

Whereas timber companies with large forest possessions took shape in twentieth-century America, landowners and the timber industry remained opposed to each other in Germany, and in many cases state forestry offices were the dominant suppliers of timber. Their declared principle of sustainability has often sounded to consumers as a cartel-like restriction on production; the forest bureaucracy has been a common bogey for the timber trade. Yet it has provided valu-able services to processors of timber, not only furnishing them with the raw material but also grading it by quality and ensuring long-term supply security. This has been fully realized only in recent times, just as forestry services are being drastically reduced everywhere. The timber market does not guarantee sustainable forestry or the long-term security of supply that the industry needs in order to make costly investments.

Until the age of ecology, sustainability was primarily a question of forest rotation and therefore a source of lasting contention. State forestry departments persisted in demanding long rotation periods, which corresponded to the high forest model that reformers devel-oped around the turn of the nineteenth century. For a long time this suited the interests of the sawmills, which until the 1980s operated with the rule that output rose and costs fell disproportionately as trunk diameter increased. But it also corresponded to a gut feeling, found even among loggers, that trees as well as people have a right to grow old.

Karl Polanyi rightly pointed out in 1944 that, 'though the institution of the market was fairly common since the later Stone Age', history knows of 'no economy prior to our own even approximately controlled and regulated by markets' (Polanyi 1957: 43f.). This may not be true of all sectors of the economy, but it certainly is of the forestry and timber sectors. There has been trading in timber since antiquity, but the idea of adapting silviculture to changing demand in order to maximize profits has spread only in recent times. It can be realized, if at all, only in plantations with rotation periods lower than twenty years, which call to mind the coppice system of old. The bulk of forest landowners are still geared more to risk minimization than to profit maximization. That is inevitable, because anything like a precise calculation of profit is impossible in the forest.

The last century was a roller-coaster for the profitability of forestry; the more woodland was given over to logging, the sharper were the ups and downs of the construction industry. The long timber boom that began in the late seventeenth century lasted until the second half of the nineteenth, when the sector underwent its first major downturn in the depression of the 1870s. The world economic crisis after 1929 again hit the forestry sector hard, causing it to operate for years at a loss. After 1945, the West German forest industry profited at first from the postwar shortages and then from the country's 'economic miracle', but in the 1960s operating profits began to fall and many companies chalked up actual losses. In the new millennium, another timber boom and fresh incentives for precise economic calculation brought to an end the lean period in which many foresters had virtually given up hope.

Intensive forestry and the switch to 'industrial timber'

Optimize and maximize, increase profits by meeting the demands of the timber trade, use every available means of intensifying production: these were the guiding aims of twentieth-century forestry, even if it remained much closer than agriculture to the natural world and hesitated to cultivate new species of trees. Many small woodland areas, whose owners earned their money elsewhere and had little interest in rational forestry, retained a whiff of the wild.

Forestry during the last hundred years has employed a number of ways to become more intensive. The oldest method is the cultivation of pure coniferous stands, whose effect can be further increased by systematic tree selection. Especially after the Second World War, when Nazi autarky policy and occupation fever had given the

German forest a 'lift', conifer plantation was given a fresh impetus in spite of frequent objections to monoculture and the risks known to be associated with it since the late eighteenth century. In Britain, conifer afforestation first began on a large scale after the First World War, under the auspices of the newly founded Forestry Commission (Rackham [1976] 1990: 102f.); it has on the whole still not marked the country's landscape.

The spruce became the proverbial 'bread and butter' tree of German forestry (Trübswetter 1983: 146), not only because it grew so fast, but because the versatility of its fairly homogeneous wood ensured good sales. With their slim trunks and thin branches, spruces grow closely together in the forest – the kind of stand that produces most wood. There is therefore a technical reason for cultivating pure stands of the same age (Zwerger 1997: 16). Spruce can be used for internal design, roof timberwork, floor boards, plywood panels, masts, joiner's wood, furniture, and the pulpwood for paper and fibreboards.

Spruce is also much sought after for engineered wood and as a resonance wood for musical instruments, where it appreciates the most in value. Antonio Stradivari, the most celebrated violinist of all time, personally scoured the forest north of Bergamo for suitable spruce trunks, preferring mixed beech stands that prevented them from growing too fast (Jörg Uitz, in Cwienk 1995: 297). Otherwise, however, the spruce is not usually thought of as outstanding. Spruce monoculture was enemy number one for the pioneers of natural silviculture – both rationally, because of its susceptibility to pests and storm damage, and emotionally, because the sight of it was depressing unless it was covered with winter snow. *Willst du den Wald vernichten / dann pflanze nichts als Fichten!* ['If you wish to destroy the forest / Plant nothing there but spruce!']: this verse became a rallying cry for advocates of natural silviculture. But, since it grew fast and straight and was easy to dry and to process, it became very popular among woodworkers and was preferred to beech and oak in the building trade. The paper and cellulose industry, and especially chipboard producers, are large consumers of light spruce. But, as in the past, the trunk wood provides the lion's share of forest yields.

In Germany, the planting of trees was traditionally female work. One of the women in question adorned the 50 pfennig coin after the West German currency reform of 1948, so symbolic of reconstruction were tree-planters at the time. There was little incentive to mechanize the work in the compact spaces of Central Europe, but things were different in North America. The Weyerhaeuser corporation was already using helicopters in the 1950s for forest-planting, and the same aircraft scattered poisoned seeds as a weapon against animal chewing (Hidy et al. 1963: 559). It was such methods that drew Rachel Carson's ire in her *Silent Spring*, later to become the bible of the American environmental movement. In Europe, by contrast, rising wages made natural rejuvenation seem attractive again, especially as the results were often better than expected. Economics and ecology tended to converge.

The yield from large-scale cultivation of indigenous conifers was surpassed by foreign imports. The American Douglas fir, with all its advantages, suited corporate objectives especially well, and it began to be planted as early as the 1880s; there was lively propaganda in favour of Douglas firs in Germany at that time, and among foresters a venturesome 'Douglas pioneer' type emerged who did not usually come from an old family of foresters. No less a figure than Bismarck, who – though he had an oak named after him – adopted a soberly economic attitude in his own forests, grew Douglas firs in Saxony and encouraged the tree nursery owner John Booth, on whose initiative eighty-eight Prussian forestry offices conducted trials with foreign wood species (Hesmer 1958: 309). Dieback in 1937 led to a temporary ban on new planting of the tree (Oeschger 1975: 130ff.). Douglas fir wood can be used for external and internal design, for parquet floors, floor boards, shipbuilding, peeled wood and mine timber; it is more resistant than spruce to destructive fungi and insects. Its seeds are today up to a hundred times more expensive than spruce seeds in Germany. But it is still a controversial tree in Europe, both economically and ecologically.

Rationalization through mechanization

In the 1950s and 1960s, sharply rising wages and social contributions in the leading industrial countries had a severe impact on the profits of labour-intensive forestry. The traditionally low wages drove many workers into sectors where pay and working conditions were better, and to counter this the forest industry had to offer large wage increases without being able to pass the higher costs on in the form of higher prices. The only businesses that could withstand the economic pressure were therefore those in a position to adopt rationalization strategies involving mechanization, speed-up and job reductions.

The wave of mechanization in Central European forestry – especially the introduction of chainsaws and de-barkers – began in the early 1960s, decades later than in the most heavily forested countries; conditions were less favourable than in Canada, the United

Figure 4.1: American illustration for the Paris World Fair of 1878. It shows the zeal with which steam power was deployed in the forest at that time, even though the economic results were not altogether convincing. The United States was then ahead of Europe in this technology and proudly presented its achievements at the World Fair. Mobile steam engines (locomobiles) were used to fell trees and even to drive frame saws.

States or the Soviet Union. To mechanize on that scale would have required larger businesses, since only sizeable surfaces permit full use of heavy machinery and interlocking work processes. Such integrated systems were on the cards only in state enterprises, where partial adjustments were indeed carried out. For the many thousands of private forest-owners, extensive mechanization was possible only in exceptional cases.

The seemingly simple chainsaw was in fact a hundred years in the making. Sawing mechanization trials started in the United States in the second half of the nineteenth century, at a time when only steam power was available (figure 4.1). But steam saws were not up to the job (Fries 1951: 33): only motors could mechanize felling operations. This proved successful, however, only when people stopped being fixated on mechanical imitation of the handsawing process.

There was a striking parallel with the development of bandsaws in sawmills. In their search for continuous rotation, nineteenth-century engineers already considered the to-and-fro gang saw to be behind the times, and in 1855 the first 'endless saw' was introduced at the Paris World Fair. But the combination of extreme firmness and flexibility necessary for a sawing business was not easy to achieve; it was bound up with advances in steel quality. The rotating sawblade of the nineteenth century was not firm enough to cut thick tree trunks with precision. Bandsaws and gang saws still sat side by side in many twentieth-century mills, the latter being used to cut valuable thick trunks (Finsterbusch and Thiele 1987: 224–43). Only in recent times has the bandsaw taken over for that purpose too.

Rotation also led to the chainsaw breakthrough: Andreas Stihl, who marketed the first model in the 1920s, became the world leader, later celebrated by Chuck Leavell, the Rolling Stones keyboard player, as the 'father of the chainsaw' (Leavell 2001: 77). In Central Europe it would take another generation for the innovation to enter general use. The early devices were too heavy, too bulky and too failure-prone; even the lightest topped 40 kilos in the 1930s and required great effort from two men working together. The chainsaw had to lose a lot of weight if it was going to catch on, and this did not happen until the 1950s. After 1955 the light one-man chainsaw scored an 'unparalleled victory' in the Alps (Bobek 1994: 310).

With a weight of just 3 kilos, it was not only a one-man but also a one-woman tool. The American writer Sue Hubbell writes in her field report *A Country Year*: 'The best chain saws are formidable and dangerous tools. My brother nearly cut off his arm with one. . . . He was very solemn when I told him that I had bought my own chain saw, and he gave me a good piece of advice. "The time to worry about a chain saw," he said, "is when you stop being afraid of it."' (1986: 45).

The hand chainsaw was for a long time the most important forest implement. It helped to make log felling – which had often been a side activity until the 1950s – into a specialized occupation. Mechanization raised skill requirements, but at the same time it reduced the workforce by so much that forestry workers almost disappeared as a distinctive social category in Central Europe. Between 1950 and 1990 the output of an Austrian logger increased tenfold, from 200 to 2,000 cubic metres per annum, and between 1965 and 1992 the numbers employed all year round shrank from 28,000 to 5,900 (Bobek 1994: 311). The triumph of the chainsaw revolutionized forestry work around the world.

Since loggers were lured out of the woods into more attractive jobs in the boom years of the 1950s and 1960s, the chainsaw came at just the right time for forest managers. It did not have to be forced onto forestry workers, as the handsaw had been two hundred years earlier, since their piece-rates initially remained at more or less the same level and, although they had to buy their own chainsaw, they were able to increase their wages several times over. The chainsaw also allowed them to work on their own, as in the days of the axe, and the high pay tempted many to saw for hours at a time without observing the prescribed rest periods. This ruined their health, confirming the truth of the old union saying: *Akkord ist Mord* [Piecework is murder]. Conditions were so scandalous that forest managers eventually switched to time rates, which did not have the bad effect on morale that they had previously feared.

Meanwhile heavy machinery (harvesters) was pushing chainsaws out in the vast forests of Canada and Scandinavia – a development that brought the greatest cost reduction for decades and ended an era of manual labour going back to time immemorial and only intensified by the chainsaw. Today it is rare for a tree trunk or the resulting timber to be touched by human hand, either in the forest or in a sawmill.

Natural limits on the use of heavy machinery lasted longer in Central and Western Europe, and up to a point still remain in force. For a considerable part of the forest there lies in small mountainous regions, where the terrain is not conducive to large-scale mechanization. In Scandinavia and Canada trees can be felled by the square kilometre, and it was worth deploying 'forwarders' (a kind of cross between crane truck and giant shears) much earlier. Indeed, in northern Canada, industrial timber is harvested with machines that fell, limb and cut in one operation; a fully grown tree can be processed into small logs in 30 seconds flat.

By now heavy machines such as pushback tractors, harvesters and forwarders have appeared in European mountain forests too. Steep terrain has proven less of an issue here than the capacity of the soil to bear heavy tyre pressure without sustaining long-term damage. All in all, the mechanization of forestry work sharpens the tension between economics and ecology at a time of heightened environmental awareness. Wood harvest trains that the Austrian government introduced after major windthrow disasters have had to be 'mothballed' again: 'They bring practical constraints that are alien to the rhythm of forest growth. The forest ecosystem sits uneasily with inflexible technological giants' (Josef Spörk, in Heinzinger 1988: 40).

Technological change also affected the skills structure of forestry work, requiring the training of specialists in everything from chainsaws to engine-driving. However, chainsaws did not remove the dangers of tree-felling and to some extent even increased them.

Workers had to look out more than before for hidden stresses, which were especially hard to detect in trees with overhanging branches; it was a skill that could be learned only by long experience, not from mere training courses.

The new heavy machinery considerably reduced accident rates in forestry work, after a period in which chainsaws had sometimes pushed them up. In particular, there were fewer dangers from tool wounds, falling trees and trunk or branch tension. Technology was specifically deployed to eliminate accidents in heavy and dangerous work such as reconditioning after wind-breakage.

2 Technological Revolution in the Timber Industry

Wood becomes an industrial raw material

Since the second half of the nineteenth century, wood has been used as a raw material in three different ways: for boards and beams (still the most important timber products); for the paper and chemical industries; and for woodwork materials such as plywood, chipboard and fibreboard. Whereas experience and craftsmanship used to be paramount in the processing industry, the new materials and engineered lumber rely upon developments in chemistry.

Raw timber has been treated in various ways and combined with other materials in order to even out quality variations and to achieve a uniform end product. Carpenters traditionally needed only a white-washed surface on which to lay out wood of the correct size for their timber joints (figure 4.2), but large hydraulic presses are needed for today's engineered lumber. A frame saw and air-dried stacks of wood used to be enough for board-making, but the production of chipboard requires ever larger industrial plant, with a long chain of work steps in a largely automatic process sequence.

The development of technology led to a reversal of traditional norms: whereas glue and ferrous compounds had once been frowned upon in the carpenter's trade – early bone glues were not watertight and therefore could not be used for external walls – such substances were at the heart of modern technology. The old division between joiners and carpenters lost much of its keenness. Whereas the old crafts had tried to use as much good-quality wood as possible, the exploitation of 'wood waste' now became the driving force of the sector. But, despite technological changes, many jobs in the timber industry remain more versatile than elsewhere and have more of a

Figure 4.2: Timber yard in Kiel, *c.*1890. It is a real-size 'drawing floor', on which pieces of construction timber are laid out and cut. Although the building industry boomed in the nineteenth century with the growth of cities, production technology still had a craft character in the expanded enterprises. The photograph illustrates the lack of machinery even towards the end of the nineteenth century.

craft character. To this day, the industry has also preserved its local and middle-class profile in large parts of Europe.

When wood becomes an industrial raw material, it loses its macro-structure and the natural properties associated with it. Only certain features of its micro-structure are still used – above all, the capacity of elements in wood to join or adhere together without the use of glue. This property is the basis for the use of wood in the paper and plasterboard industries – two branches that have become essential to the wood industry, and in which wood is the main raw material.

A raw material in paper production

In pre-industrial times paper was made from white rags, but this led to bottlenecks in the eighteenth century, provoking a search for substitutes. It is said that the idea of using wood instead was first suggested by the observation of wasps, which scrape greyed wood from which the lignin has washed away and make 'wasp paper' for their nests from the remaining cellulose. But, at the height of the panic over shortages, wood did not seem to offer good prospects for a major new consumer. Then the rag supply bottleneck was alleviated for a while by the introduction of chlorine bleach (1787), the early industrial 'revolution in the art of bleaching' (Clow and Clow 1956: 173), which made it possible to turn coloureds white and even to use them for paper.

Machine production of paper, first seen in Germany around 1840, brought a new raw material bottleneck. This was solved by means of mechanical wood-pulping, which was invented in 1843 by the master weaver and mechanic Gottfried Keller. The new material, available from timber resources released by the onward march of coal, enabled the mass production of cheap paper, especially for the printing press. Tree trunks were first de-barked and sawn into blocks, then torn into fibres on a wood grinder, mixed with water and turned into a fibrous pulp. At first this was only added to the traditional rag mixture, but the development of chemical wood-pulping in cellulose production created a perfect basis for the industrialization of wood paper. It was superior in quality to mechanical pulping, whose end product is less watertight and contains lignin, the cause of long-term yellowing. Paper containing lignin is therefore used today only for short-life products, especially newsprint.

Apart from recycled paper, the basic material for most other paper products is cellulose, which is characterized by water-tightness and a high degree of purity. Lignin, the characteristic component of wood, shows its defects in the production of paper – above all because of the yellowing process. Whereas wood pulp partly retains a fibrous structure, wood completely loses its natural character in chemical pulping. All that is left is a mushy mass, more like cotton wool than wood.

Wood pulp too developed out of practical trials, but cellulose was invented around 1870 by the chemist Alexander Mitscherlich, who was conducting research at the Hannover-Münden Forest Academy on industrial applications of wood (Greiling 1943: 247ff.). When he also founded a cellulose factory, whose emissions caused damage to the forest, he made himself unpopular with his colleagues and was eventually forced to give up his academic position. Subsequently, however, more and more foresters saw the expanding cellulose industry as a way of using scrap wood rejected by the sawing industry. With firewood on its way out, it was the demand of the cellulose industry that made thinning operations – the elimination of low-grade wood in favour of 'well brought-up' varieties – profitable again.

The paper and cellulose industry, one of the most energy-intensive, is a major source of air and water pollution. State-of-the-art mechanical defibration now has a recovery yield as high as 98 per cent, whereas nearly a half of wood mass is lost as 'waste' in chemical pulping (Sittauer 1982: 120). Water pollution, a traditional problem in paper production, was greatly increased by the switch to cellulose production, which caused the first sensational damage to the environment in a country such as Sweden. The Soviet ecological movement developed in the 1970s mainly out of disgust at the pollution of Lake Baikal, an iconic feature of the Russian landscape, whose cellulose complexes were exploiting the wealth of Siberia's forests (Pryde 1991: 84ff.). In 1938, the authorities in the Ruhr went into a real state of alarm over plans to build a cellulose factory in the upper reaches of the river; it hung over the region like a sword of Damocles and fulfilled 'the worst fears' when it was brought into wartime service against the objections of the district president (Radzio 1988: 57). Since then, filtering and wastewater treatment plants have made it possible greatly to reduce this kind of pollution.

Another delicate issue was the stench from sulphur used in the production process (Becker 1986: 35); even a chemist who wrote a specialist work on *Wood and Technology* admitted that the smell emanating from the factories in question was 'frightful' (Jellinek 1927: 55). Cellulose production is the only major branch of industry that environmentalists managed to drive out of parts of Germany long before the coming of the 'ecological age'. Recently, however, ways have been found to reduce the pollution associated with it. The largest cellulose plant in Central Europe, built between 2002 and 2004 at Arneburg near Stendal, in the former GDR, was praised by former German chancellor Gerhard Schröder as a 'beacon project' for the future (*Holz-Zentralblatt*, 29 October 2004).

New materials: plywood, fibreboard and chipboard

The still growing list of wood products may be divided into three groups: plywood, fibreboard and chipboard. These developed in three successive historical periods, each corresponding to a stage in the structural disaggregation of the material and the industrialization of the timber sector. In these groups of products, unlike in the cellulose industry, the fibrous structure of wood is still an asset, albeit in smaller particles, but glue is increasingly used to hold the material together. The old problem of warping over time, which has always affected timber buildings and wooden furniture and doors, thus ceases to be a problem, and at the same time the proportion of useable wood is considerably increased.

The new materials were initially produced with the old soluble bone glues; their huge and surprising potential for the timber industry became fully apparent only when new synthetic glues came on stream. The United States played a key role in these developments. Whereas the 'natural wood mentality' persisted for a long time in Europe, associated with a longing for solidity across generations, the more mobile Americans, who see houses and furniture as more provisional, were more prepared to experiment with new wooden materials.

Plywood was in the vanguard, dissolving the structure of wood for the first time and assembling it into a new unity. Not only did it become available in much greater quantity than solid wood with comparable uses, it also had a number of groundbreaking quality advantages. Moisture expansion, contraction and buckling – those troubles that keep recurring in the technical history of wood – were now a thing of the past. Plywood made it possible to produce large panels that revolutionized furniture production. In fact, it was based on veneer technology that went back to ancient Egypt; the novelty was that the veneer was no longer laid parallel but applied in several layers stuck on top of one another across the direction of the fibres. This meant that it was 'closed off' from buckling.

The plywood breakthrough began in the late nineteenth century in regions richly endowed with wood: the Baltic and the United States. It was thus originally a quality product, not a means of saving wood. For a long time, German craftsmen had strong reservations about the new material; it was at first restricted to barrels, boxes and chairs and only gradually found its way into furniture production. Progress was must faster in Britain, where refugees from the Baltic started mass-producing furniture with plywood around the end of the nineteenth century, and where it became a luxury material for high-quality furniture, pianos and grand pianos, panelling and doors. On the continent, people generally preferred exotic redwoods, especially *okumé* or gaboon from Equatorial Africa, which could be pared for veneer more easily than cut for boards (Bramwell 1976: 232). Whereas the tropical woods in favour on the continent had previously been high-grade hardwoods, after 1900 *okumé* became the first tropical lightwood to be imported in bulk; it gave a new dimension to deforestation in the countries in question.

Aircraft construction in the two world wars gave fresh impetus to plywood production (Hornitex 1976: 18). During the Second World War, Stanley F. Horn (1943: 162) called it 'the young mammoth of the

forest-products industries'. But in the 1930s German specialist literature described it as a 'luxury item', three times more expensive than
simply glued wooden panels (Spannagel 1939: 47f.). The decisive
innovation for the German plywood industry was the use of beechwood, the only suitable kind available internally in large enough
quantities, which could also be had quite cheaply because of its status
as a 'forgotten wood'. Not only was beech sufficiently robust and
water-tight for plywood; its other advantages were its thick trunks
and immaculate branches. While spruce and birch are preferred in
Northern Europe, and poplar in Southern Europe, the native beech is
still today the most important basis for the German plywood industry. 'It is loved by no one (even plastic has people who love it), and
yet is now used by everyone' (Clancey 2007: 127). Since the 1990s,
however, plywood has been overtaken by 'oriented strand boards'.

Durable *fibreboards* for furniture were first made in Britain in
1898, but mass production began only in the 1920s, once defibration
techniques had been perfected. As in paper production, coniferous
wood was used from thinning operations, together with low-grade
spruce showing flaws or signs of misgrowth, waste wood from other
tree species, or even rape and rice straw. This industry had a beneficial
effect on Scandinavian forestry, since it created an economic incentive
for thinning operations that speeded up the growth of the trees left
standing.

The soaring rise of *chipboard* in the second half of the twentieth
century overshadowed that of all other wood materials (Höchli 1957:
67; Hornitex 1976: 22). Its history is closely bound up with the rise
of synthetic resins and the development of the chemical industry.
Favoured by the policy of autarky in Nazi Germany, as well as in
Switzerland, it reached the stage of industrial application around
1940 and began its triumphal march in the 1950s (Deppe 1976: 21f.).
By the 1980s West Germany was leading the world in chipboard
production (Trübswetter 1983: 131). One 'generation' of technology
followed another, until the goal of Ford-style continuous flow production was reached.

Chipboard production is simple in theory, though not in present-
day practice. The raw wood – smallwood, branches, low-grade wood,
industrial or craft waste – is first machine-shredded into chips of
varied but fixed lengths. This material is coated with synthetic resin
binder in a large mixer, scattered into suitably layered moulds, and
pressed into boards under heat. Then, in a final stage, these boards
are polished and trimmed.

The wood-processing industry and woodcrafts have in chipboard a material that can be better processed by machine than solid wood or plywood, and that can also be machine-produced out of waste wood. Chipboard is versatile, its main applications being in furniture and internal fittings. Originally, softwood logs were used for its production, but soaring output in the 1950s soon made it necessary to expand the range of wood inputs. Researchers tried to bridge the gap with hardwood, and since the late 1970s waste wood has replaced log wood in most European countries. This corresponds to a general trend to exploit timber residue as an industrial raw material.

Chipboard production came under attack in the 1970s and 1980s because of its potential dangers to the environment and health; explosive high-energy gases can build up in the production process and volatile wood constituents can be put into circulation (Kossatz 1976: 24). The use of synthetic resin glues, which revolutionized wood materials, also created problems that long went unnoticed. The production of formaldehyde-based glues can be injurious to the health, since formaldehyde penetrates the nasal passages and causes skin inflammation and allergies; there is also growing evidence that it increases the risk of cancer (Lahl and Zeschmar 1985: 12). It is not only people working in the industry but also consumers who are at risk, since products made with formaldehyde leave traces in ambient air that can persist for months and years.

The formaldehyde alarm of the 1980s marked a stage in the environmental movement and created uncertainty in the timber industry that has not gone away (*Holz-Zentralblatt*, 16 November 2007). Tolerance limits for formaldehyde in ambient air have become more and more restrictive. Indeed, since the substance also occurs naturally, it is now sometimes the case that natural solid wood releases more formaldehyde into the air than chipboard does. Formaldehyde-free chipboard, containing calcium or polyurethane binding agents, has also begun to appear on the market.

From plywood to chipboard: the progression of materials seemed to be breaking the natural structure of wood down into smaller and smaller particles. But there is no linear advance in wood matters: the recent headlong rise of oriented strand boards (OSBs) shows that it is more like a zig-zag movement, which sometimes reverts to greater use of natural structures and even sets up surprising aesthetic effects that appeal to customers. OSBs consist of long rough boards arranged crosswise in three layers and glued under high pressure. Since they are cheaper than plywood, but come close to it in water-tightness, they have succeeded in pushing it out of many applications.

At a time when wood was losing a lot of ground, the new materials greatly expanded its field of application and, despite limited forest resources, gave a huge impetus to growth; the position that wood occupies today would have been unimaginable on the basis of solid wood alone. One advantage of the new materials is that they allow for precise quality standardization – a key point in modern technology that makes the traditional oversizing of timber structures unnecessary. At least in a technical sense, the new materials have brought potential unity to the timber sector: the old line of divide between joiners and carpenters has blurred; technical transfers have developed in both directions between wooden components and cabinetmaking. Joiners can no longer rely on a sharply defined sphere of competence, but must seek new industrial niches for themselves – which they have so far repeatedly managed to find (Zander 2008).

But, as in all things, progress comes at a price. The faster that new materials are developed, the less experience one has of their long-term durability and the more one has to reckon on unpleasant surprises. They cried out for research, but science often lagged behind the turbulent advances in technology (Höchli 1957: 57). As mechanization drove up fixed costs, profitability depended more on capacity utilization and was at risk from downturns in the economy; this is a typical problem of Fordist mass production, already well known from the crisis of 1929 and tending to grow sharper with the increased differentiation of consumer tastes. Although the timber industry presents wood as the ideal resource for the ecological age, produced with solar energy and free of disposal problems, the use of chemical glues in new wood materials casts doubt on this claim, particularly when they are combined with synthetic substances. In 1948 it was still an open question for Giedion what would happen when mechanization met up with organic substances. Since then the problems have become much easier to identify.

To repeat: linear concepts of progress do not apply to wood; there have been steps forward from solid wood to composite materials, but also steps back towards solid wood. The natural–synthetic composites have often been lauded as the materials of the future, but it is doubtful whether such prognoses will be confirmed in view of all ecological reservations. At the special display on 'new materials' at the Hannover Trade Fair in 1986, questions about recycling usually met with an awkward silence. This speech problem has not persisted: no limits are set today to the spirit of invention, even in the case of 'biosynthetics' that combine the advantages of wood and synthetic materials in an ecologically unobjectionable manner (GreenTech 2007: 82). But the new 'solid wood panels', which, unlike chipboard

263

and fibreboard, largely preserve the natural structure of wood, are also part of the 'renaissance of solid wood' in the ecological age (Alfred Teischinger, in Bobek 1994: 378f.).

The German timberman Ralf Pollmeier started out with glued wood particle boards, but he soon found himself undercut by East Asian competitors. So then he turned himself into Europe's largest sawyer of deciduous wood, at Creuzburg, in one of the prohibited areas of the former GDR. Today he no longer conceives of rationalization in the Fordist sense of an improved production flow, but defines it as optimal quality grading plus information about the state of the market.

The *International Book of Wood*, published in 1976, ends its chapter on wooden materials as follows:

> A glance into the future suggests that in coming years even these man-made products may be regarded as outdated and wasteful. Current research is directed at reducing the whole tree – stem, branches, bark and roots – to a mass of fibre, and rebuilding this raw material into board and moulded products which, as well as having totally controlled properties, could be impregnated during manufacture with any desired additives. (Bramwell 1976: 44)

This seems today a curious case of self-denial in a book that is carried along from beginning to end by a fascination with natural wood. The quotation illustrates just how transient are perspectives for the future.

The halting industrialization of cabinetmaking

In his lecture of 28 January 1919, 'Politics as a Vocation', Max Weber characterizes the ideal-typical politician as a 'driller through thick board' – a formulation that became the most famous metaphor for politicians but also the most famous metaphorical use of timber in the social sciences. Clearly Weber still had craftsmen before his eyes. It is true that even in those days many woodworkers used drilling machines (and many politicians did not conform to Weber's ideal!), but cabinetmaking did more or less stick with craft traditions into the early twentieth century. David Roentgen (d. 1807), who was known throughout Europe as a furniture manufacturer, met his demise during the Napoleonic wars and left no successors (Janneau 1975: 249). Formed under the French monarchy, he specialized in luxury desks with sophisticated secret compartments, but he did not produce any ordinary furniture. Steam power did not permit mechanization of the furniture sector; only the electric motor made this a possibility.

But plywood proved to be the decisive step towards industrialized furniture, offering a readily available material that could be standardized and machine-produced. It was the suppliers of so-called fixed dimension plywood panels who opened the way, since these allowed continuous-flow assembly of furniture with ready-made frames. Customary modes of construction now gave way more and more to plywood panel assembly, in which special finishing strips were sometimes used to fake a traditional frame.

The origins of industrial furniture production lie in the mid-nineteenth century, when the cabinetmaker Michael Thonet (1796–1871) took up and developed methods of bending wood under heat that were already known from shipbuilding and carriage-building. He is one of the few great inventors in the history of furniture. Having initially worked with moulded chair parts containing several layers of thick veneer, he moved on to the bending of massive blocks of timber. He first used steam to make the wood malleable and then placed it in a steel band equipped with special supports, so that the wood, with its fibrous structure intact, acquired the desired shape and retained it after drying.

No one had used the elasticity of wood fibres so elegantly before. After long trials, in 1859 Thonet produced his 'No. 14 chair', which was to become the first serially produced chair (figure 4.3). Its back-rest and seat were put together with metal screws instead of the traditional mortise joint. Of course, metal fittings had been in use for centuries, but the production of so-called bentwood furniture made screws an indispensable component in their own right (Flade 1979: 183f.).

This non-cutting process, which preserved the fibrous structure of the wood, offered solidity and elegance with the least expenditure of time and material. It was subsequently introduced into other branches such as cooperage and ship- and carriage-building (Andés [1903] 1986). Any deciduous wood could be processed in this way – most often the plentiful common beech, which was otherwise not much used and was therefore relatively inexpensive. This innovation path was quite different from the one taken by veneer technology, which relied on the paper-thin slicing of top-quality woods.

Although designed for series production, Thonet's first chairs adorned the palaces of the nobility and the upper bourgeoisie. In 1842 no less a figure than Metternich brought him to Vienna, where the poor master joiner from Boppard became rich and world-famous. This was the age of the Biedermeier style in Germany, but Metternich was not a Biedermeier man: he was a neo-conservative with a modern

Figure 4.3: Thonet's 'No. 14 Chair' from 1859. It was the first serial chair in history, produced with a process that bent the wood without cutting it and preserved its fibrous structure.

ideal of healthy living. The curved Thonet chair, adapted to the contours of the human back and popular in Viennese cafés, suited the new casual lifestyle of relaxed sitting, which had not been possible on the old dead-straight wooden chairs, or even on the famous rococo ones of Thomas Chippendale (1718–79), which had already shown a fondness for curved shapes. The bending of chairs corresponded to the nature of the human body as well as the nature of wood; we can therefore agree with Giedion (1948: 310f.) that it is a fine example of the co-evolution of culture and nature. However, since there is a tension between calm sitting and movement, the co-evolution in chairs is always in movement.

At first, the Thonet chair was an expensive and exquisite object, which still contained a lot of handiwork (Andés [1903] 1986: 73).

But a whole number of wood-bending machines were subsequently developed for a kind of series production, without ever completely eliminating the craft element. It took half a century from the first series of bentwood chairs until they became 'people's furniture'.

While Metternich was discovering how calmly one could sit on Thonet chairs, the British colonial authorities in India were similarly enthusiastic about bamboo armchairs. Bamboo became so attractive in Victorian England that this exotic giant grass was even imitated in wood. Meanwhile, the furniture of the Puritan states of New England still displayed 'the massive verticality of early colonial chairs, many of which could have easily taken their place in medieval castles' (Michael N. Shute, in Mayo 1984: 187). Many British traditions survived longer in America than in 'the Old Country'.

Many contemporaries had no eye for the charms of simple sleek shapes; beauty for them was rooted in ornament. Leading furniture designers of the nineteenth century violently rejected industrialization as a threat to the quality of their product. It was a view held not only by conservative traditionalists but also by the English romantic socialist William Morris (1834–96), the founder of the Anglo-American Arts and Crafts Movement, who campaigned for the highest degree of craft precision. He did not oppose all mechanization, but valued machines that were 'improved tools' demanding some creative input from the craftsman. What he held in horror in the modern world was 'allowing machines to be our masters and not our servants' (Morris 1973: 156). But the Arts and Crafts Movement became fashionable in the United States at a time when it was less and less possible to alter the course of mechanization. The same might be said of the kindred Deutscher Werkbund in Germany.

The advance of industrialization in the nineteenth century set new tasks for furniture producers. Office furnishings for the expanding bureaucratic apparatus, together with mass housing construction in the big cities, constituted a new kind of demand; low-cost functionalism became the standard for furniture too. Until then the larger workshops, mostly in the German-speaking capital cities of Vienna, Munich and Berlin, had specialized in expensive items. Furniture for 'ordinary people' came from small local cabinetmakers, who used the same designs and techniques for decades without ever changing them. The production of cheap furniture in large enterprises was a twentieth-century novelty in Germany.

The world fairs held between 1851 and 1900 had a big impact on furniture design (Mang 1979: 23f.). In the United States, simple furniture was already being made with the help of machines, but in

Germany things really began to change only in the early years of the twentieth century. Whereas furniture had been seen purely as a useful object among the lower classes, the aspirations of the petty bourgeoisie now brought about a marked change in consumption habits: people wanted to have furniture for its display value. The demands of this new group led furniture producers to widen their range and to move into series production.

Previously honoured as a part of tradition, furniture more and more became an object of changing fashions, especially among people with money. In 1902 Werner Sombart noted with a mixture of distaste and cultural pessimism: 'A married couple coolly refurnishes their house for their silver wedding, as if twenty-five years of joint use has not spun a thousand threads between the occupants and their furniture that a sensitive nature finds it barbaric to break' (Radkau 1994c: 51).

During this period, especially in densely wooded regions, larger enterprises that would later grow into furniture factories gradually took shape out of small craft businesses. Celebrated designers were already working with department store chains on furniture 'for the people' (Savage 1966: 252), and little by little it became accepted that the designer's goal should be to give an artistic quality to industrial products. After the First World War, a major new impetus came from municipal housing construction (Mang 1979: 245ff.) – a strictly functional area of activity, in which it soon became apparent that the kind of furniture produced until then would neither fit through doors nor have sufficient room space. A prerequisite for cheap, factory-produced furniture was the plywood that Ferdinand Kramer had been introducing into Germany.

An overview of developments since the nineteenth century would reveal two partly contrary, partly parallel paths: one sold on technological progress, one geared to the old crafts, but both addressing social needs of the modern world. Although factory production came to prevail after the First World War, the furniture sector did not experience a huge leap in industrialization (with continuous-flow production, as in the automobile industry, for example) until after the Second World War. Despite increasing mechanization, the division of labour remained at a low level. The heads of the Nazi war economy tried to apply Fordist models for the mass production of simple furniture, but this aroused the anger of both workers and managers (Detlev Heiden, in Grebing 1993: 169).

Far-reaching changes appeared only in the 1950s, based economically on huge pent-up demand – West Germany spent more per capita on furniture than any other country in the world! – and technically on the development of chipboard and fast-acting synthetic resin glues. It was now possible to introduce assembly lines, special machinery and a more advanced division of labour. While production in large series replaced production in series of fifty to a hundred pieces, semi-automated conveyor belts and the new chipboard required new designs with completely smooth, undecorated surfaces and a rectangular box construction.

Yet Fordist mass production continually came up against the fact that the furniture sector is heavily fashion-dependent, and that customers with purchasing power have individual tastes. 'Because of the very nature of wood, there could be no Henry Ford of furniture', opined Alfred D. Chandler (Hounshell 1984: 127). The invocation of nature may be passé in the age of electronic control systems, which up to a point can even automate the processing of solid wood (Zander 2008: 136ff.). But it is more than ever the case that economies of scale which are perfectly possible in technical terms are by no means necessarily rational from the customer's point of view; a fixation on technical rationalization is a distraction from marketing. All the more, however, has a trend to larger stores asserted itself; dependence on the retail market has long been a characteristic feature of the furniture industry.

Since the wave of mechanization in the 1960s, it has been technically feasible for the whole of furniture production to proceed without directly manual activity. This becomes significant only in the final assembly, although a strong division of labour means that low skill levels are required there. The cabinetmaker did need training in handiwork, but his working life was shaped by batch production and piece-rates; a fitter was not infrequently preferred for the work of adjustment. Here too electronics brought a new era, extending mechanization from uniform mass production to diversified sectors such as furniture. Electronically controlled milling even made it possible to mechanize the art of engraving; a pre-milled wooden elephant nowadays requires a mere ten minutes of manual finishing. However, expensive machinery was only profitable with a high utilization rate, and in times of crisis it threatened to choke companies to death.

Rationalization and mechanization in wood-processing

As in the timber sector generally, the advance of mechanization was quite slow in sawmills; it has accelerated only in the last few decades. The natural irregularities of raw wood here make automation especially difficult, so that the control of important operations is still

269

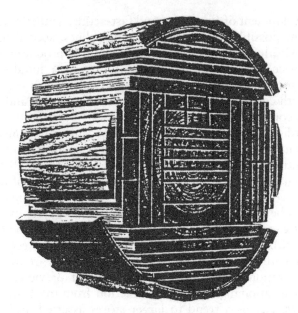

Figure 4.4: Modern bandsaw cutting pattern for a thick trunk. The illustration shows the ideal case of a stem section with virtually no defects, which can be processed into boards with very little waste. Such a result was impossible for sawmills in past centuries, and bandsaw operators still have to be very skilful and attentive. The task is made more difficult by the fact that the trunk tapers upwards; this is taken into account in computer determinations of the optimal cut, raising the useful yield to as much as 99 per cent.

entrusted to the human eye and hand. There was a bout of robot euphoria a few decades ago, but it became clear that even smoothing operations, which a person learns very quickly, cannot be taught to robots 'without an irrational amount of effort' (Radkau 1986a: 352). The once hoped-for full automation of sawmills receded again as a feasible objective, since even mechanical conveyor systems or computerized measurement and control systems could not dispense with skilled sawyers. This was true especially of deciduous wood, where attempts at full automation have so far lasted the shortest length of time.

When a tree trunk is fed into a band saw, each stage of processing involves a computerised measurement system that calculates and displays the most appropriate cutting operation (figure 4.4). The sawyer, seated at a console, must adjust his plan to the internal structure of the wood (which becomes increasingly apparent with each operation) and make decisions concerning its optimal use – for example, whether

270

to avoid defects or to comply with the customer's wishes (Mitchell 1981: 170). But the higher the degree of mechanization, the more the 'human factor' counts as a weakness to be eliminated.

Growing interest in the processing of smallwood is a particular spur to automation in the sawing industry. In this respect the profiling technology that spread from Scandinavia to Central Europe in the 1980s has had revolutionary implications; it means that a round log can be processed from all four sides in a single pass, so that the resulting raw form can be immediately dissected into boards and beams in the next pass. Profile cutters achieve much faster throughput than a saw could ever do, and only they make the cutting of thin stems a viable proposition. For centuries sawyers had carefully noted that trunks became thinner on average as old forest stands were cleared; profile cutters turned this tendency into an advantage, especially since thin stems are not only cheaper but also much more homogeneous than the thick ones traditionally preferred by sawmills. They have been the precondition for the new wood construction boom that many parts of Europe have experienced in recent years. The trend has gone so far that large-dimensioned timber is left in the forest and regains its lost value only through new wood technologies – a topsy-turvy world from the viewpoint of the past.

One general problem since the moves to partial mechanization has been the higher risk of accidents, which particularly affected the timber industry for a long time. In 1976 the average frequency of accidents was 2.8 times higher than in industry as a whole, rising to five times in the case of carpenters and nine times in that of wood processors; 43 per cent of accidents concerned a hand (*Humanisierung* 1984: 17, 48). These grim figures cast light on the tension between mechanization and the fact that, until very recently, irregularities in natural wood made the human hand irreplaceable. The circular saw has been the leading source of danger ever since it first appeared on the scene.

Electronic control systems have now significantly lowered the rate of reportable accidents, which, according to the German timber trade association, has fallen since 1980 from 150 to 65.5 per thousand full-time workers; circular table saws continue to be the worst offenders.

A quite different (and for a long time much less noticed) danger has increased as a result of mechanization – namely, the presence of ambient dust (*Humanisierung* 1984: 164). In the past, the main dangers in large mechanized enterprises were thought to come from fire and explosion; damage to the lungs from fine dust particles has only recently come to the centre of attention. Statistics for German

271

joiners in 1889 already attributed the cause of death in 60 per cent of cases to 'disease of the respiratory organs', yet in only 138 out of 7,488 enterprises was there 'provision for ventilation' at the time. Since many workshops were used for the drying of wood, joiners also frequently complained of the heat: 'As there is no provision for ventilation, the workers there simply dry out with the wood' (Grebing 1993: 32). For a long time health and safety campaigners raised the issue of ventilation, turning a workplace issue into an environmental hazard.

From craft-timbered structures to engineered timber

Wood has kept its original appearance and natural properties in housing construction: boards and beams serve their purpose in the same way today that they did centuries ago. It is true that concrete, steel and new wooden materials partly took the place of natural wood, but it has recently been winning back some of the lost ground. Even such pioneers of modern architecture as Frank Lloyd Wright, and even more Alvar Aalto, a lover of his native Finnish birch, helped to rekindle a feeling for the natural appearance of wood, with their slogan that building materials should be on open view (Giedion 1967: 416, 467, 618ff.). Such approaches, however, usually ground to a halt in the earlier part of the twentieth century, as architecture remained under the chilly spell of the concrete, steel and glass aesthetic. The modernist trailblazers set out to build functionally, but they neglected heat insulation to an extent that strikes us today as scandalous. This too was an advantage of wood construction that escaped them.

The industrialization of architecture is easier with wood than with stone, as the long tradition of prefabricated half-timbering shows. Today, the revival of wood is expressed in new kinds of structures that employ modern joinery and gluing techniques, but also in the restoration of old half-timbered buildings that has become increasingly popular since the 1970s in Germany, England and elsewhere. Until then it happened that consultancy bureaux – which 'were not uncommonly agencies of the construction company potentially involved in a project' – might mark down as many as three-quarters of the historic buildings in a town for demolition, while critical surveys showed that the so-called consultants had formed a 'thoroughly inaccurate judgement' of wood as a construction material (Großmann 1986: 172).

In fact, it was precisely in the 1970s, as metal joints consolidated their dominant position, that much of the traditional proficiency and familiarity with wood went by the board. This loss was especially noticeable in the large-scale restoration of old half-timbered houses, which were literally redeveloped out of existence. The younger generation of carpenters no longer knew how to secure a mortise and tenon by hand: mortise machines could drill holes beforehand for the construction of modern timbered houses, but restoration work had to be done manually on site, as in the old days. Visible wooden structures call for better training with the material; only an intensive learning process can ensure the necessary accuracy of fit and craft know-how, as well as the ability to draw fully on the available machinery.

Having stagnated for centuries, the technique of timbering houses has proved capable of further development since the nineteenth century, in steel structures as well as wooden. Advances in modern timber-frame construction have occurred mostly in the United States and Japan, whereas the German housing sector, despite significant take-up in panelling and prefabricated construction, has tended to lag behind (Götz 1980: 175ff.). Yet, from 1996 to 2006, the share of wooden housing in Germany doubled to approximately 14 per cent – a boom that would not have seemed possible a short time before.

Engineered timber, which has been mainly responsible for making wood competitive with steel and concrete, shows that quite different aesthetic effects can be achieved. Its advantages are most evident in constructions with an extremely damp indoor climate, such as swimming pools, or in the chemical industry, where wood is markedly less sensitive than steel or stone to aggressive substances.

Large wooden constructions are not an invention of our times. Halls 40 metres long and bridges 60 or more metres wide were already known in the eighteenth century – truly mammoth structures, for which huge quantities of timber were required. Among these were the bridges over the Rhine near Schaffhausen (1757) and over the Limmat near Wettingen in Switzerland (1777–8) (Blömer 1973: 475). All wooden structures at that time were erected on the basis of handicraft experience. The trump card of wood was its water-tightness, which made it the ideal material for roofs. Its weakness used to be the difficulty of making tension-proof connections where the width of the beams was insufficient. Builders in wood therefore used to design wide buildings in such a way that the main load-bearing elements were as far as possible subjected only to compressive stress.

Until well into the twentieth century, only solid wood was available for construction. The rise of engineered timber is as closely bound up with the development of glued laminated beams as the industrialization of furniture-making is with the development of plywood. These

Figure 4.5: The 'Expo 2000' roof in Hannover, symbol of a new age of wood and of the possibilities opening up for engineered timber and woodworking in general.

multilayered laminated beams can be produced to almost any size, depending on width and curvature of edge, as well as on systems-related length, height and shape. They also have considerably better technological and static properties than solid wood. Together with modern wood joints and glues, they have made it possible to calculate the static equilibrium of wooden buildings more or less precisely. That was scarcely possible with older wooden joints, where the specifications had to contain a large margin of error.

Glue technology revolutionized wood construction as well as wooden materials. Early glued laminated beams used glues made from casein, which a plant in the Ruhr processed from ordinary quark into a compound mass. The hot melt adhesives developed in the 1930s were, like casein glues, not completely water-resistant. Only the development of synthetic resin glues brought engineered timber construction onto a realistic agenda (figure 4.5). 'Glue use should never be a matter of what "feels right"', warned the head of the German laboratory responsible for testing plywood and wood glues (Plath 1951: 79). It is true that a master carpenter is supposed to have been the first to have glued planed boards to a beam (Teischinger and Lex 2005: 106), but the gluing then became a matter for specialists subject

274

to official supervision (Götz 1980: 69). The heavy demands that engineered timber placed upon load-bearing elements strengthened the division between designers and operators. And yet, as practical experience was accumulated, engineered timber construction too became more based upon craft know-how.

Since laminated timber is made from ready-sorted wood free of flaws, load-bearing capacities can be achieved that are out of reach in solid wood with similar dimensions. Larger diameters and curved beams become possible, and the formation of cracks is avoided. Laminated beams are thus eminently suitable for imaginative roof designs, although this is not to say they are without problems of their own. Only time will tell whether the glue will meet the demands made of it in conditions of variable moisture. A few spectacular roof collapses have given it bad headlines in recent years – for example, the collapse of the glue–tape flat roof at the Bad Reichenhall skating rink on 2 January 2006, which led to a high-profile court case that lasted several years and concluded that safety norms had not been taken seriously. At least there were no fundamental doubts as to whether the safety of large wooden constructions can be properly calculated. Besides, concrete fares no better from the point of view of safety and durability: though initially heralded as the 'material of the century', it has often needed a total overhaul after no more than a couple of decades.

Until very recently, reinforced concrete has set the standard for large buildings. In modern timber constructions, there is a gulf between what is technically possible and what is permissible in safety terms – and what clients who love large buildings want to have. Konrad Wachsmann (1901–80), who built a wooden house for Albert Einstein and later followed his friend Walter Gropius into exile in America, designed prefabricated timber buildings for series production in the restrained cubic style of the Bauhaus school. But the demand for them was not there (BDF 2007); people who wanted a wooden house had different tastes. The simple wooden houses, produced in series, were derided as 'dog kennel architecture'. Even Einstein, who loved wood and stroked the beams in his house almost tenderly, thought the modern design uncomfortable and insisted on at least a traditional interior: 'I don't want to sit on chairs that keep reminding me of a turbine hall or an operating room!'

This discrepancy means that innovative technologies are still difficult to implement in wood construction. One pioneer of engineered timber demands: 'The image of wood must shift in the direction of "wood technology" and finally get over the "cosy rustic" image'

(Ernst Giselbrecht, in Cwienk 1995: 248). Yet cosy rusticity is just what many wood fans want. Those who can afford it often prefer an opulent building style reminiscent of giant trees in the forest, rather than simple constructions that demonstrate what modern timber technology can achieve. Many sawmills, too, have no time for innovations that reduce the demand for wood, realizing that it is in their interests to stick with the traditional oversized structures. The timber construction industry therefore continues to harbour considerable unused potential.

The reconstruction of the Frauenkirche in Dresden shied away from wood more than technical considerations would have rationally dictated, no doubt because of the trauma of the great fire that followed the air raid of February 1945. As a result, the new dome in the church turned out to be too heavy, and static equilibrium problems began to appear. As far back as the High Middle Ages, it was repeatedly observed that wood was more stable than stone for the construction of cupolas, but such lessons kept being forgotten – or repressed, for fear of fire. Even today surveys show that, although nearly all Germans love wood, almost none trust that timber buildings are safe against fire.

3 Fissile Material and Bonding Agent: Forest and Wood in the Eco-Age

The situation today suggests a dramatic finale to the history of wood. But we should not forget that the history of the interaction between man and wood is never-ending, and that it is likely to hold more surprises in store. Things anyway seem to be coming full circle: wood is re-emerging from the Cinderella existence to which industrialization banished it for two centuries; several strands of development, economic and ecological, are being knotted together and making wood and the forest a major public issue again.

High praise for everything made of wood, growing fear that supplies will start running out: this is a familiar tune to anyone who has read their history. The past is returning under the sign of ecology and points to surprising perspectives for the future. No other material offers such an impressive opportunity for synthesizing economics and ecology, but the synthesis will neither happen by itself nor be problem-free – that too is a lesson of the last few decades. The trio of forestry, timber industry and environmental movement is filled with tensions. We are still a long way from a grand Green Trinity.

The beginnings of the 'ecological revolution'

The beginnings of the 'ecological revolution' – which, to be sure, played itself out more at the level of programmes and declarations than in everyday reality – are usually situated around the year 1970. On 22 April 1970 American environmental groups first solemnized Earth Day with a great media fanfare; previously it had been celebrated as Arbor Day, in a 'quasi-religious tone that suggested the cleansing of the soul and the promotion of Christian values' (Williams 1989: 383). The new environmental movement too had its spiritual side, but also, like forest conservation, early administrative moorings: the Environmental Protection Agency was founded in the same year in the United States, and the new socialist–liberal coalition government in Bonn set itself a similar objective. In 1970 the 'Tokyo Resolution' declared a healthy environment to be a human right, while the Chipko movement began its protest against deforestation on the southern slopes of the Himalayas. It was a year of fascinating simultaneity around the world.

Initiatives at the top and from below, within the state administration as well as 'civil society', coexisted with each other in partial harmony, but also in partial discord. In 1971 Greenpeace was founded in Vancouver; the 'rainbow warriors' made the oceans their arena and gave a heroic new face to ecological commitment. Already in the years before 1972, preparations for the Earth Summit in Stockholm gave a global horizon to environmental policy. In 1911, alluding to a nineteenth-century botanist and archivist, the writer Hermann Löns had sneeringly dismissed the conservationism of his day as 'Pritzel stuff'. Now, sixty years later, the situation had dramatically changed – or, at least, public perceptions of it had.

No doubt the main trigger for the change was certain unwelcome concomitants of the postwar boom: the consequences of mass motoring and the flood of synthetic and disposable goods, driven by the availability of cheap oil. There had been no sense of looming catastrophe before the turn in 1970, and afterwards it was to some extent contradictory fears that caused environmentalism to swell into a mass movement. *The Limits to Growth*, the Club of Rome study published in 1972 that became a global bestseller, invoked the old fear of resource depletion; the oil crisis of autumn 1973 gave a prompt demonstration of its topicality. In the following years, however, as atmospheric damage and the danger to the world's climate captured public attention, the opposite worry came to the fore: that carbon dioxide emissions from fossil fuels would continue to grow for the foreseeable future, with irreparable long-term consequences. Limitless growth now sounded even more menacing than the limits to growth!

The two fears did converge in one respect – that is, in the demand for greater use of renewable energy sources. At least potentially, this gave a new importance to wood. Of course, the situation could also have been turned into an argument for nuclear energy, but it was precisely nuclear power stations that were the main target of environmentalist campaigns in West Germany and many other countries. They did not emit any carbon dioxide, but they brought other risks that were no less unpleasant. Although breeding reactors promised to make atomic energy virtually renewable, their development has come to a halt nearly everywhere because of the economic and ecological risks they entail. Nuclear power has thus lost the charm of an 'inexhaustible' energy source.

But nuclear power was by no means everywhere the chief issue sparking environmental protest. Overall, and in a global perspective, a large number of environmental questions were not new. Some elements went as far back as prehistoric times – the concern for clean water, for example, as we can see from the thick walls built around wells. What was new in the early 1970s was the global horizon on which they linked up.

Ecological and emotional attitudes to the forest

As we have seen, woodland conservation has a centuries-old tradition in Europe. Concern for the forest first appears in the historical record as economically motivated: people were worried about the wood supply. 'Sustainability' too was originally an economic concept. Only occasionally do the medieval sources show some insight into the relationship between the forest and soil water dynamics; a Dominican monk from Alsace, for example, recalls around 1300 that a century earlier, before the great clearances, the rivers and streams did not swell so much, 'because tree roots in the mountains retained the moisture from snow and rain longer' (Schubert 1994: 45). By the nineteenth century this was a commonly known fact, especially in regions such as Switzerland and southern France, which experienced major floods, but also in the United States.

The man–forest relationship has never been altogether sober and rational. Modern foresters often present themselves outwardly as cool calculators – more than they are in their hearts. One need only think of the exaggerated rotation times that allow trees to grow to a venerable old age, or of the weakness that many foresters have for hunting and their tolerance of game damage to the forest, or of the social kudos that used to attach to aristocratic landowners with a wonderful forest. The demand that forestry should be 'adapted to the location' always assured the forester of some discretion; he did not simply carry out instructions from above but also followed personal preferences. That was not the least attraction of his profession.

The emotional side of the long man–forest relationship, to which the literary and folk-song heritage attests, may be found at best only between the lines of the usual forest records. The modern forester correctly presented himself as an economist, but in reality it has never been possible to calculate with any precision what constitutes the economic optimum in forestry (Kremser 1990: 721). No one can predict the state of the market in eighty years' time, when newly planted trees will be ready for felling. If much animosity has nevertheless developed between foresters and conservationists, this is probably due not only to rational differences but also to conflicting emotions. Foresters, to be sure, did not like to see a wilderness, but they had their own peculiar emotional relationship to the forest. On the other hand, those who lived from logging got upset over ecological slogans such as 'Tree down, no thanks!' or the idealization of forest untouched by human hand.

For the environmental movement, whether in Germany or elsewhere, the forest was not initially a major issue. German nature lovers and conservationists originally had mixed feelings towards it: the classical idyll was an 'Arcadian' landscape, a mixture of tree clusters, shrubbery and meadows resulting from pasturing, which forest reformers regarded as the epitome of a lack of culture. The real Eldorado for early German conservationists was Lüneburg Heath, only seemingly a virgin landscape, which in fact resulted from deforestation through pasturing and the wood consumption of saltworks. Bernhard Grzimek, who became world-famous for his campaigning to protect African big game, would have been happy to see a German Serengeti develop in the Bavarian Forest National Park that he helped to found; indeed, he even argued for extensive tree-felling to produce the savannah-like conditions that African mega-fauna loved. No wonder that forest lovers screamed blue murder! 'Nature wants forest in almost every place in our country' was for a long time the dogma subscribed to by many German conservationists (Wulf 1993: 72).

Is that really what nature wants? For more than ten years now, the 'mega-herbivore theory' has been sowing confusion among palaeobotanists, with its idea that, before human hunters appeared on the scene, big game had multiplied to the limits of the available

279

food supply and given a savannah-like character to large parts of the landscape (Gerken and Görner 1999). Palaeozoologists accuse palaeobiologists of forgetting about animals. But more and more conservationists are partial to this new theory of original unspoilt nature. A dense forest canopy that allowed for little undergrowth contradicted the new ecological ideal of 'biodiversity'. It was precisely in conservation areas that the forest, whose death had so often been predicted, grew surprisingly quickly all by itself and reduced species diversity.

The slogan 'Save the forest!' was followed by 'Save biodiversity from the forest!' So today conservationists from Scotland to the Alps are actually campaigning against the forest, which threatens to overgrow the meadows and heathland, moors and plateaux, of which they are so fond. John Muir, the prophet of America's national parks, once reviled the sheep as a 'hoofed locust' and wanted to banish it from Yosemite Valley. Today, on the contrary, EU-subsidized sheep or even goats (traditionally the forester's deadly enemy) safely graze on open landscapes that have been declared conservation areas.

Environmental protection and the forest: this is in part a different story from the relationship of conservationists to the forest. Around 1970 foresters had long been guarding sustainability in the forest, and so there was no need for environmental activists to take up the issue. But eventually they too discovered the forest. The protest movement against the planned nuclear waste disposal facility at Gorleben, which brought the whole issue of atomic energy in West Germany to a climax, found a positive objective to campaign for in the forests of the Hanoverian Wendland. A collective book edited by the journalist Horst Stern, *Rettet den Wald* (1979), found a major public echo. What was the forest to be saved from? Above all, from conifer monoculture and excessive stocks of game for hunting. This polemical work, supported by a working group of the German Association of Forest-Owners, still partly operated within the 200-year-old tradition of 'pro-wood' foresters opposed to 'pro-deer' foresters.

'Death of the forest': the nightmare scenario

The real drum roll sounded shortly afterwards, however, when *Der Spiegel* featured *Der Wald stirbt – Saurer Regen über Deutschland* as the cover title for its issue of 16 November 1981 (figure 4.6). All the old forest pathos came pouring out more sonorously than ever before: 'First the forest dies, then man' was a cry that blew concern up into panic; fear for the environment gripped layers of the population that would never have gone near a protest against nuclear power, while supporters

Figure 4.6: Cover page of *Der Spiegel*, 16 November 1981: 'The Forest is Dying: Acid Rain over Germany'.

of atomic energy breathed a sigh of relief that the new alarm was taking much of the pressure off it. The Ordinance on Large Fire Installations issued in 1983, making long-mooted desulphurization plants mandatory for coal-fired power stations, was one prompt effect that dramatically reduced one of the main causes of damage to the forest known for centuries. The new alarm had a silver lining, even retrospectively.

The alarm did not come from forest-owners. Quite a few of them had already received damages from nearby factories on account of industrial emissions, but, as wider and longer-term effects came to be seen as the main cause of harm to the forest, their demands for compensation lost more and more of their force. After sulphur dioxide, suspicion fell on nitrogen oxides and therefore on the exhaust from motor vehicles. There was not just one enemy image for the 'dying forest' alarm: power stations, the automobile culture, agricultural nitrogen emitted by livestock, even forestry itself came under fire.

In the end, the 'dying forest' turned out to be a misleading concept. Sensational press articles had predicted that no forest would be left in Germany by the year 2000, but it became clear in the 1990s that, precisely because of carbon dioxide and nitrogen in the atmosphere, the forests were growing faster than before and Germany was becoming more densely wooded than at any time in the previous centuries.

281

To some extent this was unhealthy growth, but the value of the wood did not usually fall. The 'dying forest' did not put landowners under any clear-cut economic pressure to act. There were (and still are) worrying signs of damage to the forest; the mistake was to turn chronic, partly hypothetical, damage into a clear and present disaster. But there is some evidence that the real crisis of the forest, due to soil acidification, is yet to come.

In 1982 the alarm led to the foundation of the Robin Wood Society, which, despite its English-sounding name, is a German splinter organization from Greenpeace. For these friends of the forest, the 'rainbow warriors' were too geared to the oceans, operating at a global level remote from grassroots movements. But the problem was that the forest conservationists in Germany kept losing the object of their attack: first it was the large power stations, but these were soon forced into building desulphurization plant; then it was conifer monoculture, but forest managers themselves turned more and more to mixed forest. Robin Wood also campaigned for less use of wood and the recycling of old paper, but rising wood prices anyway led to a run on old paper in the recycling branch.

After 1987, the protection of tropical forests was one of Robin Wood's main objectives. At that time there was some common ground between the concerns of environmentalists and those of the timber industry; even the International Tropical Timber Organization spoke out in favour of sustainable use of the tropical forests. The big issue then, as now, is whether sustainability has a chance in the tropical forests. Robin Wood distinguished itself by critically examining wood certificates at a time when these were becoming the object of a profitable, bluff-filled trade. Many German environmentalists were anyway fonder of the imaginary tropical forest – the old dream of paradise on earth! – than of the real German forest. But it remains unclear whether certificates can guarantee sustainable forestry in the Third World, since occasional spot checks by outsiders cast little light on faraway places, and the issuers of certificates are paid by the very firms they are supposed to check up on. Only thorough scrutiny over long periods of time might establish how trustworthy the forest managers and timber companies really are.

The turn in forestry

The 'Wiebke' windstorm of 1990 was at least as important for the history of German forestry as the warnings about the death of the forest. Whereas the new kinds of damage partly affected mixed forest

282

too, the storm demonstrated the particular vulnerability of spruces and recalled the kernel of truth in the old verse: 'If you want to destroy the forest / Plant nothing other than spruce.' Supporters of 'natural forestry' – long dismissed by the mainstream as dreamers and windbags or 'the Jehovah's Witnesses of the woods', sometimes even suspected of diehard attitudes reminiscent of the Nazis' short-lived 'continuous forest' policy (Hockenjos 2000: 125) – found a way of breaking out of their isolation.

When Hans Leibundgut (1909–93), the Swiss pioneer of forestry, urged foresters 'to be cleverly lazy', they lost no time in taking up his advice. The old schism in the forest lost some of its asperity. Will global warming force conifer monoculture into retreat and again make deciduous forest dominant in Central Europe, thereby settling the centuries-long war of beliefs? All we can say is that the conflict between 'natural' and 'economic' forestry is by no means over yet. In Europe it rumbles beneath the surface most of the time; in the disputatious civil society of the USA, where privately owned forest is the rule and the American Forest and Paper Association, founded in 1993, stands opposed to the wilderness ideal, the two front lines sometimes clash violently with each other (Hays 2007). The traditions of conservation and preservation, associated with Gifford Pinchot and John Muir, which originally joined forces to fight against forest fires and destruction, have gone their separate ways; sustainable use stands opposed to the preservation of original forest. Since the American West still has ancient forests with giant trees, such as have all but disappeared from Europe, the struggle for the 'wilderness' is much more emphatic there than in the Old World.

Spatial distance used to ensure a more or less peaceful coexistence between American preservationists and conservationists: the former had their national parks, larger than anything possible nowadays in little Europe, while the latter relied on an early arrangement with foresters. As ecological issues have come to the fore, however, the American public has shown increasing signs of wanting to extend the 'wilderness' model from the national parks to the national forests. The protagonists of 'ecological forestry' speak disdainfully of conventional 'commodity forestry'. Chuck Leavell, the former Rolling Stones keyboard player turned forest-owner, notes: 'Public opinion has now shifted so that the rights of the Northern spotted owl, for instance, are viewed as being just as important as those of the loggers wanting to remove trees from public lands. Frankly, maybe even more so' (Leavell 2001: 159).

Conservation and preservation used to go hand in hand in the global diplomacy of earth summits. The Rio summit of 1992 set 'sustainable development' as the objective for the whole world economy and, at the same time, came out strongly in support of biodiversity. One paradox of Rio is that, since Third World countries led by Brazil and Malaysia imposed a veto, no decisions could be taken on forestry – the very area where 'sustainability' had the most clearly defined meaning. After some hesitation, the word 'sustainable' was rendered into German by the old forestry term *nachhaltig*, which in the 1990s was blown up so much that it became virtually synonymous with 'good', even though many Germans do not associate it with any clear ideas. The origins of this new magic word were unknown to the wider public, indicating just how much forestry remains apart from the mainstream of the ecological movement. In Germany, *Nachhaltigkeit* – in the original sense of even tree-felling guaranteed over time – is the least of the problems facing the forest; indeed, until the recent rise in timber prices, the amount of wood being cut was generally far smaller than the new growth. Not even the 'death of the forest' scaled this back.

The charismatic and bureaucratic phases of the eco-age

The position of the ecological movement on forestry and the timber industry cannot be stated in blanket terms, since it is not a 'movement' in the classical sense, with a clearly definable common interest, but a number of interconnecting networks built around the ebb and flow of loosely related initiatives. Much takes place at the level of the media rather than practical action. Initiatives from politicians 'at the top', which already played a role in the early days of the movement, have acquired increasing importance; the 'grassroots' movement, so dear to the heart of supporters of the new social movements, is only half of the story. But, without this outside stimulus, environmental policy would have run into the ground before long.

The fortunes of the ecological movement have certainly been variable. An ideal-typical simplification, with Max Weber in mind, might distinguish between two phases in Germany and elsewhere: a first, 'charismatic', phase of naïve enthusiasm and naïve fears, in which environmental initiatives did not yet add up to a fully fledged 'movement'; and a second phase, marked by professionalism and bureaucratization, which saw the growth of research projects, legislation and certificates of environmental friendliness. But this second phase is not the end of the story either. For all the pessimistic predictions, new grassroots movements have continued to develop.

In wood and forest matters, each phase contained both opportunities and irritants. The first, naïve phase was carried along by the basic conviction that 'ecologically correct' is synonymous with 'morally good', that what is good is unambiguous, and that all good things are in harmony with one another. This way of thinking stood in the classical tradition of antiquity, although it was usually unaware of this. But it found itself in thick forest, confused by the opaqueness of the timber industry.

In fact, from the beginning, the ecological movement had a strong, though often ill-defined, longing for 'nature': for natural lifestyles, close-to-nature housing, natural materials and natural wood, spurning the contemporary boom in synthetics and plastics. In Ernest Callenbach's novel *Ecotopia* (1975), even the bath tubs are made of wood. A preference for 'organic' products reached far beyond the ecological movement: the spreading sauna culture, for example, set up an instinctive association between wellness and natural wood. This created numerous pitfalls, however, and people had to learn that 'nature' is not an unambiguous ideal. Many natural fibres that feel good on the skin are produced with as much chemistry as synthetic fibres are. A spokesman for the Swiss furniture industry complained: 'Customers keep clamouring for nature, but they won't put up with any flaws in natural products' (Catrina 1989: 168). Living close to nature made people more dependent on the motor car and involved higher energy consumption than living in a city-centre apartment block.

A spokesman for Austrian carpenters recalled in 1988 that construction timber bore the mark of a loser until the 1960s. After 1970, a 'major new upturn' (Hans Löcker, in Heinzinger 1988: 252) associated with greater demand for comfort led to an often rash use of wood preservatives that turned out to be damaging to health. It was a double-edged situation: people longed for natural wood, but they did not trust its natural properties and, misled by alarmist publicity, impregnated wood with chemicals even in well-heated rooms where they were completely unnecessary, producing an effect that was toxic not only for insects but also for human beings. Many a scandal could have been avoided if there had been better communication between the timber industry and environmental protection agencies. Klaus Töpfer, Germany's environment minister from 1987 to 1994, once rounded on a gathering of timber industrialists and called them a herd of 'cattle' (*Rindviecher*). At that time, the German timber lobby had been trying in vain to derail through the EU the government's ban on dioxin-contaminated wood preservative. In Töpfer's view, instead of complaining all the time about environmental standards and trying to gloss over the toxicity of chemical wood preservatives, they should have seized the back-to-nature trend as an opportunity to make wood as healthy and environmentally friendly as they could.

The dangers of wood preservatives were first noticed by workplace doctors in the timber industry, but the scandal broke only when it became clear that consumers too were affected. It was the time when formaldehyde emissions from new wooden materials were also hitting the headlines. One especially toxic preservative contained PCP (pentachlorophenol), a substance similar to the dioxin that caused the chemicals disaster at Seveso on 10 July 1976 and opened a new round of environmental alarms. The slogan 'Seveso is everywhere!' began to sound plausible. In 1983 people harmed by wood preservatives in Germany founded an interest group. In 1985 the US Environmental Protection Agency banned the use of PCP, and other countries followed its lead. The environmental movement also campaigned to make labour protection an issue in areas where it had been neglected for much too long. In 1985 the German trade union for the wood and synthetics sector described wood dust – especially when combined with chemical substances – as a ticking 'time bomb'; and in 1987 the timber industry recognized that certain categories of people suffering from cancer were entitled to compensation for occupational illnesses (Hemmer, in Grebing 1993: 265).

Heating with wood waste that contained chemicals also turned out to be far from always environmentally friendly, since it could cause high levels of dust particle emissions. The lessons of eighteenth-century literature on how to heat rooms most efficiently and pleasantly with wood had to be learned all over again. On top of all this, environmentalists themselves were divided as never before, keen to use wood as consumers, but unwilling to accept tree-felling as friends of nature; in favour of renewable materials (as opposed to coal and atomic energy), but hankering in their hearts after wild untouched forest. Conservationists often could not even find a common basis with campaigners for natural silviculture. The two might appear from afar to form a united 'ecological movement', while displaying close up a yawning gap between conservationism and environmental protection.

It is surprising how few attempts were made in the naïve-charismatic phase to argue out these contentious points. What was 'good' was beyond discussion; any compromise had something unprincipled about it. As the French historian Fernand Braudel once noted with visible irony about the eighteenth-century appeal to nature: 'As an argument, it brooked no contradiction' (Radkau 1994a: 283). 'Nature' cannot be discussed, weighed up or negotiated over; one can only furiously insist on it and keep dissidents out of the way. Since the wood and forestry sector was internally divided and rather averse to public attention, there was anyway no interlocutor, no partner to a discussion. And if the parties did sit round a table, each failed to understand what the other was saying.

In principle, it is quite possible to imagine joint action by the forestry sector, the timber-processing industry and environmental protection agencies, and indeed the call for a 'broad green alliance' has been around for a long time. Yet communication has often been all but non-existent among these three groups, especially between the first two and the third. Moreover, both sides were and still are internally split – another effect, perhaps, of the much vaunted versatility of wood and the forest.

As the ecological movement entered the second phase of professionalization and bureaucratization, a lot of the old ideological rigour became slacker. On the other hand, the bureaucratization and institutionalization of environmental protection developed its own special kind of rigidity. Bureaucracy as such was nothing new in the forest, but it developed a new opaqueness after the 'ecological revolution' and the alarm over the 'death of the forest'. It began to be questioned whether the forester should have sole responsibility for the forest. And the taciturn timber industry did not keep up with the environmental rhetoric.

In theory everything was so simple: wood seemed the ideal agent for bonding together economics and ecology; sustainable forestry automatically stabilized carbon dioxide in the atmosphere, so there was no need for a huge investment in regulations, controls and sanctions. The point, however, seems to be precisely that wood solutions are too simple and too conventional. Environmental agencies specialize overwhelmingly in other questions. Unlike climate research, solar hydrogen, offshore wind power, ocean wave energy or CO_2 sequestration, projects concerning wood or the forest offer little material for what counts as 'cutting-edge research', and new discoveries are not likely to put anyone in the running for a Nobel prize.

Fascinated as they are by world horizons, but also spurred on by international seminar tourism, intellectuals tend to gravitate towards models of global management. From both a historical and an ecological point of view, however, a global forest policy would seem to be the most senseless thing imaginable. Any forest success stories from the developing countries have been local in character, involving small group initiatives – whether by women in Kenya's Kitui district (Küchli 1997: 86ff.) or by the Kalibo mangrove community on the Philippines island of Panay (Durst et al. 2005: 39ff.) – to plant trees that correspond to local interests and ecological conditions.

Even attempts to develop a common EU forest policy have met with strong misgivings on the part of member states, which have an understandable horror that the EU's agricultural protectionism might acquire a wooded pendant. For all the state regulation, the history of the forest up to now has displayed a low degree of protectionism in comparison with the history of agriculture. There has been no strong movement in Germany for protective tariffs on forest products, although even Bismarck, as a forest landowner, would have had an economic interest in them. Germany was a wood-exporting country until the middle of the twentieth century, and it is about to become one again in respect of sawn timber.

Nature protection, which before the eco-age was basically run by volunteers, has been subject to a special kind of professionalization and bureaucratization. It has gone hand in hand with an increasingly scientific approach to the task: whereas people used to confess freely to their emotional involvement, acknowledging their aesthetic and nostalgic motives or seeing themselves as part of heritage protection, they now justify their work mostly by reference to ecological science – even though, on closer examination, it has always been difficult to give a precise ecological basis for norms and regulations. What nature protection has gained in professionalism, it has often lost in popularity. Its ability to make interconnections has also tended to decline: whereas many foresters used to belong to the older type of volunteer conservationist, a growing distance and hostility has developed in recent decades between the two. The old aesthetic joy used to be shared by foresters who championed mixed deciduous forest; the new cult of unspoilt wilderness, taken over from the American national parks, has also led to a break with supporters of close-to-nature forestry.

'Wilderness' experiment: concepts of protection under discussion

The two positions clashed particularly sharply in the debate over the Bavarian Forest National Park. Founded in 1970 as the Federal Republic's first national park, it was well received by many local people, who had high hopes that it would boost tourism at a time when wood was not fetching high prices on the market. The park management adopted a policy of non-intervention in nature and stuck to it so rigidly that, when a storm caused major damage to the forest in 1983, bark beetles were able to multiply at an unexpectedly fast rate in the fallen trees. Even nature lovers who were aesthetes at heart now began to lose faith in the wilderness ideal, since the beetles were creating a depressing spectacle for miles around; the tourist attraction was becoming a thing of the past. Owners of other forest land in the area feared ruin from the spread of the beetles; it was a real 'death of the forest' that threatened to produce an economic calamity.

When the Bavarian government decided on a major expansion of the park in 1995, it ran into considerable opposition. Hate-filled tirades thundered out against the 'Nazi anal park'; the management was accused of destroying nature in the name of natural conservation. Many conservationists concluded from this bitter experience that 'pure wilderness' cannot be suddenly introduced in the middle of conifer forest without risking damage that offends the aesthetic sense even of many nature lovers (Haber 2006). In fact, it came to be generally perceived that the 'wilderness' model rests on an illusion. The history books make it clear that scarcely any unspoilt forest is left in Germany: that people have been using and changing the forest for millennia, and that, whatever eco-fundamentalists and many historians may say, this process cannot be sweepingly equated with 'destruction of the forest'. The wilderness of which nature lovers are so fond is usually former plantation forest or old pasture and common – a 'cultural landscape' that will gradually disappear if left entirely to itself.

This realization suggests that natural conservation might be reconciled with natural forestry, not only in Germany, but also in other parts of the world. It is a possibility that corresponds to the 'biosphere reserve' model developed by the UN 'Man and Biosphere' project, in which protection of a traditional cultural landscape includes the people living there. Nature conservation agencies will, of course, have difficulty with the practical consequences of such a way of looking at things. There is a reason for this too. The 'wilderness' model is cheap and simple to apply and satisfies the bureaucratic demand for clear lines of demarcation; it marks out a space where no one but authorized hunters and shepherds have any business to be.

The 'protection of traditional cultural landscapes' offers a different model, in which conservancy officials are not the only competent players. The model can never be perfectly realized, since the landscapes in question are associated with human cultural forms which have passed away for ever as totalities, leaving only individual elements to go on living, sometimes thanks to subsidies. A look back into history will remind us of this too. Today's 'close to nature' supporters fear that rising timber prices will make yield maximization so attractive that natural forest will only stand a chance in the core areas of national parks, where any kind of use is forbidden.

Climate change and energy crisis: is a broad green alliance taking shape?

The current situation is that climate alarms and soaring energy prices have given wood an opportunity that it did not have at any time in the past 200 years. Forest circles are excited to learn that the Shell oil corporation is now the world's largest forest-owner, and experts are discussing how to calculate future timber prices in 'barrel equivalents'. Financial advisers recommend investing in forests – a safe haven in the long term, now that everything else has become uncertain. German forests, which seemed economically inconsequential for more than half a century, are suddenly in demand throughout the world. This is a reason for their owners to focus on them more sharply than they have done until now.

Whereas the timber industry treated German forests for decades as more or less interchangeable sources of raw materials, the worldwide shortage has now made regional forestry an interesting partner again. 'Cluster' has become the new magic word, in the sense of long-term, technically optimized regional cooperation between forestry and the timber industry. Not only representatives of the timber industry, but also environmentalists who favour wood as a renewable resource, sometimes groan – in the manner of the Wuppertal Institute for Climate, Environment and Energy – that the 'mobilization of wood' is a 'Herculean task'. Many small owners of woodland have been unwilling to sell their wood because they thought they were being cheated. A spokesman for the Finnish timber industry complained that until now the path of logs from forest to mill in Germany has been a 'hurdle race', and that it must be made into a 'relay race' (*Holz-Zentralblatt*, 18 February 2005). Lower transport costs and trusting cooperation as the new secret of success in institutional economics! It is a formula that applies especially in the timber trade, where, as we have seen, a relationship of trust has always existed between buyers and sellers; the irregularity of the raw material means that defects cannot be easily detected before a sale is concluded.

Something that was for long unthinkable has now come to pass: German timber is being exported to America and the Far East, in such quantities that it will be necessary to check that German forestry is observing the sustainability requirement. In 2004 a Charter for Wood, supported by a consensus stretching from the timber industry to the Green Party, made the increased use of wood an official goal of central government policy. Shortly afterwards, however, an unexpected rise in the demand for timber caused signs of turbulence to appear. Even forest deadwood is now sought after as a source of fuel. Whereas scrap wood was available almost gratis for decades – at a time when it was not worth using wood for heating homes, even in the forest (Hockenjos 2000: 49) – the deliberate cultivation of 'energy forests' is now in prospect.

But this situation too has its downside. The exploding demand for wood chips and pellets – which used to be made only from scrap wood – is putting lumber under increasing pressure and provoking angry reactions. The terms 'dendromass' (or 'wood-like biomass', unsuitable for 'high-grade' uses such as housebuilding or furniture) and 'quality wood' are designed to uncouple the fuel and lumber markets, but these are actually beginning to overlap as a result of energy price increases. A single, integrated wood market is taking shape as scarcely ever before in history. But this is also sharpening competition among the various users of wood.

It is hard to predict how great a role wood will play in the long term as a renewable energy source. As always in these matters, there is a wide gulf between what is theoretically conceivable and what is feasible here and now, given the other demands on the forest and, not least, the provisions of the law. Josef Krauhausen, the editor of the *Holz-Zentralblatt*, describes German plans for huge power stations fired by imported wooden pellets as a 'madness of energy policy', which would disappear overnight in the absence of state subsidies. For those who think of all the fine things that can be done with wood, it is a shame to use it for fuel.

'Repeated protestations that Germany is forest champion, with the most woodland in Europe, may be true in substance, but by themselves they will not bring the wood from the forest to the consumer', ponders Andreas Schulte, the director of the Münster Forest Centre. 'Energy forests' with short rotation periods are even more repulsive to nature lovers than the high spruce forest of old. The main point, however, is that wood will fade into the background if climate and energy alarms generate a national political clamour for immediate grand solutions on a global scale. For wood cannot offer such solutions.

In any event, that style of politics does not seem appropriate to environmental issues. The long time that trees take to grow has always been a good education for long-term, measured thinking. That is probably the best way to realize the political potential of wood and to bring a 'broad green alliance' closer. Historical surveys can sometimes help to clear obstacles along the way and to resolve policy conflicts in a rational manner. The fragmented picture that the forestry and timber sector offered to the public corresponded to a fragmentary awareness of its own history and great uncertainty about its future prospects.

Does the climate alarm offer wood a new opportunity? At the Kyoto climate conference in 1997 and in the years that followed, there was much controversy about whether reforestation could compensate for fuel emissions. The Kyoto Protocol left this possibility open, but it was precisely the environmentalists who subjected it to hefty criticism. Their doubts were well founded, since reforestation simply in order to cut down more trees in the future has a close to zero effect on the CO_2 balance in the atmosphere. Besides, the mere planting of trees does not mean much: the important thing is to water the trees, to protect them from livestock grazing and to manage them on a sustainable basis. All of that can only be accomplished over time and is difficult to check up on from a distance. There is reason to suspect that, as in the case of development aid, the payment of reforestation premiums is only an invitation to corruption (Victor 2001: 60f.).

Be that as it may, a global climate policy based mainly on controls and restrictions, without effective sanctions to back it up, appears doomed to failure. In the long run, such strategies have a chance of success only if those directly affected by them have an interest in taking them up. History shows that this is generally the only route to sustainable forestry. A larger role for wood in the world economy, combined with sustainable forestry, creates a sector in which the CO_2 balance evens out in the long term, without controls or restrictions. Forest and wood are popular, or at least have a chance of becoming so, but restrictions are never popular. There is therefore an opportunity for the forestry and timber sector to take the offensive by participating directly in climate policy formation.

At the seminar on forest and wood held in Freiburg early in 2005, 'the unanimous message from all the speakers was that outside influences will increase; that developments and ambitions in forestry will adapt more and more to external developments and demands' (*Holz-Zentralblatt*, 18 February 2005). In principle, this is nothing new. If, as the Freiburg seminar claimed, the World Bank is subordinating forestry to the war on want, this is not so different from what Pfeil demanded in Prussia 200 years ago.

A social and cultural history of wood and the forest, which goes beyond the traditional boundaries of forest history, demonstrates what many discussions, even at an international level, continue to ignore (Poore 2003: 255) – namely, that the solution to many problems is not to be found in the forest alone. In the past, too, sustainable forestry was far from being a matter for supervisors alone; it depended at least as much on the state of agriculture. Not the least of the uses of a historical retrospect is that it sharpens our eye for potential situations in today's world – situations that open up new opportunities.

— 5 —

GLOBAL PROSPECTS AND CONTRASTS

1 Lessons from Asia

The wood culture par excellence: Japan

The eyes of wood lovers light up at the sight of Japan: the 'empire of the rising sun' has the world's supreme wood culture. Until far into modern times, no other country built so many prestigious monumental buildings in wood, and in scarcely another did the art of woodwork – even outside the luxury sector – attain such a degree of sophistication. What is more, Japan is the only non-Western civilization to have had forms of sustainable forestry for centuries, and the only one which, despite being closed to the West until the nineteenth century, soon achieved rapid industrial growth and began to compete with the leading industrial nations. Does it not seem likely that these different kinds of uniqueness are somehow related to one another?

Curiously, for all the head-scratching about the causes of the 'Japanese miracle', little attention has been paid in Japan or elsewhere to the role of wood as a factor. It is not difficult to find it underlying Japan's ascent. Yet, as Gregory Clancey mockingly pointed out: 'That industrializing Japan continued to rely so heavily on wood and woodcraft well into the twentieth century was something of a dirty little secret to those for whom wood still symbolized economic and cultural backwardness' (2007: 132). The ideological use made of timber buildings by Japanese traditionalists has further concealed the wooden path to modernity.

Conrad Totman has done most to reappraise the role of wood in Japanese history, especially in the Tokugawa era (*c.*1570–1868) before the opening to the West. Hardly any historian in the world has done more than he to proceed from forest history to a reconstruction of *l'histoire totale* (Totman 1993). His works fit into a new trend in Japanese studies that developed especially after the collapse of the bubble economy around 1990 – a trend towards rehabilitation of Japan's period of closure, previously dismissed by modernizers as a time of petrification. The age of alleged stagnation was now promoted to one of great dynamism, which, at least in comparison with what had gone before and came after, achieved a reconciliation of culture and nature and laid the basis for the country's subsequent rise.

In his introduction to the forest history of pre-industrial Japan, Totman notes: 'Germany is commonly viewed as the society that first developed the practices of regenerative forestry. This study shows that such practices arose independently in Japan as early as in Germany' (1989: 6). Japan, then, offers a little noticed cross-check for historians

295

of the German and West European forest, indicating which conditions were essential to sustainable forestry and which were either marginal or replaceable.

One is immediately struck by the fact that three aspects which appear to have been dominant in the West played only a small role, if any, in the history of Japanese forestry. First of all, naval construction – which elsewhere made protection of the forest a political priority – did not shape forest policy in Japan during the Tokugawa period, when the country restricted its fishing to coastal waters and abstained from ocean travel or maritime expansion. Nor did princely hunting, so important a determinant throughout Europe, play a major role in shaping Japanese forest policy; the samurai may have resembled Western knights in many respects, but hunting in a forest landscape was not central to their way of life.

A third difference, which Germans find particularly astounding, is the much lesser role played by foresters and forestry officials in Japanese history (Clancey 2007: 124). Someone familiar only with the history of Germany tends to believe that a scientifically trained corpus of state officials is indispensable for the development of sustainable forestry. In Japan, however, even as late as the mid-twentieth century, it was not state officials but local farmers, especially small farmers, who did most of the work in cultivating the forest (Iwai 2002: 9). Forest grows faster in the Japanese climate than in Europe; those who help it along do so for themselves, not only for future generations. People in Japan understand that the ordinary needs of a farmer's life can promote woodland cultivation, without any forest science or forest ordinance. Admittedly, though, official decrees played a flanking role there.

It seems amazing that, at the very time when the government in Vienna was imposing saws on Alpine loggers, the practice of sawing was forbidden in Japanese forests. The reason was that saws produce less sound than axes and therefore make it easier to fell trees illegally (Totman 1989: 183); as we have seen, wood thieves in Germany also used saws from an early date. Moreover, in contrast to Europe and North America, the exploitation of Japan's forest was slowed down by the fact that sawmills had no significance until the nineteenth century and that timber floating and rafting, though present, clashed with the irrigation of ricefields and did not grow as dynamically as in the West (Totman 1995: 109f., 50f.). On the other hand, handicraft traditions of woodwork were more widespread and persisted longer than in the West, without interfering with industrial development. Clancey thinks it possible to conclude from the Japanese as well as the

American experience that 'wood has always been par excellence the material of innovation' (2007: 130).

A traveller who flies over the bare mountains of northern China and on to Japan is struck by the densely wooded slopes of his island destination; the contrast between the two could not be greater and is confirmed by the statistics. How is Japan's wealth of forest to be explained? At first glance, it would seem to be a perfect example of geographical determinism: two-thirds of the country consists of steep mountains, and nearly the whole of that two-thirds is wooded; nothing could be simpler than that; forest and mountain are identical in present-day Japan. But then what accounts for the bare mountains of northern China? It might be said that those regions have little rainfall, or that fertile loess stretches part of the way up the hillsides and offers a strong incentive for farming. Modern social scientists, who work without an atlas beside them, consider geographical determinism to be the worst of sins. But forest history most certainly cannot leave geography out of account.

Japan is indeed a perfect illustration of the fact that geography contains opportunities and constraints, while in no way determining what happens in history. Totman's view is the exact opposite of geographical determinism: 'Japan should be a ruined land because of the particular interaction there of geography and history' (1989: 2). In fact, Japan's history has also known periods of extensive mountain deforestation. Engelbert Kaempfer, who travelled there in 1691–2 and wrote a report that remained the best-known Western account of Japan until the nineteenth century, observed in many places that farmers gathered leaves and fir cones because of the shortage of wood (Scurla 1974: 73). It is true that in the imperial city of Kyoto, where the demand for construction timber was especially high, decrees prohibiting clear-cutting were issued as early as 793 and 804, a thousand years before the great forestation drive began in Europe (Fiévé 2008: 29, 410). The steep slopes around Kyoto must have provided constant evidence that clear-cutting leads to landslides. Yet, as we can see from old photos, even the hills around Kyoto, which are today covered with lush forest, were partly bare in the late nineteenth century. The agrarian reformer Franklin Hiram King, who held up East Asia's intensive rice cultivation as a model for American farmers, reported from Japan in 1908: 'This lack of strong forest growth, and even of shrubs and heavy herbage, on hills covered with deep soil, was our first great surprise' (King [1911] 1949: 27).

Hard-working Japanese farmers, like their counterparts in China and Indonesia, were perfectly capable of pushing field terraces up mountain slopes – and they often did as much in earlier centuries. Without a doubt, it was not nature alone that protected the Japanese forests, still less a natural instinct of the Japanese people. A brochure at the Tokyo Museum of Nature and Science tries to assure us: 'The people of the Japanese islands have been sensitive in observing the richness and diversity of nature around them since the beginning of their history. Our daily life in harmony with nature has also enabled us to acquire uniqueness in manufacturing and industry.' But, as everywhere else, if ecological wisdom came to Japan, it did so only after experiences of shortage and hardship.

Whereas the 'ecological revolution' of recent times has often involved exhibition bouts between ecology and economics, world history provides clear indications that economic and ecological energies are closely bound up with each other. Both involve an ability to react to challenges in a considered way, to plan for the future, and to work out the practical implications of those plans. It is clear that Japan has had that ability in comparatively high measure in the last few centuries, at least in situations where a crisis seemed to be around the corner. In that small island kingdom, densely populated and ecologically fragile, the limits to growth became apparent earlier and more clearly than in the vast Chinese empire across the water.

In the seventeenth and early eighteenth centuries, severe famines made Japan aware that it had reached the limits of its ability to feed itself at the existing level of technology. It responded to this by imposing birth restrictions, often probably including infanticide, and by introducing measures to protect and recultivate forest areas. At the time, a sense of crisis at the disappearance of the forest spread throughout the country, not unlike the alarm that gripped Europe in the late eighteenth century. Around 1660 Tsugaru Nobumasa, the noble patron of the artistic lacquering trade, warned that the loss of wood, one of the five elements, would rob men of their vital core: 'Wood is fundamental to the hearth; the hearth is central to the person' (Totman 1989: 77).

The effect of woodland in regulating watercourse levels seems to have been known in Japan earlier than elsewhere, no doubt because its steep mountain slopes were visible to large sections of the population, unlike in countries where they were a long way from fertile lowlands. Tree-planting – not only the regulation of clear-cutting, as in Europe – even played a role early on in forestation. To some extent Japan was also ahead of Europe in converting conifer woodland into mixed deciduous forest – another surprise, given that modern Japanese literature on the forest concentrates mainly on two species of conifer – *sugi* and *hinoki*, the Japanese cedar and cypress, both highly coveted as construction timber. But the majority of wood, in Japan as in the West, was used as firewood and grown as coppice – which meant that deciduous forest was needed. With its scant coal reserves, Japan continued to use wood and charcoal as its major fuels until the 1950s – longer than most European countries. In the nineteenth century, poor Japanese had to spend a much smaller proportion of their income on firewood than poor Central Europeans paid for their increasingly coal-based fuel supply. Forest pasturing did not have the role familiar to us in Europe, but farmers did collect leaves as fertilizer – another reason for not cultivating only *sugi* and *hinoki*. Unlike Western conifers, *sugi* cedars sprouted from stumps left behind after harvesting and could even grow into upright trees; the farmers' typical methods of forestry could therefore also be useful for the production of construction timber.

In Totman's account, there were two epochs in Japanese forest history from ancient times until the late Tokugawa era: the 'millennium of exploitation forestry' and the 'emergence of regenerative forestry' (following acute shortages in the late seventeenth century). This corresponds to the usual periodization in Germany: first the long bad times of plunder, then a glorious age of reforestation and sustainability, with scientific forest reformers as the heroes coming to the rescue. As we have seen, this view of history – which reflects the self-image of modern forestry – should be subjected to critical region-by-region analysis. So, the question suggests itself: should the same be done for Japan? In any event, the heroic figure of the forest reformer is missing there. So who were the main players in the forest? Did the *bakufu*, the central officials of the Tokugawa shogunate, constitute their own forest management? 'The heart of the deforestation problem, however', Totman suddenly throws in, 'lay in authorized, not unauthorized, logging. The protective measures were being taken by the principal forest predators as a means of assuring their own access to forest yield, not as a way of preserving forests per se' (1989: 80). Hence the same paradox as in the West: the rulers issued forest ordinance so that they could plunder the forest undisturbed. Or were discourses concerning the forest what saved the day, given that forest literature was fashionable in eighteenth-century Japan as it was in Europe? Totman is withering about any such suggestion: 'Rhetoric alone did even less to preserve timber stands than it did to stop erosion, because the rhetoricians were the chief lumber consumers' (ibid.: 97).

All this directs our attention towards the farmers and villages in whose hands the fate of the forest lay in most parts of the country. When we read in a *bakufu* decree of 1649 that farmers lack the capacity 'to reason or think ahead', our attitude should be as critical as it is towards Western sources that decry farmers as 'dolts' or 'woodworms'. Many Japanese villages had their *buraku*, similar to the common woodland and pasture of Central or Western Europe, and it is precisely these which offer counter-evidence to Garrett Hardin's 'tragedy of the commons' thesis (Margaret A. McKean, in Bailes 1985: 358–62). They support the argument in Europe that, so long as the commons retained a degree of external autonomy and closure, they were an element of preservation rather than destruction of the forest.

The numerous peasant revolts in Japan – as many as 1,500 estimated for the whole Tokugawa period – testify to great poverty, but they also suggest a high capacity for self-organization. Village autonomy was at its most extensive in mountainous districts: Schiller's motto that 'freedom lies in the mountains' is as applicable to Japan as it is to the West – at least in areas where villages were able to feed themselves. This autonomy was combined with considerable social control over use of the forest (Ushiomi 1964: 9–16). Elinor Ostrom, the 2009 Nobel prizewinner, who, in opposition to Garrett Hardin, argues that local communes often managed woodland and other common resources better than the state or private landowners, presents Japanese mountain villages as an exemplary case in point. It was precisely in mountain valleys, where nature is so unstable, that village communities were often most stable (Ostrom 1990: 65ff., 95).

Recent research on regions with farmer-managed woodland – so-called *satoyama* landscapes – reveals a symbiosis of village and forest, in which the cultivation of a wide range of species corresponds to the diverse uses that farmers make of them (Fukamachi et al. 2001). As in the West, coppices are here inherently sustainable without artificial forestation. The secret of Japan's 'forest change' appears to lie not so much in central government as in the regions; studies of regional history would seem to confirm that this is the case (Roberts 1998). From afar present-day Japan looks like an unusually uniform country, but its geography, with many steep mountain slopes, favoured decentralization and regional autonomy before the advent of modern technology. This is one crucial difference with the huge expanse of China, where levels of society between village and emperor were much weaker. But there may be an analogy with Germany, which was split historically into many different territories and could develop an effective forestry only in the proximity of forest areas. After the

Meiji Restoration in 1868, when Japan's central government weakened local autonomy and embarked on accelerated industrial growth, decades of overexploitation of the forest eventually led to a crisis that cast a retrospective light on the ecological merits of the preceding period (Fiévé 2008: 413).

It is exciting to consider – but also difficult to answer – whether Japan's highly developed woodcraft culture is connected with its tradition of sustainable forestry. At first sight, nothing seems more logical than to construct such a causal link, but here too one should not be too free and easy with the determinism. Japanese high culture originated in China, and if it now strikes us as distinctively Japanese this is because it survived better in the forested archipelago than in China. But the opposite argument is also possible: that the art of woodworking can reach special heights precisely where wood is scarce and expensive; regions such as Scandinavia or Canada scarcely feature in sections of art history that deal with wood. We should conceive of the relationship between forestry and woodcraft in Japan not as one of simple causality but as a series of interactions.

Western tourists who associate old oak buildings with the image of eternity are amazed to hear in Japan that wooden Shinto shrines are renovated every twenty years. Wood is identified there not with a philosophy of eternity, but with one of transience and constant renewal. Of course, European oak structures do not last forever either, but they make it easier to forget how transient things are. That is not possible in Japan. Yet, precisely because rebuilding is seen in advance as something that will be necessary, it is clear all along that provision must be made for an adequate supply of wood; Shintoism thus has an inbuilt compulsion to practise sustainable forestry. Shinto shrines used to have their own woodland. But, paradoxically, the Meiji regime, which elevated Shintoism to the state religion, also cleared many of these woodlands, making the state subsequently responsible for reforestation. Today the main shrine at Ise is probably the only place in Japan where everything is controlled by a single organization, from forestry via felling and cutting to construction (Henrichsen 2004: 53). Ancient wooden constructions can be found in Japan only in Buddhist temples; the Hōrū-ji near Nara is said to be the oldest large timber building in the world. Frequent fires kept up the demand for massive tree trunks, which for temple use had to be tall and branchless; the best grew in artificially cultivated forests with high rotation times. No wonder that artificial forestation began early in Japan.

In Europe, from the baroque period on, stone was the main material used for prestige architecture, while wood became increasingly confined to the dwellings of the poor. In Japan, however, wood retained its prestige and its sacred quality. This cultural status, combined with the pressure for constant renewal, also kept the old woodcraft traditions alive – not only the trivial ones practised in the making of everyday objects. Finely grained construction woods could be planed completely smooth, stimulating the architect to design plain uncovered surfaces. An affinity thus developed between the nature of the Japanese forest and the aesthetic of simplicity that has characterized the arts in Japan since early modern times.

An English specialist in woodcraft has noted: 'The more one works with wood and the more deeply one comes to understand wood, the more sensitive one becomes to the value of natural tactile surfaces, and the more appreciation one has for the appearance of wood in the raw' (Hoadley 1980: 185). Whereas other cultures clogged this impulse – assuming it was there in the first place – with decoration and metal facing, woodwork really came into its own in Japan; it is not surprising that Western fans of wood were overjoyed when they discovered Japanese art. The Western carpenter's art was technically rather crude; the sophisticated Japanese *daiku* was more akin to the Western cabinetmaker, although traditionally furniture has not developed very much in Japan. The dynamism flowing from chairs and cabinets in modern Western woodwork is missing there, but the high art of timber construction amply compensated for the deficit. In 1892, the secretary of the Japan Society in Britain compared the working methods of British joiners and Japanese *daiku*: 'Both in sawing and planing their bodies had swayed in opposite directions, the Englishman pushing the tool away from his body, the Japanese drawing it towards himself' (Clancey 2006: 47). To avoid injuring himself, he had to be more gentle with the wood than his British counterpart.

The diagonal bracing so characteristic of Western timber work, but also of Nepalese temple roofs, is strikingly absent in Japanese wooden structures. This has caused many a Western engineer to shake his head in disbelief. Even beneath wide and heavy temple roofs one finds horizontal timber elements instead of diagonal supports. After all, diagonal bracing is the simplest way of reinforcing a wooden construction, and to do without it requires elaborate and precisely tooled timber joints. These were indeed the special pride of the Japanese *daiku*.

It is sometimes claimed that the frequency of earthquakes and typhoons in Japan is the reason why builders allowed themselves this leeway in wooden constructions. That would be the 'rational choice' explanation. But it is not beyond all doubt, since one might equally argue that triangular supports precisely permit the leeway that can make wooden buildings more earthquake-proof. In the Meiji era there was a wave of propaganda in favour of the *sankuku nagaya*, the Western-inspired 'triangular house': 'The triangle and its material expression, the truss, were talismanic in Meiji Japan. Because triangles in Europe and America successfully overcame gravity and wind pressure, they came to Japan inscribed with an almost abstract resistance to natural forces in general' (Clancey 2006: 186f.).

Of course, diagonal bracing did not offer total protection against the forces of nature, but an 'earthquake culture' is not sufficient explanation for the suspicion in which it was held. Aesthetic traditions must also have played a role. We should note too that, although the wood joints were precise, they were usually simple, not complicated like dovetails. If the house collapsed, the joints were often not destroyed and it could be put together again fairly easily (Henrichsen 2004: 45). It looks as if the traditional philosophical approach to disaster centred less on prevention than on eventual rebuilding. Something like that must have been involved in the Japanese insistence on timber construction.

Nor does rational choice fully explain the heavy, overhanging roofs of traditional Japanese architecture. In a pamphlet published in 1878, *On Structures in Earthquake Countries*, two British physicists who admired Japanese architecture thought they could detect seismological wisdom behind the mighty Japanese roofs: 'It was due to the viscous resistance opposed by the numerous joints and to the lavish employment of timber that the slowly vibrating Japanese house owed its comparative security' (Clancey 2006: 67). But, two years later, the great Tokyo–Yokohama earthquake demonstrated that the 'slowly vibrating Japanese house' was not so stable after all. It is likely that the protruding, elegantly curved roofs so typical of traditional architecture in East and Southeast Asia were originally inspired by the light and elastic bamboo. But the use of heavy wood did not rob them of stability. Junichiro Tanizaki's famous book on the Japanese aesthetic, *In Praise of Shadows*, first published in 1933, explains the overhanging roof by neither technology nor seismology but by the Japanese fondness for shadows (Tanizaki 1991: 17f.). He ought to know.

The pagoda is a bizarre object of controversy among experts, some maintaining that this fragile-looking structure is an example of 'earthquake architecture', others arguing the exact opposite (Clancey 2006: 51, 163). It contrasts starkly with the wide, low churches in earthquake-prone regions of Latin America, but that architectural style corresponds to the properties of stone. Originally, the pagoda was everywhere a wooden structure; only in Japan, unlike China, did it remain so, even outwardly resembling a tree. The octagonal column in the middle is not driven deep into the ground, nor is it tightly joined to the overall structure; the idea is that its to-and-fro movement in an earthquake will have the effect of balancing the rest of the pagoda (Glauche 1995: 41). Or, if things go wrong, will it not throw the pagoda even more off balance? Technology and seismology alone certainly cannot explain the construction of a pagoda.

At first, it was not earthquakes but fires that represented the worst danger to Japanese cities built of wood; even an earthquake turned into a disaster mainly because of the fires it unleashed. Unlike in modern Europe, however, this did not lead Japan to turn away from timber, but further intensified the nexus between forestry and construction. Fires were such common events that they offered good economic prospects to the timber industry, albeit in violent lurches between boom and bust (Totman 1995: 97f.). Since in Japan's damp climate many wooden houses had to be rebuilt every few decades, there was anyway a permanent demand for wood, and fires were not as great a shock as in countries where oak gave the illusion of houses that would last for ever. Once again, the Japanese philosophy of survival aimed less at disaster prevention than at the production of simple houses that could be easily pulled down and rebuilt (Brumann 2001). Reconstruction was so much part of the history of Japanese temples that historians have suspected that stories of fires were sometimes invented. Only after 1950 did restrictions on wooden construction become the typical response to fire disasters.

In 1886 the US zoologist Edward Morse argued that Americans, who build their houses as simply and cheaply as possible, not for eternity, could well appreciate the wisdom of the Japanese approach to housebuilding. By contrast:

> An Englishman particularly . . . recognizes but little merit in the apparently frail and perishable nature of these structures. He naturally dislikes the anomaly of a house of the lightest description oftentimes sustaining a roof of the most ponderous character, and fairly loathes a structure that has no king-post, or at least a queen-post truss; while the glaring absurdity of a house that persists in remaining upright without a foundation, or at least without his kind of foundation, makes him furious. (Clancey 2006: 87)

Supporters of wood seemed to have won when many newly built Western-style brick buildings collapsed in the great earthquake at Nobi on 28 October 1891, while multi-storey wooden structures remained standing (Clancey 2006: 113ff.). The victory of concrete in Japanese cities did not begin until the 1950s. One may find it tragic that the old Japanese ideal of simplicity was transferred to concrete, since that which had appeared beautiful and sophisticated in precious woods now looked monotonous. Even the famous cityscape of Kyoto, which was spared by American bombers, has been blighted by concrete buildings. On 15 August 1991, after Japan's economic bubble burst, the Buddhist Association of Kyoto published an appeal in the *New York Times* in the hope of mobilizing world opinion against the disfigurement of the old capital (Fiévé 2008: 308), and recently a broad movement has been gathering momentum to preserve and restore traditional wooden buildings (*machiya*). Much more typical today are various hybrids of tradition and modernity – industrially produced timber structures that retain some traditional elements. So far, Japan's sophisticated aesthetic taste has at least slowed down the switch to 'Fordist' mass production.

The Second World War again led to overexploitation of the forest. There followed a large-scale reforestation drive, now conducted by the state and often involving monoculture. As firewood came to be used less and less, the interest in deciduous forest declined. But even the cultivation of new coniferous woodland did not make sense in the end, since logging on steep mountainsides, where it was expensive to build tracks and large harvesters threatened to overturn, was no longer profitable in a time of rising wages; it was much cheaper to buy timber abroad to meet requirements. In other words, only massive imports prevented Japanese wooden buildings from becoming unaffordable.

While many Japanese forests turned into overgrown 'ghost reserves' – to the chagrin of foresters and the delight of nature lovers – Japan became the world's largest timber importer. Its timber companies conducted ruthless clear-cutting in Southeast Asia, even on the Pacific coast of Latin America, provoking the disgust of forest conservationists all over the world (Dauvergne 1997). 'Never before had full-scale clearances been pursued so deliberately and radically' as in the 1970s, by the Japanese JANT corporation in New Guinea (Garbe 1985: 131). In that case indigenous people fought back: one chieftain in Papua threatened in 1981 that, if the JANT workers returned, they would be killed and eaten (Becker 1986: 7).

Although appeals by Western conservationists for a boycott of tropical woods provoked defiant local support for logging in some of the countries affected, it proved possible to mobilize the new Asian nationalism against Japanese clear-cutting. Recently there has been a trend in Southeast Asia towards restrictions on raw wood exports;

the Philippines and Sabah – previously Japan's two main suppliers – imposed a ban on further shipments, in 1986 and 1993 respectively, to ward off complete destruction of their forests. If this tendency persists, and if prices continue to rise, there is likely to be a revaluation of Japan's forests, especially as the country cannot in the long term tolerate a blatant contradiction between its internal and external ecological morality without losing face internationally. Flexible specialization, with an eye on differentiated demand, is currently the motto of Japanese forestry and is all to the good of its natural diversity. There is a future for the 'Japanese idea that a working forest is also a beautiful forest' (Reiffenstein and Hayter 2006: 522f.).

China

In the middle of the twentieth century, no less than 68 per cent of the area of Japan was forested, while in China the corresponding estimate was all of 8 per cent (Mitchell 1981: 138). Until recently, in its dealings with the forest (and not only those), China differed as much as one can imagine from Japan. Today its northern loess regions display bare mountain ridges on all sides, with gaping chasms caused by erosion; local people point them out to you without being asked. This development is hard to explain from the history of culture in China. As a famous quotation from the Confucian Mencius shows (see box 5.1), the Chinese already appreciated the value of the forest in ancient times, even if many artists had an eye above all for the aesthetic of naked cliffs. What was lacking most were practically effective institutions and vital interests.

Box 5.1 From Liang Hui Wang, by Mencius (372–289 BC)

There was a time when the trees on Ox Mountain grew in abundance, but since they are on the outskirts of a large city they are being constantly hewn with the axe. Is it any wonder that they are no longer beautiful? . . . Given the moisture from rain and dew, they do not fail to put forth new shoots and buds, but then cattle and sheep come to graze on the mountain. For this reason everything is so bare. People who see only the bare surfaces tend to think there have never been any trees on the mountain. But can that be the nature of the mountain? . . . If man turns aside from his true heart, it happens to him as with trees and axes.

Especially in southern and western China, the forest was the pre-serve of non-Chinese minorities; imperial rule expanded by clearing the forest, not by protecting it. There was not, as in Europe, a close historical link between forest conservation and royal hunting, nor did shipbuilding provide a major impetus for forestation during most of the Chinese Empire. Around 1390, apparently, a massive foresta-tion campaign that would have been unthinkable in the West at the time planted some 50 million trees in order to secure the timber for an ocean-going fleet. But that brief spurt of maritime imperial-ism soon gave way to the traditional self-absorption of the 'Middle Kingdom'.

Probably a much more important factor was that, even in areas of intensive rice cultivation, livestock-breeding did not have anywhere near the same significance for farming that it did in large parts of the West. A typical Chinese village had neither forest pasture nor common woodland. The Chinese example suggests that, contrary to the view of many historians, the use made of the forest by farmers in Central Europe generally favoured its conservation. A further element in the equation was that, from early modern times on, population growth was faster in China than in Japan.

Yet, even if conditions in China had been different, the empire would have been much too large for a state forestry policy to have real bite. It is not possible to run forests from afar. If Germany overtook centrally governed France in forestry after 1800 – at least in terms of economic yield (Badré 1983: 281) – this was due in no small measure to the *Kleinstaaterei* bewailed by German nationalists; political frag-mentation ensured that the forest doctrines applied in highland areas were not the same as those that governed the north German plain. In a country like China, the regional institutions were lacking that might have pursued effective forest conservation (Radkau 2008a: 112–15).

The communist takeover in 1949 established a strong central power, such as China had not had for centuries. Mao Zedong called for the 'conquest of nature' (Shapiro 2001), but he knew full well the value of the forest in supplying wood and guarding against soil erosion. In 1956 the government in Beijing even declared the largest forestation project of all time, comparable to the Great Wall – that is, the building of a 'great green wall' against the 'yellow dragon', to protect the forest from the advancing steppe and desert. The 'green wall' remained largely imaginary, however, in the absence of a con-sistent and coordinated forest policy. The communist dictatorship nationalized the forests, but as elsewhere this led the local population to lose interest in them.

In 1958 Mao announced the 'Great Leap Forward', one of whose most spectacular measures was the building of small smelting furnaces to operate with local wood resources. The 'Great Leap' not only resulted in a terrible famine, but spelled ruin for the already much depleted forests. Many long-distance admirers of Mao at the time thought that the decentralization of heavy industry and its gearing to local resources amounted to a rational and fascinating programme, but in reality it was a sudden, ill-considered directive from on high that took no account of regional conditions and ended in unmitigated disaster. The Great Leap period and the subsequent Cultural Revolution witnessed massive destruction of the forest.

Times have changed since then. The present Chinese government has been pursuing a campaign of major reforestation, and everywhere in China tree-planting has become at least a symbolic act of environmental protection and concern for the future. Although the government, despite its dictatorial powers, often finds it difficult to push through environmental measures that clash with regional industrial interests, it has achieved growing success in respect of forestation. China is one of the few countries in the world to have dramatically increased its forested area in recent years; possibly the 'Great Green Wall' will end up a reality after all. But natural rejuvenation is not working in northern China, where trees have to be continually planted and artificially irrigated (Küchli 1997: 186).

The traumatic experience of Maoism led Chinese environmental policy-makers after 1982 to seek salvation in the opposite extreme: in the privatization of forests. Legislation introduced in 1985 disregards land ownership in assigning trees to those who plant them, even going so far as to grant tree inheritance rights (Küchli 1997: 182). As in Europe at the beginning of the nineteenth century, the activation of private interests is seen as a magical way of improving conditions. Only time will tell whether this method is as successful in forestry as it has been in the general economy. The dynamic of private interest has its own environmental risks, especially in a system of mixed private and collective ownership. One leading Chinese forest scientist stated recently: 'Garrett Hardin's "tragedy of the commons" has stimulated China's policymakers to try to put a stop to decollectivization and privatization, to prevent selfish individuals from overusing common resources' (Liu 2009: 221).

The state of the Chinese forest appears less dire if we include bamboo in the picture and remember how important it is for southern China. Love of bamboo runs through Chinese painting, poetry and popular culture, and its cultivation is considered one of the traditional virtues. Its uses for Chinese people are similar to those of wood, although it has been the basis for a culture of a different kind: 'Adding wood to bamboo' is in Japanese a metaphor for combining the irreconcilable – but, if you look closely in East Asia, you will often find the two in combination with each other. Although China may possibly be worse off than Japan in forestry, it has almost twenty-five times more bamboo at its disposal. Since bamboo can grow where forest struggles to prosper, it is an argument on the side of optimistic ecologists who trust in the power of nature to heal itself (Farrelly 1984). Since bamboo groves are so indestructible, it has not harmed the panda's ecological image that it eats its way through such huge quantities of shoots. It even features in the logo of the World Wildlife Fund and has become the darling of Chinese conservationists.

A Central European viewpoint is not enough to understand the situation in other parts of the world. Karl August Wittfogel, who explained the course of Chinese history by reference to irrigation, wrote in 1931 of bamboo: 'Perhaps this giant grass is one of the main factors responsible for the slaughter of China's forests' (1931: 490). Today the Chinese hunger for wood is contributing to intense agitation in the international timber industry.

India

Only limited comparisons are possible between pre-modern India and China, since India developed into a political entity only under British colonial rule in the nineteenth century. In the early modern period, the Islamic moguls established their power in the broad river valleys in the north of the subcontinent – from the Indus to the Ganges and Brahmaputra – while indigenous polities hung on in mountainous areas of the south and on the southern slopes of the Himalayas. From the viewpoint of the Moguls and their British successors, many forests were the refuge of 'forest peoples', who had escaped outside rule or even rebelled against it. Here too, then, the assertion of political power meant clearing the forest rather than protecting it.

Yet the situation was clearly different from that of China: India as a whole was never ruled by a central authority comparable to that of the Middle Kingdom. Around 1670 the Maratha Prince Shivaji, leader of a Hindu revolt against Mogul rule, issued one of the few forest conservation decrees known from pre-modern India; the forest could become a popular cause as a support for regional autonomy. The 'forest peoples' also left their mark on Indian culture. Fruit trees became even more a part of village life.

Franz Heske, who travelled in the southern slopes of the Himalayas in the 1920s, described peasant India as a forest culture, in a way that makes one feel transported to pre-industrial Germany:

In India the forest plays an exceptional role in the life of the farming population. The whole of their domestic and livestock economy depends on the forest. Their animals graze there, and its leaves serve as fertilizer to replace the lost nutrients in the field. The forest yields construction timber and firewood, resin, fruits and a thousand other important things; it provides a valuable opportunity for work in the breaks between work in the fields. The forest proves its worth in lean times, when it saves man and beast from the worst hardship. (Heske 1937: 1f.)

For all the huge differences, there are also surprising analogies from the Hunsrück to the Himalayas.

The historian of gardens Marie Luise Gothein, who was travelling in India at roughly the same time, thought that, although the veneration of trees was universal, it had nowhere had 'such a long and still unbroken series of testimonies as in India' (Gollwitzer 1984: 50). Do such testimonies have the same expressive power as forest ordinance? That is an open question, and the answer to it is important for an interpretation of Indian forest history. Around 250 BC, an edict handed down by the Buddhist-inclined Emperor Ashoka forbade the burning of forest for no reason or simply to destroy the animals inside it. But subsequently Buddhism all but disappeared from India; no continuity of forest conservation is discernible from Ashoka to Shivaji.

East of Kathmandu, the capital of Nepal, the tourist joyfully discovers the beautiful forest of Deopatan, which is considered holy because the god Shiva withdrew there with his consort Parvati for a copulation that lasted a thousand years. But such events are unusual and unlikely to ensure reproduction of the forest on a large enough scale. The Indologist Axel Michaels flatly disputes that veneration of holy trees leads to forest conservation. He argues that, on the contrary, 'the tree is holy because of its uniqueness' (1999: 132).

In the end, the British Raj did establish a massive link between political rule and forest conservation, the first and strongest impetus being the supply of timber for the Royal Navy. But this very association with foreign rule made forest conservation unpopular. The British authorities were most interested in teak – indeed, it was their only concern in the case of Burma. When the king of Burma signed a secret treaty with the French in 1885, promising them access to the country's famed teak forests, London sent an expeditionary corps which, to the enthusiasm of Rudyard Kipling, captured Mandalay:

'Thus, perhaps for the only time in history, timber traders found themselves at the focal point of a war' (Latham 1957: 185f.).

The British appetite for teak clashed with traditional village use of the forest, much as conifer forestation had clashed with pasturing and leaf collection by local farmers in the Germanic world. Imperial rule was still harsher in Burma than in India, and teak from Burma dominated the world market until far into the twentieth century. But this complete subordination of local forest use to exports became the bane of Burmese life; its long-term consequences can still be seen in the present military dictatorship (Bryant 2007: 145ff.).

The German-educated botanist Dietrich Brandis, who was appointed inspector-general of forests for British India in 1864 and became a legendary figure still exalted by Kipling, realized that, in a huge land such as India, forest conservation could succeed only with the agreement of local people (Ramachandra Guha, in Poffenberger and McGean 1996: 88ff.). The Hauberg system in his native Siegerland had shown him an elaborate and successful example of this, and on later trips to Europe – in sharp contrast to most German foresters – he had been especially impressed by the management of communal woodlands. He therefore tried in India to combine teak cultivation with local subsistence economics in an early form of 'agroforestry' (figure 5.1) (Hesmer 1975: 105, 40f.). His project of drawing on the vitality of the Indian village looked ahead to Mahatma Gandhi's fundamental idea. Gifford Pinchot, the founder of American forestry, who also had to deal with giant trees, called him 'the first of living foresters'. 'He had accomplished on the other side of the world what I might hope to have a hand in doing in America' (Pinchot [1947] 1998: 9). It was a conception of forestry under conditions of grassroots democracy.

The problem remained the colonial framework. Brandis tried in vain to get the British authorities to accept that, as the precondition for sustainable forestry, village forests should have official status and that villagers should be able to rely on keeping their rights to use it (Hesmer 1975: 157f.). In the end, state conservation officials turned many anti-colonial rebels into opponents of the forest itself. According to the British forest historian Michael Williams:

> The end result was a terrible paradox. An admirable and massive administrative edifice had been constructed for the rational use of the timber resource, which had no parallel in the world for decades to come. It was one of the administrative jewels in the Imperial Crown, a model for the rest of the world, and a highly efficient and profitable enterprise. But it was also going to prove to be one of the festering sores in the body of the Indian subcontinent that has still not been healed. (2006: 346)

Figure 5.1: An example of successful 'agroforestry' in Java: maize cultivation under teak trees, which will probably be felled in the next few years and have already started dying off so that the wood can be dried by 'curling' (notching right in the heart of the wood). This process, a subject of controversy among experts, makes teak logs capable of being drifted and rafted. Maize cultivation has benefits for the forest, since the ground under the dead teak trees would otherwise become overgrown and make tree growth more difficult later on (Hesmer 1966–70: vol. 2).

'The Forest Department is the biggest enemy' became the motto of forest villages faced with criminalization of their traditional rights. As India's independence movement gathered momentum, forest-burning developed into a common method of resistance, especially in conifer plantations. Then, after independence, conservation was neglected for decades; the state wanted to keep the price of wood low for industry, so the incentive to squander resources was high.

The first sign of a change – revolts *for* the forest, no longer against it – came in the 1970s amid the worldwide 'ecological revolution'; most famously, the Chipko movement ('Embrace the Trees!'), composed largely of women and led by Gandhi supporters, protested in the name of traditional village rights against the commercial clearing operations of outside corporations (figure 5.2). It grew outwards from the edge of the Himalayas, where unusually severe flooding had occurred in 1970 and the key role of the forest in regulating the hydrologic balance was particularly evident (Guha 1989: 155ff.).

The protest movement erupted in 1972 when the Forest Department forbade a local development agency to cut down twelve trees, yet

Figure 5.2: Women from the Chipko movement in India. It harks back to
Amrita Devi, from a village in Rajasthan, who spread her arms around a tree as
she was hacked to death in 1720 by a party of loggers sent by the maharajah of
Jodhpur. She was taught to worship trees as a child – so the story goes – because
they protected her village from sandstorms, captured water and provided food
for people and livestock (Tüting 1983: 16f.). Wood use was thus considered less
important than the ecological value of trees.

allowed a sports goods company from Allahbad to fell not only ashes
and willows but even fruit-bearing walnut trees (Seebauer, in Schuler
1985: 204). The image of women embracing trees was enthusiastically taken up by the media: it fitted perfectly the 'Bollywood' film
world, one of whose favourite scenes featured women dancing round
a tree; but it also corresponded to the ideal scenarios of Western eco-
feminism. The Chipko movement developed into the best-known
ecological movement in the Third World, winning sympathy in the
Indian administration and scoring greater success than any of the
country's other environmental initiatives. But the myth associated
with it proved more effective by far than the actual movement, which
remained limited both in time and in geographical extent. The Chipko
song became famous: 'What are the blessings of forests? Soil, water
and air. Soil, water and air / are the essentials of life' (Rawat 1993:
43). It was the best proof that convergence was possible between
ecology and local needs.

Since then, however, there has been a tendency in India to puncture

313

the myth of the Chipko movement, on the grounds that it corresponded only to a momentary snapshot. In today's world, even remote villages do not remain for long outside the modern economy. The Chipko villagers eventually developed a commercial interest of their own in wood, and by weakening the Forest Department they opened the way to uncontrolled clear-cutting (Rangan 2000: 164ff.).

A similar story unfolded around the same time in Amazonia, where the Kaiapò Indians were first feted by Western environmentalists as fighters against destruction of the rainforest but then let their fans down by engaging in a lucrative trade in high-grade mahogany. The village is not per se a champion of conservation. For some time, grassroots movements have been appearing around the world that fight *against* restrictions on village forest use and the expulsion of whole villages from the forest in the name of conservation. 'Conservation refugee' is the new term for people affected by this (Dowie 2009; Pedersen 2008). On the other hand, 'joint forest management' has recently become a buzzword in India, denoting cooperation between forest-aware villages and decentralized state forestry departments (Poffenberger and McGean 1996).

Nepal as a paradigm for the Third World

More even than India, the Himalayan kingdom of Nepal has traditionally been a land of forests. Until 1982 it was a significant exporter of timber, and one can still see in its towns that it had a highly developed woodcraft tradition. Woodcarvers stand far above blacksmiths in Nepal's traditional craft hierarchy (Levy 1990: 81, 95), and they developed special skills in window frames and slanting crossbeams for temple roofs. The contrast is extreme with Japanese architecture, which achieved the geometrical clarity that fascinated modern architects precisely by foregoing door and window frames.

Like Japan, though, Nepal preserved the sacred value of wood longer than many other cultures. Here, too, woodcarvings were originally unpainted; this changed only in the 1930s, when foreign influences began to tell. The carvings on temple friezes, with their copulating gods and demons, are more sensual than similar stone sculptures in India and have a suppleness of form that makes it hard to believe they are from the hard wood of the sal tree (*Shorea robusta*). They fascinated tourists and animated the tantra fantasies of the hippies who flocked to Kathmandu from the mid-1960s on.

All the more abrupt was the scene change in 1975, when a widely noted article by Erik P. Eckholm argued that the forces of 'ecological degradation' had had a more rapid and glaring effect in Nepal than in any other mountainous country in the world. Further alarms followed in a similar vein. In 1978 a World Bank report predicted that no accessible forest would be left in Nepal in twenty years' time. The country mutated from heaven to hell in the imagination of environmentally aware globetrotters. What had happened?

As so often, the first answer that springs to mind is that rapid population growth, together with the spread of Western consumption models on the crest of a tourist wave, was the ruin of the forest in Nepal's ecologically fragile mountainous setting. This causal link is all too plausible. Yet, according to a number of reports, it was the nationalization of the forests in 1956–7 – officially in the name of conservation and the 'green forest nation's wealth' – that brought about a critical situation once villages stripped of their customary rights lost interest in forest cultivation. Paradoxically, then, 'the loss of forestry resources is partly due to the over-protective role of the forest administration, making forest area either inaccessible or denying right to manage by local inhabitants.' In the name of conservation, nearly all public attention was directed at the forest, scarcely any at the fields. 'A wolf's cry for forest and silence for farmland loss. The world seems to enjoy more the tune played by the foresters' (K. Panday, in Heide 1992: 62–9). 'Soil loss is probably Nepal's single most serious resource conservation problem', concluded an expert from the Kathmandu-based International Centre for Integrated Mountain Development (B. Bhatt, in Dahal and Dahal 1998: 69).

The authorities cast the forest as a supplier of wood, while local farmers needed it above all as a supplier of fodder for their livestock: it is a vicious circle typical of developing countries. Nationalization makes the forest a de facto social no-man's-land. Friederike von Stieglitz reports from several countries in Africa: 'The state institutions lack the capacity to enforce regulations, and the farmers have lost interest in conservation along with their rights.' As Ostrom noted, since state forestry departments are often ineffectual and corrupt, 'nationalization created open access resources where limited-access common-property resources had previously existed' (1990: 23) – and limitation of access is the important thing in forest conservation! One forest-dweller on the Indonesian island of Aru explained to two leading Western environmentalists: 'Wherever people aren't in control of their resources, nature gets hammered. This is the essence of the conservation problem' (McNeely and Sochaczewski 1988: xv). What a simple problem it is – if only people lived in their own small worlds!

Whether in parts of Africa or in the Himalayas, this depressing scenario is not the end of the story. For the crisis is partly a question of *perceptions*. Development strategists had a Western model before their eyes, and Nepalese government departments happily adopted the deforestation thesis in order to legitimize the state's control of the forest and to obtain overseas aid for reforestation programmes. In this spirit, officials announced to village gatherings that, without state forest conservation projects, farmland soil would be washed down into the Bay of Bengal.

Since then, however, a revisionist literature has cast doubt on the thesis of catastrophic deforestation, and indeed attacked it as an outright myth based upon a whole web of false assumptions, such as the idea that mountain farmers blindly reproduced and stripped the forest bare (Ives and Messerli 1989; Radkau 2008a: 281–4). Many things surprisingly recall the controversy over whether deforestation – especially deforestation due to farmers – happened on a catastrophic scale in German-speaking lands two centuries ago. Similar disputes have since then centred on African countries where the government, following in the footsteps of colonial administrators, blames local people for forest destruction as a way of legitimizing state control (Fairhead and Leach 1996).

In Nepal, as in China and other countries, the resource picture changes as soon as one includes bamboo groves. Since bamboo grows quickly, a grove can be run in the same way as coppices; the short life of bamboo products is enough to recommend sustainable forestry without a need for careful arithmetic. Bamboo groves are not as attractive as forest for development agencies, there not being much to 'develop' in them (Seeland 1980: 89–93). But Brandis – once more against the prevailing orthodoxy – recognized long ago the importance of bamboo for forestry (especially the fact that it improved the soil under teak trees) and even foresaw its value for the paper and cellulose industry (Hesmer 1975: 290).

Since the state of the forest is unclear in many parts of the world, typical stories of destruction and reforestation can easily circulate without any basis in reality. But it would probably not be accurate simply to dismiss signs of crisis for either Nepal or African regions or to write off the whole 'story of forest destruction' as an invention (Ives and Messerli 1989: xix). Purely imaginary constructs do not have the power to convince. Construction timber really has become very expensive in Kathmandu; brick really has been replacing wood there since the 1980s and filling the valley air with its smell.

In Nepal, indoor carpentry has become an art of handling

small-dimensioned wood: 'The manner in which the joistings and the frames are carried out gives the impression that Newar carpenters did not have thick long pieces of wood at their disposal or perhaps they did not deem it fit to use such wood' (Le Port, in Toffin 1991: 81, 89, 109). In the Himalayas, unlike the Alps or the Appalachians, there are no traditional systems for transporting wood, and so tree trunks have to be dealt with as far as possible on the spot – and when they are fresh, in the case of hardwood, since it can no longer be processed when it has dried out.

Deforestation in Nepal is not an acute disaster, but nor is it a pure invention. In revisionists who dismiss such stories as 'narratives', one comes across ideological preconceptions such as a belief that traditional village communities always have a rational relationship with their environment. Whether that is true or not must be verified case by case. Villages are by no means always capable of autonomous and far-sighted action; they often do not even stand together as a community, but display internal divisions and a lack of critical public awareness. It would appear that environmental protection develops best where local and transregional impulses interact with each other.

Often, however, the interaction can be of a fatal kind. In Nepal as elsewhere one has to reckon with the possibility of a vicious circle: catastrophic deforestation is used as an argument to intensify state control, but this causes local people to lose interest in sustainable forestry and results in a deepening of the crisis. Where forest conservation is combined with political rule, concern for the forest becomes entangled in the wiles of power politics. This brings us to a general problem of the present day: 'environment' can serve many different purposes, one of which is arbitrary intervention by the state. An understanding of this might form the basis for a new, much less naïve, era of environmental awareness.

In comparison with other environmental issues, the principle of forest conservation has gained a high degree of acceptance all over the world. Long before the dawning of the eco-age, forest conservation and tree-planting were held up by various governments, not least authoritarian ones, as a model of patriotic provision for the future; the 'Patriotic Society' founded in Hamburg at the end of the eighteenth century is a good case in point (Walden 2002: 271ff.). Yet the planting of trees remains a merely symbolic act if the trees are not properly watered, bring local people no tangible benefits, and have no protection from woodcutters or pasturing animals. The nexus of conservation and power is found everywhere in today's world; Europe's other tradition – consensus about the forest and a harmonization of interests through legal channels – is much less widespread. In large parts of the world, then, conservation often exists only on paper. We repeatedly hear from aid workers that tree-planting is little more than a farce to gain access to development funds; most of the seedlings are immediately afterwards eaten up by goats. A 'sustainable forestry' would chiefly mean that local people saw forest conservation as being in their own interests. Sustainability is a matter not of technology but of social policy.

2 Conflicts and (Ostensible) Solutions

Forest destruction in the tropics

Whereas earlier generations had associated the tropics with images of impenetrable jungle and inexhaustible fecundity, alarming signs of rapid destruction began to accumulate in the 1970s, bringing with them extensive soil erosion and threatening to undermine the whole future of the areas in question.

In 1980 a major report on the environment to US President Jimmy Carter, *Global 2000*, highlighted deforestation in developing countries as one of the most urgent ecological problems facing the world and predicted that, if it continued at its present rate, all the forest there would be destroyed by the year 2020. Similar prognoses have since been heard from the UN's Food and Agriculture Organization, whose competence also stretches to forestry.

The cities with the greatest say on policy in the developing world used to show limited interest in forest conservation, since their food supply seemed to depend on the conversion of large areas into farmland. Much as in Europe in the past, lifestyles and economic forms associated with the forest were held up as examples of backwardness that needed to be overcome. Only recently has it been realized that, despite the lush vegetation, tropical soil is not very fertile and that in many areas a stock of trees is the only way of safeguarding the possibility of agriculture.

From a historical point of view, it is understandable that the catastrophic tendencies in contemporary development came to be recognized so late. Swidden cultivation proved ecologically stable for thousands of years, and it was only rapid population growth that led to ruinous overexploitation of the soil in many regions. A fatal interplay developed between the timber industry and slash-and-burn clearance: loggers would drive forest aisles and roadways into the jungle even if they could use only a fraction of the trees; land-hungry settlers then followed and destroyed what was left of the forest.

For a long time the timber industry only exploited forest areas close to water and even there made relatively few incursions. But access took on new dimensions with the construction of motor roads and the spread of full forest harvesting for the paper and cellulose industry (Myers 1980). The export of tropical hardwoods alone rose from 3 million to 40 million cubic metres between 1950 and 1976 (Douglas 1983: 84).

Deforestation in the tropics reached a peak in the postcolonial period; Kenya, for example, has lost 90 per cent of its forest since independence (Ehlert 2004: 83). What Albert Schweitzer wrote in 1931 still rings true today: 'Whenever the timber trade is good, famine reigns in the Ogowe region, because the villagers abandon their farms to fell as many trees as possible. In the swamps and the forest in which they find this work they live on imported rice and imported processed foods, which they purchase with the proceeds of their labour' (Schweitzer [1931] 1998: 192).

Campaigns for a boycott of tropical wood, seeking to protect indigenous cultures as well as the forest, became popular in the environmental movement. But they increasingly faced the dilemma that the main causes of deforestation were to be found not among the big timber importers of the industrial countries but in the developing countries themselves. Campaigners therefore had to come to grips not only with their own timber industry, but even more with the modernization strategies of Third World governments, which angrily pointed to the fact that the wealthy industrial countries were systematically exploiting their own forest resources while trying to prevent poorer countries from doing the same. The movement to boycott tropical wood went into decline in the 1990s, in much the same way that the alarm over the 'death of the forest' receded. Sometimes the focus on energy-saving cut across protection of the tropical forest, since tropical hardwoods, because of their great durability and resistance to warping, experienced a new boom for the production of heat-retaining window frames. Wood harvested in the developed countries would have had to be chemically treated to produce the same effect.

As research has shown, sustainable kinds of use – though not with the same diversity of tree species – would be theoretically possible in many tropical forests. But up to now practical steps in that direction have remained modest – not surprisingly, if we bear in mind that sustainable forestry is much more complicated in the tropics than in Central Europe, and that forest authorities there are generally much worse trained. Traditional symbioses of village and forest have collapsed, and the new states often do not encourage them. Simple transfers of European reforestation experiences to the tropical rain-forest have led to 'monumental failures' (Schulte and Schöne 1996: 22). Projects that combine cash crops for export with planting for subsistence have been rather more successful, enabling the interests of local people to be articulated with a species diversity that makes the societies more resistant to economic and ecological crisis. There is no general recipe, however, only specific regional solutions.

Plantations and 'turbo forest': the case of eucalyptus

Large-scale forestation projects usually prefer eucalyptus (figure 5.3) and various sorts of pine. These require rotation times of two to ten years (eucalyptus) or fifteen years (pines) for the production of

Figure 5.3: Eucalyptus trees (*Eucalyptus haemastoma*) in Australia, where they are a native species that makes up 95 per cent of woodland. Unlike most other trees, the eucalyptus forms natural stands, though there are a number of different varieties. Its exceptional robustness and growth properties were already known in the nineteenth century. Planting began in Portugal around 1850, and many of the resulting trees are among the largest in Europe (Goes 1984). Spain, Brazil, India and other countries have since followed suit, but ecologists have tried to dampen down the enthusiasm for eucalyptus.

320

raw material for the paper and fibre industry. Many forestry departments and large farmers have switched to the cultivation of eucalyptus forest, because its fast-growing wood, which needs very little attention, often yields a higher profit than any agricultural produce. California and other parts of the world with a suitable climate experienced a veritable 'mania' for eucalyptus-growing as far back as the late nineteenth century (Tyrrell 1999: 59).

In Southern Europe, the eucalyptus played a role in the struggle against malaria in and after the nineteenth century, since its high absorption of water helped to dry out the wetlands where the carrier of the disease traditionally bred. This characteristic can be a problem in arid regions, however. Around the turn of the twentieth century, Jewish settlers in Palestine threw themselves into the cultivation of eucalyptus, and it became a symbol of the labour of the early pioneers. But fifty years later ecologists were cursing the once-celebrated tree (Tal 2002: 78f.).

As previously in Spain, Portugal or Israel, eucalyptus plantations have recently become a divisive issue in developing countries too. Some regard the tree as a 'spectacular solution to wood supply problems' (Normand 1971: 58), but for others – an Indian environmental journalist, for example – it is an 'ecological terrorist', which robs its surroundings of water, chokes them with its slow leaf replacement growth, and poisons the soil with toxic substances that emanate from its deep roots.

In India the eucalyptus has been praised for having scarcely any natural enemies (Krauß 2001: 135), but in Brazil huge new eucalyptus plantations have been wiped out by ants. Still, the incentive to grow eucalyptus trees remains high in Brazil, which has more than 400 paper and cellulose factories. Its climate is such that a tree is ready for felling there after seven years, whereas the spruce in Central Europe needs seventy more on top of that. Eucalyptus plantations in Brazil also receive favourable tax treatment (Bolius 1998).

Farmers complain that the eucalyptus provides no fodder for their livestock, and in Thailand many resisted the eucalyptus boom that was energetically promoted by the state in the 1980s (Lee and So 1999: 126). On the other hand, eucalyptus has its uses as firewood, and in southern India it has even been cultivated in combination with agriculture. As with many other environmental issues, the controversy loses much of its sharpness when one realizes that it is not a question of absolute good and absolute evil.

In the literature on development policy, the acacia tree is sometimes mentioned in the same breath as the eucalyptus but sometimes

321

presented as a contrast. It appears as a chameleon presence in the history of the forest: its many varieties, which only botanical classification joins together, are associated with quite different histories. To confuse matters even more, there is a pseudo-acacia – known to botanists as the *Robinia* – which originates from the East of the United States and, though promoted as a robust, fast-growing tree in Europe since the eighteenth century, has also been treated as an enemy by many foresters.

The true acacia has been famed since antiquity as an indestructible tree of arid regions. It was 'the appropriate wood for the Jews in the Sinai desert to make their ark, tabernacle, table, and altar' (Meiggs 1982: 59). Enthusiasm for the acacia, which in the nineteenth century swept across the almost treeless Hungarian plain, has since spread to the African Sahel region. Today it has an international circle of friends among aid workers, since it is unusually hardy in periods of drought, its thorns keep grazing livestock away, and it supplies excellent wood for jobs around the farm. Many regard it as the saviour of the Sahel. In South Africa and Australia, it is the national emblem and the pride of the landscape.

The sprawling roots of the acacia, and their exceptional capacity for regeneration, are nevertheless a nuisance to farmers or foresters who want to use the site of a stand for a different purpose. A Greenpeace flyer lumps the acacia and eucalyptus together and warns that both are usually 'marketed from plantations'. 'In many areas, the monotonous plantations crowd out primeval forest, with dire consequences. Woodland is nurtured with artificial fertilizer and pesticides; species diversity is whittled away, the soil eroded, and the water balance destroyed.' The problem of sweeping value judgements applies to it more sharply than to almost any other tree!

Firewood: still one of the world's main energy resources

In many developing countries, outside the tropical wetlands, signs of a firewood crisis have been gathering for a long time. Wood is by far the most important – and often the only – source of energy for the rural population and urban slum-dwellers. It is estimated that, in the economically underdeveloped countries of the South, a yearly average of one to one and a half tonnes of wood are used for fire per head of the population, the great majority of it for the cooking of food. The Brundtland Report, *Our Common Future* (WCED 1987), rightly dedicated a whole chapter to firewood. In 1986 a speaker at a public hearing of the Brundtland Commission in Nairobi had pointed out:

'For most of the rural population in developing countries, firewood and charcoal are and will remain the principal fuels.' But the report was divided in the conclusions it drew from this: it first noted that people are more economical with wood when it is in shorter supply, but later observed that for people living on the land it remains a 'free good' until 'the last tree is felled'.

In many regions wood has become so scarce that people are forced to travel longer and longer distances to collect it – especially the women, who are responsible for cooking and related activities, and who may 'spend half their life gathering wood' (Klüting 1981: 49). Semi-nomads in the Sahel move around in search of dwindling wood resources. Contrary to previous expectations, the substitution of wood with other fuels is not on the cards for the time being; the 'age of wood' continues, even if firewood is not a big issue in international environmental discourse. Since the 1980s 'social forestry' has become an objective of development aid, for the Food and Agriculture Organization and the World Bank too – which means, first and foremost, improving the fuelwood supply in rural areas. Often it also means planting eucalyptus trees, which in reality serve commercial interests and are damaging to the ecology of arid regions because of their high water requirement (Ives and Messerli 1989: 71ff.).

In the 1970s and 1980s, aid workers in regions with little forest tried to persuade local people to use solar cookers. To Northern eyes, the tropics and subtropics seem positively made for solar energy, but such projects were generally failures. Too little thought was given to the daily rhythm and lifestyle of the women affected by them, and the outside location of the cookers meant that it was difficult to integrate them into domestic labour. Besides, women cook in the morning and the evening, when the sun is not high in the sky (Knerr and Schmidt-Ranke 1984: 34).

Energy-saving stoves – which, as we have seen, were typical projects in early modern Germany – are a better proposition and have been undergoing a revival in the world of development aid. They can bring major gains for little expense, given that traditional open cookers make use of only a tenth of the heat generated by firewood. Nevertheless, as in the early modern age, the first experiments were disappointing; energy-saving is not a purely technical problem when ovens and stoves form such an integral part of household culture. In the past, however, people eventually learned from the mistakes, and much the same is beginning to happen now. It helps a great deal if the women in question are able to build their own energy-saving device from locally available clay. In this and other

323

areas of development aid, success depends mainly on the degree of cooperation with women.

3 Looking Back to the Future: Six Spotlights on the History of Forest and Wood

Many truths about forestry and the timber industry are local or regional in nature. The forest has an endless number of local variants, and the same is true of everything that people do with it. In the pre-industrial age, when the weight of logs precluded a transregional market unless there were suitable rivers, one sometimes had only to cross a mountain crest to reach a different world: on one side, drifting on a large scale ensured a successful timber trade; on the other side, a jungle-like realm was penetrated only by charcoal- or tar-burners.

Yet the endless diversity of regional microcosms is only one side of the coin. Analogies abound here, if only because natural laws also operate in the relationship between man and nature. Indeed, many fundamental insights lie beyond the limited horizon of regional history, obtainable only through cross-regional comparisons or even a global overview. The following points are especially important:

1 It is always a key question whether power manifests itself in forest clearance or in forest conservation. All around the world, from early times and often into the modern age, the expansion of a ruler's authority has been associated with clearances. As we have seen, a major change occurred in Central and Western Europe at least as early as the sixteenth century, when forest ordinance acquired central importance in the construction of territorial states. In other parts of the world, the nexus of forest conservation and political dominion is found only sporadically before modern times – in Iran or northern India, for instance.

2 If Europe has a plethora of archive material about the forest since the late Middle Ages, this is due not least to the fact that forest users were able to employ legal channels to fight for their interests as soon as competing claims came into play. This presupposed that the law was in some degree independent of political power – that the ruler could not simply play fast and loose with the law. This seemed to go without saying in large parts of modern Europe, but a glance at other parts of the world shows that such a function of juridical process is by no means obvious. Courtroom battles were, to be sure, not always to the benefit of the forest, but they did lead

324

to a sharper focus on the conditions prevailing there and the scale of destruction; early maps of the forest usually grew out of legal disputes. In most other parts of the world one would look in vain for comparable sources – among other reasons, because the use competition typical of Europe has not been present there.

3 The question of whether state or private ownership of the forest is more beneficial has been ideologically charged for centuries. History tells us that there is no generally applicable answer. The state is of use to the forest mainly when it strengthens regional institutions that have an interest in preserving the forest. It is a truism that you cannot have someone watching every tree. Forest conservation is successful only when it coincides at least partially with the interests of people living there and the concepts they have of legal rights. Hence, for all the wrangling over use of the forest, the degree of consensus as to its value is also important. Consensus is not as spectacular as struggle, but it too has undoubtedly been present in large parts of Europe; historians are discovering more and more evidence of this (Ernst 2000: 345). At the very time when 'forest criminal' was flying around as a term of abuse, there was a basic recognition that the use of wood must be kept 'proportionate' to the size of the forest; the only argument was over what that actually meant for everyone involved. It is a basic fact of history in Central and Western Europe that farmers too needed the forest. We should not be misled by foresters' talk of farmers as 'woodworms' or tree 'mutilators'. A global comparison makes it quite clear that the farmer's interest contributed to forest conservation – sometimes more, sometimes less.

4 If we look only at the mass of complaints about forest destruction and wood shortage that reached a peak in the late eighteenth century, one is tempted to argue – as many have done before – that Europe's industrialization based on steel and coal was a response to the growing scarcity of wood. But that is a wrong conclusion. In most regions, industrialization first proceeded on the basis of wood resources and animal and water power. A global comparison clearly shows that, in the eighteenth century, Europe was still quite rich in timber resources and was by no means suffering from exceptional shortages.

5 Sometimes the role of nature in the history of the forest and the world is clearer in the broad picture than it is in the detail. Nature in Europe is not particularly rich in species diversity, but it is relatively robust and – to use a modern turn of phrase – 'error-friendly'. Many European soils supported deep ploughing; many

forests regenerated all by themselves, even when they were badly overexploited for a considerable length of time. Foresters therefore found it fairly easy to point to successes: they needed only to restrict use of the forest for it to grow fine and strong again without artificial means. But nature is also a significant factor in another way. In regions with cold winters, where people freeze without heating, some degree of provision for firewood became second nature. This too made it easier to achieve the consensus that is essential for forest conservation.

6   On the other hand, historians who wish to grasp the full picture of man's interaction with the forest, over and above the forester's viewpoint in modern Central Europe, must not focus only on the great high forests. Even in early German history, coppices and forest pasture were more important than high forest for people's everyday needs. German foresters have often missed a feeling for the forest among Mediterranean peoples, but the relationship with fruit trees – olive, chestnut, carob, fig – has greater importance in their lives. Similarly, Indian villages cultivate their mango trees and treat the jungle as the tiger's realm. In East Asia it is necessary to look at bamboo groves as well as trees, even if for botanists bamboo is not a tree but a grass.

Historical insights might support attempts to go beyond rigid alternatives and to develop an imaginative feel for the combination of different uses ('agroforestry', for example). But history also gives many a reason for caution and scepticism. Sharply conflicting social interests cannot be harmonized in forestry any more than elsewhere, nor can the complex forest ecosystem be manipulated for ever for purely economic objectives. Why should anyone try to go on manipulating it? As far as the limits to growth are concerned, the forest is a good place where real organic growth happens before our eyes. On a wide historical horizon, the forest and wood open our eyes to opportunities that culture and nature have to evolve together.

POSTSCRIPT: THE MYSTERY OF CERTIFICATES, OR, SUSTAINABLE FORESTRY VERSUS GREENWASHING

In late 2010 I presented a paper at a conference in Chicago on environmental history. That same night I had a fright when I heard a sound in my hotel room; I switched the light on and saw that a poster of the NGO ForestEthics had been slipped under my door. It showed a steep escarpment that had been cleared of trees against all the rules of forestry: a wretched image of destruction. The heading: 'This landslide has been certified "green" by the SFI.' SFI stands for Sustainable Forestry Initiative, a leading American certification organization. On the back of the poster, beneath the title 'SFI: Certified Greenwash', a large chart showed how the SFI board of directors linked together more than two dozen leading corporations in the timber industry with the PPPPP quintet of consumers (pulp, paper, panels, printer, publisher). It was a shaft of light into the mysteries of certification such as I had never seen before.

I took the poster away with me, unable to get it out of my mind. It kept providing material for my correspondence with Josef Krauhausen, the editor of *Holz-Zentralblatt* and an independent mind with thirty years' experience in the timber industry. I was now more aware that certification lay at the heart of international forest policy and that the history behind it was dramatic and still largely opaque. The origin of wood certificates in the 1980s – whether the initiative came from conservationists or from the timber industry – is itself obscure. The Forest Stewardship Council (FSC), which was founded in 1993 and took the lead in Europe, works together with the Big Three in forest conservation (Greenpeace, Friends of the Earth and the World Wildlife Fund), while the American timber industry created the SFI as a rival to it; neither abbreviation means anything to more than a few outsiders. But the FSC faced competition in Europe too, from the Pan-European Certification System (PEFC), founded in 1998, which claimed to be better adapted to local conditions. For, although the costs of FSC certification are 'peanuts' for large state forests, they are not cheap for the smaller, privately owned ones that are quite common in Europe. The PEFC settles for all-inclusive certification of whole countries, trusting that their forestry administration will take care of sustainability. But FSC spokespersons say this is a farce, and there are non-stop battles between the two organizations. Robin Wood, the radical splinter from Greenpeace, also considers the FSC to be corrupt.

Certification has become surprisingly widespread since the late 1980s, but it remains doubtful how much of an advance this represents for sustainable forestry. A number of aspects need to be taken into account. First of all, the extent to which the market honours certification – indeed, compels leading corporations to honour it – is quite remarkable. Have people become more moral? It is mainly government organizations that have responded to public pressure by demanding certification, if only to protect themselves from criticism by NGOs. In markets where public contracts play less of a role, certification has been correspondingly less significant. Representatives of NGOs are involved in the certification process; it is thus a source of funds for them, and since they are often strapped for cash this carries the danger of corrupt practices.

The danger is increased if it is very difficult to monitor sustainable forestry from outside. Reliable certification requires the cooperation of local foresters; it must be possible to depend on the information they provide. Certification arose in response to the alarm over the destruction of tropical forests, as an alternative to the boycotting of tropical woods that many conservationists were calling for. Yet it is precisely in the tropics that certification has had the least success. Foresters there often lack a cooperative spirit or the capacity to plan ahead. On the other hand, certifiers have had lucrative results in Europe's large state-owned forests, where all they have had to do is rubber-stamp sustainable economic activity that functioned perfectly well without them. The toughest problems have affected small areas of private forest, for which the certification process is too expensive. In many cases, however, it is precisely these forests that host the greatest biodiversity.

So, is the whole history of certification a farce? Let us not be hypercritical about it: all environmental policy is piecemeal! Although certification often brings no immediate benefits for sustainability, it can advance a little in that direction over time. Malaysia, for example, which led third world opposition to a global forest regime at the Rio summit in 1992, has since developed its own conservationist NGO (MTCS, in reality a 'GONGO' – Government-Organized Non-Governmental Organization) and certification system under their control. To be sure, that is no happy end, but neither is it pure farce. The cultivation of long-term thinking is not the least purpose of forest history, which may thus be of eminently practical use.

WOOD TALK

The forest is a peculiar organism of unlimited kindness and benevolence, which makes no demand for its sustenance and generously extends the products of its life activity; it affords protection to all beings, offering shade even to the axeman who would destroy it.

Gautama Buddha

King, the master of wood carvers, once carved a bell-rest. When it was finished, all who beheld it marvelled, considering it a divine piece of work. The Duke of Lu also gazed upon it and questioned the master, saying, 'What is your secret?' To which the wood carver replied, 'I am a man who works with his hands and I have no secrets. And yet there is one thing that is truly needful. When I made up my mind to carve the bell-rest, I was careful not to expend my energies on thoughts of other things. So that my heart might be at rest, I fasted, and after three days I no longer thought of honours or reward. After five days I no longer thought of praise or blame, and after seven days I had forgotten that I had a body or limbs, nor at that stage had I any longer any thought for Your Highness's court. Thus I became truly serene and could pursue my object with complete singleness of mind, for all disturbing influence of the outer world had disappeared. I then went into the forest and looked at the trees. As soon as I set eyes on the right tree, the bell-rest appeared before me as though finished and I needed only to set my hand to work. Had I not found this tree, I would have abandoned the task. It is because I allowed my own nature to work along with the nature of my material that people now consider this to be a divine piece of work.

Zhuangzi (c.369–286 BC)

For there is a hope for a tree,
if it is cut down, that it will sprout again,
and that its shoots will not cease.
Though its roots grow old in the earth, and its stump dies in the ground, yet at the scent of water it will bud
And put forth branches like a young plant.
But mortals die, and are laid low;
Humans expire, and where are they?

Book of Job, 14:7–10

But, from the fact that each plant likes its own soil and its own mixture of air . . . it is clear that there are plants which either do not thrive at all in different places or, if they are planted, do not continue to grow and bear fruit and generally end up badly. . . . But all become finer and stronger if they grow in their own characteristic soil. Wild trees too have each their fitting place, as do domesticated ones.

Theophrastus of Eresos (c.371–287 BC)

Timber should be felled between early autumn and the time when Favonius [the spring wind] begins to blow. For in spring all trees become pregnant, and they are all employing their natural vigour in the production of leaves and of the fruits that return every year. The requirements of that season render them empty and swollen, and so they are weak and feeble because of their looseness of texture. This is also the case with women who have conceived.

Vitruvius (1st century BC), *The Ten Books on Architecture*, II: 1

[Protagoras] was the first person who asserted that in every question there were two sides to the argument exactly opposite to one another. . . . He was the first person who demanded payment of his pupils; fixing his charge at a hundred minae. . . . He was also the original inventor of the porter's pad for men to carry their burdens on . . .; for he himself was a porter . . ., and it was in this way that he became highly thought of by Democritus, who saw him as he was tying up some sticks.

Diogenes Laertius, *The Lives and Opinions of Eminent Philosophers*, IX: 1–4

For one may there see reduced to practice not only all the art that the husbandman employs in manuring and improving an ill soil, but whole woods plucked up by the roots, and in other places new ones planted, where there were none before. Their principal motive for this is the convenience of carriage, that their timber may be either near their towns or growing on the banks of the sea, or of some rivers, so as to be floated to them; for it is a harder work to carry wood at any distance over land than corn.

Thomas More, *Utopia* (1516)

I marvel how our God has given so many uses to wood for all men in the whole wide world: building timber, firewood, joiner's, cartwright's and shipbuilder's wood, wood for rooms, wood for wheelbarrows, paddles, gutters, barrels, etc. Who can tell of every use that wood has? In short, wood is one of the greatest and most necessary things in the world, which people need and cannot do without.

Martin Luther, *Tischreden* (30 August 1532)

The work of a correct and regular writer is a garden accurately formed and diligently planted, varied with shades, and scented with flowers; the composition of Shakespeare is a forest, in which oaks extend their branches, and pines tower in the air, interspersed sometimes with weeds and brambles, and sometimes giving shelter to myrtles and to roses; filling the eye with awful pomp and gratifying the mind with endless diversity.

Samuel Johnson, *Shakespeare* (1765)

Spiel du die Zauberflöte an,	If you play the magic flute,
Sie schütze uns auf unsrer Bahn.	It will protect us on our way.
Es schnitt in einer Zauberstunde	My father cut it in a magical hour
Mein Vater sie aus tiefste Grunde	For the most important reasons
Der tausendjährgen Eiche aus	Out of the thousand-year-old oak
Bei Blitz und Donner, Sturm und	During lightning, thunder, storm
Braus.	and shower.

Pamina, in Mozart's *The Magic Flute*, Act III

'Come here, Fritz!' Friedrich approached shyly; his mother seemed alien to him in her black ribbons and with her troubled expression. 'Fritz,' she said, 'are you going to be good now and make me happy, or are you going to be wicked and tell lies or drink and steal?'

'Hülsmeyer steals, Mother.'
'Hülsmeyer? God forbid! Do I have to whip you? Who tells you such wicked stories?'
. . .
'But, Mother, Brandis too says that he steals wood and game.'
'Child, Brandis is a forester.'
'Mother, do foresters tell lies?'
Margaret was silent for a while; then she said: 'Listen, Fritz, God makes wood grow in freedom and the game changes its haunts from the land of one master to that of another, it can't belong to anybody.'

Annette Droste-Hülshoff, The Jew's Beech (1842)

Fallen wood . . . has as little organic connection with the growing tree as the cast-off skin has with the snake. Nature itself presents as it were a model of the antithesis between poverty and wealth in the shape of the dry, snapped twigs and branches separated from organic life in contrast to the trees and stems which are firmly rooted and full of sap. . . . Human poverty senses this kinship and deduces its right to property from this feeling of kinship. . . . [But, for the legislator who also punishes the collection of dead wood], wood remains wood in Siberia as in France; forest owners remain forest owners in Kamchatka as in the Rhine Province. . . . This *abject materialism*, this sin against the holy spirit of the people and humanity, is an immediate consequence of the doctrine which the *Preussische Staats-Zeitung* preaches to the legislator, namely, that in connection with the law concerning wood he should think only of wood and forest and should solve each material problem *in a non-political way*, i.e., without any connection with the whole of the reason and morality of the state.

Karl Marx, Debates on the Law on Thefts of Wood (27
October and 3 November 1842)

Social policy . . . is what lurks behind the trees in the forest and beneath the rustling red leaves of last autumn. . . . It is well known that the idea of private ownership of the forest appeared only late and only gradually among the German peoples. According to an age-old German legal principle, forest, meadow and water are for the use of all members of the farming commune. . . . The poor farmer would go hungry in many parts of Germany if the traditional benefits of the forest were not a lifetime annuity for

333

him. . . . The real enemies of the forest, however, the political enemies, are the substitutes for wood that are increasing year by year, and which point, in the certainty of victory, to the no longer distant time when forests will no longer be needed and their whole area can be converted into agricultural land. . . . This thought of seeing every patch of earth upturned by human hand has something horribly sinister for the mind of any natural human being, but it is especially repulsive to the German spirit. . . . Lay the axe to the forest and you demolish civil society as historically constituted. The German people need the forest, as human beings need wine. . . . Only the forest still affords us civilized creatures the dream of a personal freedom unencumbered by police supervision.

Wilhelm Heinrich Riehl, *Natural History of the German People*
(1853)

Primeval forests . . . with the eternal ocean, are the unchanged general objects remaining to this day, from those that originally met the gaze of Adam. For so it is, that the apparently most inflammable or evaporable of the earthly things, wood and water, are, in this view, immensely the most durable.

Herman Melville, *Pierre: or, The Ambiguities* (1852)

Wild im Walde
wuchs ein Baum,
den hab ich im Forst gefällt:
die braune Esche
brannt' ich zur Kohl',
auf dem Herd nun liegt sie
  gehäuft.
Hoho! Hoho!
Hohei! Hohei!
Hoho! . . .
Des Baumes Kohle,
wie brennt sie kühn;
Wie glüht sie hell und hehr!

In springenden Funken
sprühet sie auf:
Hohei! Hoho! Hohei!
Zerschmilzt mir des Stahles
  Spreu.

In the woodland
a tree grew wild,
I felled it in the forest,
burned the brown
ash trunk to charcoal.
Now it lies piled on the
  hearth.
Hoho! Hoho!
Hohei! Hohei!
Hoho! . . .
How blithely the tree's
charcoal is burning!
How bright and splendid it
  glows!

In spouting sparks
it spurts upward:
Hohei! Hoho! Hohei!
It smelts the molten steel for
  me.

Richard Wagner, *Siegfried*, Act I

I cannot deny that my trust in the character of my successor suffered a blow when I learned that he had cut down the ancient trees on the garden side of his (formerly my) accommodation – trees that would take centuries to grow again and were thus an irreplaceable adornment of the state landholding in the compound. . . . This destruction of trees bespeaks a Slav, not a German, trait of character. . . . I would overlook many a political difference of opinion with Herr von Caprivi sooner than the wanton destruction of ancient trees, with regard to which he has abused . . . the right of usufruct.

Otto von Bismarck, *Gedanken und Erinnerungen*, vol. 3
(published posthumously in 1921)

'Wood', generally speaking, seems, in accordance with its linguistic relations, to represent feminine matter (*Materie*). The name of the island Madeira means 'wood' in Portuguese. Since 'bed and board' (*mensa et thorus*) constitute marriage, in dreams the latter is often substituted for the former, and as far as practicable the sexual representation-complex is transposed to the eating-complex.

Sigmund Freud, *The Interpretation of Dreams* (1900)

In the Arabic Middle Ages [the lute] became the instrument decisive for the fixing of the scale intervals. This parallels the function of the kithara for the Hellenic world, the monochord for the Occident, the bamboo flute for China. . . . For the effectiveness of string instruments shaping of the resonant body is decisive. A string merely firmly strung without a vibrating body does not produce a musically useful tone. The creation of resonant bodies is a purely Occidental invention . . . The handling of wood in the form of boards and all finer carpenter's and wooden inlay work is much more typical of Nordic peoples than those of the Orient.

Max Weber, *The Rational and Social Foundations of Music*
(1912)

The finest woods are not exported, because they are still unknown and therefore not sought after on the European market. Should they ever become known and sought-after, the timber trade on the Ogowe will be much more important than it already is. . . . At first I did not understand how everyone here, including those who have nothing to do with the timber trade, can take such an interest in the qualities of various woods. But over time, as a result of constant association with timber dealers, I have become what my wife calls a wood freak.

Albert Schweitzer, *Zwischen Wasser und Urwald* (1926)

When I built my own house, I at least avoided tiles, and had the floor done in camphor wood. To that extent I tried to create a Japanese atmosphere – but was frustrated finally by the toilet fixtures themselves. As everyone knows, flush toilets are made of pure white porcelain and have handles of sparkling metal. Were I able to have things my own way, I would much prefer fixtures – both men's and women's – made of wood. Wood finished in glistening black lacquer is the very best; but even unfinished wood, as it darkens and the grain grows more subtle with the years, acquires an inexplicable power to calm and soothe.

Junichiro Tanizaki, *In Praise of Shadows* (1933)

The rational conquest of the environment by means of machines is fundamentally the work of the woodman. . . . Stone is a mass: but wood, by its nature, is already a structure. . . . Wood, then, was the most various, the most shapeable, the most serviceable of all the materials that man has employed in his technology: even stone was at best an accessory. Wood gave man his preparatory training in the technics of both stone and metal: small wonder that he was faithful to it when he began to translate his wooden temples into stone. And the cunning of the woodman is at the base of the most important post-neolithic achievements in the development of the machine. Take away wood and one takes away literally the props of modern technics.

Lewis Mumford, *Technics and Civilization* (1934)

Asked about his relationship to nature, Mr K. said: 'Now and then I would like to see a couple of trees when I step out of the house. Particularly because, thanks to their different appearance, according to the time of day and the season, they attain such a special degree of reality. Also, in the cities, in the course of time, we become confused because we see only commodities . . .. In our peculiar social order, after all, human beings, too, are counted among such commodities, and so, at least to me, since I am not a joiner, there is something reassuringly self-sufficient about trees, something that is indifferent to me, and I hope that,

336

even to the joiner, there is something about them that cannot be exploited.'

Bertolt Brecht, *Stories of Mr Keuner* (1930)

Late Gothic frame construction grew organically from the properties of wood. It allows for swelling and for shrinking. It is as vital to the development of later furniture types as is the sustained development of the cross-ribbed vault in architecture – a flight from massiveness towards refinement of form.

In detail, frame construction underwent many changes. New techniques appeared, but this late Gothic construction has remained until the present day as the method of building furniture. Not until recent decades was a new principle advanced, whose supporting element was the elastic slab of plywood or plastic.

Sigfried Giedion, *Mechanization Takes Command* (1948)

'Wood' is an old name for forest. In the wood there are paths, mostly overgrown, that come to an abrupt stop where the wood is untrodden.

They are called *Holzwege*.

Each goes its separate way, though within the same forest. It often appears as if one is identical to another. But it only appears so.

Woodcutters and forest keepers know these paths. They know what it means to be on a *Holzweg*.

Martin Heidegger, *Off the Beaten Track* (1949)

Wood is only a one-syllable word, but behind it lies a world full of beauty and wonder.

But does 'the' material qua material have a formal equivalent? Early Puritanical zeal almost reached the point of assuming that this, that or the other corresponded to iron, wood or stone. . . . *All* artistic form is determined *not* by the material but by *the mind's mastery over matter*. Anyone who does not know this already should take a look at the wonderful baroque churches of Balthasar Neumann or Dominikus Zimmermann; they will teach him what secret magic (or trickery, the doctrinaire will say) the great masters achieved with their material. Matter as such *lacks* formal equivalence. But, to put it negatively, I would say that it offers resistance.

Theodor Heuss, *Was ist Qualität?* (1951)

Kemal (Atatürk) found a frequent refuge on the model farm which he was developing on the slopes around his former headquarters at the Agricultural School – an easy ride from Chakaya. Since his boyhood there had grown in him a feeling for nature. . . . The sight of a pine tree gave him a sense of almost pagan veneration. Once, while riding with Ismet (Inönü), then his chief of staff, he had exclaimed, 'Find me a new religion.' 'Let it be a religion', Ismet answered, 'whose form of worship is to plant trees.'

Patrick Kinross, *Atatürk: The Rebirth of a Nation* (1964)

Every follower of the Buddha ought to plant a tree every few years and look after it until it is safely established, and the Buddhist economist can demonstrate without difficulty that the universal observation of this rule would result in a high rate of genuine economic development independent of any foreign aid. Much of the economic decay of South-East Asia (as of many other parts of the world) is undoubtedly due to a heedless and shameful neglect of trees.

E. F. Schumacher, *Small Is Beautiful* (1973)

Not that long ago one could still hear the woodsman sing a woodcutter's song as he sawed down a tree. During transplanting, singing voices rolled over the paddy fields, and the sound of drums surged through the village after the fall harvest. . . . These scenes have changed drastically over the past twenty years or so. In the mountains, instead of the rasping of hand saws, we now hear the angry snarl of chain saws. We see mechanical ploughs and transplanters racing over the fields. . . . The disappearance of the sunken hearth from farming homes has extinguished the light of ancient farming village culture. Fireside discussions have vanished, and with them, the village philosophy.

Masanobu Fukuoka, *The Natural Way of Farming* (1985)

I noticed that much of the land that had been covered by trees, bushes, and grasses when I was growing up had been replaced by tea and coffee. I also learned that someone had acquired the piece of land where the fig tree I was in awe of as a child had stood. The new owner perceived the tree to be a nuisance because it took up too much space and he felled it to make room to grow tea. By then I understood the connection between the tree and water, so it did not surprise me that when the fig tree was cut down, the stream where I had played with the tadpoles dried up. . . . I mourned the loss of that tree. I profoundly appreciated the wisdom of my people, and how generations of women had passed on to their daughters the cultural tradition of leaving the fig trees in place.

Wangari Maathai, *Unbowed: A Memoir* (2006)

REFERENCES AND BIBLIOGRAPHY

Abel, Wilhelm (1986) *Agricultural Fluctuations in Europe: From the Thirteenth to the Twentieth Centuries*, trans. Olive Ordish. London: Methuen.

Abetz, Karl (1955) *Bäuerliche Waldwirtschaft: Dargestellt an den Verhältnissen in Baden*. Hamburg and Berlin.

Ackermann, G., and Ramazzini, B. (1780) *Abhandlung von den Krankheiten der Künstler und Handwerker*, 2 vols. Stendal.

Addy, John (1976) *The Textile Revolution*. London: Longman.

Albion, Robert G. (1926) *Forests and Sea Power: The Timber Problem of the Royal Navy, 1652–1862*. Cambridge, MA: Harvard University Press.

Albion, Robert G. (1952) 'The Timber Problem of the Royal Navy, 1652–1862', *Mariner's Mirror*, 38/1: 4–22.

Altrogge, Diethart (1984) *Waldsterben: Argumente zur Diskussion*. Regensburg: Deutscher Forstverein.

Altwasser, E. (1981) *Die Augustinergasse, Geschichte einer Marburger Straße*. Marburg: Arbeitsgruppe für Bauforschung und Dokumentation.

Andés, Louis Edgar ([1903] 1986) *Die Holzbiegerei: Herstellung der Möbel aus gebogenem Holz*. Cologne: R. Müller.

Anonymous (1788) *Reisen des grünen Mannes durch Deutschland und Ungarn*. Halle.

Appuhn, Karl (2009) *A Forest on the Sea: Environmental Expertise in Renaissance Venice*. Baltimore: Johns Hopkins University Press.

Arbeit und Umwelt: Grundlinien für ein ökologisch orientiertes Wirtschafts- und Arbeitsplatzprogramm (1983) Wiesbaden: Hessisches Ministerium für Landesentwicklung.

Armstrong, Lyn (1978) *Woodcolliers and Charcoal Burning*. Horsham: Coach.

Armytage, W. H. G. (1976) *A Social History of Engineering*. London: Faber.

Arndt, Ernst Moritz (1820) *Ein Wort über die Pflegung und Erhaltung der Forsten und der Bauern im Sinne einer höheren d.h. menschlichen Gesetzgebung*. Schleswig.

Assmann, Jan (2003) *The Mind of Egypt: History and Meaning in the Time of the Pharaohs*. Cambridge, MA: Harvard University Press.

Ast, Hiltraud, and Katzer, Ernst (1970) *Holzkohle und Eisen*. Linz: Trauner.

Åström, Sven-Eric (1975) 'Technology and Timber Exports from the Gulf of Finland, 1661–1740', *Scandinavian Economic History Review*, 23: 1–14.

Bachelard, Gaston (1964) *The Psychoanalysis of Fire*. London: Routledge & Kegan Paul.

Badré, Louis (1983) *Histoire de la forêt française*. Paris: Arthaud.

Bailes, Kendall E. (ed.) (1985) *Environmental History: Critical Issues in Comparative Perspective*. Lanham, MD: University Press of America.

Bakker, J. W. (1976) 'Der europäische Nadelschnittholzmarkt', in *Holzhandel auf neuen Wegen*, Stuttgart: DRW.

Balla, Bálint (1981) 'Ressourcenknappheit und soziales Handeln', in F. Rapp (ed.), *Naturverständnis und Naturbeherrschung*. Munich: Fink, pp. 214–26.

Bamford, Paul Walden (1956) *Forests and French Sea Power, 1660–1789*. Toronto: University of Toronto Press.

Barth, Ernst (1975) 'Brennholzpreise in Chemnitz', *Jahrbuch für Wirtschaftsgeschichte*, 4: pp. 253–67.

Barton, Gregory A. (2002) *Empire Forestry and the Origins of Environmentalism*. Cambridge: Cambridge University Press.

Bätzing, Werner (1984) *Die Alpen: Naturbearbeitung und Umweltzerstörung*. Frankfurt am Main: Sendler.

Bauer, Erich (1981) *Unsere Wälder im historischen Kartenbild*. Grünstadt: Sommer.

Bauer, Otto (1925) *Der Kampf um Wald und Weide*. Vienna: Wiener Volksbuchhandlung.

Baumgärtel, Hans (1963) *Bergbau und Absolutismus: Der sächsische Bergbau in der zweiten Hälfte des 18. Jahrhunderts und Maßnahmen zu seiner Verfassung nach dem Siebenjährigen Krieg*. Leipzig.

Baumgarten, Wilhelm (1933) *Beziehungen zwischen Forstwirtschaft und Berg- und Hüttenwesen im Kommunionharz: Ein Beitrag zur Wirtschaftsgeschichte des Harzes*. Brunswick: Waisenhaus.

Baumgartner, Hansjakob (1981) 'Die Brennholzkrise', *epd–Entwicklungspolitik*, 14–15: 16–19.

Baxandall, Michael (1980) *The Limewood Sculptors of Renaissance Germany*. New Haven, CT: Yale University Press.

Bayer, R., et al. (1985) 'Zellstofftechnologische Bewertung von Fichtenholz aus immissionsgeschädigten Beständen', *Zellstoff und Papier*, 34/4: 128–31.

Bayerl, Günter, and Pichol, Karl (1986) *Papier: Produkt aus Lumpen, Holz und Wasser*. Reinbek: Rowohlt.

BDF (Bundesverband Deutscher Fertigbau) (ed.) (2007), *80 Years of Modern Prefabrication Construction*. Bad Honnef: BDF.

Becher, Johann Philipp ([1789] 1980) *Mineralogische Beschreibung der Oranien-Nassauischen Lande*. Kreuztal: Wielandschmiede.

Becher, Udo (1981) *Die Leipzig-Dresdner Eisenbahn-Compagnie*. Berlin: Transpress.

Becker, Jörg (1986) *Papiertechnologie und Dritte Welt*. Eschborn: Vieweg.

Bedal, Konrad (1978) *Historische Hausforschung*. Münster: Coppenrath.

Bedal, Konrad (ed.) (1984) *Mühlen und Müller in Franken*. Munich: Delp.

Behr, Lothar (1984) 'Holz im Benzintank: Experimente mit Holzgasantrieb', *Das neue Universum*, no. 101: 102–7.

Beil, Anton (1846) *Forstwirtschaftliche Kulturwerkzeuge und Geräte in Abbildungen und Beschreibungen.* Frankfurt am Main.

Beilner, Wolfgang, et al. (1978) *Flößerei und Sägewerk, Mskr., Preisschrift des Schülerwettbewerbs Geschichte.* Lech.

Berg, Carl Heinrich Edmund von (1844) *Das Verdrängen der Laubwälder im nördlichen Deutschland durch die Fichte und die Kiefer.* Darmstadt.

Berg, Carl Heinrich Edmund von (1869) *Pürschgang im Dickicht der Jagd- und Forstgeschichte.* Dresden.

Berg, Maxine (1979) *Technology and Toil in Nineteenth-Century Britain.* Atlantic Highlands, NJ: Humanities Press.

Bergeret, Anne (1986) 'Ökologisch lebensfähige Produktionssysteme', in Peter Rottach (ed.), *Ökologischer Landbau in den Tropen.* Karlsruhe: C. F. Müller.

Bergmann, Jürgen, and Büsch, Otto (1973) *Das Berliner Handwerk in den Frühphasen der Industrialisierung.* Berlin: Colloquium.

Bernhardt, August (1869) *Die Waldwirtschaft und der Waldschutz mit besonderer Berücksichtigung der Waldschutzgesetzgebung in Preußen.* Berlin.

Bernhardt, August ([1872–5] 1966) *Geschichte des Waldeigentums, der Waldwirtschaft und Forstwirtschaft in Deutschland,* 3 vols. Aalen: Scientia.

Bettmann, Otto L. (1974) *The Good Old Days – They Were Terrible!* New York: Random House.

Betzhold, Uta (1986) 'Holzverknappung und Umgang mit Technik im Altenaer Drahtgewerbe: altständische Nahrungssicherung am Ende der vorindustriellen Ära', *Der Märker* [Altena], 35: 194–502.

Bevilacqua, Piero (2009) *Venice and the Water,* trans. C. A. Ferguson. Solon, ME: Polar Bear.

Biebelriether, Hans (1982) 'Die Rache der Natur', *nature,* no. 4.

Bieler, Karl (1949) *Holz als Werkstoff.* Brunswick: Westermann.

Bierter, Willy, and Gaegauf, Christian (1982) *Holzvergasung – Umweltfreundliche und effiziente Energieholznutzung.* Karlsruhe: C. F. Müller.

Binder, Josef (1909) *Geschichte des Waldwesens der Stadt Hermannstadt-Nagyszeben.* Hermannstadt.

Binding, G., Mainzer, U., and Wiedenau, A. (1977) *Kleine Kunstgeschichte des deutschen Fachwerkbaus.* Darmstadt: Wissenschaftliche Buchgesellschaft.

Birch-Hirschefeld, Hildegard (1920) 'Die holzverarbeitenden Gewerbe in Leipzig um 1500–1800', dissertation, Leipzig.

Biringuccio, Vannoccio (1925) *Biringuccio's Pirotechni: Ein Lehrbuch der chemisch-metallurgischen Technologie und des Artilleriewesens aus dem 16. Jahrhundert,* trans. Otto Johannsen. Brunswick: Vieweg.

Blab, Wilhelm (1960) *Bodenwöhr: Geschichte und kulturelle Entwicklung eines bayerischen Berg- und Hüttenortes.* Bodenwöhr: Gemeinde Bodenwöhr.

Blaschke, Karlheinz (1967) *Bevölkerungsgeschichte von Sachsen bis zur industriellen Revolution.* Weimar: Böhlau.

Blaser, Werner (1987) *Fantasie in Holz/Fantasy in Wood: Elemente des Baustils um 1900.* Basel: Birkhäuser.

Blasius, Dirk (1978) *Kriminalität und Alltag.* Göttingen: Vandenhoek & Ruprecht.

Blau, Josef (1917–18) *Böhmerwälder Hausindustrie und Volkskunst,* 2 vols. Prague.

Blickle, Peter (ed.) (1977) *Deutsche ländliche Rechtsquellen: Probleme und Wege der Weistumsforschung.* Stuttgart: Klett-Cotta.

REFERENCES AND BIBLIOGRAPHY

Bloch, Gunther W. (1984) *Beiträge zur Analyse und Synthese eines Mensch-Maschine-Systems, dargestellt am Beispiel der Motorsäge*. Hamburg: Wiedebusch.

Blömer, August (1973) 'Der Ingenieur-Holzbau im Verlauf seiner Entwicklung', *Bauen mit Holz*, no. 75.

Bobek, Hans Peter (ed.) (1994) *Österreichs Wald: Vom Urwald zur Waldwirtschaft*. Vienna: Eigenverlag Autorengemeinschaft 'Österreichs Wald'.

Bode, Wilhelm, and Emmert, Elisabeth (1998) *Jagdwende: Vom Edelhobby zum ökologischen Handwerk*. Munich: Beck.

Bode, Wilhelm, and Hohnhorst, Martin von (1994) *Waldwende: Vom Försterwald zum Naturwald*. Munich: Beck.

Bogucka, Maria (1980) 'The Role of Baltic Trade in European Development from the 16th to the 18th Centuries', *Journal of Economic History*, 9: 5–20.

Bogucka, Maria (1984) 'Der Pottaschehandel in Danzig in der ersten Hälfte des 17. Jahrhunderts', *Hansische Studien*, 6: 147–52.

Bolius, Uwe (1998) *Landnahme: Eukalyptus-Monokulturen in Brasilien*. Frankfurt am Main: Brandes & Apsel.

Bonnemann, Alfred (1984) *Der Reinhardswald*. Hannoversch Münden: Weserbuchhandlung.

Borgemeister, Bettina (2005) *Die Stadt und ihr Wald: Eine Untersuchung zur Waldgeschichte der Städte Göttingen und Hannover vom 13. bis zum 18. Jahrhundert*. Hannover: Hahn.

Born, Martin (1974) *Die Entwicklung der deutschen Agrarlandschaft*. Darmstadt: Wissenschaftliche Buchgesellschaft.

Bossel, Ulf, and Gunold, Bernd (1982) *Wärme aus Holz: Holzheizung in Theorie und Praxis*. Karlsruhe: C. F. Müller.

Bothe, Friedrich (1913) *Geschichte der Stadt Frankfurt am Main*. Frankfurt am Main.

Bramwell, Martyn (ed.) (1976) *The International Book of Wood*. London: Mitchell Beazley.

Brandl, Helmut (1970) *Der Stadtwald von Freiburg*. Freiburg: Wagner.

Braudel, Fernand (1975) *The Mediterranean and the Mediterranean World in the Age of Philip II*, 2 vols. London: Fontana.

Braudel, Fernand (1982) *Civilization and Capitalism 15th–18th Century*, vol. 2: *The Wheels of Commerce*. London: Collins.

Braudel, Fernand (1984) *Civilization and Capitalism 15th–18th Century*, vol. 3: *The Perspective of the World*. London: Collins.

Brecht, Bertolt (2001) *Stories of Mr. Keuner*, trans. Martin Chalmers. San Francisco: City Lights Books.

Briessen, Fritz van (1977) *Shanghai-Bildzeitung, 1884–1898*. Zurich: Atlantis.

Bringmann, August ([1905–9] 1981) *Geschichte der deutschen Zimmerer-Bewegung*, 2 vols. Berlin: Dietz.

Broelmann, Jobst (1983) 'Vom Holz zum Eisen', *Kultur & Technik*, 7: 28–32.

Brose, Eric D. (1985) 'Competitiveness and Obsolescence in the German Charcoal Iron Industry', *Technology and Culture*, 26: 532–59.

Bruchhaus, Eva-Maria (1982) 'Bois de Village – Aufforstung an den Graswurzeln', *E + Z* [Entwicklung und Zusammenarbeit], no. 4.

Brückner, Hans (1980) 'Die Entwicklung der Wälder des Schwarzwaldes durch die Nutzung vergangener Jahrhunderte und ihre heutige Bedeutung', in Ekkehard Liehl and W. D. Sick (eds), *Der Schwarzwald*. Baden: Konkordia.

Brumann, Christoph (2001) 'Die Blumen von Edo: Zur Brandgeschichte japanischer Städte', in Bernd Busch and J. G. Goldammer (eds.), *Feuer*. Cologne: Wienand, pp. 426–42.

Brunet, Pierre (1929) 'Sylviculture et technique des forges en Bourgogne du milieu du XVIIIe siècle', *Annales de Bourgogne*, 1: 337–65.

Brunner, Otto (1949) *Adeliges Landleben und europäischer Geist*. Salzburg: Otto Müller.

Bruns, Heinz-Hermann (1981) 'Wald und Wald-Entwicklung im Emsland', in Werner Franke (ed.), *Wald im Emsland*. Sögel: Emsländischer Heimatbund.

Bryant, Raymond (2007) 'Burma and the Politics of Teak: Dissecting a Resource Curse', in Greg Bankoff and Peter Boomgaard (eds), *A History of Natural Resources in Asia*. Basingstoke: Palgrave Macmillan, pp. 143–61.

Bücher, Karl (1899) *Arbeit und Rhythmus*. 2nd edn, Leipzig.

Bücher, Karl (1918) *Die Entstehung der Volkswirtschaft, Vorträge und Aufsätze: 2. Sammlung*. Tübingen.

Buchholz, Hans-Günter (2004) *Der Werkstoff Holz und seine Nutzung im ostmediterranen Altertum*. Weilheim: Verein zur Förderung der Aufarbeitung der Hellenischen Geschichte.

Bühler, Anton (1911) *Wald und Jagd zu Anfang des 16. Jahrhunderts und die Entstehung des Bauernkriegs*. Tübingen.

Bühler, G. C. W. von (*c*.1850) 'Hall und Limpurg: Geschichte der alten Saline Hall', manuscript, 5 vols., Stadtarchiv Schwäbisch Hall.

Bülow, Götz von (1962) *Die Sudwälder von Reichenhall*. Munich: Bayerisches Staats Ministerium.

Burger, Erich (1978) *Norwegische Stabkirchen: Geschichte, Bauweise, Schmuck*. Cologne: DuMont.

Burschel, P. (1979) 'Der Wald in seiner Umwelt', in Horst Stern (ed.), *Rettet den Wald*. Munich: Kindler.

Bus, P. H. (1797) *Einrichtung der Plattenöfen zur Ersparniß des Holzes*. Frankfurt am Main.

Cabourdin, Guy (ed.) (1981) *Le Sel et son histoire*, proceedings of a conference of the Association Interuniversitaire de l'Est. Nancy: Presses Universitaires de Nancy.

Cahen, Claude (1970) *L'Islam*. Paris: Bordas.

Cancrin, Franz Ludwig von (1805) *Vollständige Abhandlung von dem Theerbrennen in einem neuen mehr vollkommenen Theerofen*. Giessen.

Cartier, Claudine (1984a) *Cellule du patrimoine industriel: inventaire général*. Paris.

Cartier, Claudine (1984b) 'Le rôle des ingénieurs dans les innovations technologiques hydrauliques au XIXème siècle: l'exemple d'Alphonse Sagebien', in *Energie in der Geschichte*. Düsseldorf, pp. 140–51.

Cate, C. L. ten (1972) *Wan god mast gift: Bilder aus der Geschichte der Schweinezucht im Walde*. Wageningen: Centre for Agricultural Publishing.

Catling, Harold (1970) *The Spinning Mule*. Newton Abbot: David & Charles.

Catrina, Werner (1989) *Holzwege: Schweizer Holz – verkannter Rohstoff*. Zurich: Orell Füssli.

Cattaruzza, Marina (1984) 'Handwerker und Fabriksystem: Die Hamburger und Bremer Schiffszimmerer in den Anfängen der großbetrieblichen Werftindustrie', in Ulrich Engelhardt (ed.), *Handwerker in der Industrialisierung*. Stuttgart: Klett-Cotta.

REFERENCES AND BIBLIOGRAPHY

Champion, Selwyn G. ([1938] 1963) *Racial Proverbs: A Selection of the World's Proverbs Arranged Linguistically*. London: Routledge & Kegan Paul.

Clancey, Gregory (2006) *Earthquake Nation: The Cultural Politics of Japanese Seismicity, 1868–1930*. Berkeley: University of California Press.

Clancey, Gregory (2007) 'Seeing the Timber for the Forest: The Wood in Japanese Capitalism', in Gregg Bankoff and Peter Boomgaard (eds.), *A History of Natural Resources in Asia*. Basingstoke: Palgrave Macmillan, pp. 123–41.

Clow, A., and Clow, N. L. (1956) 'The Timber Famine and the Development of Technology', *Annals of Science*, 12/2: 85–102.

Cole, A. H. (1970) 'The Mystery of Fuel Wood Marketing', *Business History Review*, 44: 339–59.

Cole, John W., and Wolf, Eric R. (1974) *The Hidden Frontier: Ecology and Ethnicity in an Alpine Valley*. New York: Academic Press.

Cooper, Carolyn C. (1984) 'The Portsmouth System of Manufacture', *Technology and Culture*, 25: 182–225.

Corvol, Andrée (1984) *L'Homme et l'arbre sous l'Ancien Régime*. Paris: Economica.

Cwienk, Dieter (ed.) (1995) *Holzzeit: Natur, Mythos, Technik*. Graz: Kulturabteilung.

Dahal, Madan K., and Dahal, Dev Raj (eds) (1998) *Environment and Sustainable Development: Issues in Nepalese Perspective*. Kathmandu: Nepal Foundation for Advanced Studies.

Danzer, Karl Furnierwerke (ed.) (1979) *Holz für die Zukunft*. Reutlingen: Danzer.

Dau, Lutz (1979) 'Die Hamburger Holzschiffbauer in der ersten Hälfte des 19. Jahrhunderts', dissertation, Hamburg.

Dauvergne, Peter (1997) *Shadows in the Forest: Japan and the Politics of Timber in Southeast Asia*. Cambridge, MA: MIT Press.

Davis, Ralph (1972) *The Rise of the English Shipping Industry in the 17th and 18th Centuries*. 2nd edn, Newton Abbot: David & Charles.

Deinhard, Martin (1963) 'Die Tragfähigkeit historischer Holzkonstruktionen', *Bauen mit Holz*, no. 65.

Dengler, Alfred (1935) *Waldbau auf ökologischer Grundlage*. 2nd edn, Berlin: Springer.

Deppe, Hans-Joachim (1976) 'Holzwerkstoffe in ihrer geschichtlichen Entwicklung', in *50 Jahre Hornitex Werke*. Horn-Bad Meinberg: Hornitex.

Derry, T. K., and Williams, T. I. (1970) *A Short History of Technology*. Oxford: Oxford University Press.

Devèze, Michel (1973) *Histoire des forêts*. Paris: Presses Universitaires de France.

Devivere, Beate von (1985) 'Neunter Weltforstkongreß: Eine weltweite Kettenreaktion zur Rettung der Wälder?', *epd–Entwicklungspolitik*, 12.

Dietrich, Richard (ed.) (1981) *Politische Testamente der Hohenzollern*. Munich: Deutscher Taschenbuch.

Diogenes Laertius (n.d.) *The Lives and Opinions of Eminent Philosophers*, trans. C. D. Yonge, http://classicpersuasion.org/pw/diogenes.

Douglas, James J. (1983) *A Re-Appraisal of Forestry Development in Developing Countries*. The Hague: Nijhoff.

Dowie, Mark (2009) *Conservation Refugees: The Hundred-Year Conflict between Global Conservation and Native Peoples*. Cambridge, MA: MIT Press.

Driver, Elisabeth A., and Wigston, David L. (1982) 'Historical Ecology in the

Analysis of the Ecological Effects of Long-Term Forest Management', in *Actes du Symposium International d'Histoire Forestière*. Nancy: ENGREF.

Dubler, Anne-Marie (1978) *Müller und Mühlen im alten Staat Luzern*. Munich: Rex.

Duhamel du Monceau, Henri-Louis (1761) *Art du charbonnier*. Paris: Desaint & Saillant.

Duhamel du Monceau, Henri-Louis (1766–7) *Von Fällung der Wälder und gehöriger Anwendung des gefällten Holzes . . .*, 2 vols. Nuremberg.

Durst, Patrick B., et al. (eds) (2005) *In Search of Excellence: Exemplary Forest Management in Asia and the Pacific*. Bangkok: FAO.

Ebeling, Dietrich (1987) 'Rohstofferschließung im europäischen Handelssystem der Frühen Neuzeit am Beispiel des rheinisch-niederländischen Holzhandels im 17./18. Jahrhundert', manuscript, Bielefeld.

Ebeling, Theodor (1925) 'Die Landes-Oeconomie-Manufactur und Commercien-Deputation in Sachsen', dissertation, Leipzig.

Ebert, Hans-Peter (1981) *Mit Holz richtig heizen in Ofen, Herd und Kamin*. Ravensburg: Maier.

Eckardt, E., and Knauer, S. (1979) *Kein schöner Lan: Ein deutscher Umweltatlas*. Hamburg: Gruner & Jahr.

Eckardt, Hans Wilhelm (1976) *Herrschaftliche Jagd, bäuerliche Not und bürgerliche Kritik*. Göttingen: Vendenhoeck & Ruprecht.

Eckert, F. (1956) 'Erste Glasschmelze mit Kohle und Koks', *Internationales Journal für Silikate*, March: 79–81.

Eckholm, Erik (1975) *The Other Energy Crisis: Firewood*. Washington, DC: Worldwatch Institute.

Eglin, Jean, and Théry, Hervé (1982) *Le Pillage de l'Amazonie*. Paris: Maspero.

Ehlert, Stefan (2004) *Wangari Maathai – Mutter der Bäume*. Freiburg: Herder.

Eisenhauer, G. (ed.) (1985) *Internationales Symposium Mechanisierung in der Waldarbeit*. Hamburg: Wiedebusch.

Eliade, Mircea (1978) *The Forge and the Crucible*. 2nd edn, Chicago: University of Chicago Press.

Ellenberg, Heinz (1982) *Vegetation Mitteleuropas mit den Alpen in ökologischer Sicht*. 3rd edn, Stuttgart: Ulmer.

Ellenberg, Heinz (1990) *Bauernhaus und Landschaft in ökologischer und historischer Sicht*. Stuttgart: Ulmer.

Emmanuel, Arghiri (1982) *Appropriate or Underdeveloped Technology?* Chichester: Wiley.

Emons, H. H., and Walter, H. H. (1984) *Mit dem Salz durch die Jahrtausende*. Leipzig: Deutscher Verlag für Grundstoffindustrie.

Endres, Max (1888) *Die Waldbenutzung vom 13. bis Ende des 18. Jahrhunderts: Ein Beitrag zur Geschichte der Forstpolitik*. Tübingen.

Endres, Max (1905) *Handbuch der Forstpolitik mit besonderer Berücksichtigung der Gesetzgebung und Statistik*. Berlin.

Erkelenz, Klaus, et al. (1985) *Holzfachkunde für Tischler und Holzmechaniker*. Stuttgart: Teubner.

Ernst, Christoph (2000) *Den Wald entwickeln: Ein Politik- und Konfliktfeld in Hunsrück und Eifel im 18. Jahrhundert*. Munich: Oldenbourg.

Evans, F. T. (1982) 'Wood since the Industrial Revolution: A Strategic Retreat?', *History of Technology*, 7: 37–53.

Evelyn, John (1664) *Sylva, or a Discourse on Forest Trees*. London.

Eversmann, F. A. A. ([1804] 1982) *Uebersicht der Eisen- und Stahl-Erzeugung auf Wasserwerken in den Ländern zwischen Lahn und Lippe*. Kreuztal: Die Wielandschmiede.

Eyth, Max (1906) *Hinter Pflug und Schraubstock-Skizzen aus dem Tagebuch eines Ingenieurs*. Stuttgart.

Faber, Alfred (1950) *1000 Jahre Werdegang von Herd und Ofen*. Munich: Oldenbourg.

Fairhead, James, and Leach, Melissa (1996) *Misreading the African Landscape: Society and Ecology in a Forest-Savanna Mosaic*. Cambridge: Cambridge University Press.

Fansa, Mamoun, and Vorlauf, Dirk (eds) (2007) *Holz-Kultur: Von der Urzeit bis in die Zukunft: Ökologie und Ökonomie eines Naturrohstoffs im Spiegel der Experimentellen Archäologie, Ethnologie, Technikgeschichte und modernen Holzforschung*. Mainz: von Zabern.

Farrelly, David (1984) *The Book of Bamboo*. San Francisco: Sierra Club.

Fautz, Hermann (1941) 'Die Geschichte der Schiltacher Schifferschaft', *Die Ortenau*, 28: 3–66.

Feldhaus, Franz-Maria (1921) *Die Säge: Ein Rückblick auf vier Jahrtausende*. Berlin.

Feldhaus, Franz-Maria ([1914] 1970) *Die Technik: Ein Lexikon*. Wiesbaden.

Fellner, Josef, and Teischinger, Alfred (2001) *Alte Holzregeln: Von Mythen und Brauchbarem über Fehlinterpretationen zu neuen Erkenntnissen*. Vienna: Kunst- und Kulturverlag.

Fellner, Robert (1895) 'Beitrag zur Geschichte des Stadtwaldes von Frankfurt am Main', dissertation, Munich.

Fiévé, Nicolas (ed.) (2008) *Atlas historique de Kyoto: Analyse spatiale des systèmes de mémoire d'une ville, de son architecture et de son paysage urbain*. Paris: UNESCO.

Finsterbusch, Edgar, and Thiele, Werner (1987) *Vom Steinbeil zum Sägegatter: Ein Streifzug durch die Geschichte der Holzbearbeitung*. Leipzig: Fachbuchverlag.

Flade, Helmut (1979) *Holz: Von der natürlichen Form zur Gestaltung*. Wiesbaden: Ebeling.

Flinn, Michael W. (1959) 'Timber and the Advance of Technology: A Reconsideration', *Annals of Science*, 15: 109–20.

Flinn, Michael W. (1978) 'Technical Change as an Escape from Resource Scarcity: England in the 17th and 18th Centuries', in A. Maczak and W. N. Parker (eds), *Natural Resources in European History*. Washington, DC: Resources for the Future, pp. 139–59.

Flinn, Michael W. (1984) *History of the British Coal Industry*, vol. 2: 1700–1830: The Industrial Revolution. Oxford: Oxford University Press.

Flocken, Johann, et al. (1977) *Lehrbuch für Tischler:Teil 2*. Hannover: Schroedel Schulbuchverlag.

Fogel, Robert W. (1964) *Railroads and American Economic Growth*. Baltimore: Johns Hopkins University Press.

Foley, Mary M. (1981) *The American House*. New York: Harper & Row.

Fölster, Horst (1986) *Erhaltung und nachhaltige Nutzung tropischer Regenwälder: Elemente einer Strategie gegen die Waldzerstörung in den Feuchttropen*. Munich: Weltforum.

Forberger, Rudolf (1982) *Industrielle Revolution in Sachsen, 1800–1861*, vol. 1. Berlin: Akademie-Verlag.

Fourquin, Guy (1975) 'Le temps de la croissance', in Georges Duby and Armand Wallon (eds), *Histoire de la France rurale*, vol. 1: *La Formation des campagnes françaises*. Paris: Seuil.

Franklin, Benjamin (1909) *The Autobiography of Benjamin Franklin*, ed. John Bigelow. New York: G. P. Putnam's Sons.

Franz, Friedrich Christian (1795) *Beantwortung der Frage: Wie dem Holzmangel vorzubeugen sei?* Leipzig.

Franz, Günther (1963) *Quellen zur Geschichte des Bauernkrieges*. Munich: Oldenbourg.

Fraunhofer-Institut (2006) 'OSB aus Buche', *Wilhelm Klauditz Forum*, no. 9, July; www.wki.fraunhofer.de/publikat/WK-Forum_9_www.pdf.

Frazer, J. G. (1978) *The Golden Bough: A Study in Magic and Religion*. London: Macmillan.

Freeden, Uta von (ed.) (2002) *Spuren der Jahrtausende: Archäologie und Geschichte in Deutschland*. Stuttgart: Römisch-Germanische Kommission.

Fremdling, Rainer (1986) *Technologischer Wandel und internationaler Handel im 18. und 19. Jahrhundert: Die Eisenindustrien in Großbritannien, Belgien, Frankreich und Deutschland*. Berlin: Duncker & Humblot.

Freyre, Gilberto ([1936] 1990) *Das Land in der Stadt: Die Entwicklung der urbanen Gesellschaft Brasiliens*. Munich: Deutsche Taschenbuch-Verlag.

Fries, Robert F. (1951) *Empire in Pine: The Story of Lumbering in Wisconsin, 1830–1900*. Madison: State Historical Society of Wisconsin.

Fritsch, Franz X. (1974) *Geschichte der oberpfälzischen Forstorganisation: Ihre Entwicklung vom Mittelalter bis zur Jetztzeit (1973) im Zusammenhang mit der Oberpfälzer Eisenindustrie*. Munich: Bayern Staatsministerium.

Fruhauf, Christian (1980) *Forêt et societé*. Paris: CNRS.

Fuchs, Wilhelm Werner (1924) 'Waldwirtschaft und Holzhandel im Gebiet des badischen Schwarzwaldes vom 13. Bis 19. Jahrhundert', dissertation, Heidelberg.

Fukamachi, Katsue, Oku, Hirokazu, Kumagai, Y., and Shimomura, A. (2000) 'Changes in Landscape Planning and Land Management in Arashiyama National Forest in Kyoto', *Landscape and Urban Planning*, 52/2: 73–87.

Fukamachi, Katsue, Oku, Hirokazu, and Tohru, Nakashizuka (2001) 'The Change of a Satoyama Landscape and its Causality in Kamiseyama, Kyoto Prefecture, Japan, between 1970 and 1995', *Landscape Ecology*, 16: 703–17.

Fukuoka, Masanobu (1985) *The Natural Way of Farming: The Theory and Practice of Green Philosophy*. Tokyo: Japan Publications.

Garbe, Eckart (1985) 'Südostasien, "Ausverkauf der Regenwälder"', in Peter E. Stüben (ed.), *Kahlschlag im Paradies*. Giessen: Focus.

Garner, Philippe (1980) *Möbel des 20. Jahrhunderts*. Munich: Keyser.

Geistefeldt, Heinz (1963) 'Untersuchungen zur Geschichte der Flößerei und Flößereiverwaltung in Kursachsen', dissertation, Eberswalde.

Gerken, Bernd, and Görner, Martin (eds) (1999) *Europäische Landschaftsentwicklung mit großen Weidetieren: Geschichte, Modelle und Perspektiven*, Höxter: University of Paderborn.

German Appropriate Technology Exchange (ed.) (1984) *Fuel-Saving Cookstoves*. Brunswick: Vieweg.

GHK (Gewerkschaft Holz und Kunststoff) (1983) *Protokoll der 3. Fachtagung*

'Technischer und organisatorischer Wandel in der Holzwirtschaft – Bestandsaufnahme und soziale Herausforderung'. Düsseldorf.

Giedion, Sigfried (1948) *Mechanization Takes Command: A Contribution to Anonymous History*. New York: Oxford University Press.

Giedion, Sigfried (1967) *Space, Time and Architecture: The Growth of a New Tradition*. 5th edn, Cambridge, MA: Harvard University Press.

Gimpel, Jean (1976) *The Medieval Machine: The Industrial Revolution of the Middle Ages*. New York: Holt, Rinehart & Winston.

Gizycki, Peter von (1984) 'Keine Chance mehr für die Wälder der Dritten Welt?', *epd–Entwicklungspolitik*, 10–11.

Gläser, H. (1956) 'Zur Technik der Motorsägenarbeit beim Holzeinschlag', *Allgemeine Forstzeitschrift*, 11/10: 133–6.

Glatz, Hubert (1971) *Erinnerungen eines alten Holzwurms: Geschichten und Anekdoten rund ums Holz*. Gernsbach: Deutsche Betriebswirte-Verlag.

Glauche, Johannes W. (1995) *Der Stupa: Kultbau des Buddhismus*. Cologne: DuMont.

Gleitsmann, Rolf-Jürgen (1980) 'Rohstoffmangel und Lösungsstrategien: Das Problem vorindustrieller Holzknappheit', *Technologie und Politik*, 16: 104–54.

Gleitsmann, Rolf-Jürgen (1985a) *Die Spiegelglasmanufaktur im technologischen Schrifttum des 18. Jahrhunderts*. Düsseldorf: VDI.

Gleitsmann, Rolf-Jürgen (1985b) '"Wir wissen aber, Gott lob, was wir thuen": Erfinderprivilegien und technologischer Wandel im 16. Jahrhundert', *Zeitschrift für Unternehmensgeschichte*, 2: 69–95.

Gleitsmann, Rolf-Jürgen (1985c) 'Holzwirtschaft', in Jürgen Ziechmann (ed.), *Panorama der Fridericianischen Zeit*. Bremen: Ziechmann.

Glesinger, Egon (1949) *The Coming Age of Wood*. New York: Simon & Schuster.

Goes, Ernesto (1984) *Árvores monumentais de Portugal*. Lisbon: Portucel.

Göhrde-Seminar (1985) *Biomassenutzung im Rahmen von Energieversorgungskonzepten für den Ländlichen Raum*. Bonn: Bundesforschungsanstalt für Landeskunde und Raumordnung.

Gollwitzer, Gerda (1984) *Bäume: Bilder und Texte aus drei Jahrtausenden*. 2nd edn, Herrsching: Schuler.

Gordon, James E. (1968) *The New Science of Strong Materials, or Why You Don't Fall Through the Floor*. London: Penguin.

Gothein, Eberhard (1889) 'Entstehung und Entwicklung der Murgschiffahrt: Ein Beitrag zur Geschichte des Holzhandels', *Zeitschrift für die Geschichte des Oberrheins*, 43: 401–55.

Gothein, Eberhard (1892) *Wirtschaftsgeschichte des Schwarzwaldes und der angrenzenden Landschaften*. Strassburg: Trübner.

Götschmann, Dirk (1985) *Oberpfälzer Eisen: Bergbau und Eisengewerbe im 16. und 17. Jahrhundert*. Theuern: Bergbau- und Industriemuseum Ostbayern.

Götz, Karl-Heinz (1980) *Holzbau-Atlas*. Munich: Institut für Internationale Architektur-Dokumentation.

Götz, Wolfgang (1968) *Zentralbau und Zentralbautendenz in der gotischen Architektur*. Berlin: Mann.

Graßmann, Gottfried Ludolf (1792) *Abhandlung über die Nutzbarkeit des Torfes in der Feuerung zur Schonung der abnehmenden Wälder*. Berlin.

Greber, Josef M. (1956) *Die Geschichte des Hobels: Von der Steinzeit bis zum Entstehen der Holzwerkzeugfabriken im frühen 19. Jahrhundert*. Zurich: VSSM.

Grebing, Helga (ed.) (1993) *'Holzarbeiter, schließt die Reihen':* Das *HolzArbeiterBuch: Die Geschichte der Holzarbeiter und ihrer Gewerkschaften.* Cologne: Bund.

Green, Harvey (2007) *Wood: Craft, Culture, History.* London: Penguin.

GreenTech Made in Germany (2007) *Umwelttechnologie-Atlas für Deutschland,* ed. Bundesministerium für Umwelt, Naturschutz und Reaktorsicherheit. Munich: Vahlen.

Greiling, Walter (1943) *Chemie erobert die Welt.* Berlin: Limpert.

Grewe, Bernd-Stefan (2004) *Der versperrte Wald: Ressourcenmangel in der bayerischen Pfalz (1814–1870).* Cologne: Böhlau.

Gribl, Dorle (2002) *'Für das Isartal': Chronik des Isartalvereins.* Munich: Buchendorfer.

Grießinger, Andreas (1981) *Das symbolische Kapital der Ehre.* Frankfurt am Main: Ullstein.

Großmann, Georg Ulrich (1984) *Bielefelder Bauernhausmuseum.* Bielefeld.

Großmann, Georg Ulrich (1986) *Der Fachwerkbau.* Cologne: DuMont.

Großmann, Josef (1916) *Das Holz: Seine Bearbeitung und seine Verwendung.* Leipzig.

Grottian, Walter (1948) *Die Krise der deutschen und europäischen Holzversorgung.* Berlin.

Grüll, Georg (1963) *Bauer, Herr und Landesfürst: Sozialrevolutionäre Bestrebungen der oberösterreichischen Bauern von 1650 bis 1848.* Graz: Böhlau.

Guha, Ramachandra (1989) *The Unquiet Woods: Ecological Change and Peasant Resistance in the Himalayas.* Oxford: Oxford University Press.

Gülich, G. von ([1830–45] 1972) *Geschichtliche Darstellung des Handels, der Gewerbe und des Ackerbaus,* 5 vols. Graz: Akademische Druck- und Verlagsanstalt.

Gupta, Badal Sen (1984) 'Schlechtes Beispiel macht Schule: Historisch-politische Ursachen der Ökokrise in Indien', *epd–Entwicklungspolitik,* 10–11.

Haber, Wolfgang (2006) 'Kulturlandschaften und die Paradigmen des Naturschutzes', *Stadt und Grün,* 12: 20–5.

Hafner, Franz (1979) *Steiermarks Wald in Geschichte und Gegenwart.* Vienna: Österreichischer Agrarverlag.

Hafner, Franz (1981) 'Die Holztrift mit besonderer Berücksichtigung ihrer Ausübung in der Steiermark', in Gerhard Pferschy, (ed.), *Siedlung, Macht und Wirtschaft: Festschrift für Fritz Posch.* Graz: Steiermärkisches Landarchiv.

Hafner, Franz (ed.) (1983) *Österreichs Wald in Vergangenheit und Gegenwart.* Vienna: Österreichischer Agrarverlag.

Hägermann, Dieter, and Ludwig, Karl-Heinz (1984) 'Mittelalterliche Salinenbetriebe: Erläuterungen, Fragen und Ergänzungen zum Forschungsbestand', *Technikgeschichte,* 51: 155–89.

Haiding, Karl (ed.) (1962) *Almwirtschaft in der Steiermark.* Trautenfels: Heimatmuseum.

Haiding, Karl (1978) 'Vergehendes Holzhandwerk der Obersteiermark: Die Gabelmacher, Mühlenzimmerer und Wagner', in Martha Bringemeier et al. (eds), *Museum und Kulturgeschichte: Festschrift für Wilhelm Hansen.* Münster: Aschendorff.

Halle, Francis, Oldeman, R. A. A., amd Tomlinson, P. B. (1978) *Tropical Trees and Forests: An Architectural Analysis.* Berlin: Springer.

Halliday, E. C. (1964) 'Zur Geschichte der Luftverunreinigung', in World Health Organization (ed.), *Die Verunreinigung der Luft*. Weinheim: Chemie.

Hambloch, Hermann (1974) 'Langstreifenfluren im nordwestlichen Alt-Niederdeutschland', in Hans-Jürgen Nitz (ed.), *Historisch-genetische Siedlungsforschung*. Darmstadt: Wissenschaftliche Buchgesellschaft.

Hammersley, G. (1957) 'The Crown Woods and their Exploitation in the Sixteenth and Seventeenth Centuries', *Bulletin of the Institute of Historical Research*, 30: 136–61.

Hammersley, G. (1973) 'The Charcoal Iron Industry and its Fuel, 1540–1740', *Economic History Review*, 26: 593–613.

Handtmann, Adelheid J. (1982) 'Der technische Fortschritt im Eisenhüttenwesen der Steiermark und Kärntens von 1750 bis 1864', dissertation, Marburg.

Hansjakob, Heinrich ([1897] 1984) *Waldleute: Erzählungen*. Haslach im Kinzigtal: Stadt Haslach.

Hard, Gerhard (1976) 'Exzessive Bodenerosion um und nach 1800', in Gerold Richter (ed.), *Bodenerosion in Mitteleuropa*. Darmstadt: Wissenschaftliche Buchgesellschaft.

Hardach, Gerd H. (1969) *Der soziale Status des Arbeiters in der Frühindustrialisierung*. Berlin: Duncker & Humblot.

Hardin, Garrett (1968) 'The Tragedy of the Commons', *Science*, 162: 1243–8.

Harris, Richard (1978) *Discovering Timber-Framed Buildings*. Aylesbury: Shire.

Hart, Cyril (1971) *The Industrial History of Dean*. Newton Abbot: David & Charles.

Hartig, Georg Ludwig (1804) *Physikalische Versuche über das Verhältnis der Brennbarkeit der meisten deutschen Waldbaumhölzer*. 2nd edn, Marburg.

Hartig, Theodor (1855) *Über das Verhältnis des Brennwertes verschiedener Holz- und Torf-Arten für Zimmerheizung und auf dem Kochherde*. Brunswick.

Hasel, Karl (1967) 'Die Entwicklung von Waldeigentum und Waldnutzung im späten Mittelalter als Ursache für die Entstehung des Bauernkrieges', *Allgemeine Forst- und Jagdzeitung*, 7: 141–50.

Hasel, Karl (1968) 'Die Beziehungen zwischen Land- und Forstwirtschaft in der Sicht des Historikers', *Zeitschrift für Agrargeschichte und Agrarsoziologie*, 16: 141–59.

Hasel, Karl (1977) 'Auswirkungen der Revolution von 1848 und 1849 auf Wald und Jagd, auf Forstverwaltung und Forstbeamte, insbesondere in Baden', *Schriftenreihe der Landesforstverwaltung Baden-Württemberg*, vol. 50. Stuttgart.

Hasel, Karl (1982) *Studien über Wilhelm Pfeil*. Hannover: Schaper.

Hasel, Karl (1985) *Forstgeschichte*. Freiburg: Parey.

Hatzfeldt, Hermann Graf (ed.) (1996) *Ökologische Waldwirtschaft*. 2nd edn, Heidelberg: C. F. Müller.

Hauck, H. (1866) 'Das Steigen der Holzpreise seit dem Anfange des vorigen Jahrhunderts, dessen Ursachen und Wirkungen und die Mittel dagegen', in *Suppliment zur allgemeinen Forst- und Jagdzeitung*, 2: 47–66.

Hauff, Dorothea (1977) *Zur Geschichte der Forstgesetzgebung und Forstorganisation des Herzogtums Württemberg im 16. Jahrhundert*. Stuttgart: Landesforstverwaltung Baden-Württemberg.

Hauser, Albert (1961) *Schweizerische Wirtschafts- und Sozialgeschichte*. Zurich: Chronos.

Hauser, Albert (1966) 'Die Forstwirtschaft der "Hausväter"', *Schweizerische Zeitschrift für Forstwesen*, 117: 29–47.

Hauser, Albert (1972) *Wald und Feld in der alten Schweiz*. Zurich: Artemis.

Hauser, Albert (1980) *Waldgeister und Holzfäller*. Zurich: Artemis.

Hausrath, Hans (1924) 'Die Entwicklung des Waldeigentums und der Waldnutzungsrechte', *Allgemeine Forst- und Jagdzeitung*, 100: 185–97.

Hausrath, Hans (1941) 'Bauerntum und Waldwirtschaft', *Allgemeine Forst- und Jagdzeitung*, 117: 293–9.

Hausrath, Hans (1982) *Geschichte des deutschen Waldbaus: Von seinen Anfängen bis 1850*. Freiburg: Hochschulverlag.

Hays, Samuel P. (2007) *Wars in the Woods: The Rise of Ecological Forestry in America*. Pittsburgh: University of Pittsburgh Press.

Hazzi, Joseph (1804) *Die ächten Ansichten der Waldungen und Förste, gegenwärtig über ihre Purifikationen, sammt der Geschichte des Forstwesens, im Allgemeinen, vorzüglich in Baiern*. Munich.

Heide, Susanne von der, and Donner, Wolf (eds) (1992) *Mensch und Umwelt in Nepal*. St Augustin: VGH Wissenschaftsverlag.

Heidegger, Martin (2002) *Off the Beaten Track* [Holzwege]. Cambridge: Cambridge University Press.

Heilfurth, Gerhard (1981) *Der Bergbau und seine Kultur*. Zurich: Atlantis.

Heinzinger, Walter (ed.) (1988) *Die Chance Holz: Der andere Weg*. Graz: Leuscher & Lubensky.

Heis, Mons (1975) *Wald, Wild und Siedlung in der Leutascher Gegend und deren Umgebung*. Leutasch.

Helfrich, C. C. (1807) *Darstellung wegen Behandlung der Gemeindewälder im Amt Neuwied*. Neuwied.

Heller, Horst P. (1980) *Das ländliche Handwerk*, Museumsdorf Bayerischer Wald. Grafenau: Morsak.

Hellwag, Fritz (1924) *Die Geschichte des deutschen Tischlerhandwerks: Vom 12. bis zum 20. Jahrhundert*. Berlin.

Helm, Karl (1931) *Die bremischen Holzarbeiter vom 16. bis zur Mitte des 19. Jahrhunderts*. Bremen.

Helvarg, David (2004) *The War against the Greens: The 'Wise-Use' Movement, the New Right, and the Browning of America*. San Francisco: Sierra Club.

Hembery, Rachel, Jenkins, Anna, White, George, and Richards, Beatrix (2007) *Illegal Logging: Cut it Out! The UK's Role in the Trade in Illegal Timber and Wood Products*. Godalming: WWF–UK.

Henkel, Adolf (1908) 'Die Saline Sooden an der Werra unter Landgraf Philipp dem Großmütigen und Wilhelm IV', dissertation, Marburg.

Henning, Hansjoachim (1977) *Quellen zur sozialgeschichtlichen Entwicklung in Deutschland von 1815 bis 1860*. Paderborn: Schöningh.

Henrichsen, Christoph (2004) *Japan: Culture of Wood: Buildings, Objects, Techniques Japan*: Basel: Birkhäuser.

Herbert, Gilbert (1978) *Pioneers of Prefabrication: The British Contribution to the 19th Century*. Baltimore: Johns Hopkins University Press.

Heske, Franz (1937) *Im heiligen Lande der Gangesquellen*. Neudamm: Neumann.

Hesmer, Herbert (1951) *Das Pappelbuch*. Bonn: Deutscher Pappelverein.

Hesmer, Herbert (1958) *Wald und Forstwirtschaft in Nordrhein-Westfalen: Bedingtheiten – Geschichte – Zustand*. Hannover: Schaper.

Hesmer, Herbert (1966–70) *Der kombinierte land- und forstwirtschaftliche Anbau*, 2 vols. Stuttgart: Klett.
Hesmer, Herbert (1975) *Leben und Werk von Dietrich Brandis 1824–1907*. Opladen: Westdeutscher Verlag.
Hesmer, Herbert, and Schroeder, F. G. (1963) *Waldzusammensetzung und Waldbehandlung im niedersächsischen Tiefland westlich der Weser und in der Münsterschen Bucht bis zum Ende des 18. Jahrhunderts*. Bonn: Naturhistorischer Verein.
Heuss, Theodor (1951) *Was ist Qualität? Zur Geschichte und zur Aufgabe des Deutschen Werkbundes*. Tübingen: Wunderlich.
Hewett, Cecil A. (1969) *The Development of Carpentry 1200–1700: An Essex Study*. Newton Abbot: David & Charles.
Hewett, Cecil A. (1974) *English Cathedral Carpentry*. London.
Hewett, Cecil A. ([1980] 1997) *English Historic Carpentry*. Fresno, CA: Linden.
Heymer, Paul (1934) *Die westfälische Waldwirtschaft seit Beginn des 19. Jahrhunderts*. Bottrop: Postberg.
Heynitz, Friedrich August Freiherr von (1786) *Abhandlung über die Produkte des Mineralreichs in den Königlich-Preußischen Staaten*. Berlin.
Hidy, Ralph W., Hill, Frank E., and Nevins, Allan (1963) *Timber and Men: The Weyerhaeuser Story*. New York: Macmillan.
Hilf, Richard B. (1922) 'Die Eibenholzmonopole des 16. Jahrhunderts: Ein Beitrag zur Geschichte des frühkapitalistischen Holzhandels', dissertation, Munich.
Hilf, Richard B., and Röhrig, Fritz (1938) *Wald und Waldwerk in Geschichte und Gegenwart*. Potsdam.
Hindle, Brooke (ed.) (1975) *America's Wooden Age: Aspects of its Early Technology*. Tarrytown, NY: Sleepy Hollow Restorations.
Hinz, Frank-Lothar (1977) *Die Geschichte der Wocklumer Eisenhütte, 1758–1864, als Beispiel westfälischen adligen Unternehmertums*. Altena: Freunde der Burg Altena.
Hoadley, R. Bruce (1980) *Understanding Wood: A Craftsman's Guide to Wood Technology*. Newtown, CT: Taunton Press.
Hobsbawm, Eric (1968) *Industry and Empire*. Harmondsworth: Penguin.
Höchli, Oskar E. (1957) *Der Beitrag der schweizerischen Faser- und Spanplattenindustrie zur Erweiterung des Angebotes an hochwertigen Holzwerkstoffen: Eine Untersuchung über die Möglichkeiten der Holzabfallverwertung*. Winterthur: P. G. Keller.
Hockenjos, Wolf (2000) *Waldpassagen: Gesammelte Versuche über Baum, Wald und Flur*. Vöhrenbach: Dold.
Hocquet, Jean-Claude (1984) *Le Sel et le pouvoir*. Paris: A. Michel.
Hoering, Uwe (1984) 'Vor lauter Bäumen den Wald vergessen. ("Social forestry" zielt an den Grundbedürfnissen vorbei'), *epd–Entwicklungspolitik*, 10–11.
Hoering, Uwe (1985) 'Forstwirtschaft und Entwicklung', *epd–Entwicklungspolitik*, 12.
Hohenstein, Adolf (1856) *Die Pottaschen-Fabrikation für Waldbesitzer und Forstmänner*. Vienna.
Holan, Jerri (1990) *Norwegian Wood: A Tradition of Building*. New York: Rizzoli.
Holland, A. J. (1971) *Ships of British Oak: The Rise and Decline of Wooden Shipbuilding in Hampshire*. Newton Abbot: David & Charles.

Hollstein, Ernst (1980) *Mitteleuropäische Eichenchronologie*. Mainz: von Zabern.

Hölzl, Richard (2010) *Umkämpfte Wälder: Die Geschichte einer ökologischen Reform in Deutschland 1760–1860*. Frankfurt am Main: Campus.

Home, Francis (1754) *Experiments in Bleaching*. Edinburgh.

Horn, Johannes, and Thiemer, Erich (1981) *Einsatz von Holzschwellen unter Berücksichtigung technischer und wirtschaftlicher Aspekte*. Bonn: Centrale Marketinggesellschaft der deutschen Agrarwirtschaft.

Horn, Stanley F. (1943) *This Fascinating Lumber Business*. Indianapolis: Bobbs-Merrill.

Hornitex (1976) *50 Jahre Hornitex Werke: Leistung in Holz und Kunststoff*. Horn-Bad Meinberg: Hornitex.

Hornstein, Felix von (1951) *Wald und Mensch: Waldgeschichte des Alpenvorlandes Deutschlands, Österreichs und der Schweiz*. Ravensburg: Maier.

Hough, Romeyn B., and Sargent, Charles B. ([1928] 2007) *The Woodbook*. Cologne: Taschen.

Hounshell, David A. (1984) *From the American System to Mass Production, 1800–1932: The Development of Manufacturing Technology in the United States*. Baltimore: Johns Hopkins University Press.

Houzard, G. (1980) 'Les grosses forges ont-elles mangé la forêt?', *Annales de Normandie*, 30: 245–69.

Hroch, Miroslav, and Petráň, Josef (1981) *Das 17. Jahrhundert: Krise der feudalen Gesellschaft*. Hamburg: Hoffman & Campe.

Hubbell, Sue (1986) *A Country Year: Living the Questions*. New York: Perennial.

Hudson, Kenneth (1978) *Exploring Cathedrals*. Sevenoaks: Teach Yourself Books.

Hufnagl, Hans, and Puzyr, Hans (1980) *Grundbegriffe des Waldbaues*. Vienna: Fromme.

Humanisierung des Arbeitslebens in der Holzbe- und -verarbeitung (1984) Dortmund: Bundesanstalt für Arbeitsschutz.

Hundeshagen, Johann Christian (1830) *Die Waldweide und Waldstreu in ihrer ganzen Bedeutung für Forst-, Landwirtschaft und Nationalwohlfahrt*. Tübingen.

Hunter, Louis C. (1979) *A History of Industrial Power in the United States, 1780–1930*. Charlottesville: University Press of Virginia.

Hyde, Charles K. (1977) *Technological Change and the British Iron Industry, 1700–1870*. Princeton, NJ: Princeton University Press.

Imfeld, Al (1984) 'Tropische Wälder: Geschäft über die Grenzen', *epd–Entwicklungspolitik*, 10–11.

Imfeld, Al (1985) 'Was bringt das Tropenholzabkommen?', *epd–Entwicklungspolitik*, 12.

Imort, Michael (2005) 'Eternal Forest – Eternal *Volk*: The Rhetoric and Reality of National Socialist Forest Policy', in Franz-Josef Brüggemeier et al. (eds), *How Green Were the Nazis? Nature, Environment, and Nation in the Third Reich*. Athens: Ohio University Press, pp. 43–72.

Ingoviz, Rudolf (1909) 'Georg Huebmer – ein deutscher Holzknecht', *Österreichische Vierteljahresschrift für das Forstwesen*, 1.

Internationaler Holzhandelskongress (1976) *Holzhandel auf neuen Wegen*. Stuttgart: DRW.

Irle, Trutzhart (1964) *Landesherr und Gewerbe im Siegerland des 16. Jahrhunderts.* Siegen: Siegerländer Heimatverein.

Ives, Jack D., and Messerli, Bruno (1989) *The Himalayan Dilemma: Reconciling Development and Conservation.* London: Routledge.

Iwai, Yoshiya (ed.), *Forestry and the Forest Industry in Japan.* Vancouver: UBC Press.

Jachtmann, Samuel Heinrich (1786) *Anweisung, wie auf eine leichte Art alle nur mögliche Feuerungen zur Holzersparung eingerichtet werden können, um dadurch der in jedem Lande höchst verderblichen Holzverschwendung Einhalt zu tun.* Berlin.

Jacobeit, Sigrid, and Jacobeit, Wolfgang (1986) *Alltagsgeschichte des deutschen Volkes, 1550–1810.* Cologne: Pahl-Rugenstein.

Jacobeit, Wolfgang (1961) *Schafhaltung und Schäfer in Zentraleuropa bis zum Beginn des 20. Jahrhunderts.* Berlin: Akademie-Verlag.

Jäger, Hans (1970) 'Der Einfluß des Bergbaus und der Hütten, insonderheit der Kupfer- und Eisenverarbeitung, auf die Waldentwicklung in Thüringen', *Wissenschaftliche Veröffentlichungen des Geographischen Instituts der Deutschen Akademie der Wissenschaften*, 27–8: 263–4.

Jägerschmid, K. F. V. (1827–8) *Handbuch für Holztransport und Floßwesen*, 2 vols. Karlsruhe.

Jänichen, Hans (1967) 'Zur Geschichte der Sägemühlen im Mittelalter mit Ausblicken auf die Bestockungsgeschichte südwestdeutscher Wälder', *Mitteilung des Vereins für forstliche Standortskunde und Forstpflanzenzüchtung*, 17.

Janneau, Guillaume (1975) *Les Ateliers parisiens d'ébénistes et de menuisiers aux XVIIe et XVIIIe siècles.* Bellegarde: SERG.

Jantke, Carl, and Hilger, Dietrich (eds) (1965) *Die Eigentumslosen.* Freiburg and Munich: Alber.

Jars, Gabriel (1777–85) *Metallurgische Reisen zur Untersuchung und Beobachtung der vornehmsten Eisen-, Stahl-, Blech- und Steinkohlen-Waren in Deutschland, Schweden, Norwegen, England und Schottland, vom Jahr 1757 bis 1769*, 4 vols. Berlin.

Jegel, August (1932) 'Der Reichswald als Stolz und Sorgenkind von Alt-Nürnberg', *Forstwissenschaftliches Centralblatt*, 54: 132–55.

Jellinek, Otto (1927) *Das Holz und die Technik.* 4th edn, Stuttgart: Dieck.

Jentsch, Fritz (1881) *Die Arbeiterverhältnisse in der Forstwirtschaft des Staates.* Berlin.

Johann, Elisabeth (1968) *Geschichte der Waldnutzung in Kärnten unter dem Einfluß der Berg-, Hütten- und Hammerwerke.* Klagenfurt: Geschichtsverein für Kärnten.

Johannsen, Otto (1953) *Geschichte des Eisens.* Düsseldorf: Stahleisen.

John, Gerhart Heinz (1934) 'Die Elbflößerei in Sachsen', dissertation, Leipzig.

Johnson, Hugh (1973) *The International Book of Trees.* London: Mitchell Beazley.

Jonas, Wolfgang, Linsbauer, Valentine, and Marx, Helga (1969) *Die Produktivkräfte in der Geschichte*, vol. 1. Berlin: Dietz.

Jontes, Günther (1984) 'Zur Volkskultur des steirischen Eisenwesens', in P. W. Roth (ed.), *Erz und Eisen in der Grünen Mark.* Graz: Styria.

Jordan, Reinhard, Küchle, Hartmut, and Volkmann, Gert (1986) *Holzwirtschaft im Wandel.* Cologne: Bund-Verlag.

Jung, Johann H. ([1788] 1970) *Lehrbuch der Staats-Polizei-Wissenschaft*. Frankfurt am Main: Keip.

Justi, Johann H. G. von ([1760] 1965) *Die Grundfeste zu der Macht und Glückseligkeit der Staaten*, vol. 1. Aalen: Scientia.

Jüttemann, Herbert (1984) *Alte Bauernsägen im Schwarzwald und in den Alpenländern*. Karlsruhe: Braun.

Kaiser, Hermann, *Herdfeuer und Herdgerät im Rauchhaus: Wohnen damals*. Cloppenburg: Museumsdorf.

Kapfhammer, Günther (1969) 'Gemeindebacköfen im nördlichen Unterfranken', *Bayerisches Jahrbuch für Volkskunde*, pp. 133–75.

Kaser, Kurt (1929) 'Der Kampf um das Waldregal', *Zeitschrift des Vereins für die Steiermark*, pp. 25–46.

Kaser, Kurt (1932) *Eisenverarbeitung und Eisenhandel: Die staatlichen und wirtschaftlichen Grundlagen des innerösterreichischen Eisenwesens*. Vienna: Springer.

Kaspar, Fred (1984) *Das Hexenbürgermeisterhaus in Lemgo als Beispiel bürgerlichen Bauens und Wohnens zwischen dem 16. und 20. Jahrhundert*. Bielefeld: Westfalen.

Katz, Casimir (2005) *Die Holzbarone: Chronik einer Industriellenfamilie*. Gernsbach: Katz.

Kaufhold, Karl Heinrich (1978) *Das Gewerbe in Preußen um 1800*. Göttingen: Schwartz.

Kehr, Kurt (1964) *Die Fachsprache des Forstwesens im 18. Jahrhundert*. Giessen: Schmitz.

Kellenbenz, Hermann (ed.) (1974) *Schwerpunkte der Eisengewinnung und Eisenverarbeitung in Europa, 1500–1650*. Cologne: Böhlau.

Kellenbenz, Hermann, and Schawacht, Jürgen H. (1974) *Schicksal eines Eisenlandes*. Siegen: Industrie- und Handelskammer.

Keweloh, Hans-Walter (ed.) (1985) *Flößerei in Deutschland*. Stuttgart: Theiss.

Keweloh, Hans-Walter, and Carle, Ursula (1988) *Auf den Spuren der Flößer*. Stuttgart: Theiss.

Kieß, Rudolf (1958) *Die Rolle der Forsten im Aufbau des württembergischen Territoriums bis ins 16. Jahrhundert*. Stuttgart: Kohlhammer.

Killian, Herbert (1982) 'Die Bedeutung der Säge in der Geschichte der Forstnutzung', *Actes du Symposium International Forestière*, 1: 112–40.

Killian, Herbert (1983) 'Die Waldarbeit von der Antike bis zur Gegenwart', *Forst- und Jagdgeschichte Mitteleuropas*, 151: 38–48.

Killing, Margarete (1927) *Die Glasmacherkunst in Hessen*. Marburg: Elwert.

King, Franklin H. ([1911] 1949) *Farmers of Forty Centuries, or Permanent Agriculture in China, Korea and Japan*. London: Jonathan Cape.

Kirnbauer, Franz (1977) *Geschichte der Sprengarbeit im Bergbau*. Vienna: Montan-Verlag.

Klar, M. (1938) 'Derzeitiger Stand der Holzverkohlungstechnik', *Holz als Roh- und Werkstoff*, 4: 139–45.

Klein, Ernst (1973) *Die englischen Wirtschaftstheoretiker des 17. Jahrhunderts*. Darmstadt: Wissenschaftliche Buchgesellschaft.

Kliutschewskij, Wassilij O. (1925–6) *Geschichte Rußlands*, 4 vols. Berlin.

Klohn, W., and Windhorst, H. W. (1984) 'Die Entwicklung der Forstwirtschaft in der Bundesrepublik', *Zeitschrift für Agrargeographie*, 2: 71–93.

Klooster, Daniel J. (2006) 'Forest Struggles and Forest Policy: Villagers' Environmental Activism in Mexico', in Christof Mauch et al. (eds), *Shades of Green: Environmental Activism around the Globe*. Oxford: Rowman & Littlefield.

Klüting, Rainer (1981) 'Reiche Onkel, arme Neffen: UNO-Weltenergiekonferenz '81 in Nairobi', *Wechselwirkung*, November: 49–50.

Knapp, Hans D., and Spangenberg, Almut (eds) (2007) *Europäische Buchenwaldinitiative*. Bonn: Bundesamt für Naturschutz.

Knauer, Norbert (1988) *Holz als nachwachsender Rohstoff*. Frankfurt: Wabern.

Knerr, Günter, and Schmidt-Ranke, Elke (1984) *Technik nach menschlichem Maß: Dorftechnik für die Frau in Entwicklungsländern*. Cologne: Deutsches Komitee für UNICEF.

Knies, Karl ([1853] 1883) *Die Politische Ökonomie vom geschichtlichen Standpunkte*. Rev edn, Brunswick.

Knoke, Helga (1968) *Wald und Siedlung im Süntel*. Rinteln: Bösendahl.

Koch, Manfred (1963) 'Einfluß des Bergbaus auf die Entwicklung der Forstwirtschaft zu Beginn der Neuzeit', *Die Führungskraft* [Herne], 28: 130–2.

Kocka, Jürgen (1983) *Lohnarbeit und Klassenbildung: Arbeiter und Arbeiterbewegung in Deutschland, 1800–1875*. Berlin: Dietz.

Koder, Johannes (1984) *Der Lebensraum der Byzantiner*. Graz: Styria.

Kogler, Walter (ed.) (1993) *Der Schwarzenbergsche Schwemmkanal*. Vienna: Kogler.

Kohl, Werner (1969) *Recht und Geschichte der alten Münchner Mühlen*. Munich: Stadtarchiv.

Koller, Engelbert (1970) *Forstgeschichte des Salzkammergutes*. Vienna: Österreichischer Agrarverlag.

Koller, Engelbert (1975) *Forstgeschichte Oberösterreichs*. Linz: Oberösterreichischer Landesverlag.

Korn, Wolfgang (1976) *The Traditional Architecture of the Kathmandu Valley*. Kathmandu: Ratna Pustak Bhandar.

Kossatz, Gert (1976) 'Holzforschung im Dienste der Holzwerkstoffindustrie', in *50 Jahre Hornitex Werke*. Horn-Bad Meinberg: Hornitex.

Köstler, Hans Jörg (1984) 'Das steirische Eisenhüttenwesen von den Anfängen des Floßofenbetriebes im 16. Jahrhundert bis zur Gegenwart', in Paul W. Roth (ed.), *Erz und Eisen in der Grünen Mark*. Graz: Styria.

Köstler, Josef (1927) 'Grenzen des Kapitalismus in der Forstwirtschaft', dissertation, Munich.

Köstler, Josef (1934) *Geschichte des Waldes in Altbayern*. Munich: Beck.

Köstler, Josef (1954) *Waldwege und Holzwege der Wissenschaft*. Hamburg: Parey.

Krauß, Werner (2001) *'Hängt die Grünen': Umweltkonflikte, nachhaltige Entwicklung und ökologischer Diskurs: Eine ethnologische Fallstudie (Portugal)*. Berlin: Reimer.

Kremser, Walter (1990) *Niedersächsische Forstgeschichte*. Rotenburg (Wümme): Heimatbund.

Kriedte, Peter, Medick, Hans, and Schlumbohm, Jürgen (1981) *Industrialization before Industrialization: Rural Industry in the Genesis of Capitalism*, trans. Beate Schempp. Cambridge: Cambridge University Press.

Kroiß, Ferdinand (1928) 'Holzhandel und Holzpreisentwicklung im unteren Bayerischen Wald', dissertation, Munich.

Krüger, Horst (1958) *Zur Geschichte der Manufakturen und der Manufakturarbeiter in Preußen*. Berlin: Rütten & Loening.

Krüger, Karsten (1980) *Finanzstaat Hessen, 1500–1567: Staatsbildung im Übergang vom Domänenstaat zum Steuerstaat*. Marburg: Elwert.

Krünitz, Johann Georg (1789) *Oeconomische Encyclopädie*, vol. 24. Brunn.

Kruse, Hans (1909) 'Forstwirtschaft und Industrie im ehemaligen Fürstentum Nassau-Siegen', in F. Philippi (ed.), *Beiträge zur Wirtschaftsgeschichte des Siegerlandes*. Münster: Coppenrath.

Kubisch, Ulrich (1986) *100 Jahre Automobil*. Wiesbaden: BB.

Küchli, Christian (1997) *Wälder der Hoffnung*. Zurich: Neue Zürcher Zeitung.

Kunckel, Johannes ([1689] 1972) *Ars vitraria experimentalis oder vollkommene Glasmacher-Kunst*. Leipzig 1689, reprinted Hildesheim and New York: Olms.

Künßberg, Eberhard von (1904) 'Der Wald im deutschen Bergrecht', *Berg- und Hüttenmännisches Jahrbuch*, 52.

Lachner, Carl (1882) *Die Holzarchitectur Hildesheims*. Hildesheim.

Lackner, Helmut (1984) 'Die Brennstoffversorgung des steirischen Eisenwesens', in P. W. Roth (ed.), *Erz und Eisen in der Grünen Mark*. Graz: Styria.

Lahl, Uwe, and Zeschmar, Barbara (1985) *Formaldehyd, Porträt einer Chemikalie: Kniefall der Wissenschaft vor der Industrie?* 2nd edn, Freiburg: Dreisam-Verlag.

Landes, David S. (1969) *The Unbound Prometheus: Technological Change and Industrial Development in Western Europe from 1750 to the Present*. Cambridge: Cambridge University Press.

Lane, Frederic C. (1973) *Venice: A Maritime Republic*. Baltimore: Johns Hopkins University Press.

Lane, Frederic C. ([1934] 1992) *Venetian Ships and Shipbuilders of the Renaissance*, Baltimore: Johns Hopkins University Press.

Langendorf, Günther (1982) *Holz: Naturstoff mit Zukunft*. Leipzig.

Lannoy, Richard (1971) *The Speaking Tree: A Study of Indian Culture and Society*. Oxford: Oxford University Press.

Latham, Bryan (1957) *Timber: Its Development and Distribution: A Historical Survey*. London: Harrap.

Latham, Michael (1976) 'Der internationale Sperrholz- und Spanplattenmarkt', in *Holzhandel auf neuen Wegen*. Stuttgart: DRW.

Laurop, C. P. (1798) *Freimütige Gedanken über den Holzmangel*. Altona.

Le Play, Frederic (1854) *Grundsätze, welche die Eisenhüttenwerke mit Holzbetrieb und die Waldbesitzer befolgen müssen, um den Kampf gegen die Hütten mit Steinkohlenbetrieb erfolgreich führen zu können*. Freiberg.

Leavell, Chuck (2001) *Forever Green: The History and Hope of the American Forest*. Macon, GA: Mercer University Press.

Leckebusch, Günther (1966) 'Der Beginn des deutschen Eisenschiffbaus, 1850–1890', in Karl Erich Born (ed.), *Moderne deutsche Wirtschaftsgeschichte*. Cologne: Kiepenheuer & Witsch.

Lee, Yok-shiu F., and So, Alvin Y. (eds) (1999) *Asia's Environmental Movements: Comparative Perspectives*. Armonk, NY: M. E. Sharpe.

Lehmann, Johann Christian (1735) *Ars lucrandi lignum: Die Universal-Holtz-Spahr-Kunst*. Leipzig.

Lehmann, H.-A., and Stolze, B. J. (1969) *Ingenieurholzbau*. Stuttgart: Teubner.

Leibundgut, Hans (1981) *Die natürliche Waldverjüngung*. Berlin and Stuttgart: Haupt.

Leibundgut, Hans (1983) *Der Wald: Eine Lebensgemeinschaft*. Frauenfeld: Huber.
Leibundgut, Hans (1984) 'Über den Wandel im waldbaulichen Denken', *Allgemeine Forstzeitschrift*, 39: 17–22.
Leipert, Christian (1984) 'Ökologische und soziale Folgekosten der Produktion', *Aus Politik und Zeitgeschichte*, B19.
Lemp, Heinrich (1922) 'Die geschichtliche Entwicklung der baupolizeilichen Verordnungen, Frankfurts a. M. bis 1806', dissertation, Frankfurt.
Lenk, Anton (1974) *Die Gezeiten der Geschichte*. Düsseldorf: Econ.
Letsch, Hermann (1939) *Die Entwicklung des Holzverkaufswesens in Bayern von der Mitte des 18. bis zum Beginn des 20. Jahrhunderts*. Munich.
Levin, Simon A. (ed.) (2009) *The Princeton Guide to Ecology*. Princeton, NJ: Princeton University Press.
Levy, Robert I. (1990) *Mesocosm: Hinduism and the Organization of a Traditional Newar City in Nepal*. Berkeley: University of California Press.
Liebich, Christoph (1844) *Die Reformation des Waldbaues im Interesse des Ackerbaues, der Industrie und des Handels*, 2 vols. Prague.
Lindqvist, Svante (1983) 'Natural Resources and Technology: The Debate about Energy Technology in 18th-Century Sweden', *Scandinavian Journal of History*, 81: 83–107.
Lindqvist, Svante (1984) *Technology on Trial*. Uppsala: Almqvist & Wiksell.
Lindstedt, Joachim D. (1723) *Wohlerzogene Natur des Feuers*. Jena.
Linse, Ulrich (1993) 'Der Film *Ewiger Wald* – oder: Die Überwindung der Zeit durch den Raum: Eine filmische Umsetzung von Rosenbergs *Mythos des 20. Jahrhunderts*', *Zeitschrift für Pädagogik*, suppl. 31: 57–75.
Liu, Jinlong (2009) 'Reconstructing the History of Forestry in Northwestern China, 1949–1998', *Global Environment*, 3: 190–221.
Loebe, Karl (1943) *Bremens Holzwirtschaft*. Bremen.
Logan, William Bryant (2005) *Oak: The Frame of Civilization*. New York: W. W. Norton.
Lohberg, Rolf (1976) *Geschichte der Waldarbeit*. Waiblingen-Neustadt: Stihl.
Lohmann, Michael (1972) *Natur als Ware*. Munich: Hanser.
Lohrmann, Dietrich (1979) 'Energieprobleme im Mittelalter: Zur Verknappung von Wasserkraft und Holz in Westeuropa bis zum Ende des 12. Jahrhunderts', *Vierteljahresschrift für Sozial- und Wirtschaftsgeschichte*, 66: 297–316.
Lohse, Hans (1965) *600 Jahre Schmalkalder Eisengewinnung und Eisenverarbeitung vom 14.–20. Jahrhundert*. Meiningen: Staatliche Museen.
Lombard, Maurice (1959) 'Les Bois dans la Méditerranée musulmane (VII–XIe siècles)', *Annales ESC*, 2: 234–54.
Lombard, Maurice (1975) *The Golden Age of Islam*. Princeton, NJ: Princeton University Press.
Lönnroth, Mans, Johansson, Thomas B., and Steen, Peter (1980) *Solar Versus Nuclear: Choosing Energy Futures*. Oxford: Pergamon.
Losseff-Tillmanns, Gisela (ed.) (1982) *Frau und Gewerkschaft*. Frankfurt am Main: Fischer.
Lower, Arthur R. M. (1973) *Great Britain's Woodyard: British America and the Timber Trade, 1763–1867*. Montreal: McGill–Queen's University Press.
Lübke, Anton (1942) *Das deutsche Rohstoffwunder*. Stuttgart.
Ludwig, Karl-Heinz (1979) *Die Agricola-Zeit im Montangemälde*. Düsseldorf: Verein Deutscher Ingenieure.

Lütgering, Gaby (1985) 'Die Möbelindustrie: Produktionsstrukturen und Fertigungstechnologien und ihre Auswirkungen auf Qualitätsanforderungen, Arbeitsbedingungen und Beschäftigung', manuscript, Bielefeld University.

Lutz, Josef (1941) 'Die ehemaligen Eisenhämmer und Hüttenwerke und die Waldentwicklung im nordöstlichen Bayern', *Mitteilungen aus Forstwirtschaft und Forstwissenschaft*, 12: 277–94.

McCracken, Eileen (1971) *The Irish Woods since Tudor Times: Distribution and Exploitation*. Newton Abbot: David & Charles.

Machatschek, Michael (2002) *Laubgeschichten: Gebrauchswissen einer alten Baumwirtschaft, Speise- und Futterlaubkultur*. Vienna: Böhlau.

McNeill, John R. (1992) *The Mountains of the Mediterranean World: An Environmental History*. Cambridge: Cambridge University Press.

McNeely, Jeffrey A., and Sochaczewski, Paul S. (1988) *Soul of the Tiger: Searching for Nature's Answers in Southeast Asia*. New York: Doubleday.

Maczak, Antoni, and Parker, William N. (eds) (1978) *Natural Resources in European History*. Washington, DC: Resources for the Future.

Maderspacher, Florian, and Stüben, Peter F. (eds) (1984) *Bodenschätze Contra Menschenrechte*. Hamburg: Junius.

Mager, Friedrich (1960) *Der Wald in Altpreussen als Wirtschaftsraum*, 2 vols. Graz: Böhlau.

Mager, Wolfgang (1982) 'Protoindustrialisierung und agrarisch-heimgewerbliche Verflechtung in Ravensburg während der Frühen Neuzeit', *Geschichte und Gesellschaft*, 8: 435–74.

Mämpel, Uwe (1985) *Keramik: Von der Handform zum Industrieguß*. Reinbek: Rowohlt.

Mang, Karl (1979) *History of Modern Furniture*. London: Academy Editions.

Mantel, Kurt (1973) *Holzmarktlehre: Ein Lehr- und Handbuch der Holzmarktökonomie und Holzwirtschaftspolitik*. Melsungen: Neumann-Neudamm.

Mantel, Kurt (1975) '100 Jahre Forst- und Holzwirtschaft und ihr Weg in die Zukunft', *Holz-Zentralblatt*, 11.

Mantel, Kurt (1981) *Forstgeschichte des 16. Jahrhunderts unter dem Einfluß der Forstordnungen und Noe Meurers*. Hamburg: Parey.

Mantel, Wilhelm (1961) *Wald und Forst-Wechselbeziehungen zwischen Natur und Wirtschaft*. Reinbek: Rowohlt.

Marchand, A. (1849) *Über die Entwaldung der Gebirge: Denkschrift an die Direktion des Innern des Kantons Bern*. Berne.

Marsh, George P. ([1864] 1974) *Man and Nature, or, Physical GeographyModified by Human Action*. Cambridge, MA: Harvard University Press.

Marstaller, Tilmann (2008) 'Der Wald im Haus: Zum Wechselspiel von Holzressourcen und Hausbau', in Elisabeth Vavra (ed.), *Der Wald im Mittelalter: Funktion, Nutzung, Deutung*. Berlin: Akademie, pp. 63–84.

Martin, Claude (1985) 'West- und Zentralafrikanische Regenwälder: Kaum genutzt und doch zerstört', in Peter F. Stüben (ed.), *Kahlschlag im Paradies*. Giessen: Fokus.

Marx, Karl (1975) 'Debates on the Law on Thefts of Wood', in Karl Marx and Friedrich Engels, *Collected Works*, vol. 1. London: Lawrence & Wishart.

Matejak, Mieczysław (2008) *Das Holz in deutschen Abhandlungen aus dem 17.–19. Jahrhundert*. Warsaw: Matejak.

Matti, Werner (1956) 'Die Einführung des Gradierwesens bei der Haller Saline im 18. Jahrhundert', *Haalquelle*, pp. 31–5.

Matzek, Robert (1992) *So warn's die Holzknecht': Geschichten und Dokumente aus ihrem Leben*. Gernsbach: Deutscher Betriebswirte-Verlag.

Mauz, Albert E. (1957) *Geschichte, Zustand und Probleme des Sägewerkes, untersucht im Wirtschaftsraum Filstal*. Munich.

Maydell, H.-J. (1970) 'Waldeigentum und Formen der Holznutzung im Tropenwald', *Forstarchiv*, 41: 45–9.

Maydell, H.-J. (1978) 'Agroforstwirtschaft: Kombination von land- und forstwirtschaftlicher Bodennutzung', *Forstarchiv*, 49: 96–9.

Mayer, Johann Friedrich ([1773] 1980) *Lehrbuch für die Land- und Haußwirthe in der pragmatischen Geschichte der gesamten Land- und Hauswirtschaft des Hohenlohe-Schillingsfürstischen Amtes Kupferzell*. Schwäbisch Hall.

Mayo, Edith (1984) *American Material Culture: The Shape of Things around Us*. Bowling Green, OH: Bowling Green State University Popular Press.

Mayr, Otto (1969) *Zur Frühgeschichte der technischen Regelungen*. Munich: Oldenbourg.

Mayr, Otto, and Post, R. C. (1981) *Yankee Enterprise: The Rise of the American System of Manufactures*. Washington, DC: US Chamber of Commerce.

Mazoyer, L. (1932) 'Exploitation forestière et conflits sociaux en Franche-Comté', *Annales de l'Histoire Économique et Sociale*, 4: 239–58.

Meiggs, Russell (1982) *Trees and Timber in the Ancient Mediterranean World*. Oxford: Clarendon Press.

Meyer, Karl Alfons (1966) 'Der Wald in der Vergangenheit', in Walter Kümmerly, *Der Wald*. Berne: Kümmerly & Frey.

Michaels, Axel (1999) 'Sakralisierung als Naturschutz? Heilige Bäume und Wälder in Nepal', in Rolf Peter Sieferle and Helga Breuninger (eds), *Natur-Bilder: Wahrnehmungen von Natur und Umwelt in der Geschichte*. Frankfurt: Campus, pp. 117–36.

Miller, Harry (1980) 'Potash from Wood Ashes: Frontier Technology in Canada and the US', *Technology and Culture*, 21: 187–208.

Milnik, Albrecht (1999) *Bernhardt Danckelmann: Leben und Leistungen eines Forstmannes*. Suderburg: Nimrod.

Mitchell, Alan (1981) *The International Book of the Forest*. London: Mitchell Beazley.

Mitscherlich, Gerhard (1963) *Zustand, Wachstum und Nutzung des Waldes im Wandel der Zeit*. Freiburg: Schulz.

Mitscherlich, Gerhard (1970–5) *Wald, Wachstum und Umwelt*, 3 vols. Frankfurt: Sauerländer.

Mitterauer, Michael (1974) 'Produktionsweise, Siedlungsstruktur und Sozialformen im österreichischen Montanwesen des Mittelalters und der frühen Neuzeit', in Michael Mitterauer (ed.), *Österreichisches Montanwesen*. Munich: Oldenbourg.

Mohr, Siegmund (1897) *Die Flößer auf dem Rhein*. Mannheim.

Moles, Antoine (1949) *Histoire des charpentiers*. Paris: Gründ.

Moll, F. (1920) 'Holzschutz: Seine Entwicklung von der Urzeit bis zur Umwandlung des Handwerkes in Fabrikbetrieb', *Technikgeschichte*, 10: 66–92.

Möller, Alfred ([1923] 1992) *Der Dauerwaldgedanke: Sein Sinn und seine Bedeutung*. Oberteuringen: Degreif.

Moore, Barrington (1967) *Social Origins of Dictatorship and Democracy*. London: Penguin.

Mooser, Josef (1984) 'Furcht bewahrt das Holz: Holzdiebstahl und sozialer Konflikt in der ländlichen Gesellschaft 1800–1850 an westfälischen Beispielen', in Heinz Reif (ed.), *Räuber, Volk und Obrigkeit: Studien zur Geschichte der Kriminalität in Deutschland seit dem 18. Jahrhundert*. Frankfurt am Main: Suhrkamp.

Morris, William (1973) 'How We Live and How We Might Live', in *Political Writings of William Morris*, ed. A. L. Morton. London: Lawrence & Wishart.

Moser, H. C. (1795) 'Versuch einer Geschichte der deutschen Forstwirtschaft', *Mosers Forstarchiv*, 16.

Mücke, Burkhardt (1983) *Damit der Wald nicht stirbt*. Munich: Heyne.

Mülder, Dietrich (1980) '"Rettet den Wald": Bewegungen zu einer ganz neuen Art von Waldkunde', *Forstarchiv*, 51: 61–8.

Mülder, Dietrich (1982) *Helft unsere Buchenwälder retten!* Stuttgart: DRW.

Müller, Daniel Ernst (1837) *Des Speßart's Holzhandel und Holz verbrauchende Industrie*. Frankfurt am Main: Andreä.

Müller-Hohenstein, Klaus (1978) 'Die anthropogene Beeinflussung der Wälder im westlichen Mittelmeerraum unter besonderer Berücksichtigung der Aufforstungen', in H.-W. Windhorst (ed.), *Beiträge zur Geographie der Wald- und Forstwirtschaft*. Darmstadt: Wissenschaftliche Buchgesellschaft.

Multhauf, Robert P. (1978) *Neptune's Gift: A History of Common Salt*. Baltimore: Johns Hopkins University Press.

Mumford, Lewis ([1934] 1963) *Technics and Civilization*. New York: Harcourt, Brace & World.

Münch, Paul (1984) *Ordnung, Fleiß und Sparsamkeit*. Munich: Deutscher Taschenbuch.

Myers, Norman (1980) *Conversion of Tropical Moist Forests*. Washington, DC: National Academy of Sciences.

Nations, J. D., and Komer, D. I. (1984) 'Indianer, Siedler und Rindfleischexport: Die Vernichtung des mittelamerikanischen Regenwaldes', *epd–Entwicklungspolitik*, 10–11.

Nawka, Blasius (1966) 'Meilereien und Eisenhämmer in der Lausitz', *Letopis*, series C, no. 9: 13–73.

Nef, John U. ([1932] 1972) *The Rise of the British Coal Industry*, 2 vols. Freeport, NY: Books for Libraries Press.

Nenninger, Marcus (2001) *Die Römer und der Wald*. Stuttgart: Steiner.

Neuburg, Clamor (1901) *Der Einfluß des Bergbaus auf die erste Entwicklung der Forstwirtschaft in Deutschland*. Leipzig.

Nieß, Walter (1974) *Die Forst- und Jagdgeschichte der Grafschaft Ysenburg und Büdingen vom ausgehenden Mittelalter bis zur Neuzeit*. Büdingen.

Nitz, Hans-Jürgen (ed.) (1974) *Historisch-genetische Siedlungsforschung*. Darmstadt: Wissenschaftliche Buchgesellschaft.

Nördlinger, Hermann (1860) *Die technischen Eigenschaften der Hölzer für Forst- und Baubeamte, Technologen und Gewerbetreibenden*. Stuttgart.

Nördlinger, Hermann (1869) 'Der neuentbrannte Waldstreukampf', *Kritische Blätter für Forst- und Jagdwissenschaft*. Leipzig: Baumgärtner, pp. 51–92.

Normand, Didier (1971) *Forêts et bois tropicaux*. Paris: Presses Universitaires de France.

Nosrati, Kazem et al. (2005) *Schutz der Biologischen Vielfalt und integriertes*

Management der Kaspischen Wälder (Nordiran). Münster: Organisation für Forst- und Weidewirtschaft.

Novicki, Constantin V. (1866) 'Der metallische Bergbau und die Forstwirtschaft in Böhmen', in *Vereinszeitschrift für Forst-, Jagd- und Naturkunde*, pp. 21–72.

Oberrauch, Heinrich (1952) *Tirols Wald und Waidwerk*. Innsbruck: Wagner.

Oeschger, Hans Jörg (1975) *Douglasienanbau in Baden-Württemberg: Mit besonderer Berücksichtigung der geschichtlichen Entwickung*. Stuttgart: Landesforstverwaltung Baden-Württemberg.

Olechnowitz, Karl-Friedrich (1960) *Der Schiffbau der Hansischen Spätzeit*. Weimar: Böhlau.

Olson, Shary H. (1971) *The Depletion Myth: A History of the Railroad Use of Timber*. Cambridge, MA: Harvard University Press.

Osako, Masako M. (1983) 'Forest Preservation in Tokugawa Japan', in Richard P. Tucker and J. F. Richards (eds), *Global Deforestation and the Nineteenth-Century World Economy*. Durham, NC: Duke University Press.

Ostendorf, Friedrich ([1908] 1982) *Die Geschichte des Dachwerks, erläutert an einer großen Anzahl mustergültiger alter Konstruktionen*. Hannover: Schäfer.

Osterhammel, Jürgen (2009) *Die Verwandlung der Welt: Eine Geschichte des 19. Jahrhunderts*. Munich: Beck.

Ostrom, Elinor (1990) *Governing the Commons: The Evolution of Institutions for Collective Action*. Cambridge: Cambridge University Press.

Pacher, Josef (1964) 'Untersuchungen der Zusammenhänge zwischen der Forstwirtschaft und den Veränderungen der Staatswirtschaft sowie der staatlichen Wirtschaftspolitik in der zweiten Hälfte des 18. Jahrhunderts in Deutschland', dissertation, Freiburg.

Palladio, Andrea ([1738] 1965) *The Four Books of Architecture*. New York: Dover.

Palme, Rudolf (1983) *Rechts-, Wirtschafts- und Sozialgeschichte der inneralpinen Salzwerke bis zu deren Monopolisierung*. Frankfurt: Lang.

Papius, Kaspar (1840) *Die Holznoth und die Staatsforsten*. Munich.

Pappenheim, Louis (1858) *Handbuch der Sanitäts-Polizei*, vol. 1. Berlin.

Parsons, James J. (1978) 'Die Eichelmast-Schweinehaltung in den Eichenwäldern Südwestspaniens', in H. W. Windhorst (ed.), *Beiträge zur Geographie der Wald- und Forstwirtschaft*. Darmstadt: Wissenschaftliche Buchgesellschaft.

Paulinyi, Akos (1979) 'Die ersten "feuerfesten" Fabrikbauten in England', in ICOMOS, Deutsches Nationalkomitee (ed.), *Eisen-architektur: Die Rolle des Eisens in der historischen Architektur der ersten Hälfte des 19. Jahrhunderts*. Hannover: Vincentz.

Paulinyi, Akos (1983) 'Die Erfindung des Heißwindblasens', *Technikgeschichte*, 501: 129–45.

Pedersen, Klaus (2008) *Naturschutz und Profit: Menschen zwischen Vertreibung und Naturzerstörung*. Münster: Unrast-Verlag.

Perlin, John (2005) *A Forest Journey: The Story of Wood and Civilization*. Woodstock, VT: Countryman Press.

Perrot, Michelle (1973) *Les Ouvriers en grève : France, 1871–1890*, 2 vols. Paris: La Haye Mouton.

Perrot, Michelle (1981) 'Rebellische Weiber: Die Frau in der französischen Stadt des 19. Jahrhunderts', in Barbara Becker et al., *Listen der Ohnmacht*. Frankfurt: Europäische Verlagsanstalt.

Peters, Wiebke (1984) 'Nachhaltigkeit als Grundsatz der Forstwirtschaft: Ihre Verankerung in der Gesetzgebung und ihre Bedeutung in der Praxis', dissertation, Hamburg.

Petzoldt, Hans-Dieter (1990) *Knochenhauer-Amtshaus: Wiederaufbau 1987–1990: Chronik und gesammelte Zeitungsberichter*. Söhre: Petzoldt.

Pfannenschmidt, A. (1848) *Die Conservation des Holzes nach allen vorhandenen ältesten und neuesten Methoden*. Leipzig.

Pfeil, Friedrich W. L. (1816) *Über die Ursachen des schlechten Zustandes der Forsten und die allein möglichen Mittel, ihn zu verbessern, mit besonderer Rücksicht auf die preußischen Staaten*. Freistadt.

Pfeil, Friedrich W. L. (1839) *Die Forstgeschichte Preußens bis zum Jahre 1806*. Leipzig.

Phillips-Birt, Douglas (1979) *The Building of Boats*. London: Stanford Maritime.

Phleps, Hermann (1928) 'Die alte Holzbaukunst als Lehrmeisterin', *Deutsches Bauwesen*.

Phleps, Hermann (1942) *Holzbaukunst: Der Blockbau*, Karlsruhe: A. Bruder.

Picard, Liza (1997) *Restoration London: Everyday Life in the 1660s*. London: Weidenfeld & Nicolson.

Picker, Henry (1963) *Hitlers Tischgespräche im Führerhauptquartier, 1941–1942*, ed. Percy Ernst Schramm. Stuttgart: Seewald.

Piest, Heinz (1954) *Künstliche Holztrocknung*. Augsburg: Rösler.

Pike, Robert E. (1984) *Tall Trees, Tough Men: A Vivid, Anecdotal History of Logging and Log-Driving in New England*. New York: W. W. Norton.

Pinchot, Gifford ([1947] 1998) *Breaking New Ground*. Seattle: University of Washington Press.

Pisani, Donald J. (1985) 'Forests and Conservation, 1865–1890', *Journal of American History*, 72: 340–59.

Pitz, Ernst (1965) 'Studie zur Entstehung des Kapitalismus', in O. Brunner (ed.), *Festschrift Hermann Aubin zum 80. Geburtstag*. Wiesbaden: F. Steiner.

Plath, Erich (1951) *Die Holzverleimung*. Stuttgart: Wissenschaftliche Verlagsgesellschaft.

Plumpe, Gottfried (1982) *Die württembergische Eisenindustrie im 19. Jahrhundert*. Wiesbaden: F. Steiner.

Poffenberger, Mark, and McGean, Betsy (eds) (1996) *Village Voices, Forest Choices: Joint Forest Management in India*. Oxford: Oxford University Press.

Polanyi, Karl (1957) *The Great Transformation: The Political and Economic Origins of Our Time*. Boston: Beacon Press.

Poore, Duncan (2003) *Changing Landscapes: The Development of the International Tropical Timber Organization and its Influence on Tropical Forest Management*. London: Earthscan.

Poppe, Johann Heinrich Moritz von ([1847] 1972) *Geschichte aller Erfindungen und Entdeckungen*. Hildesheim: Olms.

Pott, Richard, and Hüppe, Rudolf (1991) *Die Hudelandschaften Nordwestdeutschlands*. Münster: Westfälisches Museum für Naturkunde.

Preßler, Max Robert (1865) *Der Waldbau des Nationalökonomen als Begründer wahrer Einheit zwischen Land- und Forstwirtschaft und deren Schulen*. Dresden.

Produktivitätssteigerung in der Sägeindustrie (1978). Stuttgart: DRW.

Das Proletariat und die Waldungen, mit besonderer Berücksichtigung der bayerischen Rhein-Pfalz (1851). Kaiserslautern: Tascher.

Pryce, Will (2005) *Die Kunst der Holzarchitektur: Eine Weltgeschichte.* Leipzig: Seemann.

Pryde, Philip R. (1991) *Environmental Management in the Soviet Union.* Cambridge: Cambridge University Press.

Pyne, Stephen J. (1984) 'Prelude to Sustained-Yield Forestry: The Origins of Systematic Fire Protection in the United States', in Harold K. Steen (ed.), *History of Sustained-Yield Forestry: A Symposium.* Santa Cruz, CA: Forest History Society.

Pyne, Stephen J. (1997) *Fire in America: A Cultural History of Wildland and Rural Fire.* Seattle: University of Washington Press.

Rackham, Oliver (1980) *Ancient Woodland: Its History, Vegetation and Uses in England.* London: Edward Arnold.

Rackham, Oliver ([1976] 1990) *Trees and Woodland in the British Landscape.* Rev. edn, Dent.

Radkau, Joachim (1983) 'Holzverknappung und Krisenbewußtsein im 18. Jahrhundert', *Geschichte und Gesellschaft*, 4: 513–43.

Radkau, Joachim (1986a) 'Zur angeblichen Energiekrise des 18. Jahrhunderts: Revisionistische Betrachtungen über die "Holznot"', *Vierteljahrschrift für Sozial- und Wirtschaftsgeschichte*, 1: 1–37.

Radkau, Joachim (1986b) 'Warum wurde die Gefährdung der Natur durch den Menschen nicht rechtzeitig erkannt? Naturkult und Angst vor Holznot um 1800', in Hermann Lübbe and Elisabeth Ströker (eds), *Ökologische Probleme im kulturellen Wandel.* Paderborn: F. Schöningh, pp. 47–78.

Radkau, Joachim (1988) 'Vom Wald zum Floß – ein technisches System? Dynamik und Schwerfälligkeit der Flößerei in der Geschichte der Forst- und Holzwirtschaft', in Hans-Walter Keweloh and Ursula Carle (eds), *Auf den Spuren der Flößer: Wirtschafts- und Sozialgeschichte eines Gewerbes.* Stuttgart: Theiss, pp. 16–39.

Radkau, Joachim (1989a) *Technik in Deutschland: Vom 18. Jahrhundert bis zur Gegenwart.* Frankfurt: Suhrkamp.

Radkau, Joachim (1989b) 'Ein Abgrund von "Holzhurerei"? Der alltägliche Holzdiebstahl im alten Bielefeld', *Ravensberger Blätter*, 1: 12–18.

Radkau, Joachim (1994a) 'Natur als Fata Morgana? Naturideale in der Technikgeschichte', in Kulturamt Stuttgart (ed.), *Zum Naturbegriff der Gegenwart*, vol. 2. Stuttgart: Frommann-Holzboog, pp. 281–310.

Radkau, Joachim (1994b) 'Holz auf dem Weg zum "Grundstoff des ökologischen Zeitalters"', *Holz-Zentralblatt*, 22 June.

Radkau, Joachim (1994c) '"Die Nervosität des Zeitalters": Die Erfindung von Technikbedürfnissen um die Jahrhundertwende', *Kultur und Technik*, 3: 51–7

Radkau, Joachim (1997) 'Das Rätsel der städtischen Brennholzversorgung im "hölzernen Zeitalter"', in Dieter Schott (ed.), *Energie und Stadt in Europa: Von der vorindustriellen 'Holznot' bis zur Ölkrise der 1970er Jahre.* Stuttgart: Steiner, pp. 43–75.

Radkau, Joachim (2001) 'Entzauberung des Feuers und Entfesselung der Feuerindustrien: Vom "hölzernen Zeitalter" zur Ära der Kohle', in Kunst- und Ausstellungshalle der Bundesrepublik Deutschland (ed.), *Feuer.* Cologne: Wienand, pp. 110–20.

Radkau, Joachim (2002) *Natur und Macht: Eine Weltgeschichte der Umwelt.* Munich: Beck.

Radkau, Joachim (2006) 'Der Wald als Lebenswelt und Konfliktfeld der alten Zeit: Szenen aus hessischen Archivalien in mikro- und makroskopischer Sicht', in Andreas Hedwig (ed.), *'Weil das Holz eine köstliche Ware . . .': Wald und Forst zwischen Mittelalter und Moderne.* Marburg: Verein für Hessische Geschichte und Landeskunde, pp. 75–103.

Radkau, Joachim (2007) 'Hölzerne Pfade und Holzwege in die Kulturgeschichte', in Mamoun Fansa and Dirk Vorlauf (eds), *Holz-Kultur: Von der Urzeit bis in die Zukunft.* Mainz: von Zabern, pp. 39–51.

Radkau, Joachim (2008a) *Technik in Deutschland: Vom 18. Jahrhundert bis heute.* Frankfurt: Campus.

Radkau, Joachim (2008b) 'Der legendäre und der wirkliche Wald: Die doppelte Geschichte des Teutoburger Waldes', in Naturschutzzentrum Senne (ed.), *Senne und Teutoburger Wald.* Bielefeld: TPK-Regionalverlag, pp. 59–68.

Radkau, Joachim (2008c) *Nature and Power: A Global History of the Environment,* trans. Thomas Dunlap. Cambridge: Cambridge University Press.

Radkau, Joachim (2009) *Max Weber: A Biography,* trans. Patrick Camiller. Cambridge: Polity.

Radzio, Heiner (ed.) (1988) *75 Jahre im Dienst für die Ruhr.* Essen: Ruhrverband und Ruhrtalsperrenverein.

Rangan, Haripriya (2000) *Of Myths and Movements: Rewriting Chipko into Himalayan History.* London: Verso.

Ranke, Winfried, and Korff, Gottfried (1980) *Hauberg und Eisen.* Munich: Schirmer-Mosel.

Rapp, Hermann-Josef, and Schmidt, Marcus (eds) (2006) *Baumriesen und Adlerfarn: Der 'Urwald Sababurg' im Reinhardswald.* Kassel: Euregio.

Rawat, M. S. S. (ed.) (1993) *Himalaya, a Regional Perspective: Resources, Environment and Development.* Delhi: Daya.

Reif, Heinz (1979) *Westfälischer Adel 1770–1860: Vom Herrschaftsstand zur regionalen Elite.* Göttingen: Vandenhoeck & Ruprecht.

Reiffenstein, Tim, and Hayter, Roger (2006) 'Domestic Timber Auctions and Flexibly Specialized Forestry in Japan', *Canadian Geographer,* 50: 503–25.

Renzsch, Wolfgang (1984) 'Bauhandwerker in der Industrialisierung', in Ulrich Engelhardt (ed.), *Handwerker in der Industrialisierung.* Stuttgart: Klett-Cotta.

Ress, Franz Michael (1957) *Geschichte der Kokereitechnik.* Essen: Glückauf.

Reuleaux, Franz (1877) *Briefe aus Philadelphia.* 2nd edn, Brunswick.

Riehl, Gerhard (1968) *Die Forstwirtschaft im Oberharzer Bergbaugebiet von der Mitte des 17. bis zum Ausgang des 19. Jahrhunderts.* Hannover: Schaper.

Riehl, Wilhelm H. ([1934] 1990) *The Natural History of the German People.* Lampeter: Mellen.

Rielat, Arno (1980) 'Energieverbrauch und Energiepolitik in vorindustrieller Zeit', manuscript, University of Marburg.

Ritter, Wigand (1982) 'Waldverwüstung und Wiederbewaldung', in Hermann Kellenbenz, *Wirtschaftsentwicklung und Umweltbeeinflussung (14.–20. Jahrhundert).* Wiesbaden: F. Steiner.

Ritter, Wigand (1983) 'Wohin mit dem Holz in Katar?', *E+Z* [Entwicklung und Zusammenarbeit], 10.

Roberts, Luke S. (1998) *Mercantilism in a Japanese Domain: The Merchant*

Origins of Economic Nationalism in 18th-Century Tosa. Cambridge: Cambridge University Press.

Rodekamp, Volker (1981) *Das Drechslerhandwerk in Ostwestfale: Ein traditionelles Handwerk im Strukturwandel des 20. Jahrhunderts*. Münster: Coppenrath.

Rodenwaldt, Ulrich (1977) *Der Wald einer alten Stadt im Spiegel der Ratsprotokolle des 17. und 18. Jahrhunderts (1600–1834)*. Stuttgart.

Rodgers, John (1941) *The English Woodland*. London: Batsford.

Roscher, Wilhelm (1854) *Ein nationalökonomisches Hauptprinzip der Forstwissenschaft*. Leipzig.

Rosenberg, Nathan (1976) *Perspectives on Technology*. Cambridge: Cambridge University Press.

Rosenhainer, Franz (1968) *Die Geschichte des Unterharzer Hüttenwesens: Von seinen Anfängen bis zur Gründung der Kommunionverwaltung im Jahre 1635*. Goslar: Geschichts- und Heimatschutzverein.

Roth, Emanuel (1909) *Kompendium der Gewerbekrankheiten und Einführung in die Gewerbehygiene*. 2nd edn, Berlin.

Roth, P. F. (1802) *Holzersparende Ofen-, Kochherd-, Kessel- und Bratofen-Feuerungen*. Nuremberg.

Roth, Paul W. (1976) *Die Glaserzeugung in der Steiermark von den Anfängen bis 1913*. Graz: Historische Landeskommission für Steiermark.

Rubner, Heinrich (1967) *Forstgeschichte im Zeitalter der industriellen Revolution*. Berlin: Duncker & Humblot.

Rubner, Heinrich (1975) 'Waldgewerbe und Agrarlandschaft im Spätmittelalter und im 19. und 20. Jahrhundert', in Hermann Kellenbenz (ed.), *Agrarisches Nebengewerbe und Formen der Reagrarisierung im Spätmittelalter und der 19./20. Jahrhundert*. Stuttgart: Fischer.

Rubner, Heinrich (1983) 'Naturschutz, Forstwirtschaft und Umwelt in ihren Wechselbeziehungen besonders im NS-Staat', in Hermann Kellenbenz (ed.) *Wirtschaftsentwicklung und Umweltbeeinflussung (14.–20. Jahrhundert)*. Wiesbaden: Steiner.

Rubner, Heinrich (1984) 'Technisch-industrielle Entwicklung, Waldzerstörung und Waldwirtschaft von der Aufklärung bis zur Gründung des Deutschen Reiches', *Technikgeschichte*, 51: 94–103.

Rubner, Heinrich (1985) *Deutsche Forstgeschichte, 1933–1945: Forstwirtschaft, Jagd, und Umwelt im NS-Staat*. St Katharinen: Scripta mercaturae.

Rubner, Heinrich (1986) 'Brauchen wir eine neue Forstgeschichte?', *Forstarchiv*, 57: 29–31.

Ruffer, Horst, and Schwarz, Eckerhard (1984) *Die Forstwirtschaft der Deutschen Demokratischen Republik*. Berlin: Deutscher Landwirtschaftsverlag.

Rupp, Erwin (n.d.) *Die Geschichte der Ziegelherstellung*. Heidelberg: Bundesverband der Deutschen Ziegelindustrie.

Sachse, Hans-Joachim (1975) *Barocke Dachwerke, Decken und Gewölbe*. Berlin: Mann.

Sachsenberg, E. (1936) 'Spanlose Formung von Holz', *Maschinen-Bau, Betrieb*, 15.

Sande, Theodore Anton (1978) *Industrial Archeology: A New Look at the American Heritage*. Harmondsworth: Penguin.

Sander, A. (1919) 'Die Gewinnung von Holzgas einst und jetzt', *Zeitschrift des Vereins Deutscher Ingenieure*, 63, July.

Sandgruber, Roman (1982a) *Die Anfänge der Konsumgesellschaft*. Vienna: Verlag für Geschichte und Politik.

Sandgruber, Roman (1982b) 'Die Agrarrevolution', in *Erzherzog Johann von Österreich, Beiträge zur Geschichte seiner Zeit*. Graz: Styria.

Sandgruber, Roman (1982c) 'Die Energieversorgung Österreichs vom 18. Jahrhundert bis zur Gegenwart', *Beiträge zur historischen Sozialkunde*, 12: 79–85.

Savage, George (1966) *A Concise History of Interior Decoration*. London: Thames & Hudson.

Sazenhofen, Carl-Josef von (1980) *Handwerksfibel Flößerei und Trift*. Munich: Staackmann.

Schäfer, Carl (1937) *Deutsche Holzbaukunst*. Dresden.

Schäfer, Herbert (1987) *Dioxin auf dem Holzweg*. Bergisch Gladbach: Lübbe.

Schäfer, Ingrid (1983) '"Gewerbehierarchie"-Instrument der Brennstoffpolitik im 18. Jahrhundert', *Scripta mercaturae*, 17: 63–90.

Schäfer, Ingrid (1992) '*Ein Gespenst geht um*': *Politik mit der Holznot in Lippe, 1750–1850*. Detmold: Naturwissenschaftlicher und Historischer Verein für das Land Lippe.

Schäfer, Ingrid (1998a) *Privatwald in Lippe: Natur und Ökonomie zwischen 1750 und 1950*. Bielefeld: Verlag für Regionalgeschichte.

Schäfer, Ingrid (1998b) *OKAL – Pionier im Fertighausbau, 1928–1998: Eine Studie zur Wirtschafts- und Technikgeschichte*. Salzhemmendorf: OKAL.

Schäfer, Ingrid, and Zandonella, Valentin (1993) *100 Jahre Buchen-Sperrholz: Aus der Geschichte der Blomberger Holzindustrie, 1893–1993*. Blomberg: Verlag der Blomberger Holzindustrie.

Scharff, Friedrich (1868) *Das Recht in der Dreieich unter besonderer Berücksichtigung der Verhältnisse des Frankfurter Stadtwaldes . . . .* Frankfurt.

Scheifele, Max (1988) *Die Murgschifferschaft: Geschichte des Floßhandels, des Waldes und der Holzindustrie im Murgtal*. Gernsbach: Katz.

Schellhaas, Walter, and Wächtler, Eberhard (1975) *Der Plan der Einrichtung einer Forstakademie in Verbindung mit der Bergakademie Freiberg (Sachsen) 1799–1809*. Freiberg.

Schenck, K. E. (1820) *Statistik des vormaligen Fürstenthums Siegen*. Siegen.

Schenk, Winfried (1996) *Waldnutzung, Waldzustand und regionale Entwicklung in vorindustrieller Zeit im mittleren Deutschland*. Stuttgart: Steiner.

Schlieder, Wolfgang (1977) *Der Erfinder des Holzschiffs E. G. Keller*. Leipzig.

Schlieder, Wolfgang (1980) *Schneeweiß und glatt – so hat man's gern: Geschichte und Geschichten vom Papier*. Leipzig: Deutsche Bücherei.

Schnabel, Franz (1965) *Deutsche Geschichte im neunzehnten Jahrhundert*, vol. 6: *Die moderne Technik und die deutsche Industrie*. Freiburg: Herder.

Schnapper-Arndt, Gottlieb (1915) *Studien zur Geschichte der Lebenshaltung in Frankfurt/Main während des 17. und 18. Jahrhunderts*. Frankfurt am Main.

Schneider, Helmuth (2007) *Geschichte der antiken Technik*. Munich: Beck.

Schneiter, Franz (1970) *Agrargeschichte der Brandwirtschaft*. Graz: Historische Landeskommission für Steiermark.

Schoch, Oswald (1985) 'Alte Waldgewerbe im nördlichen Schwarzwald', *Kultur und Technik*, 3: 146–65.

Scholz, Fred (1969) 'Die Tagelöhnersiedlungen des 18. Jahrhunderts im Nordschwarzwald', *Berichte zur deutschen Landeskunde*, 42: 289–318.

Schramm, Engelbert (ed.) (1984) *Ökologie-Lesebuch*. Frankfurt am Main: Fischer-Taschenbuch.

Schremmer, Eckart (ed.) (1971) *Handelsstrategie und betriebswirtschaftliche Kalkulation im ausgehenden 18. Jahrhundert: Der süddeutsche Salzmarkt.* Wiesbaden: Steiner.

Schremmer, Eckart (1980) *Technischer Fortschritt an der Schwelle zur Industrialisierung: Ein innovativer Durchbruch mit Verfahrentechnologie bei den alpenländischen Salinen.* Munich: Beck.

Schubert, Ernst (1986) 'Der Wald: Wirtschaftliche Grundlage der spätmittelalterlichen Stadt', in Bernd Herrmann (ed.), *Mensch und Umwelt im Mittelalter.* Stuttgart: Deutsche Verlags-Anstalt.

Schubert, Ernst (1994) 'Scheu vor der Natur – Ausbeutung der Natur: Formen und Wandlungen des Umweltbewußtseins im Mittelalter', in Ernst Schubert and Bernd Hermann (eds), *Von der Angst zur Ausbeutung: Umwelterfahrung zwischen Mittelalter und Neuzeit.* Frankfurt am Main: Fischer-Taschenbuch, pp. 13–58.

Schübler, Valentin (1852) *Der Kampf der Eisenhüttenwerke mit Holzkohlenbetrieb gegen die Hüttenwerke mit Steinkohlenbetrieb.* Stuttgart.

Schuler, Anton (1980) *Wald- und Holzwirtschaftspolitik der alten Eidgenossenschaft.* Zurich: ETH-Zentrum.

Schuler, Anton (ed.) (1985) *History of Forest Utilization and Forestry in Mountain Regions*, Symposium at the Federal Institute of Technology, 3–7 September. Zurich: Schweizerischer Forstverein.

Schulte, Andreas (ed.) (2003) *Wald in Nordrhein-Westfalen*, 2 vols. Münster: Aschendorff.

Schulte, Andreas, and Schöne, Dieter (eds) (1996) *Dipterocarp Forest Ecosystems: Towards Sustainable Management.* London: World Scientific.

Schulz, Horst (1983) 'Holz: Der Stoff, aus dem die Bäume sind', in Horst Stern et al., *Rettet den Wald.* Munich: Heyne.

Schumann, Hans Wolfgang (1989) *The Historical Buddha: The Times, Life and Teachings of the Founder of Buddhism.* New York: Arkana.

Schwappach, Adam (1886–8) *Handbuch der Forst- und Jagdgeschichte*, 2 vols. Berlin.

Schweitzer, Albert (1938) *On the Edge of the Primeval Forest.* London: Hodder & Stoughton.

Schweitzer, Albert ([1931] 1998) *Out of my Life and Thought.* Baltimore: Johns Hopkins University Press.

Schwerz, Johann Nepomuk von (1936) *Beschreibung der Landwirtschaft in Westfalen.* Münster.

Schwind, Werner (1984) *Der Eifelwald im Wandel der Jahrhunderte.* Düren: Eifelverein.

Scott, James C. (1998) *Seeing Like a State: How Certain Schemes to Improve the Human Condition Have Failed.* New Haven, CT: Yale University Press.

Scurla, Herbert (ed.) (1974) *Reisen in Nippon: Berichte deutscher Forscher des 17. und 19. Jahrhunderts aus Japan.* Berlin: Verlag der Nation.

Seeland, Klaus (1980) *Ein nicht zu entwickelndes Tal: Traditionelle Bambustechnologie und Subsistenzwirtschaft in Ost-Nepal.* Diessenhofen: Rüegger.

Seidensticker, August (1896) *Rechts- und Wirtschaftsgeschichte norddeutscher Forsten, besonders im Land Hannover.* Göttingen.

369

Sellner, Christiane (1988) *Der gläserne Wald: Glaskultur im Bayerischen und Oberpfälzer Wald*. Munich: Prestel.

Selter, Bernward (1995) *Waldnutzung und ländliche Gesellschaft: Landwirtschaftlicher 'Nährwald' und neue Holzökonomie im Sauerland des 18. und 19. Jahrhunderts*. Paderborn: Schöningh.

Senghaas, Dieter (1982) *Von Europa lernen: Entwicklungsgeschichtliche Betrachtungen*. Frankfurt am Main: Suhrkamp.

Sentance, Bryan (2003) *Wood: The World of Woodwork and Carving*. London: Thames & Hudson.

Seymour, John, and Girardet, Herbert (1986) *Far from Paradise: The Story of Man's Impact on the Environment*. London: BBC.

Shapiro, Judith (2001) *Mao's War Against Nature: Politics and the Environment in Revolutionary China*. Cambridge: Cambridge University Press.

Sharp, Lindsay (1975) 'Timber, Science and Economic Reform in the Seventeenth Century', *Forestry*, 48: 51–86.

Sheraton, Thomas ([1803] 1970) *The Cabinet Dictionary*. New York: Praeger.

Sieferle, Rolf Peter *The Subterranean Forest: Energy Systems and the Industrial Revolution*. Knapwell, Cambridge: White Horse Press.

Sieferle, Rolf Peter (1984a) 'Alternativen der Industrialisierung?', in Lutz Niethammer (ed.), *'Die Menschen machen ihre Geschichte nicht aus freien Stücken, aber sie machen sie selbst'*. Berlin and Bonn: Dietz.

Sieferle, Rolf Peter (1984b) *Fortschrittsfeinde? Opposition gegen Technik und Industrie von der Romantik bis zur Gegenwart*. Munich: Beck.

Sippel, Heinrich (1938) 'Die bäuerlichen Nutzungsrechte an den Reichswäldern bei Nürnberg', dissertation, Erlangen-Bruck.

Sittauer, Hans L. (1982) *Friedrich Gottlob Keller*. Leipzig: Teubner.

Siuts, Hinrich (1982) *Bäuerliche und handwerkliche Arbeitsgeräte in Westfalen*. Münster: Aschendorff.

Smith, Adam ([1776] 1950) *An Inquiry into the Nature and Causes of the Wealth of Nations*, vol. 1. London: Methuen.

Sombart, Werner (1928) *Der moderne Kapitalismus: Das europäische Wirtschaftsleben im Zeitalter des Frühkapitalismus*, vol. 2. 7th edn, Munich and Leipzig.

Sonnemann, Rolf, and Wächtler, Eberhard (eds) (1982) *Johann Friedrich Böttger: Die Erfindung des europäischen Porzellans*. Stuttgart: Kohlhammer.

Soom, Arnold (1961) 'Der ostbaltische Holzhandel und die Holzindustrie im 17. Jahrhundert', *Hansische Geschichtsblätter*, 79: 80–100.

Spannagel, Fritz (1939) *Der Mobelbau: Ein Fachbuch für Tischler, Architekten und Lehrer*. Ravensburg.

Späth, Johann L. (1800) *Praktische Abhandlung über das Verkohlen des Holzes in großen und kleinen Meilern für Cameralisten und Forstmänner*. Nuremberg.

Spelsberg, Gerd (1984) *Rauchplage: Hundert Jahre Saurer Regen*. Aachen: Alano.

Sperber, Georg (1968) *Die Reichswälder bei Nürnberg: Aus der Geschichte des ältesten Kunstforstes*. Munich: Spindler.

Sperber, Georg (2000) 'Naturschutz und Forstwirtschaft: Die Geschichte einer schwierigen Beziehung', in Stiftung Naturschutzgeschichte (ed.), *Wegmarken: Beiträge zur Geschichte des Naturschutzes*. Essen: Klartext, pp. 71–150.

Sperl, Gerhard (1984) 'Die Technologie der direkten Eisenherstellung', in Paul W. Roth (ed.), *Erz und Eisen in der Grünen Mark*. Graz: Styria.

Spindler, Konrad (1994) *The Man in the Ice*. London: Weidenfeld and Nicolson.

Sporhan, Lore, and Stromer, Wolfgang von (1969) 'Die Nadelholzsaat in den Nürnberger Reichswäldern zwischen 1469 und 1600', *Zeitschrift für Agrargeschichte und Agrarsoziologie*, 17: 79–99.

Spring, Anselm, and Glas, Maximilian (2005) *Holz: Das fünfte Element*. Munich: Frederking & Thaler.

Srbik, Heinrich Ritter von (1917) *Studien zur Geschichte des österreichischen Salzwesens*. Innsbruck.

Stark, Walter (1973) *Lübeck und Danzig in der zweiten Hälfte des 15. Jahrhunderts*. Weimar: Böhlau.

Steen, Harold K. (ed.) (1983) *History of Sustained-Yield Forestry: A Symposium*. Santa Cruz, CA: Forest History Society.

Steinlin, H. (1970) 'Wandlungen von Arbeitsweise und Sprache der Waldarbeiter', *Alemannisches Jahrbuch*, pp. 332–40.

Steinsiek, Peter-Michael (2008) *Forst- und Holzforschung im 'Dritten Reich'*. Remagen: Kessel.

Stieglitz, Friederike von (2002) 'Blickwechsel . . . von ganz nah: der Reinhardswald . . . bis ganz fern: Wald in Afrika', in Hermann-Josef Rapp (ed.), *Reinhardswald: Eine Kulturgeschichte*. Kassel: Euregio-Verlag, pp. 26–35.

Stoll, Hermann (1954) 'Das Eisenwerk Eberfingen und dessen Holzversorgung', *Alemannisches Jahrbuch*, pp. 238–78.

Strehlke, E. G. (1961) 'Amerikanische Einflüsse auf die Gestaltung der deutschen Waldarbeit', *Forstarchiv*, 32: 217–22.

Ströker, Elisabeth (1982) *Theoriewandel in der Wissenschaftsgeschichte*. Frankfurt am Main: Klostermann.

Stuber, Martin (2008) *Wälder für Generationen: Konzeptionen der Nachhaltigkeit im Kanton Bern (1750–1880)*. Cologne: Böhlau.

Stürmer, Michael (1982) *Handwerk und höfische Kultur*. Munich: Beck.

Suhling, Lothar (1983) *Aufschließen, Gewinnen und Fördern: Geschichte des Bergbaus*. Reinbek: Rowohlt.

Sydow, Jürgen (ed.) (1981) *Städtische Versorgung und Entsorgung im Wald der Geschichte*. Sigmaringen: Thorbecke.

Tabak, Faruk (2008) *The Waning of the Mediterranean, 1550–1870: A Geohistorical Approach*. Baltimore: Johns Hopkins University Press,

Tal, Alon (2002) *Pollution in a Promised Land: An Environmental History of Israel*: Berkeley: University of California Press.

Tanizaki, Junichiro (1991) *In Praise of Shadows*. London: Jonathan Cape.

Teischinger, Alfred (2007) *Ressourcenverknappung in der Holzwirtschaft als Herausforderung für Technologie und Innovation: Thesen, Gedanken und Vorschläge zur Frage der Ressourcenverknappung von Holz in Europa*. Vienna: Ihf.

Teischinger, Alfred, and Lex, Rüdiger (eds) (2005) *Holzwirtschaft Österreichs: Ein Rückblick auf die letzten 60 Jahre, geschildert von 22 Zeitzeugen, die diese Epoche wesentlich geprägt haben*. Vienna: BOKU.

Terlau, Karo, and Kaspar, Fred (1985) 'Städtisches Bauen im Spannungsfeld zwischen Bautechnik: Baugesetzen und Parzellenzuschnitt', in *Stadt im Wandel*. Stuttgart: Cantz [exhibition catalogue].

Thiele, Jürgen (1980) *Alternative in der Energiegewinnung*. Freiburg: Öko-Institut.

Thieme, Hartmut (2007) 'Die ältesten Speere der Welt: Altpaläolithische Fundplätze mit Holzgeräten aus Schöningen', in Mamoun Fansa and Dirk Vorlauf (eds), *Holz-Kultur: Von der Urzeit bis in die Zukunft*. Mainz: von Zabern, pp. 78–86.

Thier, Manfred (1965) *Geschichte der schwäbischen Hüttenwerke: Ein Beitrag zur württembergischen Wirtschaftsgeschichte, 1365–1802*. Aalen: Verlag Heimat und Wirtschaft.

Thirgood, J. V. (1981) *Man and the Mediterranean Forest: A History of Resource Depletion*. London: Academic Press.

Thirgood, J. V. (1987) *Cyprus: A Chronicle of its Forests, Land, and People*. Vancouver: UBC Press.

Thomas, Keith (1983) *Man and the Natural World: Changing Attitudes in England, 1500–1800*. London: Allen Lane.

Thompson, Edward P. (1970) 'The Moral Economy of the English Crowd in the Eighteenth Century', *Past and Present*, 50: 76–136.

Thompson, Edward P. (1977) *Whigs and Hunters: The Origin of the Black Act*. Harmondsworth: Penguin.

Thunell, B. (1970) 'Holzbearbeitung, gestern, heute und morgen', *Forstwirtschaftliches Zentralblatt*, 89: 257–68.

Timm, Albrecht (1960) *Die Waldnutzung in Nordwestdeutschland im Spiegel der Weistümer*. Cologne: Böhlau.

Toffin, Gérard (ed.) (1991) *Man and his House in the Himalayas: Ecology of Nepal*. New Delhi: Sterling.

Torekull, Bertil (1999) *Leading by Design: The IKEA Story*. New York: HarperBusiness.

Totman, Conrad (1989) *The Green Archipelago: Forestry in Preindustrial Japan*. Berkeley: University of California Press.

Totman, Conrad (1993) *Early Modern Japan*. Berkeley: University of California Press.

Totman, Conrad (1995) *The Lumber Industry in Early Modern Japan*. Honolulu: University of Hawaii Press.

Toynbee, Arnold (1946) *A Study of History*, abridgement of vols. 1–6 by E. C. Somervell. London: Oxford University Press.

Tremel, Ferdinand (1954) *Der Frühkapitalismus in Innerösterreich*. Graz: Leykam.

Treue, Wilhelm (1965) *Achse, Rad und Wagen: 5000 Jahre Kultur- und Technikgeschichte*. Munich: Bruckmann.

Trier, Jost (1952) *Holz: Etymologien aus dem Niederwald*. Münster: Böhlau.

Trier, Jost (1963) *Venus: Etymologien um das Futterlaub*. Graz: Böhlau.

Troßbach, Werner (1984) 'Bauernprotest als "politisches" Verhalten', *Archiv für hessische Geschichte und Altertumskunde*, 42: 73–124.

Troßbach, Werner (1985) 'Widerstand als Normalfall: Bauernunruhen in der Grafschaft Sayn-Wittgenstein-Wittgenstein, 1696–1806', *Westfälische Zeitschrift*, 135: 25–111.

Trübswetter, Thomas (1983) 'Holz als Rohstoff', in GHK (Gewerkschaft Holz und Kunststoff), *Protokoll der 3. Fachtagung 'Technischer und organisatorischer Wandel in der Holzwirtschaft – Bestandsaufnahme und soziale Herausforderung'*. Düsseldorf.

Trunk, Johann Jakob (1802) *Neuer Plan der allgemeinen Revolution in der bisherigen Forstökonomie-Verwaltung*. Frankfurt am Main.

Tucker, Richard P. (1984) 'The Historical Context of Social Forestry in the Kumaon Himalayas', *Journal of Developing Areas*, 18: 341–55.

Tucker, Richard P., and Richard, J. E. (eds), *Global Deforestation and the Nineteenth-Century World Economy*. Durham, NC: Duke University Press.

Tüting, Ludmilla (1983) *Umarmt die Bäume: Die Chipko-Bewegung in Indien*. Kiel: Magazin-Verlag.

Tüting, Ludmilla (ed.) (1987) *Menschen, Bäume, Erosionen: Kahlschlag im Himalaya: Wege aus der Zerstörung*. Löhrbach: Pieper's Medienexperimente.

Tunner, Peter (1846) *Gemeinfaßliche Darstellung der Stabeisen- und Stahlbereitung in Frischherden in den Ländern des Vereins zur Beförderung und Unterstützung der Industrie und Gewerbe in Innerösterreich, dem Lande ob der Enns und Salzburg*. Graz.

Turner, Frederick J. (1920) *The Frontier in American History*. New York: Holt.

Tyrrell, Ian (1999) *True Gardens of the Gods: Californian–Australian Environmental Reform, 1860–1930*. Berkeley: University of California Press.

Ulshöfer, Kuno, and Beutter, Herta (eds) (1983) *Hall und das Salz*. Sigmaringen: Thorbecke.

UNESCO (ed.), *Sauver Venise*. Paris: Robert Laffont.

Ure, Andrew ([1835] 1967) *The Philosophy of Manufactures*. London: Cass.

Usemann, Klaus W. (1980) *Lönholdt's Patent-Feuer-Closett*. Düsseldorf: VDI.

Ushiomi, Toshitaka (1964) *Forestry and Mountain Village Communities in Japan: A Study in Human Relations*. Tokyo: Kokusai Bunka Shinkokai.

Veblen, Thorstein ([1914] 1964) *The Instinct of Workmanship*. New York: Kelley.

Vecchio, Bruno (1974) *Il Bosco negli scrittori italiani del Settecento e dell'eta napoleonica*. Turin: Einaudi.

Velter, André, and Lamothe, Marie-José (1976) *Le Livre de l'outil*. Paris: Hier et demain.

Verhey, Hans (1935) 'Waldmark und Holtingerleute in Niedersachsen im Lichte der Volkskunde', dissertation, Cologne.

Victor, David G. (2001) *The Collapse of the Kyoto Protocol and the Struggle to Slow Global Warming*. Princeton, NJ: Princeton University Press.

Vitruvius (1914) *The Ten Books on Architecture*, trans. Morris Hicky Morgan. Cambridge, MA: Harvard University Press.

Voit, Johann Peter (1804) *Faßliche Beschreibung der gemeinnützlichsten Künste und Handwerke für junge Leute*, 2 vols. Nuremberg.

Vorreiter, Leopold (1940) *Handbuch für Holzabfallwirtschaft*. Berlin: Neudamm.

Wachter, A. (1978) 'Deutschsprachige Literatur zum Weißtannensterben (1830–1978)', *Zeitschrift für Pflanzenkrankheiten*, 85: 361–81.

Wagenführ, Rudi (1980) *Anatomie des Holzes unter besonderer Berücksichtigung der Holztechnik*. 2nd edn, Leipzig: Fachbuchverlag.

Wagner, E. (1930) *Die Holzversorgung der Lüneburger Saline*. Düsseldorf: Fritz.

Walbe, Heinrich (1979) *Das hessisch-fränkische Fachwerk*. Giessen: Brühl.

WCED (World Commission on Environment and Development) (1987) *Our Common Future*. Oxford: Oxford University Press [Brundtland Report].

Walden, Hans (2002) *Stadt-Wald: Untersuchungen zur Grüngeschichte Hamburgs*. Hamburg: DOBU Wissenschaftlicher Verlag.

Warth, Otto (1900) *Die Konstruktionen in Holz*. Leipzig.
Waß, Barbara (1985) *Mein Vater, Holzknecht und Bergbauer*. Vienna: Böhlau.
Weber, Wolfhard (1982) 'Die industrielle Durchdringung', in Ulrich Troitzsch and Wolfgang Weber (eds), *Die Technik: Von den Anfängen bis zur Gegenwart*. Brunswick: Westermann.
Weber, Wolfhard (1986) *Technik und Sicherheit in der deutschen Industriegesellschaft 1850 bis 1930*. Wuppertal: Gesellschaft für Sicherheitswissenschaft.
Weck, Johannes, and Wiebecke, Claus (1961) *Weltforstwirtschaft und Deutschlands Forst- und Holzwirtschaft*. Munich: BLV.
Wehdorn, Manfred (1982) *Die Baudenkmäler des Eisenhüttenwesens in Österreich: Trocken-, Röst- und Schmelzanlagen*. 2nd edn, Düsseldorf: VDI.
Weisz, Leo (1983) *650 Jahre zürcherische Forstgeschichte*, 2 vols. Zurich: Regierungsrat des Kantons Zürich.
Wessely, Joseph (1853) *Die österreichischen Alpenländer und ihre Forste*. Vienna.
Whitman, Sidney (1912) *German Memories*. London: Heinemann.
Wiebecke, Claus (1963) 'Wirtschaftsziele und Rationalisierung in der Forstwirtschaft', *Schriftenreihe der Forstlichen Fakultät der Universität Göttingen*, 33, Frankfurt.
Wiebecke, Claus (1975) 'Jagd, Jagdwirtschaft und Forstwirtschaft – oder "Die Jagdgesellschaft"?', *Forstarchiv*, 46/2: 40–2.
Wießner, Hermann (1951) *Geschichte des Kärntner Bergbaues*, vol. 2. Klagenfurt: Geschichtsverein für Kärnten.
Williams, Michael (1989) *Americans and their Forests: A Historical Geography*. Cambridge: Cambridge University Press.
Williams, Michael (2006) *Deforesting the Earth: From Prehistory to Global Crisis*, Chicago: University of Chicago Press.
Williams, Richard L. (1976) *The Loggers*. New York: Time-Life.
Wilsdorf, Helmut (1957) 'Zur Theorie und Praxis der Braunkohlenverwertung um 1800', *Freiberger Forschungshefte*, series A, no. 60: 151–207.
Wilsdorf, Helmut, Herrmann, Walther and Löffler, Kurt (1960) *Bergbau, Wald, Flöße: Untersuchungen zur Geschichte der Flößerei im Dienste des Montanwesens und zum montanen Transportproblem*. Berlin: Akademie.
Wirz, Waldemar (1953) 'Die Forstpolitik der südwestdeutschen Forstordnungen', dissertation, Freiburg.
Wislicenus, H. (1932) 'Die Entfaltung der technischen Holzchemie und ihr Einfluß auf die Forstwirtschaft', *Der Deutsche Forstwirt*, 14/83–4.
Wittfogel, Karl August (1931) *Wirtschaft und Gesellschaft Chinas*. Leipzig: Hirschfeld.
Witthöft, Harald (1976) 'Struktur und Kapazität der Lüneburger Saline seit dem 12. Jahrhundert', *Vierteljahrschrift für Sozial- und Wirtschaftsgeschichte*, 63: 1–117.
Wohlfahrth, E. (1959) 'Natur und Technik im Waldbau', *Allgemeine Forstzeitschrift*, 18.
Wohlleben, Peter (2008) *Holzrausch: Der Bioenergieboom und seine Folgen*. St Augustin: Adatia.
Wolsey, Samuel Wilfred, and Luff, R. W. P. (1968) *Furniture in England: The Age of the Joiner*. London: Arthur Barker.
Woronoff, Denis (1979) 'La crise de la forêt française pendant la Révolution et l'Empire', *Cahiers d'histoire Lyon*, 24/1: 3–17.

Woronoff, Denis (1984) *L'Industrie sidérurgique en France pendant la Révolution et l'Empire*. Paris: EHESS.
Worster, Donald (1977) *Nature's Economy: A History of Ecological Ideas*. Cambridge: Cambridge University Press.
Wulf, Andreas (1993) *Urwald Senne: Neue Wege im Naturschutz*. Paderborn: Gemeinschaft für Naturschutz Senne und Ostwestfalen.
Wunder, Heide (1986) *Die bäuerliche Gemeinde in Deutschland*. Göttingen: Vandenhoeck & Ruprecht.
Wyrobisz, Andrzej (1973) 'La crise de combustibles dans l'industrie polonaise, au tournant du XVIe et XVIIe siècles', *Studia historiae oeconomicae*, 8: 259–69.
Young, Charles R. (1979) *The Royal Forests of Medieval England*. Leicester: Leicester University Press.
Zaminer, Eduard (1891) *Geschichte des Waldwesens der königlich freien Stadt Kronstadt*. Kronstadt.
Zander, Christian F. (2008) *Vom Hobel zum Computer: Zur Wirtschaftsgeschichte des modernen Tischler- und Schreinerhandwerks in Deutschland*. Leinfelden-Echterdingen: DRW.
Zangger, Eberhard (2001) *The Future of the Past*. London: Weidenfeld & Nicolson.
Zanthier, August Carl Alexander von (1802) *Freymüthige Gedanken über Holzmangel, Holzpreise, Holzersparniß und Holzanbau von A–Z*. Göttingen: Dieterich.
Zimmermann, Ludwig (1954–5) 'Forstschutz und Bauordnungen zur Blütezeit des hessischen Fachwerkbaues', *Zeitschrift des Vereins für hessische Geschichte und Landeskunde*, 65/66: 91–105.
Zischka, Anton (1936) *Wissenschaft bricht Monopole: Der Forscherkampf um neue Rohstoffe und neuen Lebensraum*. Leipzig.
Zwerger, Klaus (1997) *Das Holz und seine Verbindungen: Traditionelle Bautechniken in Europa und Japan*. Basel: Birkhäuser.

INDEX

376

wood consumption
  controls, 145–9
  iron industry, 217
  large-scale, 92–134
  measures, 136
  rising, 249
wood courts, 58–60, 159, 185
  activities, 58–9
  rulings, 59, 60
wood defects, 50–5, 74
  exploitation, 54
wood economies, 136–56
  and construction sector, 219–21
  and fire, 206–9
  and iron industry, 217–18
  and saltworks, 215–17
  and time, 206–9
wood engravers, 83
wood harvest trains, 255
wood importation
  duties, 249
  England, 73
  Japan, 305
wood joints, 274, 302, 303
wood management, and technological
    advancement, 209–15
wood particle boards, glued, 264
wood preservatives, health risks,
    285–6
wood-processing
  literature, 3
  machinery, 236
  mechanization in, 269–72
  modern, 27–8
  rationalization in, 269–72
wood procurement, 72, 82
wood products
  classification, 259
  mass production, 163
wood-saving
  bricks and, 220
  coal and, 223–8
  forest crafts and, 212
  furnaces, 133, 211
  inventions and, 130–4, 209–15

measures, 136
technology of, 131–2, 240–3
wood science
  literature, 28
wood shortages, 3, 23–6, 81–2,
    156–71
  beginnings of, 70–6
  churches and, 70–2
  coal industry, 102
  complaints about vs. justifications
      for, 164–7
  and conflicts, 31
  controls, 146
  ecological vs. institutional crises,
      157–9
  economic issues, 31
  eighteenth-century alarms,
      historians and, 156–7
  fear of, 130–1
  and forest ordinances, 179–88
  history of, 4–6
  impacts, 101–3
  metal industry, 100, 102
  and technological advancement,
      210–15
  and trades, 94–5
wood supplies
  Baltic, 73, 75
  controls, 145–9
  for shipbuilding, 70–6, 137–40
wood tariffs, 234, 249
wood technology, vs. rusticity,
    275–6
wood waste
  exploitation, 256
  heating with, 286
wood yards, 147
woodcarvers, 39, 314
woodcutters, 189–93, 194–7, 335
  characteristics, 193
  experienced, 194
  guilds, 193
  rights, 197
  and saws, 198
  songs, 194–6